WAR PRIZES

**An illustrated survey of
German, Italian and Japanese aircraft
brought to Allied countries
during and after the Second World War**

WAR PRIZES

An illustrated survey of
German, Italian and Japanese aircraft
brought to Allied countries
during and after the Second World War

PHIL BUTLER

Midland Counties Publications

Copyright © 1994
P H Butler

Published by
Midland Counties Publications
24 The Hollow, Earl Shilton
Leicester, LE9 7NA, England
Tel: 01455 847 256 Fax: 01455 841 805
E-mail: midlandbooks@compuserve.com

Worldwide distribution (except North America):
Midland Counties Publications (Aerophile) Ltd
Unit 3, Maizefield, Hinckley Fields
Hinckley, Leics., LE10 1YF, England
Tel: 01455 233 747 Fax: 01455 233 737
E-mail: midlandbooks@compuserve.com

North American trade distribution:
Specialty Press Publishers & Wholesalers Inc.
11481 Kost Dam Road
North Branch, MN 55056, USA
Tel: 800-895-4585 (toll free) Fax: 612-583-2023

ISBN 0 904597 86 5

First published 1994
Reprinted 1998

Printed in England by
The Alden Press
Oxford

Photograph on previous page:
**View taken at Wright Field, Ohio
of Bf 109E AE479 after delivery to the USA
in April 1942 aboard the *SS Drammesfjord*.
AE479 continued to fly in RAF markings
in the USA, having previously flown with the
French Armée de l'Air as well as the RAF and the
Luftwaffe.**
J. Mutin collection

Contents

The Arado Ar 234B 'AIR MINISTRY 24' and Messerschmitt Me 262A 'USA 1' at Schleswig on 27th August 1945. *G/Capt E. Shipley collection*

Foreword

by Captain E.M. (Winkle) Brown, CBE, DSC, AFC, MA, FRAeS, RN
Chief Naval Test Pilot at RAE Farnborough 1944-1949

Captain E. M. Brown, RN, Chief Naval Test Pilot 1944-49,
C.O. Captured Enemny Aircraft Flight 1945-46,
C.O. Aerodynamics Flight 1947-49.
E. M. Brown

With the collapse of the Third Reich the Allies found themselves in a virtual Aladdin's cave of aviation treasures, and so mounted an effort to collect these prizes of war for the evaluation of their technology. Because I was a test pilot at RAE Farnborough and also German speaking, I was deeply involved in this and shall never forget the scenario of chaos that prevailed at that time in defeated Germany. The mood of the Allies was a mixture of relief and vengeful anger, and that of the former enemy was one of apprehension and surly defiance. In such an atmosphere there was little patience on our side for keeping records of events, and the Germans had been quite meticulous about destroying their documentation wherever possible. Therefore the author of *War Prizes* faced a daunting task in compiling the story of this treasure trove, and the end result represents some really fine research against the odds, and this is not just true of the European theatre of war but also of the Middle East and Far East.

Amid this post-war confusion there was little sense of history among those in the field, and destruction rather than preservation was the order of the day, for everyone was fed up to the teeth with the war and all the attendant paraphernalia. In consequence there was much unorthodoxy in the methods employed to secure the better prizes that had survived the holocaust of World War II, and this has made it particularly difficult to dig out the real facts of events up to the end of 1945. *War Prizes* has done much to bring order to this jumbled era, and although there are inevitably gaps in the information, which the passage of time will make more difficult to fill, this book is an invaluable record in its own right of a fascinating subject.

Eric Brown

October 1993

Preface and Acknowledgements

This book owes its origin to my previous title *Air Min* published in 1978 by the Merseyside Aviation Society, and now long out-of-print. This book started life as an intended second edition of *Air Min* and was to include a significant quantity of new material brought to light as a result of comments and contributions received following the publication of the first edition.

However the scope of this publication has been considerably expanded to encompass all aircraft which came to the United Kingdom (UK) and the United States of America (USA), and also those aircraft taken post-war to France. The coverage includes acquisitions from Italy and Japan, as well as from the German Third Reich.

The claim made in *Air Min* that 'this publication is the most comprehensive compilation of information yet to appear in print about "Air Min" aircraft' is likewise applicable to this book, which also includes information on other aircraft from similar Axis sources, such as the aircraft flown in the United States with 'EB-', 'FE-' or 'T2-' numbers.

Information used in the compilation of this book includes material extracted from the surviving Aircraft Movement Cards and Aircraft Accident Cards held by the Ministry of Defence (Air) AHB.2; flight records and reports filed at the Public Record Office (PRO), Kew; the Royal Aircraft Establishment Library, Farnborough; unit Operational Record Books and other 'AIR' and 'AVIA' series records at the PRO. Further information has been provided by the Accident Investigation Branch (AIB) of the UK Department of Transport; the Royal Air Force Museum at Hendon; the Smithsonian Institution of Washington, DC; the Alfred H. Simpson Historical Research Center of the Air University, Maxwell Air Force Base, Alabama, USA, US National Archives, Washington DC, ECPA, Paris and the South African Museum of Military History at Saxonwold, Johannesburg.

Much useful information has been gleaned from examination of surviving examples of those captured aircraft on display in museums, including the Royal Air Force Museum (Battle of Britain Museum) at Hendon, and the station museums at RAF Cosford and RAF St Athan, as well as in other museums around the world.

Thanks are due to the staffs of all the above organisations for their assistance, and to the staff of the Imperial War Museum photo library at Lambeth. From the USA, there were many invaluable contributions from the staff of the National Air and Space Museum, including Bob Mikesh, Richard Horrigan, Dana Bell and Larry Wilson.

Thanks are also extended to the many individuals who have contributed valuable information and photographs over the years, including Rear Admiral Charles C. Andrews (USN Ret'd), Ashley Annis, Lieutenant Robert Anspach, John Bagley, Mrs Isolde Baur, Serge Blandin, David Birch, Steve Bond, Roy Bonser, Captain Eric Brown, Roy Brown, Captain Theodore T. Brundage, Charles Cain, Rollo Campbell, Marion C. Carl, Derek Collier Webb, Eddy Collyer, Steve Coates, John Cross, Alan Curry, Phil Dale, John M. Davis, Bert Earnest, Ken Ellis, John Ellingworth, Jeff Ethell, Bob Esposito,

John K. Foster, Eugene Freiburger, Ray Frisby, Wal Gandy, Peter Green, Bert Haggas, Dr Ken Hammer, Tony Hancock, Jim Heaton and others of the Australian War Memorial, Karel Hellebrand, Leif Hellström, Ron Henry, Thomas H. Hitchcock, Cliff Hodgson, Ken Holt, Siegfried Kahlert, G. Stuart Leslie, Howard Levy, Knut Maesel, Edwin Maxfield, John May, Joe McCarthy, Fred McIntosh, Tony Morris, Jacques Mutin, Gunther Ott, Frank Phripp, the late Steve Piercey of *Flight International*, Brian Pickering of Military Aircraft Photographs, Jim Reason, Bruce Robertson, Brian Robinson, Geoff Rowe, Nigel A. Rumble, G/Capt Edwin Shipley, Graham J. R. Skillen, J. Richard Smith, Russ Snadden, Ian Somerville, Tony Speir, Hans-Heiri Stapfer, Sheri Street, John Stroud, Bob Strobell, Ray Sturtivant, Lou Thole, Chris Thomas, John Underwood, Denys J. Voaden, Idwal Walters, Tom Weihe, N. D. Welch, Kenneth S. West, Tom Willis, Chris Wills of the Vintage Glider Club of Great Britain, Tim Woodman, Mrs J. Woolams.

Thanks are also due to the many people who contributed photographs from their collections and who are individually acknowledged adjacent to each photo caption.

It should be borne in mind that whilst we have used the most modern methods to accurately reproduce the photographs that appear in this book, the vast majority of the images were originally 'captured' on film around 50 years ago. In this work, priority for inclusion has been given to photographs of historical significance and in the case of the colour section, our choice was influenced by a preference for subjects originally photographed in authentic colour schemes, even though the ravages of time may have affected the end result.

Particular mention must be made of the assistance given over the years by members of the British Aviation Research Group, especially by Mike Draper, Phil Spencer and Trevor Stone of the *Roundel* team, and to the publishers Midland Counties Publications, notably to Neil Lewis and Chris Salter.

Very special thanks are extended to Norman Malayney of Pittsburgh, Pa, USA, without whose contributions this book could not have been so comprehensive. Many are the hours that Norm has spent tracing photographs, researching material and the people who were actually involved with the aircraft described in the book. Norm is an especially dedicated, assiduous and proactive researcher. Norm, once again, my grateful thanks!

To conclude, I exhort any readers who may have any contribution, great or small, to add to the information in this book to write to me via the publisher, so that such further knowledge can be published in due course. All photographs and other information will be gratefully received, acknowledged and returned on request.

Phil Butler
Wigan, Lancashire   December 1993

Introduction

ROYAL AIR FORCE (RAF)

Aircraft captured during the Second World War were usually not flown by the RAF until British nationality markings had been applied, although this requirement was sometimes waived if the aircraft were to be flown from the point of capture to a test establishment under escort by other RAF aircraft. It was usual for an RAF serial number to be allocated within a few days of capture, as soon as an intention to fly the aircraft had been confirmed. In a small number of cases no serial numbers were issued because the aircraft concerned crashed within a few days of capture, before markings could be allotted or applied.

In the first instance, Axis aircraft captured in the United Kingdom, after landing in error or receiving battle damage, were normally flown to the Royal Aircraft Establishment (RAE) at Farnborough for initial evaluation. Then they were handed over to the RAF Air Fighting Development Unit (AFDU), initially at Northolt and later at Duxford and then Wittering, for assessment in mock combat of suitable Allied fighter tactics against these fighter types.

In 1941 No. 1426 (Enemy Aircraft) Flight was formed at Duxford to provide demonstrations of Luftwaffe aircraft at RAF (and later USAAF) airfields, to familiarise Allied aircrew with the performance and recognition features of available Luftwaffe types. No. 1426 Flight received aircraft from the RAE or AFDU initially, although later a number were received direct from their points of capture if they were of types which had already been investigated by the RAE.

The Aeroplane and Armament Experimental Establishment (A&AEE) at Boscombe Down - and its marine aircraft equivalent, the Marine Aircraft Experimental Establishment (MAEE) at Helensburgh - was also involved in trials of particular aircraft from time to time.

Towards the end of the war in Europe, the AFDU was absorbed into the Fighter Interception Unit (FIU) and No. 1426 Flight was disbanded. Their German aircraft and some of their personnel were transferred in March 1945 to the Enemy Aircraft Flight of the Central Fighter Establishment (CFE) at Tangmere.

Because of its distance from the UK, and the tenuous nature of secure communications links in wartime, 'Royal Air Force Middle East' was responsible for the immediate assessment of any aircraft captured in its operational area. These assessments were generally carried out by No. 209 Group RAF which was based in Egypt. The Group was able to rely on an extensive engineering back-up organisation in Egypt and in the Suez Canal Zone, together with a number of experienced test pilots. The aircraft were usually flown with British nationality markings although not in all cases with RAF serial numbers - this despite the fact that RAF Middle East had batches of serial numbers allocated to it for its own local use. In many cases such serial numbers were allocated, although details of all allotments have not survived because the complete record does not seem to have been transferred to the UK at the end of hostilities.

The RAF in the Far East under South-East Asia Command was in a similar situation to that in the Middle East, but no examples are known of serial numbers being allocated to captured Japanese aircraft. In 1943 a joint RAF/US unit entitled 'Allied Technical Air Intelligence Unit, South-East Asia' (ATAIU-SEA) was set up at Calcutta to carry out technical evaluations of Japanese aircraft captured or shot down in Allied territory. So far as is known this unit did not fly any aircraft while it was based in India, because, generally speaking, only badly-damaged examples became available to it. In September 1945 Singapore was re-occupied and the ATAIU moved to Tebrau in Johore State on the Malayan mainland opposite Singapore. Here a large number of surrendered Japanese aircraft were brought together and flown in British markings. Most of these carried the acronym 'ATAIU-SEA', but British serial numbers were not worn. The 'Zeke', 'Dinah' and 'Cypress' examples brought to the UK are known to have come from this unit. The Ki-100-Ib in the UK may also have been from this source.

ROYAL NAVY (RN)

The Royal Navy (Fleet Air Arm – FAA) did not directly evaluate any Axis aircraft. FAA personnel contributed to the activities of such units as the AFDU and CFE as well as to experimental establishments such as the RAE and A&AEE. There was therefore no need for a separate Naval evaluation organisation with its own group of captured aircraft. The Naval Air Fighting Development Unit, which was located at the same base as the equivalent RAF Unit, borrowed German aircraft from the RAF as required.

UNITED STATES ARMY AIR FORCE (USAAF)

The USAAF test organisation at Wright Field, Dayton, Ohio, was based on the Air Force Engineering Laboratories. It was the main centre for the test of German and Italian aircraft captured in both Europe and the Middle East. Initially, some Axis aircraft, held by the RAF in the UK, were handed over to the USAAF in April 1942, and others were later shipped direct from the Middle East. On two occasions Junkers Ju 88s were flown from the Mediterranean Theatre to the USA, via the South Atlantic route.

Later Colonel Harold E. Watson was attached to the USAAF in Europe and was responsible for the despatch of further aircraft captured by US forces on the continent of Europe, culminating in the post-surrender shipment aboard HMS *Reaper* in July 1945. Aircraft were painted in US national markings at their point of surrender, and flown to a suitable port for onward shipment to the USA, or, in exceptional cases, air-ferried or air-freighted to the USA.

After receipt at Wright Field identities incorporating the letters 'EB-' (Engineering Branch), 'FE-' (Foreign Evaluation) or 'T2-' (for the T-2 Office of Air Force Intelligence) were painted on the aircraft. The identity numbers were specific to the aircraft and were rarely duplicated although the prefixes EB-, FE- and T2- were valid at different times as the intelligence organisation underwent change. It was usual for the prefix to be changed if the aircraft remained in use after one of the organisational changes - hence several 'EB-' aircraft changed to 'FE-' and later most 'FE-' aircraft became 'T2-'.

After the end of the war in Europe, Freeman Field, Seymour, Indiana, was transferred to the control of Wright Field, for use as a subsidiary centre where many of the prizes received from Europe were re-assembled. The aircraft were usually flown from Freeman Field to Wright Field for the evaluation testing to be carried out there, because Freeman Field did not have equipment to support flight tests under properly controlled conditions.

With the end of the war against Japan, the priority for assessment of German aircraft disappeared, as the main thrust was to ensure that any developments, which might have been transferred from Germany to Japan, were fully understood before they were met in combat during an invasion of the Japanese main islands. Freeman Field was soon closed, and the Axis aircraft dispersed to Wright Field, or to storage at Davis-Monthan Field in Arizona, or to No. 803 Special Depot in the former Douglas C-54 factory at Park Ridge, Illinois, (at Chicago O'Hare Airport). A list of available Axis aircraft and equipment was published. The listed items were released for study by approved US industrial organisations. When the Park Ridge store was required for other purposes, at the time of the Korean War, the survivors were scrapped or moved to the Smithsonian Institution store at Silver Hill, Maryland.

UNITED STATES NAVY (USN)

The USN bore the brunt of the air war in the Pacific since its aircraft-carriers were the main means of bringing the Japanese air forces to combat. It was therefore natural that the USN made a major contribution to the Technical Air Intelligence Center (TAIC) which was the primary evaluation unit concerned with flying Japanese aircraft in the USA. The first captured Japanese 'Zero' was flown at NAS North Island, San Diego, and later at other Naval Air Stations. At a later date a 'Captured Enemy Aircraft Unit' was set up at NAS Anacostia, Washington, DC. This unit was concerned with rebuilding and maintaining German and Japanese aircraft selected for evaluation at US Navy establishments.

This Unit formed the basis of the joint USAAF/USN Air Intelligence organisation set up in the USA following the withdrawal of the joint service TAIU from Australia in 1944. This led to there being a centralised joint service organisation at NAS Anacostia, under the US Division of Naval Intelligence but with assistance from US Army and Allied personnel. This became the TAIC, whose functions included 'to receive, catalogue, examine, overhaul, and rebuild captured airplanes, engines, and air equipment as necessary, and to arrange for or conduct required tests'. In practice, many of the tests were delegated to NAS Patuxent River, in nearby Maryland, which was the base of the Naval Air Test Center (NATC). Subsidiary to the TAIC, were regional Technical Air Intelligence Units (TAIU), whose task was to find and evaluate enemy aircraft and equipment found in the field and to pass those of value back to Anacostia. The details of these units can be found in Chapter Fourteen.

Post-war, a batch of German aircraft evaluated by the USN at NAS Patuxent River was allotted USN Bureau of Aeronautics'

(BuAer) serial numbers, but none of the other aircraft evaluated received such official numbers.

Test Philosophies

Test flights which were made in the various Allied countries involved, generally arose in three phases, dependent on conditions prevailing at the time.

First came the initial need for any tests - namely the capture of a new and possibly previously unknown Axis aircraft which might be met in combat. In all countries the first reaction was to have the aircraft flown by a number of experienced pilots familiar with that class of aircraft. During this phase it was unusual to make any attempt at exact performance measurements. The aim was to arrive at a concensus of subjective opinion about the strengths and weaknesses of the aircraft from a combat viewpoint, in order that an immediate assessment might be given to pilots in the front-line. Much emphasis was laid on the aircraft handling qualities and diving/climbing/turning abilities. At a later stage of this assessment the aircraft might be loaned to other Air Force units - usually those concerned with developing fighting tactics - for mock combat with the Allied fighters likely to encounter the aircraft in anger. This might also include comparisons with prototypes or early production models of Allied aircraft yet to enter service, to see how they fared in a realistic situation. Any of these tests might also involve test pilots from the aircraft industry as well as serving military pilots.

Second, when these initial assessments were complete, serious measurements of performance would really begin. More scientific measurements would be made, to evaluate the absolute performance of the aircraft. This information would still be of interest to combat pilots but was, from their viewpoint, a fine tuning of the first subjective assessment. The detailed analyses probed the strengths and weaknesses of the prizes in great depth and were widely reported both within the military services and in Allied industry. Their aim was to identify improvements existing in the design which would be of value for incorporation into later Allied aircraft, and to assess the effect of ways by which the enemy might improve his own designs in due course. The analyses included firing trials with the armament, exhaustive engine performance tests, tests of radios, radars and other equipment such as de-icers, instruments and so on - each had its part to play.

Third, although rarely applied during the war period itself, was the use of aircraft for empirical research for possible application to new designs of Allied aircraft. This phase included exploration of the entire flight envelope of the aircraft, to establish basic aerodynamic information on one or more of its features, and might be combined with wind-tunnel tests of the aircraft, either complete or in model form. These were used by the British in their tests of the Messerschmitt Me 163B and Horten Ho IV, to establish information of use for later tailless jet aircraft. In the USA similar tests of the Lippisch DM-1 in the wind-tunnel at Langley were used in the development of the Convair XF-91/F-102/F-106 delta-wing fighters. Information from German design reports of their advanced projects and wind-tunnel analyses (sometimes in German wind-tunnels rebuilt in Allied countries after the war) led to the production of the next generation of fighter aircraft, such as the North American F-86 Sabre. The project work would make a fascinating study in itself, but is, unfortunately, outside the scope of this book.

Chapter One

Royal Aircraft Establishment Farnborough 1939-1945

The RAE at Farnborough was the main British centre for the testing of captured German and Italian aircraft for the duration of the Second World War and for the years immediately thereafter.

The history of the RAE can be traced back to the British Army's first balloon experiments at Woolwich Arsenal in 1878. In that year a Balloon Equipment Store was established at the Arsenal. This moved to Chatham in 1882 and thence to Aldershot in 1890.

In 1894 the unit was renamed the Balloon Factory although, almost concurrently with this renaming, experiments began with heavier-than-air machines – the man-lifting kites of Captain B. F. S. Baden-Powell (brother of the founder of the international Boy Scout movement). Later, in 1904, Samuel F. Cody, a United States' citizen, interested the British War Office in his own system of man-lifting kites, such that in 1906 he was appointed 'Chief Instructor in Kiting' to the Balloon School, which was a section of the Factory organisation. In the spring of 1906 the Balloon Factory moved to South Farnborough, where the RAE still is today. Colonel J. E. Capper, Royal Engineers, the Superintendent of the Balloon Factory, in association with Samuel Cody, constructed the non-rigid airship *Nulli Secundus* ('Second to None', named after one of King Edward VII's racehorses), which made its first flight in September 1907. It was the first of several airships made by the Factory.

At the same period the Factory began experiments with powered heavier-than-air aircraft. These included experimental powered versions of Samuel Cody's man-carrying kites. One of these, built by Cody on his own initiative, made a free flight at Farnborough in 1907. In the winter of 1907, Cody began to build his 'Army Aeroplane No. 1' in the Balloon Factory. This aircraft made a flight of seventy metres at Farnborough in September 1908.

In December 1909, His Majesty's Balloon Factory and its associated 'Balloon Section, Royal Engineers' were separated. Colonel Capper was appointed Commander of the Balloon Section, which became the embryo of the later Royal Flying Corps (RFC), and his job as Superintendent of the Factory was taken by Mervyn O'Gorman, a consulting engineer. In 1911, the Factory became the Army Aircraft Factory, although its main preoccupation was initially the production of Army airships. At this time Assistant Engineers of Design, Physics and Machine Shops were appointed, laying the foundations for the later work of the Establishment. In 1912 it was further renamed as the Royal Aircraft Factory and was charged, amongst other duties, with '. . . tests with British and foreign engines and aeroplanes; experimental work; . . . '.

During the early years of the First World War, the Royal Aircraft Factory was in almost a monopoly situation with regard to the design of aircraft for the RFC, such that it produced not only prototype aircraft designs but also supervised the production of those designs which were accepted for military service. This involved setting up production by a large number of privately-owned aircraft industry sub-contractors to the government, to the exclusion of aircraft designed by the private aircraft industry. The Factory also became involved in the production of its own aircraft and engine designs. The total of 100 employees in 1910 had increased to 4,000 by mid-1915, and activities extended not only to aircraft design and production, but also to the use of wind-tunnels and to the development of materials, instruments, propellers, stressing methods (including testing aircraft to destruction), and many other practical matters.

The monopoly position of the Factory was much criticised and in 1916 an official enquiry was set up which deliberated and ruled that the Factory should no longer be concerned with the design and construction of aircraft. Henceforth it concentrated on theoretical and consultative aspects. New wind-tunnels were commissioned, and the test-flying concentrated on theoretical aspects, such as that of spinning.

With the creation of the Royal Air Force (RAF) on 1st April 1918, the Royal Aircraft Factory came to be renamed the Royal Aircraft Establishment. This not only avoided a confusion in initials but also correctly reflected the changed role of the organisation - i.e. it no longer manufactured complete aircraft.

In 1924 a further official Committee was set up to report on the organisation of the Establishment, and this (the Halahan Committee) confirmed the primary function of the RAE as providing 'a full-scale aeronautical laboratory for the Air Ministry' and defined its main activities as:
– development work on experimental aeroplanes and engines
– testing of experimental instruments and accessories
– development of special flying instruments for which there is little commercial demand
– investigations of failures
– liaison with contractors' research
– technical supervision of the construction of experimental machines
– stressing of new types of machine, approval of designs and the issue of airworthiness certificates
– the issue of certain technical publications

In the inter-war period, subject to the severe financial restraints of the time, much work was done in the fields of aero engine development, especially with regard to engine superchargers and automatic engine controls. Other areas included aircraft fire extinguishing research, a comprehensive programme of work on aerofoils and wind-tunnel testing of models for general aerodynamic research, catapult launching and pilotless aircraft developments, and pioneering work on Gas Turbine development for aircraft applications. The whole of the RAF radio communications network was reconstructed under RAE supervision. These tasks were undertaken with a technical staff of about 150 people, until the numbers began to build up from 1934 with the prospect of a European war looming.

With the outbreak of the Second World War, the technical staff of the RAE – who at that period totalled about 550 – became increasingly involved in the investigation of crashed enemy aircraft and captured equipment. The investigation work drew on the experience of all departments of the Establishment. This experience had been built up during the formative years of peace.

These activities resulted in the issue of the 'Enemy Aircraft' (EA) series of special technical reports. From June 1940, when the Experimental Flying Department became involved in flight tests of a captured Messerschmitt Bf 109E fighter, these reports included flight test results, engineering appraisals and descriptions of complete aircraft received at the Establishment or examined 'on site' at other experimental units or at the locations where they had been shot down. The main appraisal work was co-ordinated by Mr W. Sutcliffe who was put in charge of an Enemy Aircraft and Engine Section of the Mechanical Test Department of the Establishment. RAE staff from this Section were available at short notice to carry out on-site examinations of enemy aircraft which had crashed or been shot down in the United Kingdom.

The majority of complete German and Italian aircraft captured after force-landing (or landing in error) in England were brought to Farnborough for examination and test. Later in the war examples of aircraft types or variants which had already been assessed at the RAE were sometimes sent to No. 1426 Flight or other units without coming to Farnborough, although even in these cases technical specialists from the RAE often examined them and wrote reports describing any new features or equipment found.

The main flight test work was carried out by the Aerodynamics Flight of the Experimental Flying Department, although the Wireless & Electrical Flight (W&EF) also flew many hours, especially with investigations of radar-equipped aircraft later in the war. Typical organisation charts for the Experimental Flying Department are shown on pages 20 and 21.

There follow details of the aircraft flown at the RAE during the period from 1940 to the end of the war in Europe in May 1945, and at the end is a table summarising the number of flights and flying hours accumulated by ex-Axis aircraft during the period.

AE479   Messerschmitt Bf 109E-3   WNr 1304

This Bf 109, coded 'White 1' of JG76, made a forced landing at Woerth in the Bas-Rhin Department of France on 22nd November 1939. It was later flown to the Armée de l'Air 'Centre d'Essais du Matériel Aérien' (CEMA), a test establishment located at Orleans/Bricy airfield. It was painted with French national markings although retaining its code '1'. It was flown there in comparison with the current French fighters, and probably also the French Armée de l'Air single Spitfire I which was on the strength of the same unit, before being handed over to the RAF at Amiens on 2nd May 1940, although it had in fact previously been examined by experts from the RAE at Orleans in January. It was ferried to England on the following day, after being demonstrated to RAF Hurricane squadrons based at Amiens. It routed via Chartres and Tangmere on its way to the A&AEE at Boscombe Down.

On 14th May 1940 it was flown from Boscombe Down to RAE Farnborough and commenced a series of trials. In June 1940 the RAF serial number AE479 was allocated. Records show that, at the time the serial number was allocated, the '109 was regarded as being the property of the French Government, on loan to the British. The Bf 109E was flown frequently at the RAE until 20th September when it departed to Northolt for use by the AFDU, the RAF unit concerned with the development of fighter tactics, and it remained there until its return to Farnborough on 20th November. After a landing accident at Farnborough on 5th January 1941 and repair using the tail unit of Bf 109E Werk Nummer (WNr) 1480, AE479 recommenced test flying in February 1941. During its time at Farnborough it was flown by a large number of different pilots, including Flying Officer (F/O) J. E. Pebody, Flight Lieutenant (F/Lt)

Bf 109E AE479 of the AFDU photographed at Duxford during 1941. *MAP*

J. F. Tobin, Squadron Leaders (S/Ldrs) Wilson and Heycock, Wing Commander (W/Cdr) G. H. Stainforth (the Schneider Trophy race pilot of 1931), S/Ldr A. E. Clouston (a pre-war Farnborough test-pilot and maker of many record-breaking long-distance flights), and others.

While at RAE Farnborough AE479 made flights as follows:

Month	Hrs	Mins	Flights	Activity
May 1940	19hrs	15 mins	28 flights	Handling
June	15	10	25	Handling, radio & engine tests
August	3	00	5	Handling
September	0	55	2	Engine cooling, ferry to Northolt
October	0	35	2	Demonstration, ferry from Northolt
November	0	25	2	Ferry flight, air test
December	0	15	1	Air test
January 1941	0	25	1	Handling
February	0	35	2	Air test, performance
March	2	30	3	Performance
May	0	15	1	Air test
June	3	20	4	Performance
July	1	20	2	Performance

On 24th July 1941 AE479 was flown to Duxford by Wing Commander I. R. Campell-Orde to rejoin the AFDU which had moved there in the meantime. On 11th December 1941 AE479 joined the then newly-formed No. 1426 (Enemy Aircraft) Flight, also based at Duxford. The duty of this unit was to demonstrate airworthy ex-Luftwaffe aircraft at RAF and USAAF airfields to familiarise aircrew with their recognition features. After only a short period on this unit it was flown to No. 47 MU Sealand by F/Lt R. F. Forbes, CO of No. 1426 Flight, on 28th January 1942, for crating and shipment to the USA. AE479 sailed from London aboard the SS *Drammesfjord* on 7th April 1942, consigned to Wright Field, Dayton, Ohio. It arrived there on 14th May 1942 but had only a short career in the USA, being damaged beyond repair in a forced landing at Cambridge, Ohio, on 3rd November 1942.

AW177   Heinkel He 111H-1   WNr 6853

This aircraft, coded '1H+EN' of II/KG26, was based at Sylt/Westerland and force-landed with only minor damage on open moorland at North Berwick Law, close to North Berwick on the south side of the Firth of Forth, after combat with a Spitfire of No. 602 Squadron on 9th February 1940. The Heinkel was taken by road to Turnhouse and after two test flights on 13th August was flown from there to Farnborough via Finningley on 14th August 1940.

While with the RAE, AW177 made flights as follows:

August 1940	3hrs	30mins	4 flights	Test and ferry to RAE
October	1	35	4	Handling
March 1941	1	05	3	Air test, handling
April	1	00	2	Handling
July	0	10	1	Air test
August	2	30	8	Handling
September	0	45	2	Handling
October	5	55	7	Handling
November	4	05	8	Handling
December	0	40	2	Air test, handling

Among the pilots who flew the He 111 at Farnborough were S/Ldr L. D. Wilson, Lt Lewin (RN), F/Lt J. F. Tobin, F/Lt Humpherson, F/Lt D. B. S. Davie and Group Captain (G/Capt) A. H. Wheeler, who was the Commanding Officer of the RAE Experimental Flying Department at the time.

During these trials at RAE, AW177 flew on 12th September 1941 to Duxford for further tests by the AFDU, returning to RAE on 6th October 1941. Towards the end of the series of flights, handling experience was given to F/O R. F. Forbes, Pilot Officer (P/O) E. R. Lewendon, and Flight Sergeant (F/Sgt) D. G. M. Gough, who were to fly the He 111 later in its career with No. 1426 Flight. On 7th December 1941 it returned to Duxford on delivery to No. 1426 (EA) Flight and remained with that unit until being destroyed in an accident at the USAAF airfield at Polebrook on 10th November 1943. The He 111 was landing when its pilot saw Ju 88 HM509 of the same unit landing from the opposite end of the same runway. The He 111 took avoiding action and spun-in off the resulting stall; seven of the eleven personnel on board were killed including the pilot, F/O F. A. Barr.

An official air-to-air shot of He 111H AW177 showing the 'Lion Geschwader' badge behind the cockpit. *IWM, E(MoS)1226*

AX772 Messerschmitt Bf 110C-5 WNr 2177

This aircraft coded '5F+CM' belonged to Aufklärungsgruppe 14 [4.(F)14] and had been built by Gothaer Waggonfabrik AG. It had taken off from its base in the Cherbourg area on 21st July 1940 and was shot down by Hurricanes of No. 238 Squadron close to their home base at Goodwood. It was repaired using parts from the Bf 110C-5 '2N+EP' which had been shot down at Povington Heath near Wareham in Dorset on 11th July 1940. WNr 2177 made its first flight after repair at the RAE on 25th October 1940, as AX772. Flights made were as follows:

October 1940	0hrs	35mins	2 flights	Handling
November	1	15	3	Handling
December	4	05	8	Handling
January 1941	1	00	2	Performance
February	3	05	4	Performance
March	2	15	2	Air test, performance
May	5	20	7	Performance
June	5	20	7	Performance
August	1	10	4	Air test, handling, performance
September	2	10	3	Handling, performance
October	1	15	3	Performance, handling

Flights were made by S/Ldr L. D. Wilson, F/O J. F. Pebody, F/O R. J. Falk, F/O J. F. Tobin, F/Lt Humpherson, and others.

AX772 was flown extensively at Farnborough until it was eventually transferred to the AFDU at Duxford on 13th October 1941. Further transferred to No. 1426 Flight on 5th March 1942, it remained with the Flight until that was disbanded in January 1945. Then it was taken on charge by the EAF of the CFE at Tangmere on 31st January 1945 and flown by this unit, or other sections of the CFE, for several months until transferred to the charge of No. 47 MU Sealand on 1st November 1945. In fact AX772 probably remained at Tangmere until selected for transfer to Sealand by the AHB in the spring of 1946. It remained in storage until late 1947

The Bf 110C AX772 during one of No. 1426 Flight's 'Circus' tours.
Steve Coates collection

AW177 and AX772 on the ground at Honington during a visit by No. 1426 Flight in 1942; the He 111H still wears the badge of KG 26, known as the 'Lion Geschwader', on its nose behind the cockpit with the motto 'Vestigium Leonis'. The track between the two aircraft is part of the airfield camouflage, intended to break the pattern of the airfield into separate 'farm fields'.
Peter Green collection

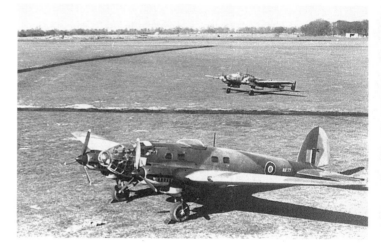

when pressure on available space at Sealand and elsewhere forced a review of aircraft held for museum purposes. At that point AX772 was put up for disposal and almost certainly went to No. 34 MU at Sleap for reduction to scrap between November 1947 and February 1948.

'AX774'   —

This serial number has been reported as applying to a second Bf 110C-5 shot down at about the same time as AX772. This aircraft was allegedly the one coded '2N+EP' shot down near Wareham on 11th July 1940 which is referred to under AX772. The RAF serial number AX774 was not allocated to any aircraft and the report of it applying to the Messerschmitt in question is therefore erroneous.

AX919   Junkers Ju 88A-1   W Nr 7036

This aircraft, coded '9K+HL' of I/KG 51, force-landed at Buckholt Farm, north of Bexhill, on 28th July 1940 after running out of fuel and was taken to the RAE for examination. The RAF serial number AX919 was allocated and the aircraft taken on charge by the RAE on 31st August 1940. Although this example was studied closely by the RAE and reports were written about its undercarriage, hydraulic system, bomb gear and automatic dive pull-out system, it was not flown in RAF colours until 3rd April 1941. It seems to have been difficult to keep serviceable and was not flown after the arrival of EE205 later in the year. Flights were as follows:

April 1941	1hrs 40mins	3 flights	Air test, handling
June	0 30	1	Performance

All these flights were made by S/Ldr L. D. Wilson. No reports were written about its flying characteristics. On 12th June 1942 the Ju 88 was taken by road to Duxford for use as a source of spares for the other airworthy Ju 88s on the strength of No. 1426 Flight.

BT474   Fiat CR 42   C/no 326, ex MM 5701

This single-seat biplane fighter of the Regia Aeronautica was the only one of the Italian aircraft shot down in the Battle of Britain to be repaired and made airworthy for test purposes. Coded '13-95', it belonged to the 95ª Squadriglia Caccia Terrestre (of the 18° Gruppo, 56° Stormo), the Squadriglia being indicated by the '95' in the code on the aircraft. This unit was attached to the Corpo Aereo Italiano (Italian Air Corps) which was the overall title of the Regia Aeronautica units, under the command of the Luftwaffe's Luftflotte 2, which took part in the Battle of Britain. It was based at Maldegen in Belgium and was shot down by RAF Hurricanes from Martlesham Heath on 11th November 1940, force-landing near Orfordness with a fractured oil-pipe but otherwise undamaged.

It was taken by road to Martlesham Heath and then, on 27th November, to Farnborough. The CR 42 was subsequently allotted the RAF serial BT474. Only limited flights were made at RAE by S/Ldr L. D. Wilson before it was flown to the AFDU at Duxford by W/Cdr I. R. Campbell-Orde on 28th April 1941, to enable that unit to develop tactics against the type, which was the standard Italian fighter in use in the Middle East theatre, by mock combat with various types of fighter in service with the RAF.

During 1943 the AFDU lost interest in the type because of its obsolescence and the aircraft was selected as potential museum material. It is recorded as being dismantled for permanent storage on 12th December 1943. It was initially stored at No. 16 MU Stafford and later at a dispersed site of No. 16 MU near Reading, before going to No. 52 MU Cardiff for a period before the end of the war. It was almost certainly the Fiat packed and despatched from No. 76 MU Wroughton in August 1946 and it probably then went to No. 47 MU Sealand although there is no specific note of it in the latter unit's records. By 1949 BT474 was certainly in the German Air Force Equipment Centre (GAFEC) at Stanmore Park and was seen there by the writer in 1955. It followed the rest of the AHB aircraft from Stanmore Park to Biggin Hill via Wroughton and Fulbeck. It ended up at St Athan, where it stayed for many years in the Station Museum and was allotted the ground instructional number 8468M there for book-keeping purposes. In 1979 the CR 42 was transferred to Hendon for display in the Battle of Britain Museum which opened in 1980 and it is currently there.

An air to air shot of Fiat CR 42 BT474 taken after the Fiat was repaired and repainted in RAF markings. *MAP*

A shot of Ju 88A AX919 taken at RAE Farnborough. It is said that this aircraft may have been repaired with a wing from another aircraft. There is a story that a German prisoner, taken to Farnborough to see why one of the captured Junkers did not fly well, fell about laughing when he saw that the aircraft had dissimilar port and starboard wings! *PRO from AIR 40/126*

BV207   Gotha Go 145B   W Nr 1115
This two-seat biplane trainer, coded SM+NQ and in use as a communications aircraft by Stab/JG 27 at Cherbourg, arrived at Lewes racecourse on 28th August 1940 as a result of a navigational error. It was flown from Lewes to RAE Farnborough on 31st August by S/Ldr H. J. Wilson. Brief test flights were made on 6th and 10th September 1940 by Wilson and F/O Pebody and the Gotha then remained grounded until an air test at the RAE on 12th December made by S/Ldr Fulton, prior to the aircraft departing to No. 20 MU, Aston Down, on 1st January 1941 in the hands of F/O Alsop. By this time it had been allotted the RAF serial number BV207. It was issued from No. 20 MU to No. 2 School of Technical Training (SoTT) at RAF Cosford as an instructional airframe in September 1941. Its ground instructional number, 2682M, was allocated on 18th September. The Gotha was struck off charge (SoC) at a census on 1st April 1942, so its instructional life was quite short.

EE205   Junkers Ju 88A-5   W Nr 3457
This aircraft, coded '4D+DL' of I/KG 30, landed intact at RAF Lulsgate Bottom on 23rd July 1941. It had taken off from Lanveoc-Poulmic in Brittany to bomb Birkenhead and landed at Lulsgate in error, probably as a result of British radio deception measures – the so-called 'Meaconing' system by which radio beacons in England were set up to broadcast on the same frequencies as Luftwaffe beacons on the Continent; this resulted in aircraft homing on a point between the two beacons. The Ju 88 was ferried to RAE Farnborough on 1st August 1941 by S/Ldr H. J. Wilson and was allocated the RAF serial number EE205. It made its first flight as such, from Farnborough to Boscombe Down and return, on 14th August, piloted by Wilson. From 19th August to 1st September EE205 was attached to the AFDU at Duxford for tactical trials, then returning to Farnborough where it was flown frequently until transferred to No. 1426 Flight at Duxford on 28th August 1942.

While at Farnborough, EE205 was flown very extensively. Pilots involved included F/Lt L. D. Wilson, F/Lt J. F. Tobin, S/Ldr D. A. Letts, S/Ldr Fulton, S/Ldr R. J. Falk (RAE Chief Test Pilot

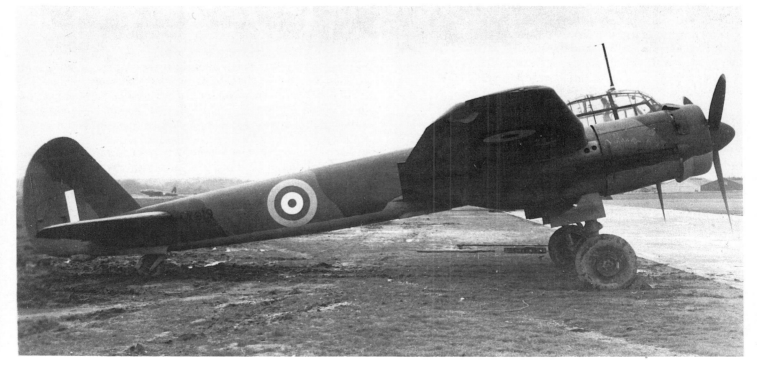

after W/Cdr H. J. Wilson), S/Ldr W. R. Cox, F/Lt R. A. Kalpas, F/Lt D. B. S. Davie, G/Capt A. H. Wheeler (CO Experimental Flying), Lt K. J. Robertson (RN), F/Lt A. D. Moffett, F/Lt C. G. S. McClure, F/O R. V. Keeling and others. The range of flying extended far beyond handling evaluation and performance measurement. It included extensive testing of the dive-bombing sight, de-icing trials, tests of the radio and direction-finding loop installation and so on. In March 1942 EE205 was detached to RAF Martlesham Heath for photography of incendiary bomb-dropping from the aircraft. Other detachments from the RAE included a visit to Heathrow, the present London Airport, in September 1941.

EE205 remained with No. 1426 Flight until that was disbanded in January 1945, then being handed over to the EAF of the CFE at Tangmere. In September 1945, the CFE moved to West Raynham, leaving most of its German aircraft behind at Tangmere. In March 1946 the AHB of the Air Ministry visited Tangmere to survey the weathered remnants of these aircraft. The Ju 88s, a Bf 109, and a Bf 110 were selected for storage and were transported to No. 47 MU, Sealand, during March and April. EE205 was packed for storage on 1st August 1946 and was still there in November 1947. At about this time the AHB was under great pressure to reduce its holdings because of lack of storage space and early in 1948 several ex-Luftwaffe aircraft, almost certainly including EE205, were disposed of to No. 34 MU, Sleap, for reduction to scrap.

ES906   Messerschmitt Bf 109F-2   W Nr 12764

This aircraft belonged to Major Rolf Peter Pingel, Gruppen-Kommandeur of I/JG 26 and carried his double-chevron insignia in lieu of a code number. It was shot down near St Margaret's Bay, Dover, after combat with RAF Spitfires on 10th July 1941. It was not badly damaged in its belly-landing and after replacement of its propeller and other repairs at RAE Farnborough it was allotted for flight trials. After its RAF serial number, ES906, was allocated on 27th August 1941, it was test-flown for the first time at RAE Farnborough by S/Ldr H. J. Wilson on 19th September 1941. Later flights were made by F/Lt L. D. Wilson and F/Lt J. F. Tobin. On 11th October it was delivered to the AFDU at Duxford by F/Lt Simpson for comparative trials with various marks of Spitfire.

Its life with the AFDU was very short since it crashed at Fowlmere in Cambridgeshire on 20th October 1941 after its pilot, F/O M. Skalski, was overcome by carbon monoxide poisoning. It was officially SoC on 28th October 1941.

MP499   Focke Wulf Fw 190A-3   W Nr 313

This III/JG 2 aircraft wore the single-chevron insignia of the Gruppen-Adjutant of III Gruppe/JG 2 in place of any code number. It was flown by Oberleutnant Arnim Faber and had taken off from Morlaix on 23rd June 1942 to combat RAF Spitfires which had attacked its base. After making a navigational error, Faber landed at RAF Pembrey in South Wales. The Fw 190 was a most important capture for the RAF and it was taken by road to Farnborough for examination.

The RAF serial number MP499 was allocated on 29th June, prior to its first flight from the RAE on 3rd July 1942 which was made by W/Cdr H. J. Wilson. All the early flights were made by Wilson, during which it was flown intensively in comparative trials with Allied fighter types. These trials involved aircraft and pilots of the AFDU at Duxford, who were detached to RAE Farnborough for the purpose. The reason for this was that Duxford was still a grass airfield at the time and it was thought too risky to fly the Fw 190 from grass.

During the course of these trials, the '190 took part in the famous demonstration (on 22nd July 1942) in which it was flown past an official delegation, in parallel with the Griffon-engined Spitfire, a standard Spitfire IX and a Hawker Typhoon. This was in effect a speed trial which was won by the Griffon-engined Spitfire. It directly led to large orders being placed for the Griffon Spitfire.

The later flights involved F/Lt Tobin, Lt K. J. Robertson (RN), Capitaine M. P. Claisse (a French pilot who was a member of the Aerodynamics Flight), and S/Ldr S. Wroath. The last of 29 recorded flights of MP499 was made on 29th January 1943 by Lt Robertson. MP499 was SoC on 18th September 1943, the fuselage being used for firing trials, the wings for destructive testing in a structural test rig and the engine for bench tests. Twelve hours 15 minutes of test flying had been accomplished at the RAE at the time the aircraft was SoC.

TS439   Heinkel He 177A-5/R6   W Nr 550062

This He 177, coded 'F8+AP' of II/KG 40, was captured by the French Resistance at Toulouse-Blagnac where it was under overhaul in the Ateliers Industriel de l'Air facility in September 1944. It also had the radio call-sign 'KM+UK' and wore the number '60' in yellow on its fin. It was flown from Toulouse to Farnborough by W/Cdr R. J. Falk on 10th September. It wore French markings, including the title 'Prise de Guerre'. By 20th September it had received RAF markings and the serial TS439. Its first flight was made by S/Ldr A. F. Martindale on that day. It was flown on a number of occasions at Farnborough, its last recorded flight being on 20th February 1945, when it landed at Boscombe Down. From here it is believed to have been shipped in dismantled condition to the USA where it became 'FE-2100' on arrival. On its last flight the '177 had sustained irrepairable damage to one of its DB610 engines and the Americans had obtained a stock of spare engines. (The USAAF had received another He 177A in Europe, but this was destroyed at Paris/Orly in a take-off accident at the start of its delivery flight to the USA). Also see 'FE-2100' in Chapter 16.

TS439 made twenty flights under RAE control (including its ferry flight), totalling 19 hours 35 minutes. Trials covered aspects as varied as tests of the spring tab controls, bombsight and altimeter tests and checks of the crew's air heating system. Pilots who flew the aircraft included S/Ldr Weightman, F/Lt Turner, S/Ldr Keeling, F/Lt Wellwood, S/Ldr Randrup and G/Capt A. F. Hards.

This shot shows the He 177A TS439 complete with black and white invasion stripes, its prototype 'P' marking and the 'Prise de Guerre' (war prize) marking – just visible below the 'P' – applied by the French resistance group which captured the aircraft. *NASM courtesy Norm Malayney collection*

The use made of the seventeen aircraft which were flown at Farnborough is summarised in the following Table:

Serial No	Type	Time Period	No of flts	Flying hours	EA Report No
AE479	Bf 109E-3	May 1940/Jul 1941	78	47:00	EA2/14
AW177	He 111H-1	Aug 1940/Dec 1941	42	22:30	
AX772	Bf 110C-5	Oct 1940/Oct 1941	45	27:30	EA22/1 &c
AX919	Ju 88A-1	Apr 1941/Jun 1941	4	2:10	
BT474	Fiat CR 42	Apr 1941/Apr 1941	2	1:00	EA32/1 &c
BV207	Gotha Go 145B	Aug 1940/Jan 1941	4	1:40	
EE205	Ju 88A-5	Aug 1941/Aug 1942	85	67:20	EA14/16 &c
ES906	Bf 109F-2	Sep 1941/Oct 1941	14	6:55	EA2/17
MP499	Fw 190A-3	Jul 1942/Jan 1943	29	12:15	EA44/1 &c
PE882	Fw 190A-4/U8	Apr 1943/Apr 1944	97	52:20	
PJ876	Ju 88R-1	May 1943/May 1944	83	66:55	EA35/9
PM679	Fw 190A-5/U8	Jun 1943/Jul 1943	18	8:35	
PN999	Fw 190A-4/U8	Jun 1943/Sep 1943	34	14:00	
TF209	Me 410A-3	May 1944/Aug 1944	16	4:50	EA53/2 &c
TP190	Ju 88G-1	Jul 1944/May 1945	33	32:35	EA225/1
TP814	Bf 109G-6/U2	Jul 1944/Aug 1944	10	5:05	
TS439	He 177A-5/R6	Sep 1944/Feb 1945	19	17:55	EA200/5 &c
		Totals (17 aircraft)	613	390:35	

The 'EA' Reports noted are representative rather than exhaustive. Other EA Reports were written about these aircraft as were Reports on other aircraft, used by No. 1426 Flight and other units, which were examined at their bases. For example, Report EA 14/26 was written about the No. 1426 Flight Ju 88 HM509 and EA 49/1 about its Hs 129 NF756.

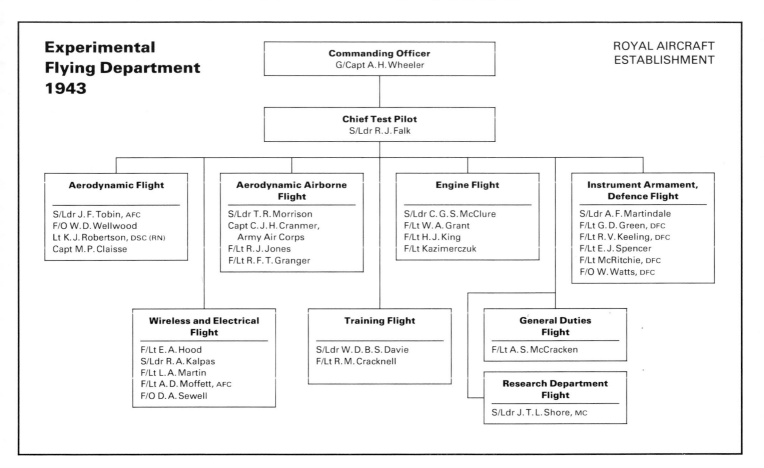

Experimental Flying Department 1943

ROYAL AIRCRAFT ESTABLISHMENT

Commanding Officer
G/Capt A. H. Wheeler

Chief Test Pilot
S/Ldr R. J. Falk

Aerodynamic Flight

S/Ldr J. F. Tobin, AFC
F/O W. D. Wellwood
Lt K. J. Robertson, DSC (RN)
Capt M. P. Claisse

Aerodynamic Airborne Flight

S/Ldr T. R. Morrison
Capt C. J. H. Cranmer, Army Air Corps
F/Lt R. J. Jones
F/Lt R. F. T. Granger

Engine Flight

S/Ldr C. G. S. McClure
F/Lt W. A. Grant
F/Lt H. J. King
F/Lt Kazimerczuk

Instrument Armament, Defence Flight

S/Ldr A. F. Martindale
F/Lt G. D. Green, DFC
F/Lt R. V. Keeling, DFC
F/Lt E. J. Spencer
F/Lt McRitchie, DFC
F/O W. Watts, DFC

Wireless and Electrical Flight

F/Lt E. A. Hood
S/Ldr R. A. Kalpas
F/Lt L. A. Martin
F/Lt A. D. Moffett, AFC
F/O D. A. Sewell

Training Flight

S/Ldr W. D. B. S. Davie
F/Lt R. M. Cracknell

General Duties Flight

F/Lt A. S. McCracken

Research Department Flight

S/Ldr J. T. L. Shore, MC

In addition to the aircraft which were flown during this period, large numbers of investigations were undertaken into materials, equipment and components recovered from crashed or captured aircraft. In a number of cases complete aircraft were examined – these are detailed below.

| — | **Arado Ar 234B** | **W Nr 140173** |

This was the first example of the Ar 234B to be captured by the Allies, after it was shot down by US 9th AAF P-47s of 366 FG near Selgersdorf on 22nd February 1945. Coded 'F1+MT' of III/KG 76, it was scarcely damaged in the forced landing and was shipped virtually intact to the RAE Farnborough on 21st March 1945 for examination. The aircraft was not flown at RAE but was subject to detailed examination of its airframe and engines. Its fate is unknown.

| — | **Caproni-Campini CC2** | **C/n 4849, ex MM487** |

The second prototype of the Caproni-Campini CC 2 'jet' aircraft was handed over to the Allied Control Commission in Italy at the Centro Sperimentale at Guidonia near Rome, in June 1944. It was shipped to RAE Farnborough and received there in about October 1944. It was transferred to No. 47 MU, Sealand, on 12th October 1945, only very shortly before the German Aircraft Exhibition, and was packed for museum storage during January 1946. It was later taken to the GAFEC at Stanmore Park but was declared surplus to requirements in November 1947 due to a combination of pressure on storage space and the poor condition of the airframe which was severely corroded. It was taken to No. 58 MU at RAF Newton and scrapped there during 1949. The CC 2 was not a true jet, being powered by a form of ducted fan driven by a piston engine combined with a primitive afterburner. The RAE Report written after completion of its assessment on the type was EA 234/1.

SL538   Gotha Go 242   W Nr *unknown*

This RAF serial number was allotted on 17th January 1944 to a Gotha Go 242 troop-carrying glider. It must be assumed that the aircraft concerned had been captured in N. Africa and shipped to the United Kingdom; the serial was outside the series of numbers allotted for use in the Middle East. However, there is no known record of such an aircraft being flown in the UK, nor indeed of a complete Go 242 being noted at any RAF unit in the UK.

The RAE received a Go 242 on 3rd July 1943 and report EA43/2 was issued in December of that year by the Structures and Mechanical Engineering Department following analysis of the design. It is believed that the aircraft described was that allocated the serial number SL538, but that it was in too poor a state of repair to be made airworthy.

| — | **Junkers Ju 87B-1** | **W Nr 087/5600** |

This 'Stuka', coded 'S2+LM' of II/St G 77, was shot down near Ventnor, on the Isle of Wight, on 8th August 1940. It was an example built by Weser Flugzeugbau in May 1940.

Although one of the crew members was killed in the crash, the aircraft was not badly damaged – its only battle damage was a shot through a petrol feed pipe. On force-landing it had collided with a gate and suffered damage to its wing-tips, propeller, spinner, engine cowling and radiator attachments. It was removed to Farnborough for examination and serious consideration was given to its repair for test flying. In the event this was not done, although the fuselage of this aircraft was still at Farnborough during the post-war German Aircraft Exhibition and it was noted in the scrap area as late as 15th December 1946. EA Report EA 26/2 was written about this Ju 87.

This official shot of Bf 109G TP814 is typical of that appearing in Allied Second World War intelligence material. It was taken at the Air Fighting Development Unit and dated 18th September 1944 and shows the '109G to advantage from four different angles. *PRO, AIR 40/192*

*   *   *

The tests of the aircraft described above represent the main trials of German aircraft at the Royal Aircraft Establishment in the period from 1940 to the end of the war in Europe in May 1945. Activities after May 1945 are described in Chapter Five.

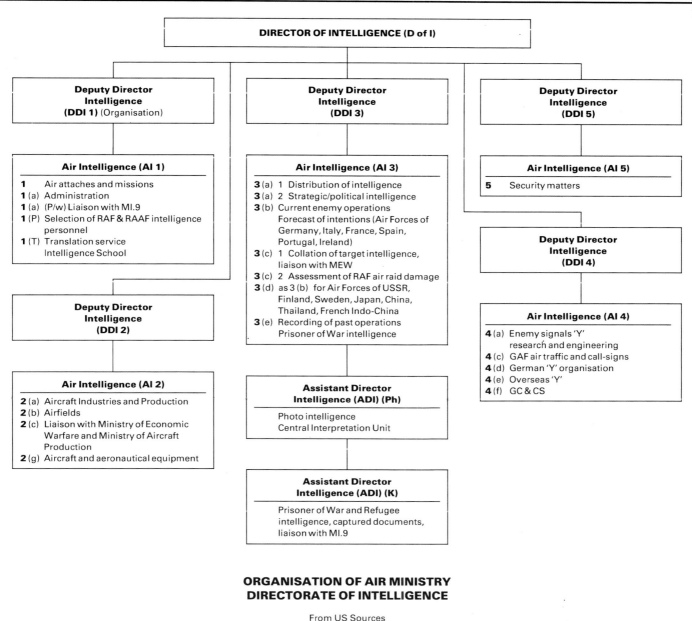

DIRECTOR OF INTELLIGENCE (D of I)

Deputy Director Intelligence (DDI 1) (Organisation)

Air Intelligence (AI 1)

1 Air attaches and missions
1 (a) Administration
1 (a) (P/w) Liaison with MI.9
1 (P) Selection of RAF & RAAF intelligence personnel
1 (T) Translation service
     Intelligence School

Deputy Director Intelligence (DDI 2)

Air Intelligence (AI 2)

2 (a) Aircraft Industries and Production
2 (b) Airfields
2 (c) Liaison with Ministry of Economic Warfare and Ministry of Aircraft Production
2 (g) Aircraft and aeronautical equipment

Deputy Director Intelligence (DDI 3)

Air Intelligence (AI 3)

3 (a) 1 Distribution of intelligence
3 (a) 2 Strategic/political intelligence
3 (b) Current enemy operations
     Forecast of intentions (Air Forces of Germany, Italy, France, Spain, Portugal, Ireland)
3 (c) 1 Collation of target intelligence, liaison with MEW
3 (c) 2 Assessment of RAF air raid damage
3 (d) as 3 (b) for Air Forces of USSR, Finland, Sweden, Japan, China, Thailand, French Indo-China
3 (e) Recording of past operations
     Prisoner of War intelligence

Assistant Director Intelligence (ADI) (Ph)

Photo intelligence
Central Interpretation Unit

Assistant Director Intelligence (ADI) (K)

Prisoner of War and Refugee intelligence, captured documents, liaison with MI.9

Deputy Director Intelligence (DDI 5)

Air Intelligence (AI 5)

5 Security matters

Deputy Director Intelligence (DDI 4)

Air Intelligence (AI 4)

4 (a) Enemy signals 'Y' research and engineering
4 (c) GAF air traffic and call-signs
4 (d) German 'Y' organisation
4 (e) Overseas 'Y'
4 (f) GC & CS

ORGANISATION OF AIR MINISTRY DIRECTORATE OF INTELLIGENCE

From US Sources
dated 1942

The chart above shows the organisation of the Air Ministry's Directorate of Intelligence. The main section involved with the enemy aircraft included in this book was AI 2(g), which gathered and disseminated intelligence on German and Italian aircraft and their equipment. The USAAF intelligence organisation was initially modelled on the operation and methods of the British, which had been closely studied by the USAAF prior to the US entry to the war.

AI 2(g) worked closely with other arms of the Air Intelligence organisation and received major inputs from air intelligence officers working in the various theatres of war, the Allied Technical Air Intelligence Unit in Washington, DC, after that was set up in 1944, the RAE at Farnborough, the Central Photographic Interpretation Unit at RAF Medmenham, and reports produced by the Prisoner of War interrogation unit of ADI(K). Other contributions came from the 'Y' service – i.e. the stations which picked up and decoded enemy radio traffic.

Often the first knowledge of a new aircraft type was obtained from photographic reconnaissance over enemy airfields such as the Luftwaffe Erprobungstelle (test establishment) at Rechlin. Until a type could be positively identified it would be known by the location at which it had been found by the combined Allied staff at RAF Medmenham, combined with its wing span in feet as estimated by the photographic interpreters, e.g. a 'Rechlin 66'. A specific example of this was the 'Peenemunde 16', the first identification of the Fieseler Fi 103 or V-1 flying bomb.'

Chapter Two

No. 1426 (Enemy Aircraft) Flight

No. 1426 (Enemy Aircraft) Flight, Royal Air Force, was formed at Duxford on 21st November 1941. Its duty was to demonstrate ex-Luftwaffe aircraft, at various locations in the UK, to familiarise Allied personnel with their recognition features and performance. Many visits were made to RAF and USAAF airfields to demonstrate the various aircraft. Initially the visits were made to RAF and then USAAF 8th AF bomber airfields, but the demonstrations were extended to cover ground defence organisations such as anti-aircraft artillery units and personnel of the Royal Observer Corps (ROC).

The latter organisation maintained a network of ground-based observation posts all over the United Kingdom, each linked by telephone to the fighter and other anti-aircraft defences. Accurate aircraft recognition was an essential skill of the ROC observers and much effort was put into their training; while much of this was theoretical classroom study (or study of books at home, for almost all Observer Corps personnel were people with civilian jobs working as Observers in their spare time), flying displays of aircraft were held from time to time as a training exercise.

No. 1426 Flight was initially staffed by a small number of RAF pilots who had previously been test pilots at Maintenance Units (MUs). These were organisations which stored aircraft received from their manufacturers pending service or aircraft received from units for re-allocation, modification or repair. Their test pilots were experienced men, who might often fly up to a dozen different aircraft, of a variety of types, each day. These first pilots were Flying Officers R. F. Forbes and Kinder, Pilot Officer E. R. Lewendon and Flight Sergeant D. G. M. Gough. They had spent eleven days prior to the formation of the Flight on attachment to the Air Fighting Development Unit (AFDU) at Duxford, familiarising themselves with the aircraft; they had also visited RAE Farnborough to fly those German aircraft which were still based there prior to being transferred to the Flight.

The selection of test pilots to staff the Flight showed considerable prescience on the part of the planners. The records of the unit show that almost all flights made by the German aircraft were of the nature of test flights, many of them ending prematurely due to some emergency or a prudent return to base because of an anticipated or actual problem. The 'tours' of other flying stations included a constant catalogue of cancelled demonstrations and shuttles in communications aircraft to the Flight's base (initially at Duxford, and then at Collyweston from 12th April 1943) or to RAE Farnborough to obtain spares or specialist tools needed to get one or other of the aircraft back into the air.

The first 'tour' carried out by the Flight commenced on 11th February 1942. This exercise was flown by the He 111 AW177 and the Ju 88 HM509. They flew from Duxford to Lakenheath with an escort of Spitfires, en route overflying the airfields of Oakington, Upwood, Marham, West Raynham, Swanton Morley and Mildenhall. At Lakenheath the aircraft landed for inspection by Observer Corps personnel. On 13th February the tour continued – the pair flew to RAF Watton, giving further displays at Lakenheath and Mildenhall on the way. Another display was given at Watton on 14th February and on the following day the aircraft flew to Coltishall and gave two flying displays there on 16th February. On 17th February both aircraft flew to Bircham Newton where the display included a dogfight between the Ju 88 and one of the locally-based Lockheed Hudsons. On 18th February the pair flew to nearby Docking and performed dogfights with a Beaufighter before returning to Bircham Newton. On 19th February the aircraft flew to Sutton Bridge and on the next day carried out mock dogfights with the Hurricanes of the Sutton Bridge-based Operational Training Unit. On 23rd February the Flight moved on to Wittering; the next day the Ju 88 made two demonstration flights but the Heinkel remained on the ground because of a propeller problem. Finally, on 27th February, the aircraft returned to their base at Duxford.

The pattern for 'tours' made by the Flight was very much as set by the first one described above. Occasional local flights were made from the base to nearby Army training ranges to give demonstrations. Other quite frequent flights were made for the benefit of the RAF Film Unit or other organisations which were making recognition films or taking sound recordings of the various aircraft types. The fifth tour was the first to include a visit to a unit of the USAAF, during which (on 29th July 1942) the Flight's Bf 109E, Ju 88 and He 111 arrived at Atcham, then a training base for the first 8th AF Fighter Group, equipped with Spitfires. After being escorted to Heston by Spitfires of 31st Pursuit Group, the tour continued from Heston to Northolt, the Bf 109, He 111 and Ju 88 HM509 then flying to Boscombe Down on 6th August. Here the aircraft, joined a few days later by the Bf 110 from Duxford, were flown by pilots of the Aeroplane and Armament Experimental Establishment. This was mainly a familiarisation exercise for A&AEE pilots, although the Ju 88 made at least one night test flight to assess the visibility of its flame damping exhausts. Twenty A&AEE pilots made fifty-one flights in the German aircraft before they moved on to Bovingdon on 16th August.

The seventh tour began mundanely with the ferry flight of Ju 88 EE205, Bf 110 AX772 and He 111 AW177 to Atcham on 4th September 1942. The tour began in earnest with a demonstration flight to the nearby RAF airfields of High Ercall, Rednal and Hawarden, on 6th September, under the escort of USAAF P-38s.

Tours continued in the same manner during the next two years, culminating in a series of demonstrations over the assembling D-Day invasion fleet in May 1944. On 12th April 1943 the Flight moved from Duxford to RAF Collyweston, a satellite airfield of Wittering. Collyweston is, in fact, now incorporated into the western end of the present-day Wittering airfield (now a base for RAF Harrier vertical-take-off fighters). In May 1943 the Flight took some of its aircraft to the RCAF base at Digby where they were reviewed by King George VI and Queen Elizabeth.

In June 1943 the first aircraft captured in the Middle East arrived. This was a Macchi MC 202, almost complete, but too badly corroded to be worth rebuilding to fly. Nevertheless, two engineers from the Enemy Aircraft Section at RAE Farnborough visited the Flight to report on the aircraft. Later in the month components of the Henschel Hs 129B, which was later to fly as NF756, began to arrive. This was also examined by engineers from the RAE to enable them to write one of their 'EA' reports. A party of airmen from No. 65 MU, Blaby, was attached to the Flight to assist in the Henschel's rebuild.

Late in September 1943 a group of Polish pilots was attached to the Flight to enable them to familiarise themselves with the aircraft. The senior Polish pilots, Squadron Leaders Bialy and Iszkowski, were allowed to fly the He 111, Ju 88 and Bf 110, totalling 23 flying hours by 14th October.

On 10th November 1943 the Flight ended a demonstration at Goxhill at 17.30 hours and flew to Polebrook, led by the He 111 flown by F/O Barr. On arrival at Polebrook the He 111 put its wheels down, followed by the Ju 88. The '88 turned in to land on the duty runway, which was illuminated. The '111 continued its circuit and started to approach the same runway from the upwind end. Its pilot saw the Ju 88 landing and opened up to avoid him, making a steep left hand turn. The aircraft spun in from 100 feet, hitting the ground vertically. Seven of the passengers were killed by the impact, but four others escaped with injuries. The Bf 110, which was following the He 111, and a Bf 109 following the Ju 88, both landed safely.

In February 1944 the unit took on additional duties, with the Flight's Bf 109G, flown by F/Lt E. R. Lewendon, being used for comparative performance trials with a Hawker Tempest I of the AFDU. Later in the month, further trials were carried out against a Mustang III and a Spitfire XIV also of the AFDU. In March, this series of tests continued against a Seafire III, F4U Corsair and Hellcat of the Naval AFDU, followed by tests of the Hellcat and Seafire against an Fw 190.

On 8th May 1944, No. 1426 Flight was instructed to proceed to Thorney Island to form part of an 'Air Show Circus' with eighteen British and American aircraft types. The purpose of this 'Circus' was to fly over various Allied units during the build-up to D-Day to provide instruction in aircraft recognition. On 9th May, Ju 88 HM509, Fw 190s PE882 and PN999, and Bf 109 RN228 positioned to Thorney Island, to be joined on 26th May by the Bf 110 AX772 and the Ju 88 PJ876. Flights continued until the invasion on 6th June enabled a return to normal duties.

On 18th September 1944, Fw 190 PN999, Bf 110 AX772 and Ju 88 EE205 flew to Chipping Ongar for a demonstration to the USAAF Air Disarmament School. On 24th September, a Ju 88S-1 was collected from Villacoublay in France, after it had been made service-

able by Flight personnel. On 13th October, F/Lt E. R. Lewendon was killed, when the Fw 190 PE882 crashed near Collyweston. Lewendon had been a founder member of the Flight, and was its Commanding Officer at the time of his death.

On 21st January 1945, official notification was received that the Flight had been disbanded. All aircraft and personnel were then posted to the Central Fighter Establishment at Tangmere, where they were to become the Enemy Aircraft Flight of that unit. The actual movement of aircraft and spare equipment took some time, so the last aircraft did not fly to Tangmere until April 1945. The full list of aircraft flown by the unit is:

AE479*	Messerschmitt Bf 109E	11 Dec 1941 to 28 Jan 1942	(to USA)
AW177*	Heinkel He 111H	7 Dec 1941 to 10 Nov 1943	(accident)
AX772*	Messerschmitt Bf 110C	5 Mar 1942 to 31 Jan 1945	
DG200	Messerschmitt Bf 109E	28 Apr 1942 to (about September 1943)	
EE205*	Junkers Ju 88A	28 Aug 1942 to 31 Jan 1945	
HM509	Junkers Ju 88A	11 Dec 1941 to 19 May 1944	(accident)
NF754	Focke Wulf Fw 190A	12 Dec 1943 to 31 Jan 1945	
NF755	Focke Wulf Fw 190A	12 Dec 1943 to 31 Jan 1945	
NF756	Henschel Hs 129B	27 Jun 1943 to 31 Jan 1945	
NN644	Messerschmitt Bf 109F	21 Aug 1943 to 31 Jan 1945	
PE882*	Focke Wulf Fw 190A	19 Apr 1944 to 13 Oct 1944	(accident)
PJ876*	Junkers Ju 88R	6 May 1944 to 31 Jan 1945	
PN999*	Focke Wulf Fw 190A	28 Sep 1943 to 31 Jan 1945	
RN228	Messerschmitt Bf 109G	26 Dec 1943 to 31 Jan 1945	
TS472	Junkers Ju 88S	25 Sep 1944 to 31 Jan 1945	
VD364	Messerschmitt Bf 109G	(arrived 14 February 1945, as the unit disbanded)	
VX101	Messerschmitt Bf 109G	9 Apr 1944 to 19 May 1944	(accident)

The histories of seven aircraft marked * above are given in full in Chapter One since they started their RAF careers at RAE Farnborough. The histories of aircraft which started their RAF life with No. 1426 Flight are given below:

DG200.   Messerschmitt Bf 109E-3   W Nr 4101

Coded 'Black 12' of I/JG 51. This aircraft force-landed at Manston on 27th November 1940, after combat with RAF Spitfires. It had previously served with II/JG 52 and had the radio call-sign 'GH+DX'. It was made airworthy with parts from other Bf 109s and arrived at Rolls-Royce Ltd, Hucknall, on 14th December 1940. It made its first flight at Hucknall on 25th February 1941. The serial number DG200 was allotted prior to this flight. After a period at Rolls-Royce for engine performance investigations, during which it made 32 flights totalling 23 hours 25 minutes, DG200 was transferred to de Havilland at Hatfield (by 8th February 1942) for tests of the variable pitch propeller installation. Shortly afterwards, DG200 was transferred to the A&AEE at Boscombe Down. On 24th March 1942, it took off from Boscombe to fly to No. 1426 Flight at Duxford, but returned with hydraulic trouble. It was eventually delivered to Duxford by road on 28th April. It was repaired and later flown by No. 1426 Flight, initially on 1st June 1942, but by this time its cockpit canopy had been lost and it was therefore of only limited use.

When a newer Bf 109 became available in 1943, DG200 was retired to No. 16 MU, Stafford, for long-term museum storage. It followed the other 'Museum' stock around the country, as described under BT474 in Chapter One. During the post-war period, it was several times displayed in Horse Guard's Parade, London, during Battle of Britain week, by that time wearing an unrepresentative 'Galland'-type clear-view canopy. During this period also, it wore the incorrect code '12+GH', derived from various earlier markings found during re-painting. After storage at Biggin Hill in the early 1960s, DG200 was at RAF Henlow in 1967-8

The Bf 109E 'Emil' DG200 airborne after its cockpit canopy had been lost. This aircraft is now in the Battle of Britain Museum at Hendon. *MAP*

during the making of the 'Battle of Britain' film. After this, it was at St Athan for a number of years, apart from a period in 1976, when it appeared at the 'Wings of the Eagle' exhibition at the RAF Museum, Hendon. In 1980, it was finally transferred from St Athan to be exhibited in the Battle of Britain Museum at Hendon. While at St Athan, it had been allotted the identity 8477M for book-keeping purposes. Prior to 1976, it had received the correct type of cockpit hood once again, obtained from RN228.

HM509   Junkers Ju 88A-6   W Nr 6073
Coded 'M2+MK' of KuFlGr 106. This aircraft landed at RAF Chivenor on 26th November 1941. It had taken off from Morlaix in France for an anti-shipping sortie over the Irish Sea and due to a navigational error mistook Chivenor for an airfield in Brittany. The aircraft was flown on 11th December 1941 to Farnborough and onwards to Duxford. The serial HM509 is amongst those allotted to No. 41 Group RAF for impressed civil aircraft. Although recorded to have been built in March 1940 as a Ju 88A-1 this aircraft had the wings of the A-5 sub-type and the electrical equipment of the A-6.

It was usually described in No. 1426 Flight records as an A-6. It was handed over to No. 1426 Flight and remained on its strength until SoC on 26th July 1944 for use as spares for other Ju 88s of the Flight. The Junkers had been damaged on 19th May 1944 in a landing accident at RAF Thorney Island, where the Flight had been giving an aircraft recognition demonstration to the assembling Normandy invasion fleet off the South Coast of England. The pilot of the Ju 88 saw another aircraft taking off on a cross runway, as he was landing. He put power on to clear the other aircraft but was only able to stop his aircraft by ground looping at the end of the landing run, causing damage when a wing tip hit a ground obstruction. The aircraft was dismantled and its engines installed in another Ju 88 of the Flight. The total of flying hours accumulated by No. 1426 Flight on HM509 was 163.00.

HX360   Junkers Ju 88A-5   W Nr 6214
Coded 'V4+GS' of III/KG 1. This Ju 88 landed at RAF Steeple Morden on 16th February 1941 with engine trouble while returning to its base after a raid on Liverpool. It was taken by road to the RAE on 7th May 1941. It was not flown at Farnborough and was taken to RAF Duxford on 12th June 1942 for use as spares for other Ju 88s flown by No. 1426 Flight. The RAF serial number HX360 was issued for this aircraft on 23rd December 1941 pending its use by No. 1426 Flight, but in the event it was not restored to airworthy condition.

NF754   Focke Wulf Fw 190A   W Nr *unknown*
Aircraft captured in Sicily and shipped to the UK. It arrived at RAF Collyweston, the base of No. 1426 Flight, on 12th December 1943. There is no specific record of this aircraft being flown by the unit, although the '190 was retained on strength until the Flight's disbandment and was transferred to the EAF of the CFE at Tangmere. It was allocated to No. 47 MU, Sealand, on 1st November 1945, although there is no specific record of its physical transfer to this unit. Several ex-CFE aircraft have this record on their 'movement cards' but most of them did not, in fact, go to Sealand until some time in 1946 after the AHB had surveyed the surviving German aircraft at Tangmere.

NF755   Focke Wulf Fw 190A   W Nr *unknown*
The history of this aircraft is identical to that shown above for NF754 except that on 17th May 1945 the serial VG913 was allocated to it. It is presumed that the later serial was not, in fact, used.

NF756   Henschel Hs 129B-1   W Nr 0297
Aircraft of I/SG 2. This aircraft was captured in the Middle East and was shipped to the UK, arriving at Collyweston on 27th June 1943. The aircraft was in a bad state of repair and more than a year was to elapse before it could be flown. The first flight at Collyweston took place on 3rd September 1944 although it was recorded on the strength of No. 1426 Flight from 13th May 1944. It was transferred to the EAF of the CFE at Tangmere after the disbandment of No. 1426 Flight. Allocated to No. 47 MU, Sealand, on 1st November 1945, but, in common with other EAF/CFE aircraft, it stayed at Tangmere until examined by the AHB in March 1946. When examined, it was considered too 'weathered' to be worth preserving and then went direct to No. 6 MU, Brize Norton, where it arrived during the week ending 15th August 1946. It was SoC on 14th August 1947, at the same time as most of the other ex-German aircraft held there. The aircraft was not W Nr 0397, as has been reported: the correct number has been confirmed by photographic evidence.

Note: The serial numbers of the above three aircraft were among a batch of identities allocated late in 1942 to No. 41 Group, RAF, for use on impressed civilian aircraft.

NN644   Messerschmitt Bf 109F-4   W Nr 7232
Coded 'White 11' of IV/JG 26. This Bf 109 made a wheels-up landing on Beachy Head on 20th May 1942 after being damaged by anti-aircraft fire whilst attacking a coastal shipping convoy in the English Channel near Newhaven. It was taken by road to RAE Farnborough for examination and the RAF serial number NN644 was allotted on 20th January 1943 for possible flight tests. In the event the '109 was not made airworthy at Farnborough.

The aircraft was taken by road to RAF Collyweston on 21st August 1943 and was restored to flying condition by No. 1426 Flight. After replacement of the engine damaged in its forced landing, the Bf 109 was test flown on 24th October 1943, before the application of its British markings. NN644 remained with No. 1426 Flight at Collyweston until the Unit's disbandment, and was then transferred to the EAF of the CFE at Tangmere. The 'movement card' records its transfer to No. 47 MU at Sealand on 1st November 1945 although this cannot be confirmed from other records.

RN228   Messerschmitt Bf 109G-2/Trop W Nr 10639
Coded 'Black 6' of III/JG 77. Radio call-sign 'PG+QJ'. This Erla Maschinenwerk-built Bf 109 was normally flown by Lt Heinz Ludemann. It was captured at LG 139/Gambut Main on 13th November 1942, and was made airworthy by personnel of No. 3 Squadron, Royal Australian Air Force, who painted it as 'CV-V'; 'CV' was the code of the Squadron and 'V' was normally reserved for captured trophy aircraft flown by the unit.

Its first flight under new management was made by S/Ldr R. H. Gibbes on 10th November. It followed the next few moves of the unit, to LG 150/Gazala No. 2 on 15th, and Martuba No. 4 on 19th November 1942. It was last mentioned in the Squadron's record book on 1st December, when it was flown by S/Ldr Gibbes and F/Lt R. J. Watt. Ferried to Heliopolis on 2nd December.

Meanwhile, on 29th November, No. 209 (Fighter) Group had ordered that the '109G should be subjected to flight tests and on 15th December it was ferried to Lydda in Palestine. A comprehensive series of flight tests was flown at Lydda between 29th December 1942 and 29th January 1943 by W/Cdr G. Mungo Buxton. While there, it was serviced by a party from No. 451 Squadron, RAF. The '109 was ferried back to Shandur in the Suez Canal Zone on 21st February.

Above: **An air-to-air shot of the Bf 109F-4 NN644 still wearing its 'White 11' and 'falling bomb' markings dating from service with JG 26.** *MAP*

Right: **An official photograph of Henschel Hs 129B NF756 of No.1426 Flight taken at RAF Collyweston.** *IWM, CH15612*

Below: **A photograph of the No.1426 Flight Ju 88A-6 HM509 taken at the USAAF airfield of Goxhill in Lincolnshire in 1943 or 1944.** *Peter Green collection*

G. Mungo Buxton was an experienced pilot with an engineering background, who had been a leading sailplane pilot and designer in England before the war. He was later the Engineering Officer of the CFE at Tangmere in 1944/5. In May/June 1945 he was to be closely involved, with other CFE officers, in the recovery of early German jet aircraft for post-war evaluation in England. The thorough tests he carried out on the '109G enabled detailed performance curves to be drawn and sent to England for dissemination by Air Intelligence 2(g).

The '109G was then shipped to England for further evaluation. After unloading at Liverpool, it arrived in crates at RAF Collyweston on 26th December 1943. The RAF serial number RN228 had in the meantime been allocated to the aircraft on 1st November 1943, at the request of the RAE.

It was first flown at Collyweston by No. 1426 Flight on 19th February 1944 and was shortly afterwards painted with its RAF serial number. A number of comparative trials were flown against various types of Allied fighter, including the Tempest V, although this duty was outside the normal remit of No. 1426 Flight. After the disbandment of the Flight, RN228 was flown from Collyweston to Tangmere on 27th March 1945, on its transfer to the EAF of the CFE. Like most of the other ex-Luftwaffe aircraft at Tangmere, it was nominally recorded on the strength of No. 47 MU from 1st November 1945 but it was still at Tangmere when inspected by the AHB in March 1946. It was transferred to Sealand in April 1946 and was packed for museum storage during May. RN228 was at Stanmore Park by 1949 and followed the other AHB aircraft to Wroughton and Fulbeck. By 1961 the aircraft had moved to Wattisham where a project was under way to restore it to airworthiness under the supervision of Flt/Lt J. R. Hawke. Eventually this project was abandoned and RN228 languished at Wattisham for some time before being taken to Henlow in connection with the film 'Battle of Britain' in 1968.

By October 1972 it was at Lyneham where its restoration to flying condition recommenced, led by F/Lt Russ Snadden, and in 1975 it moved to Northolt, where the project remained for some years before moving again, to Benson in 1983. The aircraft was allocated the ground instructional identity 8478M for book-keeping purposes. On 26th October 1990 the aircraft entered the UK civilian aircraft register as G-USTV under the ownership of J. J. Chadwick, trading as the Imperial War Museum. This was a prelude to its first post rebuild flight, which took place at RAF Benson on 17th March 1991. It has been based at the Imperial War Museum airfield at Duxford since 12th July 1991 and it is intended that it will be flown on the show circuit for three years and then grounded for permanent static display.

RN231   Messerschmitt Me 210   W Nr *unknown*
This serial number was allotted on 1st November 1943, at the request of RAE Farnborough. It is presumed to have been intended for an Me 210 being shipped to the United Kingdom in company with the Bf 109G and MC 202 which were allotted as RN228 and RN236, respectively. Nothing further is known about this aircraft and no records have been traced for any Me 210 being captured by the Allies.

RN236   Macchi MC 202 Folgore
Serial no & C/n unknown. This British serial number was allotted on 1st November 1943 at the request of RAE Farnborough. The aircraft was received by road at Collyweston on 20th January 1944 after shipment from the Middle East, for use by No. 1426 Flight. The aircraft was in too bad a state of disrepair to be made airworthy and was SoC as Category E2 on 20th May 1944. Although this can-

not be confirmed, it is probable that the MC 202 was ex-MM 7779, coded '96-4', which was the subject of an 'EA' Report on the type, prepared by RAE Farnborough staff.

TS472   Junkers Ju 88S-1   W Nr 140604
Coded 'RF+MT'. This aircraft was captured at Villacoublay in September 1944. After repair to a damaged tail wheel, the Ju 88 was air tested there on 22nd September, flown to Hawkinge on 24th September and to Collyweston on 25th September, on delivery to No. 1426 Flight. The RAF serial number TS472 was allotted on 14th October 1944.

The Ju 88S remained at Collyweston for some time after the disbandment of No. 1426 Flight in January 1945, before being flown to Tangmere on 18th April for use by the EAF of the CFE. Although nominally allotted to No. 47 MU, Sealand, on 1st November 1945, it did not leave Tangmere. It was examined by the AHB at Tangmere in March 1946 and it may have been one of the four Ju 88s which left Tangmere for No. 47 MU shortly afterwards, but there is no specific record of its receipt by that unit. It was almost certainly scrapped at Sealand or Sleap in the early post-war period.

VD364   Messerschmitt Bf 109G-14/U4   W Nr 3114/2484?
As with the example which later became VD358 (see Chapter Three), this Messerschmitt was captured at Gilze-Rijen in the Netherlands. It was taken to Antwerp-Deurne in Belgium for restoration to flying condition by No. 1426 Flight personnel. Both these examples were painted with the code letter 'P'. VD364 was flown from Antwerp to Hawkinge on 9th February 1945. Its ferry flight continued from Hawkinge to Collyweston on 14th February. The RAF serial number VD364 was allotted on 7th April 1945 and the aircraft taken on charge with the EAF of the CFE at Tangmere on 26th April. VD364 was SoC after a landing accident at Tangmere on 17th May 1945. (See also entry for Messerschmitt Bf 108 'VD364' in Chapter Six under Royal Air Force Cranwell, section 6.10).

VX101   Messerschmitt Bf 109G-6/Trop   W Nr *unknown*
This aircraft was received in damaged condition from the Middle East on 4th February 1944, via the Packing Depot at Southport. It was corroded and had been damaged by machine-gun fire. At first it was not considered worth repairing and its engine was donated to one of the Flight's other '109s. Later it was repaired and made its first flight on 10th April 1944, flown by F/Lt E. R. Lewendon. On 19th May 1944, the aircraft was damaged beyond repair when its starboard undercarriage leg collapsed while it was landing at Thorney Island. This was on the same day that the Flight lost its Ju 88, HM509. On 26th September, VX101 was SoC as Category E2, for use as spares, after 11 hrs 10 mins flight time.

*   *   *

At the disbandment of the Flight, it had a total of seven pilots, two radio operators and thirty-two ground personnel. All of these were transferred to form the Enemy Aircraft Flight of the CFE Tangmere. The pilots were F/Lt D. G. M. Gough (Flight Commander), F/Lt F. T. Roberts, F/Lt R. H. Pattison, F/Os R. A. Gordon and H. A. Fox, and P/Os R. F. Lee and H. E. Gray.

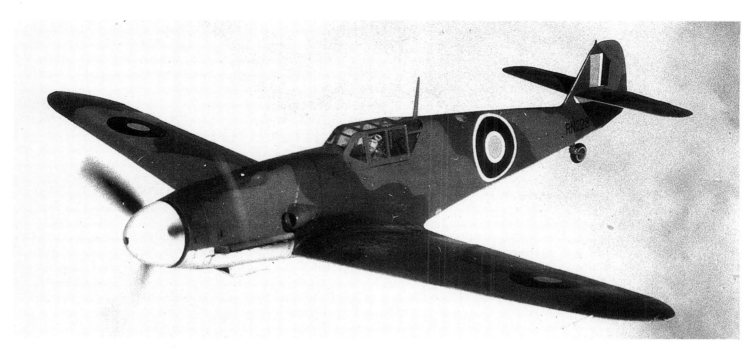

Above: **An official air-to-air photograph of the Bf 109G RN 228 in its days with No. 1426 Flight. This is the aircraft recently restored to airworthiness at RAF Benson and now flying from Duxford.** *IWM, E(MoS)1375*

Right: **The Ju 88S-1 TS472 of No. 1426 Flight, photographed at Collyweston.** *MAP*

Below: **A ground shot of the Bf 109G VX101 captured in the Middle East, during its brief service in 1944 with No. 1426 Flight. The origin of its RAF serial number, VX101, is obscure since chronologically numbers prefixed 'VX' were not allotted until late 1947.** *J. Mutin collection.*

Chapter Three

Other Units
in the United Kingdom

These included the following RAF units:
- Aeroplane and Armament Experimental Establishment, Boscombe Down.
- Air Fighting Development Unit (and the associated Naval Air Fighting Development Unit). This was formed at RAF Northolt and later moved, in turn, to Duxford and then Wittering.
- Airborne Forces Experimental Establishment, at Ringway, Sherburn and later at Beaulieu.
- Maintenance Command Communications Squadron, at Andover.
- Marine Aircraft Experimental Establishment, at Helensburgh.
- Telecommunications Flying Unit, at Christchurch and Hurn.
- No. 24 Squadron.
- No. 271 Squadron.

In addition, the civilian air ferrying organisation known as the Air Transport Auxiliary and British Overseas Airways Corporation both had an involvement with ex-Axis aircraft, as did Rolls-Royce Limited, the aero-engine manufacturer.

Finally, the Royal Norwegian Navy operated a Flight of Heinkel He 115 floatplanes under RAF control from Dundee/Woodhaven and elsewhere, for a period. This unit was later re-equipped with Consolidated Catalinas and became No. 1477 Flight, RAF.

3.1   AEROPLANE AND ARMAMENT EXPERIMENTAL ESTABLISHMENT (A&AEE)

The A&AEE is concerned with the more practical service trials of new British military aircraft. Whereas the RAE is concerned with theoretical aspects, basic research, and the solution of problems within its expertise, the A&AEE is more oriented to 'wringing out' new aircraft types, testing them and their equipment for their Service applications and finally issuing the formal airworthiness clearances, pilot's manuals, and dealing with the other preliminaries prior to the entry of a type into service.

The unit was first formed at RAF Martlesham Heath in 1924, although it can trace its ancestry to the Experimental Flight of the joint Royal Flying Corps/Royal Naval Air Service Central Flying School at Upavon in 1914. The units which became the A&AEE first moved to Martlesham Heath in 1920. The A&AEE itself moved to Boscombe Down at the start of the Second World War, to be further away from the possibility of German air attacks.

Although the A&AEE was the first unit to fly the Messerschmitt Bf 109E AE479, prior to its delivery to RAE Farnborough, it did not subsequently have any Axis aircraft on its permanent strength. In August 1942, the aircraft of No. 1426 Flight were detached to Boscombe Down to give flight experience of German aircraft to A&AEE test pilots. During this exercise, twenty of the pilots made a total of fifty-one flights in Junkers 88, Heinkel 111, Messerschmitt 109 and 110 aircraft. Later, examples of the Focke Wulf Fw 190 and Messerschmitt 410 were loaned to Boscombe Down by the RAE for similar exercises.

3.2   AIR FIGHTING DEVELOPMENT UNIT (AFDU) AND ASSOCIATED UNITS

The AFDU was formed at Northolt to act as a centre for the development of fighter tactics, and to provide a cadre of air combat expertise which could be used to train potential Squadron and Flight commanders in the lessons learned by the most experienced combat pilots. Late in 1940, the Unit moved to Duxford, and in 1943 it transferred again, to Wittering.

Closely associated with the RAF AFDU was the Royal Navy's Naval Air Fighting Development Unit. This was formed as No. 787 Squadron in March 1941. In June 1941 this unit moved from Yeovilton to Duxford. The NAFDU's operations were closely allied to those of the AFDU and the Axis aircraft flown by AFDU were frequently used as the object of tactical trials with new Naval fighter aircraft. The NAFDU moved to Wittering in March 1943, at the same time as the AFDU itself. In January 1945 the NAFDU moved to Tangmere to be located with the new RAF Central Fighter Establishment, and later followed that unit to West Raynham in November 1945.

The Fighter Interception Unit (FIU), a similar entity to the AFDU but specialising in the development of night fighter tactics, moved early in 1944 to Wittering from its normal base at Ford, to allow space at Ford to be used by squadrons involved in the forthcoming invasion of Europe. While at Wittering, the FIU was involved in trials of the Messerschmitt 410 TF209, details of which appear in Chapter One. After the invasion, the FIU returned to Ford and the AFDU moved there also. Both units were disbanded and their personnel and equipment used as the basis of a new unit, the Central Fighter Establishment (CFE). No. 1426 Flight also joined the new unit in February 1945, its resources becoming the Enemy Aircraft Flight (EAF) of the CFE.

The AFDU and CFE flew many of the aircraft already referred to under the RAE and No. 1426 Flight in Chapters One and Two. In addition, they were involved with the following:

VD358   Messerschmitt Bf 109G-14/U4   W Nr 413598
This Bf 109, with VD364, was found at Gilze-Rijen, near Breda, in the Netherlands, and was taken by road to Antwerp-Deurne where it was re-assembled and then flown to RAF Hawkinge on 9th February 1945. Photographs taken at Deurne show that both VD358 and the aircraft which became VD364 were painted in RAF colours including 'invasion stripes', and both carried the code letter 'P'.

On 24th March it was flown to Tangmere and later taken on charge by the EAF of the CFE. The serial VD358 was allocated on 7th April 1945 and the official date of allocation to the EAF was 26th April. It received the code 'EA-2' with the Flight. VD358 was ferried from Tangmere to the RAE, to appear in the German Aircraft Exhibition. The precise flight date has not been traced, but it had arrived there by 21st September 1945.

After the Exhibition closed, VD358 was flown to No. 6 MU Brize Norton on 10th January 1946. It wasn despatched from No. 6 MU to an unknown destination during the week ending 18th July 1946 (at the same time as the Fw 190 PN999). Its fate is obscure.

VF204 Fiat G 55 Centauro ex MM 91150

MM91150 was surrendered by a defecting Aeronautica D'Italia SA test pilot who landed at Piombino airfield on 4th August 1944. It was recorded on charge with the EAF of the CFE at Tangmere on 17th March 1945, although the CFE Operations Record Book states that it was 'being unpacked' on 7th April and its RAF serial number was not allotted until 27th April 1945. It is believed not to have been flown because of serious corrosion which had taken place during its shipment to the UK. The aircraft was examined *in situ* by the RAE, and an 'Enemy Aircraft' Report (EA 273) was written about it. It is presumed to have been scrapped at Tangmere.

* * *

Below: **The Fiat G 55 VF204 in semi-derelict condition at Tangmere probably in 1946.** *Steve Coates collection*

Bottom: **These two Bf 109Gs are shown at Antwerp/Deurne, where they were assembled by personnel from No. 1426 Flight after being found dismantled at Gilze-Rijen in the Netherlands. Both aircraft wear British markings and camouflage and both are coded 'P', possibly as a mis-application of the 'P for prototype' marking. These aircraft became VD358 and VD364 after delivery to England.** *RAFM, P11490*

The equipment of the AFDU and CFE was flown for familiarisation purposes by most of the unit pilots. Pilots took turns to fly the different types of aircraft in mock combat, to assess the types' strengths and weaknesses and to recommend future tactics accordingly.

The AFDU had a parallel Royal Navy unit, the Naval Air Fighting Development Unit (NAFDU), based alongside it at Duxford and Wittering. This assured that there was a suitable interchange of information on air tactics between the two Services. This arrangement continued under the CFE regime.

A typical AFDU pilot was F/Lt A. E. Rumble, who flew with the Unit at Duxford from December 1941 to June 1942. During his first month there, Rumble flew the Hurricane, Spitfire, Defiant, Lysander and Messerschmitt Bf 110 for 'Type Experience', making his first solo in Bf 110 AX772 on 28th December 1941, a trip of 25 minutes. In the following month, his experience was expanded to include the Douglas Boston, de Havilland Mosquito, Fiat CR 42 and Messerschmitt Bf 109E.

The Bf 109E was AE479, and Rumble made its last flight in England before the 'Emil' was shipped to Wright Field. On 28th January 1942, Rumble flew from Duxford to Sealand in a Westland Lysander of the AFDU. His duty was to bring the ferry pilot, F/Lt Forbes, CO of No. 1426 Flight, back to Duxford after flying the '109E to Sealand, where it was to be crated for shipment to the USA via Liverpool. It had been arranged that, on reaching Sealand, Rumble would be allowed a 30-minute familiarisation flight in the '109.

Rumble was duly briefed and after being assured that all local fighter units and AA batteries had been warned of the flight, he took off from Sealand for his trip. After seven minutes of uneventful flight, Rumble suddenly noticed tracer bullets arcing past his wing tip. As he took evasive action, excited chatter could be heard over the radio, and he saw a number of Spitfires chasing him. By great good luck, he was able to escape into cloud and return, somewhat chastened, to Sealand. The radio chatter had been in Polish, and research shows that the Spitfires were probably from No. 308 (Polish) Squadron, RAF, which was based at Woodvale, a few miles north of Sealand, along the Lancashire coast. This incident highlights the danger inherent in flying an enemy aircraft in Allied colours without a close escort of friendly aircraft. No. 1426 Flight always used such an escort unless the cross-country distance was less than ten miles or so.

In seven months with the AFDU, Albert Rumble flew over 150 hours on a variety of aircraft types which included, in addition to

those listed above, the GAL Hotspur troop-carrying glider, Vultee L-1 Vigilant, Wellington bomber, Hornet Moth communications aircraft, Blackburn Skua and Fairey Fulmar naval fighters, N A Mustang, Hawker Typhoon, Gloster Gladiator, Stinson Reliant, Airspeed Oxford trainer, Heinkel He 111, Junkers Ju 88, Tiger Moth, Miles Magister and Curtiss Kittyhawk. Over eleven flying hours were on the ex-Axis types.

3.3 ### AIRBORNE FORCES EXPERIMENTAL ESTABLISHMENT (AFEE)

The AFEE was formed as part of the 'Central Landing Establishment' (the initial cover-name for the unit responsible for airborne forces' training and development). Its days at Ringway and Sherburn were concerned with the trials of British airborne equipment including parachutes and troop-carrying gliders.

During the early development period, trials were conducted with rotary wings as an alternative means of delivery to the parachute and the glider. These involved trials with a single-seat rotary kite, the Rotachute, designed by Raoul Hafner. Hafner was an Austrian citizen who had designed autogiros in Austria and England before the war. The Rotachute was intended as an alternative to the parachute for the delivery of men behind enemy lines, the theory being that the rotor-kite had a carrying capacity for extra equipment and allowed a more controllable descent, in particular that it could be steered more easily towards a selected objective. In parallel, a 'Rotajeep' was built to try out the delivery of a jeep by attachment of a two-bladed rotor.

These projects led to the accumulation of considerable knowledge in the characteristics of rotary-wing aircraft at the AFEE. When the first Focke Achgelis Fa 330 was found on U-boat *U-852*, captured after being beached on the coast of Somaliland in May 1944, it was delivered to Beaulieu for assessment. Further examples of the Fa 330 were delivered in the post-war period, together with an example of the Focke Achgelis Fa 223E twin-rotor helicopter.

3.4 ### MAINTENANCE COMMAND COMMUNICATIONS SQUADRON (MCCS)

This unit qualifies for inclusion because, for most of the war, it was the sole RAF user of the Messerschmitt Bf 108B Taifun (or 'Aldon', as it was called in RAF service).

The unit was based at Andover, adjacent to the Command HQ which it served. The first 'Aldon' was received on 28th March 1941. The name 'Aldon' was derived from the name of the British sales' agent for the Messerschmitt 108, Mr H. J. Aldington of AFN Ltd, who had imported two examples of the type prior to September 1939. These aircraft were impressed into RAF service, together with a German civilian example left at Croydon Airport by the German Embassy in London on the declaration of war.

AW167   Messerschmitt Bf 108B-1   W Nr 370114
Ex D-IJHW of the RLM. This was a German-owned aircraft based at London's Croydon Airport for the use of the German Embassy. On the declaration of war on 3rd September 1939 it was unable to leave Croydon because of a flat tyre and was abandoned by its owners. It was flown away by the RAF on an unknown date but force landed due to engine trouble, eventually arriving at No. 10 MU, Hullavington, by road, on 6th December 1939. Impressed on 30th June 1940 with the RAF serial AW167, it was allotted to No. 110 (Anti-Aircraft Co-operation) Wing at Ringway on 30th June 1940 and then transferred to the Station Flight at RAF Abingdon on 14th July 1940. On 1st July 1942, it was transferred to RAF Andover for use by the MCCS, receiving the code 'S6-K' of that unit. It served with the Squadron until flown to No. 5 MU, Kemble, on 12th August 1946. It flew to Heston on 26th September 1946 to be cannibalised to service ES955 (see below), and later was civilianised with the registration G-AFZO, which properly belonged to ES955. It was then sold to Switzerland in April 1950 as HB-ESM. Still current as such in 1991, but the German registration D-ESBH was reserved for it in 1992.

DK280   Messerschmitt Bf 108B-1   W Nr 2039
Ex G-AFRN of AFN Ltd. This was a demonstrator, owned by the British agents for Messerschmitt, which had been imported by H. J. Aldington, the proprietor of AFN Ltd. This Taifun was first used by the RAE at Farnborough in connection with the tests car-

An unidentified RAF 'Aldon', as impressed civilian Bf 108s were known in RAF service. *NASM courtesy Norm Malayney collection*

ried out there on the Bf 109E AE479. Flights were made at Farnborough on 10th August 1940 and again on 18th March 1941. G-AFRN was ferried from Farnborough to Andover on 28th March 1941 by W/Cdr Elwin Jones; the '108 was impressed on 17th April 1941 and received the RAF serial DK280. It was allotted to the MCCS at Andover and was SoC on 8th September 1942, after its undercarriage collapsed on landing at Weston Zoyland, but it was later repaired and brought back on charge on 30th November 1943 with the same unit.

DK280 crashed at Boughy Fall Farm, Colton, near Rugeley in Staffordshire, on 20th July 1944. It was finally SoC as Category E2 on 17th August 1944.

ES955 Messerschmitt Bf 108B-1 W Nr 1660

Ex G-AFZO of AFN Ltd. This aircraft was imported shortly before the outbreak of war by AFN Ltd having previously been D-IDBT of Margarethe Guttermann. Although registered as G-AFZO on 28th September 1939, after the war started on 3rd September, the new registration may not have been painted on the aircraft; a list of civilian aircraft held at Heston on 22nd June 1941 still included D-IDBT. Impressed on 23rd September 1941 with the serial ES955, which was actually painted on the aircraft as ES995 (correctly the number of a Wellington). Initially allotted to No. 24 Squadron at Hendon, before joining the other 'Aldons' at Andover on 9th

August 1942 when it was transferred to the Station Flight there; to the Station Flight at Northolt from 10th January to 22nd April 1943, after which it returned to Andover. Flown to No. 5 MU, Kemble, on 24th May 1946 and restored to its original civilian owner as G-AFZO on 19th September 1946. Flew from Kemble to Heston on 26th September and was briefly repainted as G-AFZO before reappearing as G-AFRN. The latter marks correctly belonged to the preceding DK280 which had been written off while in RAF service. It remained in these incorrect markings until sold in Switzerland in April 1950 as HB-ESL. In 1955, HB-ESL was sold to the Government of the Saarland as SL-AAV. In June 1959, the aircraft was 'sold' to West Germany as D-EDIH, the Saarland having been incorporated into the Federal Republic in the meantime. It crashed at Walsrode after engine failure on take-off on 7th September 1980. Registration cancelled on 12th September 1980.

ES995 see foregoing text for ES955.

Below: **An ex-RAF Messerschmitt Bf 108B HB-ESM W Nr 3701, previously AW167, photographed by the author at Ascona, Switzerland, in July 1970.**

Bottom: **Another ex RAF Bf 108B D-EDIH photographed by the author at Liverpool-Speke, 19th May 1967, while *en route* to an Air Rally being held at Jurby in the Isle of Man. This was W Nr 1660, formerly ES955 of the RAF.**

3.5   MARINE AIRCRAFT EXPERIMENTAL ESTABLISHMENT (MAEE)

The MAEE was formed at Felixstowe to cover the development of marine aircraft in the same manner as the A&AEE at Martlesham Heath carried out trials with British land-based aircraft. The bases of the two units were only a few miles apart, to promote co-operation between them. In 1939, the MAEE moved to Helensburgh on the Clyde in Scotland, to reduce the risk of damage and disruption from enemy air activity in the South-East of England.

The MAEE first became involved with the trials of an Arado Ar 196 captured in Norway in 1940, and the tests of Royal Norwegian Navy Heinkel He 115 floatplanes which were similar to Luftwaffe aircraft of the same type – indeed one of the Norwegian aircraft was itself a captured Luftwaffe example.

After the invasion of Norway on 9th April 1940, one Heinkel He 115 of the Royal Norwegian Navy was flown to the UK and taken over by the MAEE at Helensburgh. This is believed to have been 'No. 52', which was flown to Helensburgh on about 1st May 1940. After the surrender of Norwegian forces to the Germans on 8th June 1940, three further He 115s arrived at Sullom Voe and then flew onwards to Helensburgh. In February 1941 all these aircraft were put in the hands of Scottish Aviation Ltd, for overhaul and repainting in RAF markings.

At the time that the Heinkel He 115s were flown to Scotland, a captured Arado Ar 196A seaplane accompanied them from Norway to Sullom Voe, an RAF advanced seaplane base in the Shetlands. The Arado took off from Sullom Voe on 16th or 23rd April 1940 (reports conflict about the date) en route to Inverkeithing/Tayport. Due to bad weather at its intended destination, it was forced to land in the River Eden, adjacent to Leuchars land airfield, and to be beached there by its pilot until it could be refuelled. The Ar 196 was ferried from Leuchars to the MAEE at Helensburgh. No RAF serial number was allocated to this aircraft because it crashed at Rhu, near Helensburgh, on 26th April 1940, when its pilot, Cdr C. W. Byas, RN, misjudged his landing on flat calm water and flew into the sea. The aircraft sank and was written off. A few small parts were salvaged and taken to RAE Farnborough for examination. No Werk Nummer is known for this aircraft.

This Ar 196 had originally been captured by Norwegian forces on 8th April 1940 after it had made a forced landing near Lyngstad after running short of fuel. It was briefly operated by the Royal Norwegian Navy (unit FA 2) prior to its flight to Scotland.

Further trials of German marine aircraft were conducted in the immediate post-war period.

Bü 131 Jungmann W Nr 4477 'GD+EG' of the Luftdienst, photographed at RAF Christchurch shortly after it was stolen. *Ron Henry collection*

3.6   TELECOMMUNICATIONS FLYING UNIT (TFU)

The TFU was a radar development Unit, primarily for airborne radar equipment. Its flying arm was initially formed as the 'Special Duties Flight' (SDF), later becoming the TFU. It was originally formed at Worth Matravers on the south coast of England, although the flying elements of the Unit were based initially at Christchurch airfield, later moving to Hurn. Later the Unit formed the basis of the new Telecommunications Research Establishment (TRE), established at Defford airfield, near the TRE main site at Malvern. The Unit has, in recent years, become the Royal Signals and Radar Establishment, still based at Malvern.

Flying activities are now carried out at Bedford/Thurleigh, co-located with the RAE there.

The TFU involvement with an ex-Axis aircraft arose solely because one such aircraft landed at its base and was taken over by the Unit.

DR626   Bücker Bü 131B   W Nr 4477

This two-seat biplane trainer, coded 'GD+EG' of Luftdienst, was stolen from Caen-Carpiquet by two French pilots and flown to RAF Christchurch on 29th April 1941. It was taken to London by road on 22nd May for a 'War Weapons Week' display. It was returned to Christchurch on 13th June, having been allotted the RAF serial DR626 in the meantime, and was allocated to the strength of the SDF based at Christchurch. The SDF was concerned with providing target aircraft for the development of improved radar systems and was later absorbed by the TFU at Hurn.

The Bücker had been too badly damaged by souvenir hunters during its display in London for it to be repaired! It was nominally transferred to the TFU on 1st August 1941, before finally being SoC on 5th November 1941.

3.7   No. 24 SQUADRON, RAF

This unit briefly used three examples of the Savoia-Marchetti SM 73P three-engined transport aircraft. The squadron was a transport unit, based at Hendon, to the north of London.

These were aircraft of the Belgian national airline, SABENA, which escaped to England following the German invasion of Belgium on 10th May 1940. Two aircraft, OO-AGX and OO-AGZ, were delivered to the Squadron on 11th May and a third, OO-AGY, on 14th May. These aircraft were all licence-built examples of the SM 73P, manufactured by the Belgian firm, SABCA. The three aircraft were attached to 'E' Flight of the Squadron.

OO-AGZ was damaged on the ground by enemy action, at Merville in northern France, on 23rd May 1940, and captured by the advancing German forces.

OO-AGX and OO-AGY were recorded as 'missing' in France on 23rd May 1940, but they appear to have subsequently been restored to the ownership of SABENA.

Later, on 16th September 1940, both aircraft were seized by the Vichy French authorities at Oran in Algeria, while en route to the Belgian Congo. It is believed that the aircraft were then handed over to the Italian government.

The Squadron later used an example of the Messerschmitt Bf 108B. Details are given under aircraft serial number ES955 (see entry in this Chapter for 'Maintenance Command Communications Squadron', section 3.4). No RAF serial numbers were allocated to the SM 73Ps of this Squadron.

3.8   No. 271 SQUADRON, RAF

This squadron also used four SABENA Savoia-Marchetti SM 73P airliners, during May 1940. These aircraft were delivered to the squadron at Doncaster on 12th May 1940. The SM 73Ps of this unit were allotted the RAF serial numbers X8819 to X8822, inclusive. Although RAF markings were painted on the No. 271 Squadron aircraft, the serial numbers were not used. These aircraft were used in the evacuation of British forces from northern France. The four SM 73Ps used by No. 271 Squadron were:

OO-AGL Savoia-Marchetti SM 73P   **C/n 30001**
OO-AGO Savoia-Marchetti SM 73P   **C/n 30005**
OO-AGQ Savoia-Marchetti SM 73P   **C/n** *unknown*
All SABCA-built. Returned to SABENA on 31st May 1940. Subsequently interned at Oran, on 22nd September 1940.

OO-AGS Savoia-Marchetti SM 73P   **C/n** *unknown*
SABCA-built. Shot down by enemy ground forces near Calais in northern France on 23rd May 1940, while returning to England after delivering ammunition to Merville.

Below: **An ex-SABENA Savoia Marchetti SM 73P in RAF colours after delivery to No. 271 Squadron at Doncaster.** *RAFM, P7377*

Bottom: **The former Danish Airlines Fw 200 with its British civilian registration G-AGAY applied. The registration was underlined with red, white and blue stripes to highlight the civilian status of the aircraft, a ruling that applied to all civilian aircraft at the time.** *PRO, from AIR 40/124*

3.9   AIR TRANSPORT AUXILIARY (ATA)

The Air Transport Auxiliary was a civilian organisation set up with Government support at the start of the war to carry out aircraft ferrying and related duties. The organisation had its headquarters at White Waltham aerodrome, near Maidenhead in Berkshire. Its pilots were drawn from civilian volunteers, many of them former military pilots who were too old for military service. Others in their ranks were women or ex-airline pilots who, for one reason or another, were not eligible for military service. Because many of them were mature in years, their ATA title came to be unkindly interpreted as 'Ancient and Tattered Airmen'. When the ex-DDL Focke Wulf Fw 200 was considered to be unsuitable for BOAC service because of the dangers inherent in its German silhouette, it was transferred to the ATA for possible use as a multi-engined training aircraft, since no other suitable aircraft were available.

DX177   Focke Wulf Fw 200A-02 Condor   W Nr 2894
Ex OY-DAM of DDL. This aircraft was owned by the Danish national airline, DDL, and was named *Dania*. It was at Shoreham on 9th April 1940, when Germany invaded Denmark. It was seized and ferried to Bristol/Whitchurch on 18th April. When registered as G-AGAY to the Secretary of State for Air on 15th May 1940 it was intended for service with BOAC between the UK and Egypt via Marseilles but this plan was dropped after the fall of France. It was then allotted to the Cairo-Takoradi route but it lacked the range for the ferry flight and was modified to carry extra tanks in the cabin for the trip to Africa. It flew to Eastleigh for overhaul by Cunliffe Owen Aircraft on 9th June 1941 but was then allotted to the ATA for multi-engined training and delivered to White Waltham on 5th July. The registration G-AGAY was cancelled on 30th June and the RAF serial DX177 allotted. The Condor was test flown at White Waltham on 12th July 1941, but was damaged beyond repair on landing when it skidded on the wet grass and its undercarriage collapsed. SoC on 18th January 1942 and taken to No. 1 Metal Produce and Recovery Depot at Cowley, for reduction to scrap.

3.10   BRITISH OVERSEAS AIRWAYS CORPORATION (BOAC)

BOAC's involvement with Axis aircraft was very limited. On 9th April 1940, the date of the invasion of Denmark, the Danish Air Lines (Det Danske Luftfahrt, DDL) Focke Wulf Fw 200 airliner

OY-DAM was at Shoreham, near Brighton in Sussex. Shoreham was then the UK terminal for those few European air services still operating under wartime conditions. The Fw 200 was taken over by the British authorities and was handed over to BOAC. (See ATA section 3.9).

At the same period, the RAF acquired a number of Heinkel He 115 seaplanes from the Norwegians. These aircraft were later overhauled at the BOAC flying-boat maintenance base at Hythe. (See section 3.12).

3.11   ROLLS-ROYCE LIMITED

(See entry for Messerschmitt Bf 109E DG200 in Chapter Two).

3.12   ROYAL NORWEGIAN NAVY FLIGHT

This unit was formed at Dundee/Woodhaven on the south bank of the River Tay. It mainly comprised escaped Norwegian personnel who had flown their Heinkel He 115 float-planes to Scotland. The Flight initially operated as a detachment of No. 210 Squadron, RAF. Earlier histories are shown under the MAEE, (section 3.5).

Among the intended duties of the original Norwegian unit were the delivery of undercover agents to Norway and other covert activities. Little has come to light of the detail of such operations. Details of the aircraft used are:

BV184   Heinkel He 115A-2
Ex '56' of Marinens Flyvevaesens. From Norway to Sullom Voe on about 8th June 1940, then to MAEE Helensburgh on 9th June. Taken on RAF charge on 24th September 1940 and ferried from Helensburgh to Calshot in November. The RAF serial number was allotted on about 12th December under AM Requisition No. 566196, which recorded that the aircraft was still the property of the Norwegian government. BV184 was flown to Scottish Aviation for maintenance and painting in RAF markings on 8th February 1941. To BOAC at Hythe on 3rd May 1941 for modification in connection with its intended use for covert operations in Norway

and elsewhere. To RAF Calshot on 24th August 1941 and flown from there on clandestine operations in the Bay of Biscay. BV184 was damaged when it was attacked in error on 23rd April 1942 by Spitfires of No. 303 Squadron, while returning from a sortie over the Bay of Biscay. To RAF Wig Bay for repair, but was damaged beyond repair by an explosion during take-off from there on 31st May 1942 and SoC.

BV185   Heinkel He 115A-2
Ex '58' of Marinens Flyvevaesens. From Norway to Sullom Voe on 7th June 1940, then to MAEE Helensburgh on 9th June. Flown by MAEE for performance assessment and then ferried to RAF Calshot on 14th November 1940. To Scottish Aviation and to BOAC as per BV184. To Calshot on 20th June 1941 and thence to Gibraltar and Malta, arriving at Kalafrana on 23td June. BV185 flew on clandestine operations to North Africa before being destroyed in its hangar in an Italian air raid on 9th July 1941. SoC on 1st April 1942.

BV186   Heinkel He 115A-2
Ex '52' of Marinens Flyvevaesens. The history of BV186 is identical to that for BV184 up to the Scottish Aviation entry. To BOAC at Hythe on 17th September 1941 for modification, and thence to No. 57 MU Wig Bay for storage on 14th July 1942. To the Royal Norwegian Navy Flight at Dundee/Woodhaven on 15th August. Scrapped in December 1942, prior to the re-establishment of the unit as No. 1477 Flight on 17th February 1943.

BV187   Heinkel He 115B-1
Ex '64' of Marinens Flyvevaesens. This had previously been a Luftwaffe aircraft which had been captured by the Norwegians during the fighting in Norway and taken over by the Marinens Flyvevaesens. It was one of two Luftwaffe Heinkel He 115 which force landed at Helgelandskysten on 13th April 1940. The He 115 was flown to Tromso/Stattorn on 30th April and numbered '64'. It operated with FA 3 of the Royal Norwegian Navy until evacuated to Britain in June 1940. Thereafter its history is as per BV185 up to the BOAC Hythe entry. From Calshot to RAF Mountbatten on 27th October 1941, *en route* to Malta. Destroyed by strafing Luftwaffe Bf 109s at Kalafrana early in 1942 and SoC on 1st April.

Chapter Four

Aircraft Captured by the Royal Air Force in the Middle East

The numbers of Axis aircraft captured in the Middle East and the timing of their capture depended to a large degree on the swings and fortunes of war in the Libyan Desert and elsewhere. At the outbreak of war between Great Britain and Italy, on 10th June 1940, the main strength of the RAF in the Middle East was in Egypt, with smaller contingents in Palestine, the Sudan, Kenya, Aden, Iraq and Gibraltar, in all totalling about three hundred aircraft. Their main strategic purpose was the defence of the Suez Canal. The Italians had nearly three hundred aircraft in Libya, one hundred and fifty in East Africa, and fifty on the island of Rhodes, with a further twelve hundred in Italy itself.

There were several campaigns in the Middle East, not all of which yielded aircraft captures. Those campaigns which did are summarised here, as essential background to the understanding of events.

There is little doubt that the 'ace' collectors and restorers of ex-enemy equipment were the personnel of No. 3 Squadron, Royal Australian Air Force (RAAF), which, together with other squadrons of the RAF, RAAF and South African Air Force (SAAF), formed 'Royal Air Force Middle East'. After the USA entered the war, these squadrons were supplemented by units of the USAAF.

Not all the known examples of ex-Axis aircraft flown in British or US markings have been traced to specific RAF or USAAF units. All examples flown by the RAF should (in theory at least) have received RAF serial numbers in the 'HK' range, these numbers being allocated to Air Headquarters, RAF Middle East, for local allotment to acquisitions in its area. However, the master record of these allocations was not transferred to the UK at the end of the

war and the information has therefore been lost. Known examples of 'HK' serial numbers are given below, as is a listing, by type, of other aircraft known to have been used by various units.

4.1   **EGYPT & LIBYA**

Soon after the outbreak of war, the Italians in Libya began preparations for the invasion of Egypt. The British defence plan was based on holding a line at Mersa Matruh, some one hundred and twenty miles inside Egypt. The Italians at first advanced about half way to this position and began to gather resources for a major attack. This was pre-empted by a British attack on 9th December 1940, which took the Italians off balance, resulting in a headlong retreat. The British advanced and by 7th February 1941 had captured all of Cyrenaica (the Eastern province of Libya) including the city of Benghazi. This enabled No. 3 Squadron, RAAF, to open its score at Martuba in Libya, after the squadron's arrival there in January 1941, with the capture of a Fiat CR 42 from among the two hundred abandoned Italian aircraft.

This Fiat CR 42 biplane fighter of the Regia Aeronautica was coded '7-70'. It was repainted in silver with British markings and the 'serial number' A421 (signifying 'Australian CR 42 No. 1'). The number was somewhat after the style of RAAF aircraft serial numbers, which are prefixed by the letter 'A' followed by a number unique to the type of aircraft, and then an individual aircraft number (e.g., A58-1 was the first Supermarine Spitfire of the RAAF). The CR 42 was flown by No. 3 Squadron at Benina in Libya, in March 1941. When Rommel's Afrika Korps drove back British forces at the end of that month, the CR 42 was burned at Got-es-Sultan Landing Ground on 4th April, during the retreat, to prevent its recapture. On 12th February 1941, General Erwin Rommel arrived in Tripoli to take command of his 'Afrika Korps'. On 31st March, Rommel's forces attacked the British and scored an outstanding success, largely because the forces which had beaten the Italians had been despatched to help Greece (which Mussolini had invaded in October 1940), or to the Sudan to repel possible advances from Italian territories in East Africa. British forces were forced to retreat to the Egyptian border, while leaving a large garrison cut off at Tobruk in Libya.

Few British aircraft fell intact into Axis hands during these campaigns. The only example known to the writer is the Hurricane I V7670, operated by No. 261 Squadron, RAF. V7670 was SoC as a result of a 'Flying Battle' on 16th August 1941. The circumstances are unknown, but some months later (probably during Operation 'Crusader') this aircraft was recovered in the Western Desert and was taken on the strength of No. 208 Squadron, RAF.

During the period after the British retreat, one incident yielded some captures – a formation of Junkers Ju 87Bs of the Regia Aeronautica ran out of fuel on 8th September 1941 and force-landed behind British lines. At least one of these aircraft was repainted in RAF markings.

Opposite: **RAF He 115 BV186 shown in an official photograph taken for publication in aircraft recognition material.** *IWM, E(MoS) 1230*

Below: **This photograph is included to show that traffic was not all one-way. It shows an RAF Hawker Hurricane 1 V7670 in the Western Desert in Luftwaffe markings after recapture by the RAF.** *RAFM, P9602*

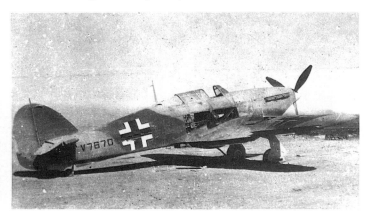

Top: **This photo shows Ju 87B WNr 5763 flying in Italian markings with the addition of RAF roundels and fin flash. Later the Italian unit code '209' – indicating 209 Squadriglia – was painted out and the RAF serial number HK827 applied.** *IWM, CM1378*

Above centre: **The Fi 156 Storch is shown soon after capture, with RAF roundels and fin flash superimposed over the Luftwaffe crosses, but still showing its code 'NM+ZS'. This aircraft was probably later flown in full RAF camouflage.** *USAF Museum courtesy N. Malayney collection*

Above: **A former Regia Aeronautica Fiat CR 42 in the hands of No. 238 Squadron at El Gubbi, near Tobruk in Cyrenaica (Libya).** *RAF Museum*

Below: **This shot shows Bf 109G 'CV-V' of 3 Squadron, RAAF, the aircraft later to be in England as RN228, and now flyable at Duxford.** *IWM, CM4171*

HK827   Junkers Ju 87B   WNr 5763

This Stuka had previously served with the 209ª Squadriglia of the Regia Aeronautica (Italian Air Force). It force-landed in Libya on 8th September 1941 after running out of fuel and was in service in December 1941 when it was flown by pilots of No. 39 Squadron based at Ikingi Maryut. It was still in service when the unit moved to Landing Ground (LG) 86, on 27th December. The Stuka continued to be flown in British hands for nearly three years, its last recorded flight being made at El Ballah in the Suez Canal Zone on 27th September 1944 by F/Lt W. A. Sutton. The airframe was scrapped soon after this date due to corrosion of the wing structure.

*   *   *

Also during this period the British forces are believed to have captured their first Fieseler Fi 156. This may have been the example identified as 'NM+ZS', flown by No. 3 Squadron, RAAF. This Storch was painted in British markings, but retained its Luftwaffe code letters. The fate of this aircraft is unknown, but it may well have been one of the anonymous Fi 156s which acquired British desert camouflage and served the British in a communications/liaison role.

A further British offensive took place in November 1941, Operation 'Crusader', which eventually advanced into Cyrenaica. A total of 458 German and Italian aircraft was captured, in various states of repair, at Gambut, Martuba, El Adem, Derna, Gazala, Berka and Benina. By January 1942, the British had reached El Agheila, the strategic defence point which had been their previous objective, in 1940. However, after receiving reinforcements, Rommel struck back swiftly and by 14th February 1942 the British were forced to retreat to Gazala, west of Tobruk. Nevertheless, several Axis aircraft captured during the 'Crusader' advance were flown in British marks.

These examples included a Fiat CR 42 flown by No. 238 Squadron at El Gubbi, during the unit's residence there between 19th January and 5th February 1942.

It is also probable that a Bf 109F, flown from Heliopolis between February and July 1942 by No. 267 Squadron, was captured in Cyrenaica during Operation 'Crusader'. Approximately six hours were flown, mostly on demonstration sorties to Army training camps for recognition purposes. The precise origin and fate of this aircraft are not known.

Rommel attacked again in May and June 1942, and after fierce fighting the Germans entered Egypt. The British Eighth Army withdrew to El Alamein, a long planned defence line sixty miles west of Alexandria. By contrast with the Axis losses in the previous British advance, only five RAF aircraft were left behind on airfields during this attack.

At El Alamein the opposing sides faced each other for several months. During this period, General Bernard Montgomery arrived from England to take command of the Eighth Army. On 23rd October 1942, the Battle of El Alamein began. When that battle was won, the Axis troops never stopped their headlong flight out of Africa for more than short-term rear guard actions. On 8th November, Operation 'Torch' started, a combined Anglo-American invasion of French North Africa, two thousand miles west of El Alamein, to complete a pincer movement from west and east.

The next captures by No. 3 Squadron, RAAF, were a Bf 109G and Bf 109F, following the Battle of El Alamein. The Bf 109G was found at LG 139 in the Western Desert on 9th November 1942 and was first flown by the Squadron CO, S/Ldr R. H. Gibbes, on the following day. This '109G is one which still exists in the UK; its full history is given in Chapter Two under the serial number RN228.

The Bf 109F was found at Martuba No. 4 LG and was flown for the first time by S/Ldr Gibbes on 20th November 1942. After a few other flights by Gibbes and F/Lt R. J. Watt, the '109F was ferried away to Gazala on 8th December 1942 by P/O R. V. Pfeiffer.

No. 7 Squadron, SAAF, also acquired a Bf 109F at this period. The example was found at LG 12. It was flown to Shandur on 27th November 1942 by the CO of the Squadron, Major Blaauw. There is no further record of the unit flying the '109. It had previously flown with III/JG 53, with the code '12'.

No. 4 Squadron, SAAF, was another inhabitant of Martuba No. 4 LG at this period. The unit arrived on 10th December 1942; its Bf 109F made a first flight under new management on 6th January 1943, in the hands of the Squadron CO, Major du Toit. This aircraft burst a tyre on landing on this day, but was not seriously damaged. There is no further mention of it in the unit records, beyond a note that it was hoped to have the Messerschmitt flying again soon. Photographs show that the '109 was marked as 'KJ-?', KJ being the code of No. 4 Squadron.

No. 213 Squadron, RAF, captured a Junkers Ju 87D at Sidi Haneish (LG 101), in November 1942. This aircraft was coded as 'AK-?' with RAF markings and was test flown on 12th November 1942.

No. 260 Squadron, yet another unit to fly from Martuba No. 4 LG, took over a Heinkel He 111H, previously '5J+CR' of III/KG 4. This was made airworthy by the Squadron and was painted in British markings, with the No. 260 Squadron code letters as 'HS-?'. This aircraft was named *Delta Lily* and was handed over to No. 211 Group for use as a communications aircraft. It made its first flight from Martuba to Alexandria on 7th December 1942, piloted by F/Lt R. Cundy. 'HS-?' was noted on a scrap dump at Fanara in the Suez Canal Zone in April 1947.

Most of the final tally of captured aircraft was added when British forces reached Tripoli, where the main airfield was at Castel Benito. Once again, No. 3 Squadron, RAAF, was amongst the first on the scene, arriving on 22nd January 1943. No. 3 Squadron chose a Caproni Ca 309 Ghibli, a twin-engined light transport and reconnaissance type, to use as a unit communications hack. This example made its first flight with the Squadron on 1st February 1943, in the hands of S/Ldr Gibbes. It was yet another coded 'CV-V'. On several occasions it made long flights, for example, to Cairo and Alexandria in Egypt, and it remained in service for several months. On 9th July 1943, No. 3 Squadron flew from North Africa to Takali, Malta, to take part in the build-up for the invasion of Sicily. The unit landed at Agnone in Sicily on 1st August. The Ghibli had, in the meantime, been flying with the Squadron's back echelon in North Africa and joined the unit at Agnone on 10th August. It was last noted in the unit's records on 4th September 1943.

The Squadron also acquired a Caproni Ca 164 two-seat light aircraft; this was also possibly found at Castel Benito, although it was first mentioned in the records on 2nd March 1943 when it was flown from El Assa to Castel Benito by P/O H. J. Bray. It was also flown frequently in North Africa until at least 29th May 1943, when it was flown from Zuara to Gabes by F/Sgt Ulrich.

Other examples of aircraft 'liberated' at Castel Benito included a Savoia Marchetti SM 79 taken over by No. 145 Squadron, RAF, on the unit's arrival there on 8th February 1943. This aircraft was repainted in British markings, with the Squadron code letters 'ZX'. It was previously MM 22174 of the Regia Aeronautica. It was used extensively as a Squadron communications aircraft and wore the name *Gremlin HQ*. F/O Jim Pickering flew this SM 79 for 88 hours 55 minutes on Squadron duties between 24th February and 19th May 1943. Later this aircraft was handed over to an unknown USAAF unit, but was destroyed by fire before it could be flown.

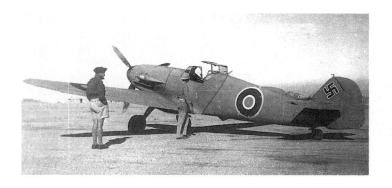

Top: **Another captured Bf 109, this time an 'F', in the hands of No. 7 Squadron SAAF. British roundels have been applied, but the fin swastika remains. It was captured at LG 12 Sidi Haneish in November 1942, after the battle of El Alamein and is the aircraft now preserved at Saxonwold, Johannesburg.** *MAP*

Above centre: **Coded 'AK-?' of No. 213 Squadron, this Ju 87B Stuka was captured at LG 101, another of the Sidi Haneish landing grounds, in November 1942.** *J. M. Bruce/G. S. Leslie collection*

Above: **This Heinkel 111H, coded 'HS-?' of No. 260 Squadron was captured in the period immediately after the battle of El Alamein.** *IWM, CM4446*

Below: **A slightly later capture was this SM 79 Sparviero, taken over by No. 145 Squadron at Castel Benito, Tripoli, in February 1943. The Squadron code letters 'ZX' of No. 145 appear on the fuselage and name 'Gremlin HQ' appears on the nose.** *Jim Pickering courtesy Roy Bonser collection*

Another Castel Benito trophy was a Fiat G 50 single-engined fighter. This was painted in RAF markings and was flown by a so-far untraced unit. It was later handed over to the USAAF 79th Fighter Group.

Operation 'Torch' had landed British and US troops in Algeria and Morocco, but the operation had not been able to cover Tunisia. The German reaction to 'Torch' was swift – on the day following the Allied landings, German forces began to land at El Aouina airfield at Tunis, soon to be reinforced by shiploads of men and equipment from Italy and Sicily. These German moves merely postponed the inevitable. German resistance in Tunisia came to an end on 13th May 1943.

An ex-Yugoslav Air Force Dornier Do 17Ka in RAF markings but without an RAF serial number, possibly at Heliopolis, photographed in 1941.
J. M. Bruce / G. S. Leslie collection

4.2   GREECE & YUGOSLAVIA

The German invasions of Greece and Yugoslavia in April 1941 introduced several more aircraft of German and Italian origin into British service. These were Dornier Do 17K and Savoia Marchetti SM 79K bombers of the Royal Yugoslav Air Force, and Dornier Do 22/See seaplanes of the Royal Yugoslav Naval Air Service. These were flown from Yugoslavia to Egypt, via Greece.

AX706   Dornier Do 17Ka
No. 3363 ex '3363' of the Yugoslav Air Force, arrived at Heliopolis on 19th April 1941 carrying gold bullion from Yugoslavia. From 6th May 1941 it was on charge with RAF Middle East, and was SoC on 12th September 1941.

AX707   Dornier Do 17Ka
This aircraft, ex '3348' of the Yugoslav Air Force, details as for AX706 above. At least one of these aircraft was painted in RAF markings, although possibly the RAF serial number was not applied. At least one (and possibly both) of these aircraft was burned out in a Luftwaffe air attack on Ismailia airfield on 27th August 1941.

An ex-Yugoslav Naval Air Service Dornier Do 22Kj '306' of No.2 (Yugoslav) Squadron taxiing for take-off at Aboukir. This example was allotted the RAF serial number AX709 but this was probably never applied since all these aircraft are believed to have continued to fly in Yugoslav markings.
IWM, CM2257

This Fiat G 12 transport was taken over by No. 223 Squadron, RAF, part of No. 232 Wing, after the seizure of Brindisi airfield at the end of September 1943, and was used by the unit during September and October for flights to Malta and North Africa. No RAF serial number is known for this example. *Courtesy J. W. Chilton*

Once on the Italian mainland, No. 3 Squadron, RAAF, set its sights on a CANT Z 501 single-engined reconnaissance flying boat. This aircraft was located at Bari, and was painted with the usual 'CV-V' codes, but this example was never actually flown by the Squadron.

4.6   **AUSTRIA**

The North-West African Air Forces (or at least some of its constituent units) became part of the Allied occupation forces in Italy and Austria in the immediate post-war period. Most of the Axis aircraft found in these areas were destroyed, although a small number were taken over for further service.

The main known user of ex-Luftwaffe aircraft in Austria was the RAF Austria Communications Flight. In 1946 this unit operated one Junkers Ju 52/3m, one Fi 156, one Bf 108 and at least one Klemm Kl 35. Earlier, the RAF is believed to have briefly flown a Junkers W 34, which was present in derelict condition at Klagenfurt in June 1947 wearing RAF markings and the code 'DV' belonging to No. 93 Squadron, a Spitfire unit which operated from Klagenfurt between May and September 1945. During July 1945, No. 93 Squadron also flew a Messerschmitt Bf 108; this may have been the aircraft later used by the Austria Communications Flight.

The Austria Communications Flight was formed at Klagenfurt on 5th October 1945. Its Fi 156 was first flown by F/Lt King on 3rd December 1945 and was still in service in April 1946. The Bf 108 was allotted to the Flight from No. 324 Wing at Zeltweg on 22nd December 1945 and was also still in service in April 1946.

The Ju 52/3m was found some time after the end of the war. At first, it was held for possible issue to Yugoslavia, whose government had requested a number of these aircraft from the Allies. However it was deemed politically unacceptable to give any aircraft to Yugoslavia, since a similar request from Greece had been turned down prior to this particular aircraft being found. Official authority was given for the Flight to carry out an air test of the aircraft on 28th February 1946. There is no later mention of the aircraft in the Flight records.

Although the Austria Communications Flight records make no mention of a Klemm Kl 35 two-seat light aircraft, photographs exist showing an example wearing the unit badge, in the Flight's hangar at Klagenfurt. The photographs are believed to have been taken in about June 1947, after the unit had been renamed the Austrian Commission Flight.

Further examples of aircraft which were allotted RAF serial numbers in the Middle East theatre included the following:

HK846   Messerschmitt Bf 110
This aircraft was test flown in Egypt and carried the code letter 'G'. It was taken on charge on 1st January 1942 and may therefore be the *Belle of Berlin* described among the aircraft above.

HK848   Savoia Marchetti SM 79   C/n *unknown*
This SM 79 was captured in Eritrea and was flown to Egypt on 3rd March 1942. No other details have been traced.

Below: **This photograph was taken at Klagenfurt in Austria by Peter Green in 1948. It shows a wrecked Junkers W 34 in RAF markings, with the unit code letters 'DV' belonging to No. 93 Squadron, which was based at Klagenfurt from May to September 1945.**

Centre: **This shot shows Bf 110D HK846 in RAF marks, with the code letter 'G', possibly at Heliopolis. This may be W Nr 4035 *Belle of Berlin* but positive confirmation is lacking.** *Steve Coates collection*

Bottom: **The Bf 109F HK849 shown here was taken on charge on 1st April 1942. It may have been captured in Cyrenaica during Operation *Crusader* in November 1941, and was possibly the '109F flown by No. 267 Squadron at Heliopolis between February and July 1942.** *RAF Museum, P013904*

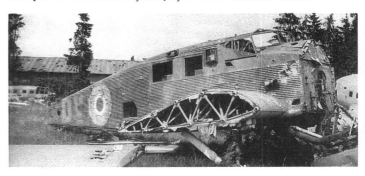

HK849   Messerschmitt Bf 109F   W Nr *unknown*

The Messerschmitt was taken on charge on 1st April 1942. It has been reported as being in service with No. 3 Squadron, RAAF, in 1943, but this seems unlikely. It is possibly the aircraft described earlier, flown by No. 267 Squadron.

HK858   Junkers Ju 88   W Nr *unknown*

No details have been traced of this reported allocation.

HK859   Caproni Ca 101   C/n *unknown*

This aircraft was shot down on 13th February 1942 by British troops, while being ferried in RAF markings by a crew from the detachment of No. 208 Squadron based at Acroma.

Top: **The Saiman 202 'MU 1' (later HK860) of No. 131 MU and later of No. 73 OTU.** *G/Capt E. Shipley courtesy N. D. Welch collection*

Above: **This Cant Z 501 single-engined reconnaissance flying boat HK976 was taken over by the RAF in Italy following the Italian surrender of September 1943, being taken on RAF charge in December of that year. It was one of a number of Cant marine aircraft of the Regia Aeronautica's 147 Squadriglia which received RAF serial numbers.** *RAF Museum, P018987*

Below: **This Ju 88D in RAF markings at Heliopolis in Egypt is W Nr 430650, otherwise FE-1598 of the USAAF and currently extant with the USAF Museum at Wright-Patterson Air Force Base. The W Nr is visible on the fin of the aircraft in the original print.** *PRO, AIR 40/126*

HK860   Saiman C 202   C/n *unknown*

This was a light communications aircraft of a type in Regia Aeronautica service. The aircraft was captured at Addis Ababa in April 1941 and was taken to Aden by W/Cdr Edwin Shipley of No. 131 MU, Khormaksar. It was flown by the MU on communications duties initially with the serial number 'MU 1'. When Shipley was posted to No. 73 OTU, Sheik Othman, the Saiman followed him there arriving on 28th September 1942. In January 1943, Shipley transferred to No. 71 OTU at Cathago in the Sudan, taking the Saiman with him. No. 71 OTU transferred to Ismailia in Egypt and the Saiman arrived there on 9th May 1943. Its last recorded flight was from Ismailia to El Gamil on 24th July 1944, after which Shipley was posted away.

HK914   Caproni (type unknown)   **C/n** *unknown*

This was received by the RAF from Saudi Arabia and was taken on charge on 31st January 1943. No further details are known. It would be a reasonable assumption that this aircraft had fled to Saudi Arabia from Italian territory in East Africa, prior to the Italian defeat, and had later been released to British custody.

HK919   Junkers Ju 52/3m   W Nr *unknown*

Taken on charge on 31st January 1943. From 4th February 1943 it was with No. 173 Squadron at Heliopolis. In May 1943, it was transferred to the British Airways' Repair Unit there. The remaining fragmentary records of the BARU suggest that this was the Ju 52/3m which was flown by the unit for 70 hours 40 minutes in August 1943, making a total of twenty-one flights. HK919 was still in service with the Middle East Communications Squadron in August 1945 but is believed to have been scrapped at Heliopolis before the end of that year.

HK920   Junkers Ju 52/3m   W Nr 5005

Taken on charge on 31st January 1943. From May 1943, HK920 was used by the British Airways' Repair Unit Servicing Flight at Heliopolis. By October 1943, it had been re-engined with three Pratt & Whitney Wasp engines. HK920 suffered a flying accident on 28th January 1944 and was SoC.

HK940   Fiat G 12   C/n *unknown*

This three-engined transport aircraft was brought on charge on 1st May 1943 and was used by the British Airways' Repair Unit Servicing Flight at Heliopolis from June 1943. The BARU flying hours return for August 1943 shows that the G 12 was only flown once during the month, on a test flight of twenty minutes duration, which suggests that the aircraft was little used. The aircraft was SoC on 27th July 1944.

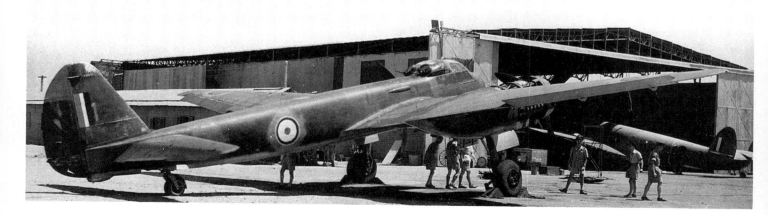

HK959   Junkers Ju 88D-1/Trop   W Nr 430650
This Ju 88 belonged to the Rumanian Air Force fighting alongside the Axis. It came from the 2nd (Rumanian) Long-Range Reconnaissance Squadron based at Mariupol and was flown by Serjeant Theodore Nikolai. On 22nd July 1943, Nikolai flew his aircraft to Limassol in Cyprus, defecting to the Allies. In August 1943 the Ju 88 was flown to Heliopolis for servicing by the British Airways' Repair Unit. It was repainted in RAF markings, although no photographs have been found showing that its RAF serial number was applied. Later the aircraft was handed over to the USAAF intelligence organisation at Cairo and, in October 1943, it was flown via Wadi Halfa, Freetown, Ascension Island, Natal in Brazil, Georgetown (British Guiana), Puerto Rico, Morrison Field in Florida and Memphis, to Wright Field. It was identified by the Foreign Evaluation number FE-1598 after arrival and, between 16th November 1943 and 9th March 1944, it was test flown for a total of 36 flying hours. Wright Field report ENG-47-1727A was written, to detail the test results. The aircraft was then put into store at Davis-Monthan AFB in Arizona but by 1963 it was on display in the USAF Museum at Wright-Patterson Air Force Base, Fairborn, Ohio. It remains on display at the time of writing.

HK974   Fieseler Fi 156   W Nr 1267
HK974 was taken on charge on 13th December 1943 and SoC on 27th October 1944. No other details have been traced but it is probable it was captured in Italy.

HK976   Cant Z 501   C/n *unknown*
Ex-Italian Air Force aircraft, coded '147-11', taken on charge on 20th December 1943 – i.e. after Italy had surrendered.

HK977   Cant Z 506B   C/n *unknown*
Ex-Italian Air Force aircraft, coded '147-4', taken on charge on 20th December 1943.

HK978   Cant Z 506B   C/n *unknown*
Ex-Italian Air Force aircraft, coded '147-7', taken on charge on 20th December 1943.

HK979   Cant Z 506B   C/n *unknown*
Ex-Italian Air Force aircraft, coded '147-2', taken on charge on 20th December 1943.

HK986   Fieseler Fi 156   W Nr *unknown*
This Storch was captured on the island of Rhodes. It was taken on charge on 26th July 1945 and transferred to the Royal Hellenic Air Force on 25th April 1946.

HK987   Fieseler Fi 156   W Nr *unknown*
Taken on charge by RAF Air Headquarters Greece on 18th September 1945. No further details have been traced.

In addition to the aircraft with identified serial numbers, the following other aircraft are known, although they cannot in all cases be related to specific units or dates:

?   Breda   C/n *unknown*
An unidentified Breda aircraft, probably a Breda 65 fighter-bomber, was flown from Addis Ababa to Sheik Othman in the Aden Protectorate by G/Capt F.O. Soden, arriving on 28th December 1941, for use by No.73 OTU. The unit makes no mention of any subsequent flight by this aircraft.

?   Caproni Ca 309-VI   C/n *unknown*
Ex MM 12444. The ground-attack version of the Ca 309 with a fuselage-mounted 20mm cannon. Noted in RAF markings at Brindisi in December 1943.

?   Caproni Ca 311   C/n *unknown*
An example in RAF markings noted at Foggia/Main in November 1943.

Below: **The Fi 156 Storch shown in this photograph was captured on the island of Rhodes in 1945. Its Luftwaffe code is 'SQ+PL' with faded RAF marks and the code letter 'C' superimposed. A second Storch is parked behind. One of these aircraft may be the example serialled HK986 described in the text.** *Ê. Barber courtesy I. A. Simpson collection*

Centre: **The Ca 309-VI Ghibli shown in this photograph in RAF marks was previously MM12444 of the Regia Aeronautica. It was seen at Brindisi on Christmas Day 1943.** *Howard Levy collection*

Bottom: **Another Caproni, this time a Ca 311, in RAF marks, at Foggia, 28th November 1943.** *Howard Levy collection*

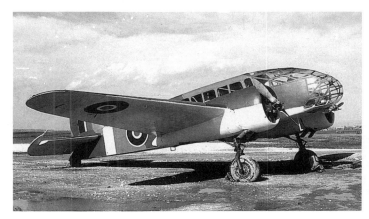

?   Fiat G 50   C/n *unknown*
Example flown by No. 260 Squadron, reportedly with the Squadron identity 'HS', while the unit was in Palestine. If correct, this report must refer to the August/October 1941 period.

Top: **An anonymous Fiat G 50 Freccia in RAF markings.** *RAF Museum, P8509*

Above: **The Ju 52/3m Junkers in RAF markings shown here was named 'Libyan Clipper'. It may be HK919 but this is unconfirmed.**
J. M. Bruce/G. S. Leslie collection

Below: **This Fi 156 Storch is typical of those flown by the Desert Air Force and its successors – it has RAF camouflage and markings but no code letter or serial number. The Vultee L-1 Vigilant in the background was one of a batch transferred to the Desert Air Force Communications Flight in February 1943. The Vigilant was struck off charge in February 1944.** *IWM, CNA2286*

?   Fieseler Fi 156   W Nr *unknown*
Several 'anonymous' examples of this type were flown by the Desert Air Force Communications Flight and its successors, and by other RAF units, from 1941 to 1946. They included an example, previously operated by 1 Wustennotstaffel, in service in RAF colours at Hergla, Tunisia, in June 1943. Photographs of Fi 156s in RAF markings in use in the Western Desert appeared as early as 1941. On 21st June 1945, the Desert Air Force Communications Flight (by that time based in Italy) had three Fi 156s on its charge, identified as nos 1, 2 and 3. On the same census date, the Mediterranean/Middle East Comms Squadron had two Fi 156s with no recorded identities.

?   Henschel Hs 126   W Nr *unknown*
One example is reported to have been coded 'OK' of No. 451 Squadron, RAAF.

?   Junkers Ju 52/3m   W Nr *unknown*
Several captured examples remained in service with communications units from February 1942 until after the end of the war.

?   Junkers Ju 87D   W Nr *unknown*
Example flown by No. 601 Squadron in RAF colours and wearing the Squadron's identity letters 'UF', after capture at LG 13/Sidi Haneish in November 1942. Abandoned at Hazbub Main on 1st March 1943.

?   Junkers Ju 87   W Nr *unknown*
One example was known to have been coded 'GA-S' of No. 112 Squadron, RAF.

?   Junkers Ju 88T-1   W Nr 1407
This aircraft, coded '8H+ZH' of Aufkl Gr 33, was shot down forty miles east of Oran on 3rd July 1944. The aircraft was damaged but was thought of sufficient intelligence interest for instructions to be given for the aircraft to be shipped to England. In the event it is probable that the instruction was cancelled with the capture of a Ju 88S in France a few weeks later.

?   Macchi MC 202
One example was painted in RAF markings, with the code letters 'AN' of No. 417 Squadron, at Castel Benito in early 1943.

?   **Messerschmitt Bf 108**   **W Nr** *unknown*
One example flown in RAF markings was photographed at RAF Heliopolis in 1941 or '42.

The files of 'Aircraft Movement Cards' show a Bf 108 with 'Med/ME' on 10th January 1946, identified as 'No. 4' and previously of the USAAF.

Further records show other 'Med/ME' operated Bf 108s on 30th August 1945, identified as 'A', 'B' and 'C'. On 21st June 1945, No. 40 Squadron, SAAF, held an unidentified Bf 108.

?   **Messerschmitt Bf 109F**   **W Nr** *unknown*
One example was known to have been coded 'EY' by 80 Squadron, RAF.

?   **Messerschmitt Bf 109G**   **W Nr** *unknown*
One example was flown by No. 72 Squadron at Pachino South airstrip in Sicily during August 1943.

F/O Hughes of this unit baled out of the '109 on 15th August after it developed a glycol leak.

?   **Messerschmitt Bf 109G**   **W Nr** *unknown*
One example flown by No. 185 Squadron with the code 'GL-?'. Dates of use unknown.

?   **Messerschmitt Bf 109G**   **W Nr** *unknown*
One example flown by No. 318 (Polish) Squadron at Treviso in 1946 with the code 'LW'. Photographed at Treviso in March 1946.

?   **Saiman 200**   **C/n** *unknown*
An ex-Italian Air Force Saiman 200, MM51235 was flown by No. 72 Squadron at Panebianco and Cassala in Sicily during September 1943.

?   **Saiman 202/I**   **C/n** *unknown*
Example flown in Italy in RAF markings with the code letters 'DS'. Noted at Foggia/Main in November 1943.

?   **Savoia Marchetti SM 79**   **C/n** *unknown*
One aircraft, reported as HK753, was written-off in a flying accident at Heliopolis on 28th February 1942.

The 'HK' number quoted is not within the series allotted to RAF Middle East.

?   **Savoia Marchetti SM 81**   **C/no** *unknown*
One example flown in RAF markings by No. 112 Squadron, with the unit code 'GA'. Possibly the SM 81 previously flown at Aden/Khormaksar (see 'East Africa', section 4.3).

Top: **The late-production Bf 109G with 'Galland' cockpit hood shown here wears the code 'LW' of No. 318 (Polish) Squadron. Note the Polish red-and-white 'checkerboard' marking on the engine cowling. The photograph was taken at Treviso, Italy, in March 1946.** *RAFM, P5118*

Above: **Depicted in this photograph is a Messerschmitt Bf 108 photographed in Egypt, possibly at Heliopolis, apparently silver overall with a dark cheatline along the fuselage.** *Steve Coates collection*

Below: **The Ju 87D Stuka wears the code 'UF' of No. 601 Squadron. The period when the unit flew the Ju 87 was Nov 1942 - Feb 1943.** *Steve Coates collection*

Chapter Five

Royal Aircraft Establishment
Post VE-Day, 8th May 1945

The RAE took a leading part in the post-war trials of German aircraft in the United Kingdom. This was carried out in three phases:
- the collection of aircraft from continental Europe, from May 1945 onwards, culminating in the 'German Aircraft Exhibition' at Farnborough in October/November 1945
- an initial evaluation period, commencing with the arrival of the first Luftwaffe aircraft at Farnborough, during which brief handling trials were conducted by Farnborough test pilots on a number of types, together with more extensive engineering assessments and performance measurements of technically innovative types (mainly the jets); during this phase also some were used for routine communications and transport duties
- from 1946 to 1948, the extended aerodynamic assessment of a number of types for reasons of empirical research - e.g..flight trials of the Messerschmitt Me 163B, Horten Ho IV, etc.

When one considers the large number of aircraft retrieved with great effort from Europe, it is perhaps surprising that many of these were never flown after their arrival in England, and that so little was recorded of those flight tests that were made. It is easy to forget that the aircraft were brought back to test establishments which were being severely cut back as the Allied war machine flung itself into reverse gear. Many people had made great efforts during the war, but now their thoughts were on peace and a return to the routine of civilian life. Governments, too, were changing their priorities and the military establishments were being starved of funds and being urged to release their personnel for peacetime employment. Their own internal priorities were changing to the support of the post-war civilian aviation industry. Even the tests of Axis aircraft were influenced by this trend – among the last trials carried out at Farnborough during Phase 2, in early 1946, were cabin noise measurements made in the Focke Wulf Fw 200 Condor and the Savoia Marchetti SM 95 for comparison with British commercial aircraft types.

At this point it is appropriate to mention that a possible fourth phase of trials was considered – that of completing (or building from scratch) a number of types of German aircraft for which parts or design details had been discovered by the Allies. The Ministry of Aircraft Production listed eighteen types of aircraft which, it was proposed, might be assembled in Germany under British supervision. These types were listed in order of priority (with annotations) as follows:

Also mentioned, but not in the list of numbered priorities, was the Blöhm und Voss Bv 238 flying-boat.

The comments shown against the aircraft appear as in the original document. The proposal to complete and fly these aircraft was abandoned due to lack of funds and personnel, but it is interesting to speculate on what might have been!

Details of the captured Bachem Natter, Horten (Gotha) 229, DFS 228, Bv 155 and Messerschmitt P1101 appear elsewhere in the book. The DFS 346 was an advanced swept-wing successor to the DFS 228; the '346 was constructed in the USSR after the war.

The Junkers Ju 287 was notable as the first jet aircraft with swept-forward wings. Two Ju 287s were flown by the Soviets after the war. The Bf 109S was an experimental prototype to have been used for research into boundary-layer control techniques. No details have been traced of a turbo-jet powered version of the Fi 103 (flying bomb).

The Junkers Ju 248 (previously the Me 163D) was a development of the Me 163 with a retractable tricycle undercarriage. The Tank Ta 183 was an advanced jet fighter design, with a T-tail and 40-degree wing sweepback. The Henschel Hs 132 was a jet powered dive-bomber of similar layout to the Heinkel He 162 jet fighter. The Junkers EF 126 was a project, again of similar layout to the He 162, for a pulse-jet powered fighter.

The 'Do 335 with jet rear engine' was the proposed Dornier/Heinkel 535, while the Do 635 was a proposal comprising two Do 335s joined by a common wing centre section. The Messerschmitt Me 264 was a conventional four-engined bomber prototype; the proposed example to have been constructed under British supervision was probably a version to have been powered by an experimental aircraft steam turbine. No details have survived of these designs making progress under British auspices.

The Hütter Hü 211 was a proposed high-altitude reconnaissance aircraft contrived by adding a new wing to a Heinkel He 219 fuselage; the partly complete hydraulic press tool to make the sparless, laminated plywood, wing for the prototype was found at Lindengarten, near the Schempp-Hirth works at Kircheim. Finally, the Bv 238 was a very large flying boat powered by six piston engines, for which an incomplete fuselage and other parts were found at Hamburg. Although they were not included in the original list, significant effort was addressed to completing various Horten tailless designs, including Horten Ho VII training aircraft found in the Peschke works in Minden and the larger Horten Ho VIII transport

1	DFS 346	(in US hands, to go to USSR)
2	Bachem Natter	(one complete at Wolf Hirth works, Nabern, two nearly complete at DFS St Leonards)
3	Horten Ho 229	(one removed from Gotha works)
4	DFS 228	(one at Ainring, to go to USSR)
5	Junkers Ju 287	(in US hands, to go to USSR)
6	Messerschmitt Bf 109S	(Boundary-layer control research aircraft)
7	Bv 155	(at Finkenwerder, promised to the USA)
8	Fieseler Fi 103	(turbo-jet version)
9	Junkers Ju 248	(in US hands, to go to USSR)
10	Tank Ta 183	
11	Messerschmitt P1101	
12	Henschel Hs 132	
13	Junkers EF126	
14	Dornier Do 335	(version with jet rear engine)
15	Messerschmitt Me 264	
16	Dornier Do 635	
17	Hütter Hü 211	

prototype, WNr41, which was found three-quarters complete at Minden and was moved to Göttingen to be completed in the original Horten factory. In the end these efforts came to nothing.

The main thrust for the proposal to complete these aircraft came from the Air Ministry. It was proposed that the work would be centred on the experimental establishment at Volkenrode, the former Luftforschungsanstalt (LFA) *Hermann Goering*, which was taken over as RAF Volkenrode, under the command of W/Cdr G. Mungo Buxton. In the event the proposal to complete the aircraft was abandoned due to lack of funds and resources. Instead much effort was expended in studying the material found at the Establishment and in dismantling major items of equipment, such as wind tunnels, for transport to the UK to be used at British research establishments. The main product in terms of hardware was a quantity of Walter 109-509 rocket engines manufactured after the end of the war by the Walter factory, to be tested at the RAE, Farnborough.

This photograph shows part of the internal aircraft exhibition, in the foreground the Bf 109G-14 WNr 413601 '7' with RAF markings on its starboard wing top surface, with the Fw 190A WNr 171747 and Ju 88G-6 Air Min 31 behind. Also visible are a Focke Achgelis Fa 330, two Heinkel He 162, Air Min 64, and Air Min 66 (partly sectioned), and the DFS 108-70 Olympia-Meise sailplane 'LF+VO'. *Crown Copyright, RAE 66107.*

5.1 PHASE ONE

The collection of ex-Luftwaffe aircraft for evaluation had been initiated by the British Air Ministry's Branch AI 2 (g), the group which had been the intelligence gatherers and collators of Luftwaffe aircraft information since before the start of the Second World War. It was this group which, with assistance from the British wartime Ministry of Aircraft Production, had drawn up a 'Requirements List' of items needed for evaluation in the UK after the war.

The list had been initiated during 1944 and was in the hands of Air Technical Intelligence teams in Europe prior to the German collapse in May 1945. The list was amended as new requirements were identified; these amendments included previously unknown aircraft or items of equipment found on the ground by the intelligence teams. With the end of hostilities the Air Technical Intelligence teams were reinforced by experienced pilots and engineers, many of them from the RAF Central Fighter Establishment at Tangmere. The personnel included members of the former No. 1426 Flight which had been incorporated into the CFE shortly before the end of the war.

It was soon decided that the ferrying of unfamiliar aircraft types was best carried out by trained test pilots and, to this end, the whole process of selecting and ferrying German aircraft to the UK

was handed over to the RAE. Lt/Cdr E. M. 'Winkle' Brown was placed in charge of the reception of German aircraft at Farnborough, and his superior, G/Capt Alan F. Hards (Commanding Officer Experimental Flying at RAE), took over responsibility for the selection of suitable aircraft. The servicing of aircraft prior to their delivery to Britain remained an RAF responsibility and this task was carried out by No. 409 Repair and Salvage Unit, based at Schleswig in northern Germany. The RAE set up an outpost at Schleswig, commanded by S/Ldr Joe McCarthy, to co-ordinate the delivery of selected aircraft to Schleswig for overhaul, and to control the acceptance test flights of individual aircraft at the completion of their servicing routine. The RAE then took over the delivery of the aircraft to England via one or more established staging posts in Holland or Belgium which were provided with jet fuel and other support facilities.

The collection phase commenced on 18th May 1945 when W/Cdr R. J. Falk flew the Messerschmitt Me 262B night fighter 'Air Min 50' from Schleswig to Gilze-Rijen, continuing onwards to Farnborough on the following day. The exercise was completed on 18th January 1946 when the Focke Wulf Fw 58 insecticide-sprayer 'Air Min 117' arrived at Farnborough from Schleswig, via Gütersloh and Melsbroek. In the meantime approximately seventy-five ex-Luftwaffe aircraft had made the journey from Schleswig to Farnborough. Nearly fifty others had arrived at Farnborough by surface transport and a few more had flown in from other places. The whole operation was safely conducted – one Ar 234B was damaged beyond repair on landing at Farnborough and one Siebel Fh 104 had force-landed in the sea *en route*, but there were no crew injuries.

Those aircraft arriving by surface transport included twenty-three Me 163, eleven Heinkel He 162 and the Messerschmitt Me 262C prototype. Others involved in the move by surface means included a prototype Blöhm und Voss Bv 155B high-altitude fighter and the first prototype DFS 228 high-altitude reconnaissance aircraft. These last two aircraft were loaned to the British by the US authorities for investigation at Farnborough before their intended shipment to the USA.

Following their arrival at Farnborough, very many of the aircraft were flown or taken by road to the RAF's No. 6 Maintenance Unit at Brize Norton to be stored, pending allocation to a series of tests.

The details of the aircraft collected and flown to Farnborough are given under the individual aircraft entries in Chapter Seven. The collection of the many and varied types enabled the RAE to mount a 'German Aircraft Exhibition', which was held at Farnborough from 29th October to 9th November 1945. The Exhibition included displays of aircraft and associated displays of equipment in various hangars and workshops, a static display of some of the larger aircraft on the airfield, and, on some days, a flying display of a few of the more interesting types, including the jets. For this Exhibition, several aircraft were recalled from storage at Brize Norton to be shown to the public. Photographs and details of the static aircraft exhibition display appear below and on previous page.

This photograph of the internal aircraft exhibition shows the other end of the shed in more detail, with the Bv 155B, Olympia Meise, Horten Ho IV 'LA+AC', Me 163B W Nr 191912 and Heinkel He 162 Air Min 64. In the background is the fin of a Do 217 and the rear fuselage and tail braking parachute of the Arado Ar 234B Air Min 24. *Crown Copyright, RAE 66311*

FS, and Captain Ordway, Engineering Officer of 61st FS). It was flown for a short period by the 56th FG, until it was flown to RAF North Weald on 12th September 1945 because of the impending return of the Group to the USA. By 14th October it had moved from North Weald to Heston, still in US markings and on 3rd November 1945 it was flown to RAE Farnborough by G/Capt J. Cunningham, with RAF roundels painted over the US stars, to appear during the last few days of the German Aircraft Exhibition. Although selected for museum use by the AHB in May 1946, it was noted in the scrap area at Farnborough on 15th December 1946. By May 1947, it had been taken to RAF Sealand and was packed for storage on 19th May. It then progressed to Stanmore Park, Wroughton, Fulbeck and Biggin Hill with the other AHB aircraft, before arriving at St Athan where it eventually became 8471M. After being taken to Henlow in 1967/8 for use in the film *Battle of Britain* and returning to St Athan, it moved to Hendon for incorporation in the Battle of Britain Museum in 1979 and is currently on display there. It is possible that this aircraft had a so-far untraced 'Air Min' number in the RAE 200-series of numbers.

— Messerschmitt Me 262B-1a/U1   W Nr 111980

This Me 262 night-fighter, coded 'Red 12' of IV/NJG 11, was surrendered at Schleswig and was flown from there to Gilze-Rijen on 19th June 1945 by S/Ldr A. F. Martindale. It overshot on landing there, coming to rest in a ditch, but was later repaired. It arrived at RAE Farnborough on 6th December 1945 from Gilze-Rijen, again flown by Martindale. 111980 was noted in the scrap area at RAE on 15th December 1946, but in July 1947 it was exhibited at the Blackpool Air Pageant at Squires Gate airport, Blackpool. Presumably it was taken to No. 47 MU, Sealand, or some other RAF unit, for museum or display purposes, but did not survive the reduction in AHB holdings of such aircraft at the end of 1947. Although there is no record of this aircraft having an RAF serial number or 'Air Min' number, it seems possible that it was the Me 262 which the writer believes to be the real owner of the number 'Air Min 53' (see comments under that entry in Chapter Seven).

Me 262A W Nr 500443 photographed at Schleswig in June 1945. The starboard side of the aircraft wore the serial number 'USA 1'. *PRO file AIR 37/1442*

— Messerschmitt Me 262A-1a   W Nr 500443

Coded 'Yellow 5' of JG 7, this Me 262 was surrendered at Schleswig and was initially allocated to USAAF Intelligence as 'USA 1'. In the event the USAAF recovered sufficient single-seat Me 262s for its needs in the US Zone of Occupation and did not take delivery of this aircraft. It was therefore brought to the UK, probably via the 'Return Ferry Service', and transported by No. 71 MU, Slough, to No. 6 MU, Brize Norton. It was on the strength of 6 MU by 29th November 1945 and remained with it, until transferred to No. 47 MU, Sealand, on 1st May 1946. At Sealand it was prepared for shipment and left Birkenhead aboard the SS *Perthshire* on 20th October 1946, bound for Cape Town in South Africa, where it arrived on 6th November. It was allotted the SAAF serial number '201', presumably for intended flight trials, but no flights were made and the aircraft was declared surplus to requirements and sold as an instructional airframe to the Benoni South Technical School in about 1950. It was scrapped in about 1953.

— Messerschmitt Me 262C   W Nr 130186

The Me 262C-1a Heimatschutzer I prototype was a mixed power-plant modification of the original Me 262 with the addition of a Walter 509A-2 rocket-motor exhausting from the rear fuselage. This motor was the same type as that which powered the Me 163B and was intended to boost the climb performance of the Me 262 for interception duties. This aircraft, also designated Me 262V-186,

Me 262B W Nr 111980 'Red 12' at Blackpool during an Air Pageant in July 1947. *Steve Coates collection*

made its first flight on 16th October 1944 and its first flight using its rocket-motor on take-off on 27th February 1945. After the surrender, the fuselage (at least) of this aircraft was brought to RAE Farnborough for investigation. It may have been the unidentified Me 262 fuselage noted in the scrap area at Farnborough on 15th December 1946.

—   Focke Wulf Ta 154   W Nr *unknown*

The Ta 154 was a twin-engined night-fighter of wooden construction. It was to a degree inspired by the British de Havilland Mosquito, which was a supremely successful application of wooden construction to a high-performance aircraft. The Ta 154 was unofficially called the 'Moskito', perhaps in recognition of its progenitor. In practice, the Ta 154 did not come up to its expectations, mainly due to development problems with the bonding agents used in its construction. Only the first few aircraft entered service and these were very quickly withdrawn from use.

Because of British interest in the structural techniques employed in the Ta 154 design, it had appeared in the Category One Requirements List, and three dismantled aircraft were selected to be shipped to the RAE. These aircraft were found at the Luftpark (Storage Depot) at Paderborn, by No. 2002 ADW. At least one arrived at Farnborough, where it was the subject of an engineering investigation, resulting in the issue of Report EA 262/1. It is possible that one or more received an untraced 'Air Min' number.

5.3   **PHASE THREE**

After the accident to the Dornier Do 335, a reassessment of the use of the ex-Axis aircraft was made. For some time, only the Fieseler Fi 156 and one of the Junkers Ju 352A transports were flown. Then, in March 1946, flight trials of the Messerschmitt Me 163B VF241 recommenced. These trials were made mostly at the nearby airfield of Wisley, to avoid the busy circuit traffic at Farnborough, since the Me 163B was towed off as a glider by a Spitfire and released at altitude to make its own way back to earth. These trials were primarily to explore the handling characteristics of the Me 163B's tailless configuration, to provide information for other tailless designs on the drawing boards of British manufacturers in the post-war period. The 'tailless' design concept had been attracting aircraft designers for years, as evidenced by the experimental designs of Northrop in the USA, Lippisch and the Horten brothers in Germany, and innovative designs by Handley-Page and Miles Aircraft in the United Kingdom. During the war years, the British Ministry of Aircraft Production had placed several contracts for experimental tailless aircraft with the aircraft industry. These resulted in extensive trials of the Baynes Carrier Wing tailless glider at the RAE. Another contract was for a series of tailless gliders with different tailless plan-forms, placed with General Aircraft Ltd, resulting in the GAL 56 'Medium V', 'Medium U', 'Maximum V' and GAL 61 prototypes. The GAL designs were tested at RAE and by GAL's own test pilots (notably Robert Kronfeld) at the company's Lasham airfield, close to Farnborough. The tests of the Me 163B, and of the Horten Ho IV sailplane, were conducted as part of this overall programme. In April 1946 decisions were taken about the long-term use of the German aircraft, resulting in the allocation of RAF serial numbers to those which it was intended to maintain in flying condition. These aircraft were:

VP543   Horten Ho IV sailplane
VP546   Fieseler Fi 156 Storch
VP550   Junkers Ju 352A
VP554   Messerschmitt Me 262A

VP559   DFS 108-14 Schulgleiter SG 38
VP582   DFS 108-14 Schulgleiter SG 38
VP587   DFS 108-49 Grunau Baby
VP591   DFS 108-30 Kranich II sailplane

In addition to these, the Messerschmitt Me 163B had previously been given an RAF serial number, VF241. The Messerschmitt Me 163B was flown initially to provide general experience in the handling of tailless aircraft. At a later stage the main purpose of the flights was to accumulate experience in the skid landing technique. The Me 163 was launched on a wheeled trolley which was jettisoned after take off. Landings were made on a hydraulically-sprung skid which was lowered prior to landing. Interest in this technique arose because two German aircraft designers, Drs Winter and Multhopp, were employed at the RAE at the time, designing a high-speed experimental jet aircraft which was to land on skids. Also at this time a naval jet fighter programme was under development based on the presumption that, to save weight, the aircraft would not have a conventional undercarriage, but would land on a rubberised 'flexible deck' on the aircraft carrier. After the trials of the Me 163B, which ended when the aircraft was damaged beyond repair following a high-speed skid landing at Wittering, interest in the skid-landing concept waned.

The Multhopp project was never built, due to a government policy decision not to risk pilots' lives in supersonic flight, a decision which later cost Britain its lead in jet fighter development. The naval fighter project, although the aircraft eventually appeared as the Supermarine Scimitar, was to see the light of day with a conventional undercarriage. This was possibly because of the Me 163B's demise at Wittering, and other unpromising trials with a modified version of the Vampire single-seat jet fighter, which was landed on a 'flexible deck' at Farnborough and on the modified aircraft-carrier, HMS *Warrior*. The Ho IV made its first flight (after being grounded to appear at the German Aircraft Exhibition) on 27th March 1946, and again on 18th April 1946. Thereafter there is no record of it making further flights until a new series of nine flights was made in April, May and June 1947. It seems possible, however, that the official Flight Log does not contain a complete record of the flights made by gliders. Most of the Ho IV flights are believed to have been made by Robert Kronfeld, who had been instrumental in bringing the sailplane to England in the first place, and after the Ho IV was withdrawn from use at Farnborough, it was sold to him.

Opposite: **A sample sheet from the RAE's technical record of German Aircraft received at Farnborough. Note the RAF serial number against He 162 W Nr 120097 should actually read VN153.**

Below: **The RAE's Fi 156C Storch VP546 photographed at Wolverhampton at an air race meeting in 1950 or '51.** *MAP*

The Fi 156, VP546, was maintained in flying condition at Farnborough until 1955, when it was grounded, due to lack of spare parts. It was used for a large variety of different projects. These included aircraft-carrier deck landings (on HMS *Triumph* in 1946, flown by 'Winkle' Brown), formation flying with helicopters to allow air-to-air photography of rotor blade behaviour, glider-towing, and routine communications flying. In 1948, another Fi 156, which had been used by AV-M H. E. Broadhurst as a personal transport, was added to the RAE fleet (serial number VX154). This was flown for two years on similar duties, until it was grounded to act as a source of spares for the original aircraft.

The Ju 352, VP550, only made two return trips to Germany after April 1946, before it was grounded due to servicing problems, while the proposed trials with the Messerschmitt Me 262 VP554 were cancelled and the aircraft was shipped to Australia, where it is still in the hands of the Australian War Memorial.

The remaining aircraft listed, all of them gliders, were taken on charge for use by the RAE Technical College Glider Flight. Their main duty was to give elementary flight training to the apprentice engineers under training at the Royal Aircraft Establishment's own training establishment. These aircraft were also used to give glider experience to RAE test pilots who might have to conduct trials with unpowered aircraft. In later years the two-seat Kranich

was fitted with blind-flying instruments and two-stage amber screens in one cockpit to conduct a series of simulated blind-flying experiments, in conjunction with the Empire Test Pilot School, which was also based at Farnborough at the time.

The only other significant trials of an ex-German aircraft took place in 1947. At that time, there was some concern at the level of light aircraft accidents, and also pressure from some quarters to see the possibility of pilot training carried out on single-seat aircraft. The authorities were giving consideration to this being allowed, providing that the aircraft concerned was 'unstallable'. A series of trials were therefore carried out at Farnborough, involving the Brunswick Zaunkönig V-2 light aircraft, which had been built at the Brunswick Technical High School in 1944. This design featured a wing with full-span slots and flaps and was intended to be unstallable. The prototype was brought to Farnborough and was first flown there on 18th September 1947. After a long series of flights in 1947 and early 1948, the Zaunkönig was handed over to the Civil Aviation Flying Unit of the (then) Ministry of Civil Aviation on 16th July 1948. This unit, based at Gatwick Airport near London, carried out further trials. In March 1949 the aircraft was returned to the RAE and then sold in May 1949 to the Ultra Light Aircraft Association (ancestor of the present-day Popular Flying Association). As part of the same series of trials, the Ministry of

FOREIGN AIRCRAFT — SHEET 2

Aircraft Type	Airframe Serial Numbers			Engine Particulars					Movement Dates		Destination	Remarks
	German	A.Min.	R.A.F.	Type	Single or Port Outer or Centre	Port or Port Inner	Starb'd or Starb'd Inner	Starb'd Outer	Arrival	Despatch		
HE 162	120076	59	V.H.523	B.M.W. 109/003.E.2	T.L. 395845				15-6-45	1-8-45	Brize Norton	
"	120098	67	V.H.513	"	T.L. 395843				11-6-45	18-7-45	Aero Flight	
"	120221	58	V.H.526	"	T.L. 395919				16-6-45			Being used as spares for other aircraft
"	120072	61		"	T.L. 395537				31-7-45	28-9-45	Aero Flight	Crashed 9-11-45 Cat "E"
"	120091	66		"	T.L. 395306				31-7-45			
"	120097	64	V.N.158	"	T.L. 395905				31-7-45			
"	120227	65		"	T.L. 395914				31-7-45			
"	120074	60		"	T.L. 394681				10-8-45	10-8-45	Brize Norton	
"	120095	63		"	T.L. 394308				10-8-45	10-8-45	Brize Norton	
"	120235			"					10-8-45	10-8-45	Brize Norton	
"	120086	62		"					22-8-45	22-8-45	Brize Norton	
HE 219	290126	20		Daimler Benz 603		1402977	82064		3-8-45	21-8-45	Brize Norton	
"	310109	21		"		3625			3-8-45	30-8-45	Brize Norton	
"	310180	22		"		01300146	01300163		27-8-45			On Exhibition
"		44		"					19-10-45	19-10-45	Brize Norton	
Ju. 52	641038	104		B.M.W. 132 A		358880	60084		18-7-45			On Exhibition
"	6567	103		"	351903	72993	351164		19-7-45	26-7-45	Brize Norton	
"	6840	102		"	53339	53300	53397		28-7-45	30-7-45	Brize Norton	
"			VM900	B.M.W. 132 A/3	70879	62244	58021					Direct to Brize Norton from Germany 17-11-45
"			YM 914	"	997	58283	67946					"
Ju 86												
Ju 88	621642		VK 888	Jumo 213		1061520904	1061521609		2-6-45	18-7-45	Tangmere	
"	622838	3	VK 884	"		1021521066	1061522469		16-6-45	23-7-45	Brize Norton	By road dismantled at Farnboro
"	621186	33		"		1061521595	1061521602		6-7-45	17-7-45	Brize Norton	
"	620968	47		"		1021520316	1021520856		6-7-45	17-7-45	Brize Norton	
"	621965	9	VL.991	"		1061522759	1061522650		13-7-45	27-7-45	Brize Norton	Returned to RAE for Inst. Flight 3/7/45
"	622811	48		"					22-8-45	30-8-45	Brize Norton	
"	0660	112		"		106152001	106152033		27-8-45	18-12-45	Gosport	
"	623193	31		"					12-9-45			On Exhibition
"	6492	77		Jumo 211		J1/404/441	J2/1041303163		21-9-45			On Exhibition
"	622461	41		Jumo 213		1061522620	1061522559		13-10-45	14-11-45	Brize Norton	
"	712273		T.P. 190	"					17-10-45			On Exhibition
Ju 188	190335			Jumo 213		1061520172	106152819		26-5-45	30-5-45	Brize Norton	
"	150245	35		"		1021522598	1021522235		6-7-45	18-7-45	Brize Norton	
"	180485	45		"		1021521035	1021520465		13-7-45	18-7-45	Brize Norton	
"	0327	113		"		1021520354	1061521571		27-8-45	8-7-45	Gosport	
"	230776	108		"		1021522036	1021521411		15-9-45			On Exhibition

Supply bought an Erco 415CD Ercoupe (serial number VX147), which was also subjected to flight evaluation at Farnborough.

VP543	See Chapter Nine
VP546	See AM 101 entry)
VP550	See AM 8 entry) Chapter Seven
VP554	See AM 81 entry)
VP559	)
VP582	)
VP587	) See Chapter Nine
VP591	)
VT762	)

VX154   Fieseler Fi 156C   W Nr *untraced*

This Storch was surrendered in an area under British control (i.e. North Germany, Denmark or Norway) in 1945, and was at first flown without a serial number, as the personal aircraft of AV-M Harry Broadhurst, AOC of No. 83 Group, British Air Forces of Occupation, with the code letters 'HB'. It was later based at Kenley in the same markings when the AV-M was posted to the UK. On 17th January 1948, it was allocated the RAF serial VX154 at Kenley. At this point the previous identity was recorded as '40747.52', but this is believed to have been the engine serial number. The RAF serial number was allocated for use at RAE Farnborough where VX154 was to be a back-up aircraft for VP546, and VX154 made its first recorded flight at RAE on 20th February 1948. It was grounded and used for spares from 2nd January 1950 and was SoC on 4th April 1950. Noted by the writer in the scrap area at Farnborough in September 1954 in its blue colour scheme of Harry Broadhurst days.

VX190   Brunswick LF 1 Zaunkönig   W Nr V2

D-YBAR of Akaflieg Brunswick. The experimental Zaunkönig light aircraft, designed by the Akaflieg (Akadamische Fliegergruppe) of the Braunschweig (Brunswick) Technische Hochschule, made its first flight at Brunswick/Waggum on 3rd May 1944. It was surrendered to the British authorities at Bad Harzburg, following the end of hostilities. The designation 'LF1' – Langsamflugzeug 1 (slow-flying aircraft number one). It was eventually transported to RAE Farnborough and flown there (still as D-YBAR) on 18th September 1947 and used for handling trials of its slotted and flapped wing. It was flown very frequently and was allotted the RAF serial number VX190 on 3rd February 1948,

making its first flight as such on 12th February 1948. Some of its flights at RAE are noted below to show the extent of its use:
18, 26 and 30 September 1947
1, 2, 3, 6, 7, 8, 9, 10, 16 October 1947
5, 17, 24, 26, 28 November 1947
2, 31 December 1947
22, 23 January 1948

Delivered to Gatwick on 16th July 1948 for trials with the Civil Aviation Flying Unit of the Ministry of Civil Aviation. Returned to RAE Farnborough on 15th March 1949, and sold to the Ultra Light Aircraft Association (ancestor of the present-day Popular Flying Association) on 7th May 1949.

It was registered as G-ALUA with the ULAA on 28th June 1949 and received an Authorisation to Fly (rather than a full Certificate of Airworthiness) on 1st July 1949. The 'A to F' was a restricted authorisation given to only a very few experimental civilian aircraft at that time. The Zaunkönig was ferried from Farnborough to Cardiff/Pengam Moors on 2nd July 1949 by John Fricker.

G-ALUA remained in the UK with various owners until April 1974 when it went to Ireland as EI-AYU. The British owners were:
– Ulair Ltd (an associate of the ULAA), from 13th April 1951 to 1st April 1953
– I. G. Le Mesurier Carling (trustee of the PFA Ipswich Group), from 23rd October 1953 to 2nd January 1955
– J. O. Isaacs and partners, from 7th February 1955 to 31st December 1955
– P. J. Sullivan, from 16th January 1956 to 5th March 1969
– Vintage Aircraft Flying Ltd, from 7th March 1969 to 7th September 1971
– M. G. Loyal and R P Green, from 18th October 1971 to 25th July 1972
– Fairoaks Aviation Services Ltd, from 8th August 1972 to 16th April 1974

After being reported at Calais in France late in 1978, still with its Irish registration, the Zaunkönig disappeared. It is reported to have been bought by a Belgian owner who did not fly the aircraft. It eventually reappeared in West Germany, where it was rebuilt. It was registered as D-EBCQ on 17th November 1986 under the ownership of L. Meeder at Biberach.

Zaunkönig VX190 photographed during a visit to Redhill, probably during 1949. *George Jenks collection.*

Chapter Six

Other UK Test Centres Post-war Period

This Chapter covers the activities of the organisations, other than the RAE, which were concerned with ex-Luftwaffe aircraft in the post-Second World War period. The organisations concerned were:

- Aeroplane and Armament Experimental Establishment
- Air Torpedo Development Unit
- Airborne Forces Experimental Establishment
- British Army (2nd Army Communications Flight)
- Central Fighter Establishment
- Chemical Warfare Establishment
- Marine Aircraft Experimental Establishment
- Orfordness Experimental Establishment
- RAF Brize Norton (No. 6 MU)
- RAF Cranwell
- RAF Kenley
- RAF Sealand (No. 47 MU)
- RAF Stanmore Park (German Air Force Equipment Centre)
- RAF Woodley (Miles Aircraft Ltd)
- Auster Aircraft Ltd
- Bevan Brothers Aero Engineers Ltd
- Chilton Aircraft Ltd
- The College of Aeronautics, Cranfield
- Other Civilian Operators

6.1 AEROPLANE AND ARMAMENT EXPERIMENTAL ESTABLISHMENT (A&AEE)

The A&AEE at Boscombe Down had originally been formed at Martlesham Heath in the inter-war period. The unit had been involved in various trials of Luftwaffe aircraft during the war, although no aircraft had been transferred to the unit's permanent strength.

No trials were conducted in the post-war period, with the exception of a series of performance evaluations conducted on a French-built Fieseler Fi 156 Storch. These trials were probably connected with the issue of British military requirements for the development of post-war observation and liaison aircraft, as described in the previous Chapter.

VG919   Morane Saulnier MS 500
Although shown in some records as a Fieseler Fi 156, this was a Morane Saulnier MS 500, c/n 130, from the French production line at Puteaux which had been continued under French auspices following the liberation. The aircraft was handed over to the Ministry of Aircraft Production at Issy-les-Moulineaux on 17th May 1945 and ferried to Boscombe Down via Amiens and Le Havre on the following day. It was allotted to 'D' Squadron of the Aeroplane and Armament Experimental Establishment for trials, until transferred to No. 6 MU at Brize Norton on 26th February 1946. It was transferred to the Royal Air Force College at Cranwell on 18th September 1946 for exhibition in the Station Museum. Its fate thereafter is not known.

6.2 AIR TORPEDO DEVELOPMENT UNIT (ATDU)

The ATDU was an RAF unit based at Gosport in Hampshire. Its duties encompassed the development of air-dropped torpedoes, mines, and associated equipment, for use by the RAF and Royal Navy. Some years after the war, it was disbanded and its role transferred to the A&AEE. In 1945, one Ju 188A and one Ju 88A anti-shipping strike aircraft were transferred from Farnborough to the unit. Their intended purpose was the investigation of German air-dropped torpedoes. So far as is known, the aircraft were not flown at Gosport. The aircraft were sold as scrap in 1948.

The aircraft concerned were, respectively:
VN143   See AM 113 entry in Chapter Seven
VN874   See AM 112 entry in Chapter Seven

The French-built Criquet VG919 at A&AEE, Boscombe Down. Note the French 'Cross of Lorraine' on its fin. *RAF Museum P5774*

6.3   **AIRBORNE FORCES EXPERIMENTAL
           ESTABLISHMENT (AFEE)**

The AFEE was set up in 1940 to carry out development work in connection with airborne forces' equipment such as parachutes, troop-carrying gliders and glider tugs and all the ancillary equipment required for the Airborne Forces. The unit started life at the experimental section of the 'Central Landing Establishment' formed at Manchester/Ringway in June 1940. The Central Landing Establishment was a cover name to disguise the real purpose of the unit. The CLE later became No. 1 Parachute Training School and the other functions of the unit were transferred elsewhere. The experimental work became the job of the AFEE, initially at Sherburn-in-Elmet in Yorkshire. Finally, the AFEE was moved to Beaulieu in Hampshire. In September 1950, the AFEE was disbanded and its functions incorporated into the Aeroplane and Armament Experimental Establishment at Boscombe Down.

As part of studies into methods of airborne delivery other than the parachute, the AFEE became involved in rotor-kites. The Austrian rotary-wing pioneer, Raoul Hafner, was engaged to assist in the studies. Hafner had been involved pre-war in the development of a series of 'Gyroplanes' both in Austria and later in England. He designed a one-man rotor-kite called the 'Rotachute', as a substitute for the parachute. This was to be launched from parent aircraft to deliver its cargo of one man and his equipment. A number of prototypes of different versions of the design were built by Hafner's company and initial flights were made at Ringway. Post-war, at least one prototype was taken to the USA and formed the basis of the Bensen Gyroglider/Gyrocopter family; another prototype is held by the Royal Air Force Museum (currently on loan to the Museum of Army Flying at Middle Wallop).

Parallel projects were for a 'Rotajeep' and a 'Rotatank'. The jeep with a rotor was also built in prototype form, although the tank project, which involved fitting a rotor to the British Infantry Tank Mark III 'Valentine', remained only on paper.

Involvement with these projects meant that the AFEE had built up rotary-wing expertise and as a consequence when the first Focke-Achgelis Fa 330 was captured in June 1944 it came to Beaulieu for examination. Post-war, a large number of Fa 330s was recovered in Germany and many of these came to Beaulieu. The AFEE was also chosen as the appropriate centre for trials of the Focke-Achgelis Fa 223 twin-rotor helicopter.

Focke-Achgelis Fa 330 Rotor-Kites
The Fa 330 Bachstelze rotor-kite was developed to serve as an airborne observation platform for German submarine (U-boat) crews in order that they might detect enemy shipping over their normally rather restricted horizon. Approximately two-hundred Fa 330s were built under sub-contract by Weser Flugzeugbau at Hoyenkamp, Delmenhorst, near Bremen from 1942. The type was used as standard equipment by Type IX U-boats, mainly in the Indian Ocean. The kite was not popular with its crews, since the pilot/observer was likely to be abandoned if the submarine were forced to dive to avoid detection by patrolling aircraft – the recovery and stowage of the kite taking several precious minutes. Its existence was known to the Allies on 2nd May 1944, following the capture at Bender Biela in Italian Somaliland of U-boat *U-852* equipped with an example, which was taken to the AFEE for examination in August of that year. No details of the example concerned have yet been traced. However, it is believed that it was flight-tested.

Operational examples of the Fa 330 were found on a number of surrendered U-boats on the cessation of hostilities but it is not known whether any of these were brought to the UK. Three examples were found in the Weser works at Hoyenkamp. These were used to produce one composite, but non-flyable, example for shipment to the UK.

A further twenty-nine complete examples, each with the standard issue of two sets of rotor blades, were surrendered to the RAF at a farm building near Kiel, which was being used as a dispersed store by Luftpark 4/XI based at Kiel/Holtenau airfield. It is believed that most if not all of these kites were either brought to the UK, or handed over to the USAAF intelligence organisation and shipped to the USA. The type was tested quite extensively in both countries and in each case the kite was considered as the basis for further type development by Allied organisations.

No record has been traced (indeed, probably none was made) of the Werk Nummern of the surrendered Fa 330s. Details will be given later of known examples, most of which still survive.

Most examples were delivered to the Airborne Forces Experimental Establishment at Beaulieu. Other examples were delivered to the RAE at Farnborough and to the College of Aeronautics at Cranfield. Most of the flying trials were conducted by AFEE Beaulieu and consisted of towed flights from the back of a three-ton truck driven along the main runway at Beaulieu airfield, with the kite on a 20 foot cable. Later trials involved towing a kite from the deck of an RAF marine craft from the flying-boat base at RAF Calshot, on a 120 foot cable. The Beaulieu and Calshot trials took place between January 1948 and July 1949 and were described in Report MoS/AFEE Rota 7. These tests resulted in little conclusive information beyond confirmation of the ingenuity of the original concept and the pleasant handling characteristics of the kite under the right conditions. It is believed that several examples of the kite were damaged or lost during the tests at Beaulieu, particularly during the critical take off and landing phases. Some of the early flights were carried out by Robert Kronfeld, although other pilots were also involved, particularly after Kronfeld's death in a flying accident in February 1948 (as described in Chapter Nine).

The tests behind a short cable were not very satisfactory, but the flights on the longer 120 foot cable were smooth and trouble free. In the UK, the Fa 330 was used as a basis for the development of the Bevan E1/48 light jet helicopter, designed to a Ministry of Supply contract, for possible military use. Several Fa 330s were handed over to Bevan Brothers Aero Engineers Ltd for trials use in un-modified or modified form at its Chelmsford works. The RAF serial numbers VX259 and VX266 were allocated to the modified version of these kites. Bevan Bros had a contract (6/Acft/2079/CB9(a)) to develop a new rotor, powered by tip-mounted ram-jets to be fitted to the Fa 330 frame. The serial number VX850 was allocated on 10th July 1948 to an Fa 330 which was the subject of a further series of trials at Beaulieu. Its details are given below:

VX850   Focke-Achgelis Fa 330A   W Nr *unknown*
This serial number was allotted to an Fa 330 held at the AFEE, Beaulieu, the aircraft being taken on charge on 10th August 1948. It is probable that the RAF serial number was allotted for the kite used in the trials during which a kite was towed behind a motor launch at RAF Calshot, although this has not been confirmed. On 11th November 1949, the kite was recorded as being in temporary storage. On 13th September 1950, it was transferred to the A&AEE at Boscombe Down following the closure of the AFEE and transfer of its responsibilities to the A&AEE. On 18th April 1951, the Fa 330 was SoC, following its sale to Bevan Brothers Ltd for use in the development of its E1/48 jet helicopter design.

Known examples of the Fa 330 brought to the UK are:
WNr:

100032	Was at RAE Farnborough – to Denmark, displayed at Egeskov
100143	Imperial War Museum, Duxford
100406	Shipped to Cranfield from Kiel as an exhibit in 1946 under *Operation Medico* – to the Hubschrauber Museum (Helicopter Museum) at Bückeburg, West Germany
100502	Was at RAE Farnborough, currently with The Aeroplane Collection Ltd, but on loan to the Lincolnshire Aviation Heritage Centre at East Kirkby
100503	Was at RAE Farnborough, e.g. in 1961 – believed to RAF Museum
100509	Currently in the Science Museum annexe at Wroughton
100545	Was at Cranfield – at Torbay Aircraft Museum, until its closure in 1987, now loaned to the Fleet Air Arm Museum, Yeovilton
100549	Was at RAE Farnborough – later to Historic Aircraft Preservation Society, Biggin Hill; Reflectaire Ltd, Blackpool/Squires Gate; Merseyside Aviation Society, Liverpool. Currently in the Air & Space Wing of the Greater Manchester Museum of Science and Industry

In addition, in 1977 two Fa 330 in the possession of a farmer who owned part of the former Beaulieu airfield were put up for disposal on his death. It is not known what happened to these two kites, nor are their identities known.

VM479 Focke-Achgelis Fa 223E Drache WNr 00014

The Fa 223 was a twin-rotor helicopter, developed from the smaller Fa 61 which was successfully flown in 1936, several years before the Sikorsky VS-300 in the USA. The Fa 223 was initially developed as a six-seat transport helicopter for Deutsche Luft Hansa, but with the start of the Second World War it was modified for military applications. These included anti-submarine patrol duties, cargo heavy-lift with underslung loads, and air-sea or mountain rescue roles with an electric rescue winch.

The production of the Fa 223 was delayed many times by Allied bombing attacks and only about ten of the 130 examples ordered ever flew. At the end of the war, two examples were in service with Transport Staffel TS 40, at Ainring. Eventually these aircraft, together with one of the unit's two Flettner Fl 282 helicopters, were surrendered to US forces at Ainring. The Staffel to which the aircraft belonged had been formed to support German Army units which had been preparing to make a last stand against the Allies in the so-called 'Southern Redoubt', in the mountainous regions of Bavaria and Austria.

The Fa 223E which came to England was the V14 prototype 'DM+SR'. This aircraft was delivered from Focke-Achgelis at Ochsenhausen to TS 40 at Ainring on 16th April 1945. On 2nd May the squadron moved to Aigen/Enns to escape from the advancing Allies, and then on 8th May to Schwarzach/St Veit. The helicopter pilots, on receiving news of the cessation of hostilities on this day, decided to fly their machines back to Ainring, where they were surrendered to the occupying US troops. The helicopters were repainted in US markings and flown to Munich, and then to the US Air Technical Intelligence Unit at Nellingen, near Stuttgart. On 15th June, the Fa 223 and an Fl 282 left Nellingen for Villacoublay, near Paris, en route to Cherbourg where they arrived on the following day. Here, the Fl 282 was prepared for shipment to the USA aboard the carrier *Reaper*, but because of lack of shipping space the Fa 223 returned to Villacoublay on 20th June and was soon afterwards released for handover to the British.

On 4th September 1945 the Fa 223 was flown from Villacoublay to Le Havre/Octeville by its test pilot, Hans-Helmut Gerstenhauer. After waiting for favourable weather, Gerstenhauer left Le Havre on 6th September for Abbeville, where he refuelled before taking off for Lympne. This flight was the first crossing of the English Channel by a helicopter. Later in the day, the helicopter continued its flight, to arrive at the AFEE, Beaulieu.

By 21st September, the Fa 223 had been repainted in olive-green camouflage with British roundels. A short test flight was made on this day and a further one on 2nd October. On 4th October the Fa 223 was flown again, but whilst taking off for a second flight later in the day the aircraft crashed. This was due to a transmission

Four views of the Fa 223E taken at AFEE, Beaulieu, in October 1945 after it had been repainted in RAF markings. *PRO file AVIA 21/238*

failure, arising from incorrect tensioning of the engine mountings. Because no tensiometer was available to enable the tensions to be checked, permission had been given for limited test flights while the checking equipment was awaited.

This ended the life of the Fa 223E in England. An AFEE Report was written on the type, together with a detailed accident analysis of its crash. For further details of this helicopter, serial number VM479, see 'AM 233' in Chapter Seven.

The Flettner Fl 282V-20, which was brought to England, was not taken to the AFEE. The reason for this is not known, although it may be relevant that, at the time of its surrender, the aircraft was under maintenance - i.e., it was in partially dismantled condition, and no personnel familiar with its technical aspects could be traced in areas under British control.

Troop-carrying Gliders
Although the Messerschmitt Me 321 Gigant and its six-engined powered version, the Messerschmitt Me 323, had been on the Category One requirements list for evaluation at AFEE Beaulieu, no examples of either type were captured in airworthy condition in areas under British control in Germany, Denmark or Norway. Reports of an example having been seen in the UK in 1945 are therefore in error. The intelligence interest in the Me 323 was more than academic, for in addition to three examples for type evaluation at Beaulieu, the Category One List included requirements for a further 150 examples of the type, to be used by British forces in South-East Asia for the 'carriage of bulldozers and other heavy equipment'. The requirement was not far short of the total production of the Me 323!

<hr>

6.4   **BRITISH ARMY
(2nd ARMY COMMUNICATIONS FLIGHT)**

<hr>

Before the surrender of German forces on 8th May 1945, a Fieseler Fi 156 Storch had been acquired by No. 658 Air Observation Post Squadron, based at Lüneburg. The Squadron had been the AOP unit supporting the British 2nd Army, part of the 21st Army Group. With the end of the war, the duties of an AOP unit changed and some of No. 658 Squadron's personnel were formed into a separate (but unofficial) Flight known as the 2nd Army Communications Flight. This was commanded by Major A. Lyell, the former CO of No. 658, and included Captain O. M. G. Murphy. The Storch was used as the aircraft of General Sir Miles Dempsey, the 2nd Army Commander, and was usually flown by Oliver Murphy, who was checked out on the aircraft on 11th May. On 25th June 1945 Dempsey returned to England with members of his staff to supervise the writing of an official history of the 2nd Army campaign, and the Flight (equipped with the Storch and two Austers) followed him, to be based at RAF Chipping Norton in Oxfordshire.

Murphy flew the Storch for 32 hours 30 minutes from Lüneburg between 11th May and 24th June 1945. On 25th June he left Lüneburg en route to Brussels, and flew to Hawkinge in Kent on 27th June. After some internal flights in England, the Storch arrived at Chipping Norton on 2nd July. These flights totalled 14 hours 35 minutes. Further flights in England up to 8th August 1945 (when Dempsey departed to the Far East to command the 14th Army) added up to a further 22 hours 40 minutes by Murphy. Major Lyell flew the Storch back to Chipping Norton after the General had departed from Hurn aboard an RAF transport aircraft.

Dempsey had asked for the Storch to be retained for future use after his return to England and in preparation Major Lyell flew it

to Rearsby on 27th July to arrange for Auster Aircraft to look after the Storch in the General's absence. During this visit the Auster test pilot Geoffery Edwards was checked out on the type. After General Dempsey left for the Far East, the Storch was flown to Rearsby by Major Lyell on 17th August. It was certainly flown by Austers during September 1945, but they later wrote to Major Lyell to say that it required considerable maintenance work carrying out and General Dempsey relinquished his claim to the aircraft. The Storch was noted in external storage at Auster's Rearsby airfield on 21st July 1946. It was probably the Storch which arrived at No. 6 MU, Brize Norton in August 1946, only to be sold as scrap in the following year.

<hr>

6.5   **CENTRAL FIGHTER ESTABLISHMENT (CFE)**

<hr>

The CFE was formed late in 1944 at Tangmere, with Ford as a satellite airfield. It was concerned with the development of fighter tactics and the assessment of new aircraft types and associated equipment. Soon after its formation, it took over the equipment and personnel of the former No. 1426 (Enemy Aircraft) Flight. Many of its personnel were involved in the initial selection of German equipment to be brought to England for post-war evaluation.

The Enemy Aircraft Flight of the CFE took over the ex-No. 1426 Flight aircraft. These aircraft were:

AX772	**Messerschmitt Bf 110C**
EE205	**Junkers Ju 88A**
NF754	**Focke Wulf Fw 190A**
NF755	**Focke Wulf Fw 190A**
NF756	**Henschel Hs 129B**
NN644	**Messerschmitt Bf 109F**
PJ876	**Junkers Ju 88R**
PN999	**Focke Wulf Fw 190A**
RN228	**Messerschmitt Bf 109G**
TS472	**Junkers Ju 88S**
VD364	**Messerschmitt Bf 109G**

Below: **The ex-2nd Army Communications Flight Storch in RAF marks at Rearsby on 1st September 1945. The badge of the British 2nd Army is worn below the cockpit.** *I. O'Neill collection*

Bottom: **The long-serving Ju 88A EE205 of No. 1426 Flight after its transfer to the Enemy Aircraft Flight of the CFE. Its 'EA-' code, possibly 'EA-9', is visible.** *FAA Museum courtesy Ray Sturtivant collection*

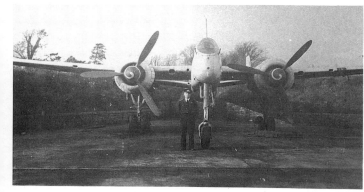

Top: **The anonymous He 219A coded 'E' at Ford after the airfield was taken over by the Royal Navy.** *Neville Franklin collection*

Above: **This Ju 88G-6, photographed at Ford after it became a Royal Naval Air Station, shows the late type 'Morgenstern' radar aerials. It is believed to be 'Air Min 16'.** *Neville Franklin collection*

Right: **Enemy Aircraft Flight Fw 190A PN999 coded 'EA-4' at Ford in 1945. Note the RAF serial number appears on its fin above the fin flash.** *FAA Museum courtesy Ray Sturtivant collection*

Below: **The Enemy Aircraft Flight Bf 109G VD358 at RAE Farnborough, coded 'EA-2', at the German Aircraft Exhibition during November 1945.** *Steve Coates collection*

The following aircraft were received from other sources:

TF209	Messerschmitt Me 410A	
	– from the Fighter Interception Unit	
TP190	Junkers Ju 88G	
	– from RAE Farnborough on 17th May 1945	
VD358	Messerschmitt Bf 109G	
	– delivered from RAF Hawkinge on 24th March 1945, after overhaul at Antwerp	
VF204	Fiat G 55 Centauro	
	– received in crate from Italy, 17th March 1945	
VK888	Junkers Ju 88G	
	– from RAE Farnborough	

The CFE was involved in the selection of many of the 'Air Min' numbered aircraft, and many of the first batch of these aircraft were delivered to Tangmere. These included:

AM 1	Junkers Ju 88G	
	– later transferred to West Raynham	
AM 2	Junkers Ju 88G	
	– later transferred to Swanton Morley	
AM 14	Junkers Ju 88G	
	– crashed at Tangmere, 18th July 1945	
AM 15	Messerschmitt Bf 110G	
	– fate unknown	
AM 16	Junkers Ju 88G	
	– abandoned at Ford	
AM 32	Junkers Ju 88G	
	– crashed at Heston, 15th October 1945	
AM 43	Heinkel He 219A	
	– abandoned at Ford	

AM 44	**Heinkel He 219A**
	– to storage at Brize Norton, 19th October 1945
AM 46	**Siebel Si 204D**
	– believed to West Raynham
AM 50	**Messerschmitt Me 262B**
	– abandoned at Ford
AM 86	**Messerschmitt Bf 110G**
	– unconfirmed allotment

In September 1945, the CFE was moved to its post-war base at West Raynham in East Anglia. Most of the German aircraft remained at Ford or Tangmere, where, in March and April 1946, they were surveyed by the Air Ministry's Air Historical Branch and a number were selected for long-term storage as potential museum exhibits. It had been intended to continue to fly the Me 262B at West Raynham. The accident involving the Ju 88 'Air Min 32' was at the end of a flight from Germany to collect spares to make the Me 262 airworthy, for its ferry flight to West Raynham. In the event, only three Ju 88s were taken to West Raynham and their subsequent lives were quite short. It is believed that the Si 204 was also taken to West Raynham, disappearing from official records for over two years, reappearing on the books of No. 6 MU in 1948.

Little was recorded of the trials carried out at the CFE and it is clear that most of the flying was 'type experience' for CFE pilots. Some evaluation was certainly carried out of the performance of German night-fighter radars using RAF aircraft as targets, and the Si 204 was used for the evaluation of German blind-flying instruments, which were in some respects ahead of Allied equipment in use at the time. Details of aircraft used by the CFE which are not included elsewhere are:

VG913   Focke Wulf Fw 190A

This serial number was allotted on 17th May 1945 to the Fw 190 previously allotted the serial NF755. See entry for NF755 in Chapter Three for details. The allotment of the serial number may have indicated an intention to fly the '190, but no flights were made.

VK888   Junkers Ju 88G-6   W Nr 621642

This Ju 88G, coded 'D5+GH' of I/NJG 3, landed at the Irish Air Corps airfield of Gormanston to the north of Dublin on 3rd May 1945 with a defecting Luftwaffe crew. After negotiations with the British government, the aircraft was flown to RAF Valley on 2nd June 1945 and then to RAE Farnborough on 3rd June. On 18th July 1945, it was ferried to RAF Tangmere on delivery to the Night Fighting Development Wing of the CFE. Believed to have been scrapped at Tangmere following the departure of the CFE to West Raynham, although it may conceivably have gone to No. 47 MU, Sealand, as a museum aircraft and been scrapped there later.

Below: **The Me 262B night-fighter 'Air Min 50' at Ford on 14th June 1946, months after the CFE had moved away to West Raynham.** *John Stroud collection*

The CWE, located at Porton Down in Wiltshire, was concerned with the development of chemical weapons – primarily gases, their means of delivery and counter measures against them. Any air support required by the CWE and associated Army units was provided by the Communications & Special Duties Flight of the Aeroplane and Armament Experimental Establishment (A&AEE) at nearby Boscombe Down.

These units were all involved in the investigation of the Raubkammer chemical weapons plant in Germany and in the selection of suitable German aircraft to carry out weapons trials on Lüneberg Heath in 1945. These aircraft included the Focke Wulf Fw 58 insecticide sprayer AM 117, a Junkers Ju 188E and two Ju 88Gs. The Junkers aircraft had suitable fittings to carry chemical weapons and were flown from Fassberg. After the completion of the trials in September 1945, the Ju 188 and one of the Ju 88s were flown to Boscombe Down where they were later scrapped without any further flights being made. The Fw 58 was sent to Farnborough where its equipment was studied for post-war application to crop-spraying from the air (see Chapter Seven).
The Junkers aircraft were:
Ju 188E W Nr 280032 'F2+UN' (arrived at AAEE 7 September 1945)
Ju 88G W Nr 622138 '4R+BA' (arrived at AAEE 22 September 1945)
Ju 88G W Nr 620452 or 620852 '..+MB' (scrapped at Fassberg)

The flying was carried out by F/Lt R. G. Wyatt and other pilots of the C&SD Flight of the A&AEE during August and September 1945.

6.7   MARINE AIRCRAFT EXPERIMENTAL ESTABLISHMENT (MAEE)

The MAEE was formed at Felixstowe immediately after the First World War. At the start of the Second World War, the unit was moved to Helensburgh on the Clyde in Scotland, since Felixstowe was considered to be at high risk of enemy air attack, situated as it is on the east coast of England.

The MAEE was involved in the selection of a number of German marine aircraft for evaluation. These included three examples each of the Dornier Do 24 and Blöhm-u Voss Bv 138 three-engined flying boats, three Arado Ar 196 seaplanes, an Arado Ar 199A and the FGP-227. This last design was a flying-scale-model of the large Bv 238 six-engined flying-boat. Separately, the RAE had selected an example of the Bv 222 Wiking six-engined flying-boat. This was flown to RAF Calshot on Southampton Water by an RAE crew and later handed over to MAEE jurisdiction.

The first to arrive in England was the Bv 138B 'Air Min S-2', which was flown to Calshot by an RAE crew on 20th June 1945. It was ferried to the MAEE at Helensburgh on 7th July 1945.

Later deliveries did not go to Helensburgh because the unit returned to its pre-war base at Felixstowe during August. The first Do 24 arrived at Calshot on 21st August 1945 and was then flown to Felixstowe on 23rd August. In the meantime, the Bv 222C-012 Wiking had arrived at Calshot from Norway on 17th July 1945. This aircraft was test-flown at Calshot on 24th July and 23rd August 1945, but it was not ferried to Felixstowe because of trouble with its six Jumo 207C diesel engines. Two engines were removed for servicing, but the big flying-boat did not fly again. In April 1946, the RAF serial number VP501 was painted on the aircraft, which was launched after minor repairs, still minus two engines. Later, its test programme was abandoned and it was scrapped. Its

Top: **The Junkers Ju 188E W Nr 280032, previously 'F2+UN' of an unknown Luftwaffe unit, photographed at Fassberg in August 1945 prior to ferrying to Boscombe Down.** *Above Centre:* **The Junkers Ju 88G coded 'MB' at Fassberg in August 1945.** *Above* **The Junkers Ju 88G W Nr 622138 '4R+BA' being loaded with gas at Fassberg for evaluation of a chemical weapon delivery system on the Lüneburg Heath ranges.** *R. G. Wyatt collection*

Below: **An Arado Ar 196A floatplane at MAEE, Felixstowe. This example is probably Air Min 91.** *N. Franklin collection*

remaining engines were sent to D. Napier & Sons Ltd at Luton to help in the development of compression-ignition aero-engines, resulting in the Napier Nomad turbo-compound diesel engine.

Two of the Arado Ar 196A floatplanes arrived at Felixstowe in September 1945. One of these, VM748, seems to have been flown quite often, being retained on MAEE strength to provide floatplane experience for the Establishment pilots. At the time, the unit had no British floatplanes available to provide such experience. The aircraft concerned ('Air Min 91') survived in flying condition for twelve months, while the other aircraft, ('Air Min 92'/ VM761) was used as a spares source.

The first Do 24 did not survive for long, since it sank during a gale in October 1945. Two further Do 24 arrived in December 1945. The aircraft were allotted for type trials, but it is not likely that they were flown very much. By June 1946 they were 'awaiting disposal'.

The Bv 138 which had flown to Helensburgh followed the unit to Felixstowe, although it also seems to have been little flown. A second Bv 138 arrived at Felixstowe at the end of 1945. This example was allotted for 'full armament trials', but once again seems to have flown little. The Bv 138s were also 'awaiting disposal' by June 1946. The second example was reprieved, since in 1947 it was in use to train RAF marine craft crews to tow and handle flying-boats.

The FGP-227 was shipped from Travemünde to Felixstowe during September 1945. It was not flown at Felixstowe, possibly because a full set of propellers could not be found for it, although flight trials had been intended and the RAF serial VM743 was therefore allotted to the aircraft.

The records of the MAEE show that the unit did not have the resources to service its collection of German marine aircraft. The MAEE was probably thankful when the ex-Luftwaffe aircraft were removed by a scrap merchant in 1947 or '8.

Details of aircraft flown by the MAEE which are not shown elsewhere are given below:

VK895   See AM S-2 under the entries for AM 69 to AM 71 incl. in Chapter Seven

VM483   See AM 115, in Chapter Seven

VM743   Flugtechnische Fertigungsgemeinschaft Prag FGP 227

Coded 'BQ+UZ', this aircraft was a half-scale flying model of the large six-engined Blöhm und Voss Bv 238 flying-boat. It was surrendered in a dismantled condition at Erprobungsstelle Travemünde in May 1945 and was investigated by the RAF Air Disarmament organisation on 11th June 1945. The aircraft was complete apart from two missing propellers. It was almost certainly allocated a so far untraced 'Air Min' number. The flying-boat was transported to MAEE Felixstowe by sea and road during September 1945 for further investigation. It arrived at Felixstowe on 1st October and the RAF serial number VM743 was allocated on 10th October 1945. So far as is known the aircraft was never flown at Felixstowe and it was recorded as 'awaiting disposal' at MAEE on 1st June 1946. It was sold for scrap to J. Dale & Co, with the other ex-Luftwaffe aircraft at Felixstowe, and collected by them on 14th November 1947. It should be noted that the 'movement card' for VM743 in the AHB records shows it as a Blöhm und Voss Bv 138 and that the various statistics for surrendered Luftwaffe aircraft also assume so, but the details shown above are definitely correct.

VM748   See AM 91
VM761   See AM 92
VN865   See AM 114   See Chapter Seven
VN870   See AM 116
VN881   See AM 70

VP501   Blöhm und Voss Bv 222C-012   W Nr 330052

This six-engined flying-boat, coded 'R' of Stab/FAGr 130, was surrendered at Sorreisa in northern Norway and flown to Trondheim during June 1945. After a test flight early in July at Trondheim, by Lt/Cdr E. M. Brown, it was later ferried to the United Kingdom. The Bv 222 flew from Trondheim to Copenhagen/Kastrup-See on 14th July, made a local test-flight from Kastrup-See on 15th July, and then continued from Kastrup-See to 'Travemünde and Sylt/ Rantum on 16th July. Finally, it flew from Sylt to Calshot on 17th July 1945. It made a local test flight from Calshot on 24th July and again on 23rd August, flown by pilots from Farnborough, but the Jumo 207C diesel engines gave a lot of trouble and it is doubtful whether it was flown again. The ferry flight from Trondheim totalled 12 hours 55 minutes and the tests at Calshot a further 1 hour 45 minutes. The RAF serial VP501 was allotted on 5th April 1946, for further intended flights by the MAEE at Felixstowe and this serial number was then painted on the aircraft, although it was never actually taken to Felixstowe. Delays had been experienced in obtaining suitable beaching gear and replacement engines. The beaching gear was received and the aircraft was slightly damaged when beached at Calshot by MAEE personnel on 30th March 1946. The Bv 222 was slightly damaged again when re-launched on 21st June 1946, but was repaired by a working party from Short Brothers at Rochester and re-launched on 1st August 1946, still minus two starboard engines. At this point, the intended further trials were suspended and the aircraft offered to the aircraft industry for study. No interest was evident and the Bv 222 was scrapped at Calshot between April and June 1947. It was officially SoC on 11th June 1947, with No. 49 MU, with the note that its Jumo engines had been removed and delivered to D. Napier & Sons Ltd at Luton. These items were used by Napiers in the development of diesel engines for aircraft applications, culminating in the Napier Nomad turbo-compound engine in 1949/50.

There has been speculation elsewhere that the Bv 222 was flown by No. 201 Squadron, a Sunderland unit based at Calshot, but there is no evidence whatsoever to support this. The 201 Sqdn ORB makes no mention of the Bv 222 and it could not have been aircraft 'R' of that unit as has been suggested since 'R' was Sunderland NJ264 during the period concerned. The identity AM 138 has been quoted in error for this aircraft (see explanation under 'AM 138' at the end of the first series of AM numbers in Chapter Seven).

Note: VP501 was not the only Bv 222 to be flown in RAF markings. The Bv 222V-2 was also surrendered at Sorreisa. The '222V-2 was flown to Trondheim in RAF markings. It was then allotted to the USA Intelligence organisation. US markings were painted on the aircraft, and a US Navy crew was flown to Trondheim to collect the aircraft. However, there is a record of a Bv 222 being scuttled at Trondheim, which is presumed to be the V-2, since only two Bv 222s were surrendered in Norway. It seems probable that the V-2 suffered from similar engine problems to those experienced by the RAF with VP501 and that these problems precluded any attempt to ferry the Bv 222V-2 to the USA.

6.8   ORFORDNESS EXPERIMENTAL ESTABLISHMENT

The Orfordness Experimental Establishment was concerned with aircraft weapons development. During the selection of aircraft for evaluation in the United Kingdom, one example each of the Messerschmitt Me 262, Arado Ar 234B and Heinkel He 162 types was selected for transfer to Orfordness. It is uncertain whether the He 162 actually arrived there, but the Me 262 and Ar 234B were

shipped from Schleswig to Orfordness during October 1945. It is believed that the aircraft were intended for firing trials - i.e., they were to be used as targets for various weapons to assess how their structures would stand up to battle damage.

—   Arado Ar 234B

An unidentified Arado Ar 234B left Schleswig by surface transport for the United Kingdom during the week ending 6th October 1945. It seems certain that this aircraft was destined for the Orfordness Experimental Establishment for weapon firing trials. It is likely that the Ar 234 concerned had originally been surrendered at Schleswig.

—   Heinkel He 162A

The statistics for surrendered Luftwaffe aircraft brought to the UK imply that an He 162A may have been allocated to the Experimental establishment at Orfordness, although the original list of requirements only makes mention of an Ar 234 and an Me 262 needed by that organisation. There is no record of an He 162A being shipped to Orfordness, but it is not possible to rule out the possibility that He 162A W Nr 120235, for which no Air Min number is known, may have been intended to go there. See entry under Air Min No. 68. Another possibility is that W Nr 120235 in fact had an untraced 'USA' number.

—   Messerschmitt Me 262

An unidentified Me 262 left Schleswig by surface transport for the United Kingdom during the week ending 6th October 1945. It is reasonably certain that this aircraft was selected to fulfil a requirement of the Experimental Establishment at Orfordness. No identity of the aircraft has been traced, although it was almost certainly one of the eight Me 262 originally surrendered at Schleswig. It has not been possible to trace the eventual fate of the aircraft although it is believed that it was used as a target during weapon firing trials.

6.9   RAF BRIZE NORTON (No. 6 MAINTENANCE UNIT)

No. 6 MU, at Brize Norton, was selected to be the storage unit for German aircraft received in the UK. Its task covered both 'Category One' aircraft, which were stored on behalf of the RAE at Farnborough, and the Junkers Ju 52/3m aircraft, which were held on behalf of the British Ministry of Civil Aviation.

No. 6 MU, Brize Norton, was one of about twenty-five Aircraft Storage Units located in the United Kingdom. The first ex-Luftwaffe aircraft were flown to Brize Norton in May 1945. Although some aircraft returned to Farnborough or were despatched to other countries, most of the aircraft remained at Brize Norton until they were sold as scrap in 1947 or 1948.

Opposite top: **Bv 222C-012 VP501 photographed at RAF Calshot during 1946 after painting with its serial number allocated in April. Note that engines are missing. It was never flown after its serial number was allocated.** *Quadrant Picture Library, Aeroplane neg 12270/2*

Bottom: **The impressive Wiking Bv 222V-2 flying-boat in RAF marks at Trondheim in 1945. This example was later painted with large 'Stars & Stripes' insignes on its hull, but was not flown to the United States.** *US National Archives 80G-427163*

The pilot painted RAF roundels on the wings and effected various minor airframe repairs. He then flew to the UK via Darmstadt, Brussels and a number of other airfields, before arriving at Shoreham on 24th December 1945. The Storch was then flown to Chilton's works at Hungerford on Christmas Day 1945, where a number of German aircraft instruments and accessories were unloaded. The aircraft then took off with the Hon. Andrew Dalrymple, one of the directors of Chilton Aircraft Ltd, as a passenger, intending to fly to Chester where the two persons intended to spend Christmas. During a low run past another employee of the company who had remained on the ground, the starboard aileron was seen to flutter and then become detached, causing the aircraft to bank steeply and side-slip into the ground and catch fire, killing both occupants. It was later established that during the ferry flight from the Continent the starboard aileron trim tab connecting rod had become disconnected and a temporary repair had been made by locking the servo tab. This induced an asymmetric loading on the aileron hinge, causing it to fail at a glued joint which had deteriorated during the months the Storch had been left standing in the open in Germany. The Aircraft Accident Card in AHB 2 quotes a WNr for the aircraft, but the number quoted is in fact the engine serial number. Further details are given in AIB Accident Report No. W2313.

The Chilton company was also involved in the construction of a British version of the DFS 108-70 Olympia-Meise sailplane. See Chapter Nine for details.

6.18 ## THE COLLEGE OF AERONAUTICS, CRANFIELD

The College of Aeronautics was a government-sponsored training college for aeronautical engineers, founded in 1946. It was located at Cranfield airfield in Bedfordshire. Besides providing the site, the government was generous with many other forms of assistance. Many ex-German training aids were provided, including research equipment from the Volkenrode experimental establishment. The Inspector-General of the RAF, Air Chief Marshal Sir Edgar Ludlow-Hewitt, was a member of the Board of Governors of the College, and it was he who had set in train a search of German research establishments for suitable equipment. The search was known as Operation *Medico*. It was commenced by an order dated 16th August 1945, and completed in February 1946.

Among complete aircraft provided as training airframes, were the Flettner Fl 282B (V-20) helicopter, a Focke-Achgelis Fa 330 rotor-kite, a Focke Wulf Fw 190, a Junkers Ju 388L, a sectioned Junkers Ju 88 and a Messerschmitt Me 163B. The Ju 88 fuselage was a product of Operation *Medico* directly, having been removed from the fifth storey of the bomb-damaged Luftfahrt Akademie in Berlin. The Akademie also contributed heavily to a very extensive collection of complete and partly-sectioned aero engines. Over 1,000 tons of equipment was shipped to Cranfield under Operation *Medico*.

Several of these items survived for many years in the College's 'Library of Flight', which was a hangar full of complete aircraft, components and equipment, where prospective aircraft designers could examine features of many innovative designs of the past. In the nineteen-sixties, the College expanded the scope of its activities and became the Cranfield Institute of Technology. At

The Fl 282V-20 'CJ+SN' at Wittering 1950, on temporary loan from the College of Aeronautics at Cranfield. *IWM HU 1858*

around this time the 'Library' hangar was required for other purposes and its contents were dispersed. The Fl 282 went to a museum in the British midlands, the Me 163 to the Museum of Flight at East Fortune in Scotland and the Fa 330 returned to Germany to become an exhibit in a helicopter museum. By this time, the other items of German origin had been scrapped.

— **Flettner Fl 282B (V20)** W Nr 280020

This helicopter, coded 'CJ+SN', was surrendered at Travemünde and sent to No. 6 MU, Brize Norton, arriving there by 22nd July 1945. Although it was of great technical interest, it was not flown in the UK. When captured, it was partially dismantled for maintenance, and no engineers with knowledge of the type could be found at Travemünde to assist with its reassembly. It may have had a so-far untraced 'Air Min' number. It was despatched from Brize Norton to Cranfield on 1st August 1946 for use as an exhibit in the College of Aeronautics 'Library of Flight'.

It remained there until about 1976 when it was removed to storage with the Midlands Aircraft Preservation Society. Although at least one German museum has since negotiated to obtain this historic helicopter, it still remains in store near Coventry.

— **Junkers Ju 88**

The sectioned fuselage of a Junkers Ju 88, used as a training item at an aeronautical engineering school in Berlin, was removed from the fifth floor of the bomb-damaged building and shipped to the United Kingdom for use by the College of Aeronautics at Cranfield. No further details are available except that such a fuselage was in fact in use at Cranfield in 1948.

— **Focke-Achgelis Fa 330** W Nr 100406

Shipped from Kiel.

See also Chapter Seven – entries for AM 83, AM 111, AM 215.

6.19 **OTHER CIVILIAN OPERATORS**

Details of the civilian users of the Junkers Ju 52/3m are given in Chapter Eight.

Two private owners attempted to fly ex-Luftwaffe aircraft in private ownership, after purchasing surplus 'Air Min' aircraft. (For details, see 'Air Min 87' and 'Air Min 122' in Chapter Seven). In neither case was their attempt successful.

The Zaunkönig tested at RAE Farnborough was purchased by the Ultra Light Aircraft Association Ltd and this was successfully flown by a number of private owners in the UK. It was later sold to Ireland and then finally returned to West German ownership. (See further details in Chapter Five).

The Brunswick LF1 Zaunkönig (see page 60) after sale to civilian owners, as G-ALUA, photographed at Panshanger. *Steve Coates collection*

Chapter Seven

The 'Air Min' Numbers

The purpose of the 'Air Ministry' numbers in the first instance was to identify aircraft of intelligence interest at their place of surrender in Germany or Denmark, and to clearly segregate such aircraft from the far larger number of aircraft which were to be destroyed as being of no further use. A typical airfield at the time of the surrender in May 1945 held perhaps four-hundred or more Luftwaffe aircraft of which perhaps ten were selected as being 'Category One' for evaluation in the United Kingdom, and a similar or slightly larger number of communications or trainer types would be allocated to other categories assigning them to use by the Royal Air Force in Germany or for transfer to Allied governments for re-equipment of their own air forces.

The 'AIR MIN' designation derived from the fact that the original team who travelled around ex-Luftwaffe bases in north Germany and Denmark, selecting aircraft for evaluation, reported directly to the Air Ministry in London. Its selections were made against a list of requirements which had been compiled by department Air Intelligence 2(g) at the Air Ministry, in consultation with the Ministry of Aircraft Production. Within a short time, the selection process and responsibility for ferrying the selected aircraft to the UK was handed over to the Royal Aircraft Establishment at Farnborough, largely because it was decided that it would be safest for RAE test pilots to fly the unfamiliar types of aircraft.

The USAAF intelligence teams operating in Europe had their own list of requirements, but the British and American lists were soon amalgamated into one. US requirements selected in British controlled areas were initially numbered in a parallel series of identities starting at 'USA 1'.

The identities were painted in a contrasting coloured paint (usually but not always white), the 'Air Min' numbers on the port side of the rear fuselage, the 'USA' numbers usually on the starboard side. Some of the larger aircraft had their identities painted on both sides and (very rarely) under the wings. Most commonly the identity was 'Air Min', although occasionally 'AM', or in full as 'Air Ministry'.

Many aircraft did not receive 'Air Min' numbers at their points of surrender – these included the Messerschmitt Me 163B rocket-powered fighters, which were selected by a separate team of mainly RAE personnel formed solely to investigate that type of aircraft. Other categories which did not at first receive numbers were aircraft selected in the US Zone of Germany, against British requirements identified in the joint US/UK list, and aircraft surrendered in Norway. The latter area had not been considered of prime intelligence interest and was not visited by the Air Ministry team, but several aircraft were reported by No. 88 Group, the RAF organisation which moved to Norway to assist the Norwegians to liberate their country. In fact the intelligence assessment had been almost correct, given that most of the 'Category One' aircraft selected in Norway had flown there from Denmark on the day that German forces in that country surrendered, 5th May 1945.

Aircraft in the three categories listed in the previous paragraph arrived at Farnborough and were allocated 'Air Min' numbers in the series 200 onwards. By this time the responsibility for allocating 'Air Min' numbers in the original series had been transferred to the Royal Aircraft Establishment, the selection of suitable aircraft generally being made by Group Captain Alan Hards, Commanding Officer Experimental Flying at RAE.

It is known that the first forty-two numbers were allocated by the Air Ministry team, between 18th May 1945 and the end of May. On 9th June 1945, G/Capt Hards visited Copenhagen/Kastrup and Vaerløse in Denmark and selected three Blöhm und Voss Bv 138 flying-boats at Kastrup-See and three Messerschmitt Me 410 at Vaerløse. These aircraft became Air Min 69 to 74 inclusive, although strangely they initially had identities such as 'Air Min S-2' and 'Air Min V-3' painted on them. The reason for these identities is not known but the writer suspects that they mark the transition point from allocation by the original 'Air Ministry' team to allocation by the RAE. It is at least plausible to consider that when he selected the six aircraft on 9th June G/Capt Hards invented some identities on the spot, because he did not know what point the allocations had reached in the numerical series. The anomaly was certainly corrected prior to the arrival of the Messerschmitts at Farnborough, for although they flew in with numbers such as 'Air Min V-1' painted on them, their Flight Log entries show both identities, as does the inventory of German aircraft received. The 'S' of the non-standard identity indicated Kastrup-'See', while the 'V' indicated 'Vaerløse'. At least two aircraft from the Kastrup land aerodrome had the letter 'K' added to their previously allocated 'Air Min' numbers (AM K41 and K42). Probably other aircraft selected at Kastrup also had this added letter, but none of them came to the UK for this to be noted by observers. It may be relevant that the three aerodromes (Kastrup, Kastrup-See and Vaerløse) were run by the same squadron of the RAF disarmament organisation, No. 5 Squadron of No. 8403 Air Disarmament Wing.

By early July 1945 the 'Air Min' numbers had passed the 100 mark, after which allocations tailed off in quantity, the final allocations in Germany being made in September 1945. The allocations made at Farnborough, from AM 200 onwards, were all made prior to the German Aircraft Exhibition in October 1945.

There follows the list of aircraft with known 'AIR MIN' numbers quoting the history of each.

7.1   **ALLOCATIONS MADE AT PLACES OF SURRENDER**
       (AM 1 to AM 123 inclusive)

AM 1   Junkers Ju 88G-6   W Nr 622983
Surrendered at Schleswig, coded '4R+RB' of NJG2. Selected for investigation of FuG 218 and FuG 350 radars. Air tested at Schleswig on 16th June 1945 and later ferried to the CFE at Tangmere. Flown from Ford to Foulsham on 12th September 1945 on delivery to the Radio Warfare Establishment (RWE) but overshot the runway on landing, suffering Category B damage. The RWE was then being formed from the Bomber Support Development Unit and

other radio warfare organisations. By 4th October 1945 the aircraft was recorded as being at the CFE, which was by then at West Raynham, probably awaiting repair. Since no other record is shown, it may be inferred that the aircraft was assessed as being beyond economical repair.

AM 2   Junkers Ju 88G-6   W Nr 620560

Surrendered at Schleswig, coded '4R+CB' of NJG2. Selected for investigation of FuG 220 and FuG 350 radars. From Schleswig to Gilze-Rijen on 4th June 1945 and to Tangmere on 7th June. From Ford to the Bomber Support Development Unit (BSDU) at Swanton Morley and flown by S/Ldr Tim Woodman on 14th September 1945. The BSDU was at the time being absorbed into the newly-formed Radio Warfare Establishment at Watton. With the RWE on 28th February 1946. SoC at No.54 MU, Cambridge, on 30th April.

AM 3   Junkers Ju 88G-6   W Nr 622838

Surrendered at Flensburg, coded '3C+AN' of II/NJG 4. Selected for investigation of FuG 217 and FuG 224 radars. Flown from Schleswig to Farnborough on 16th June 1945 by S/Ldr McCarthy and allocated the RAF serial number VK884 on 26th July 1945 for intended flight tests. In the meantime the aircraft had been taken by road to No. 6 MU, Brize Norton, on 23rd July 1945 and prepared for static exhibition in Hyde Park, London, during September 1945. It then returned to No. 6 MU and was despatched from that unit to RAE Farnborough on 11th December 1945. The further use made of this aircraft at Farnborough is not known.

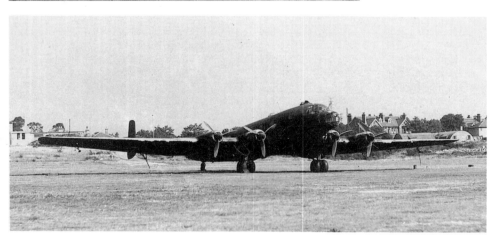

Top: **The Ju 88G-6 'Air Min 2' on its delivery flight at Gilze-Rijen in the Netherlands.** *Ross Finlayson, courtesy N. Malayney collection*

Above: **Ju 88G-6 AM 3 on display in London's Hyde Park in September 1945. German markings have been reapplied over the British marks used for its ferry flight from Germany.** *R. S. Punnett collection*

Left: **The maritime-reconnaissance version of the Junkers Ju 290A, Air Min 6, photographed at Farnborough in July or August 1945.** *Joe McCarthy collection*

Below: **Air Min 4, the radar-equipped Siebel Si 204D, at Flensburg.** *A. H. Fraser, courtesy Chris Thomas collection*

AM 4   Siebel Si 204D-1   W Nr 322127

Surrendered at Flensburg, coded 'BU+PP'. A radar trainer aircraft equipped with FuG 217 and FuG 218. Flown from Flensburg to Schleswig on 21st June 1945. Used for ferry flying within Germany initially, e.g. 22nd June Schleswig - Flensburg, 27th June Flensburg - Schleswig - Flensburg, 28th June Flensburg - Schleswig - Leck. Ferried from Schleswig to Farnborough via Gilze-Rijen on 12th September 1945 by F/Lt Taylor. At Hendon from 14th to 17th September 1945 for static display during the Battle of Britain 'At Home' day. From 18th to 26th September 1945 flown over the route Farnborough - Jever - Schleswig - Grove - Stavanger - Grove - Schleswig - Grove - Schleswig - Wisley - Farnborough, supporting the ferry flights of Arado Ar 234B jet bombers from Stavanger to Farnborough. (See AM 226 to 229 inclusive). Visited Brize Norton on 5th October 1945 but returned to Farnborough, no further flight being recorded after that date. Appeared at the German Aircraft Exhibition at the end of October 1945, but its final fate is unrecorded.

AM 5   Siebel Si 204D-1   W Nr 321523

Like AM 4 above this aircraft was surrendered at Flensburg (no code recorded) and was ferried to Schleswig on 21st June 1945. Test flown at Leck by S/Ldr McCarthy on 29th June. Ferried onwards to Farnborough on 30th June 1945 by F/Lt Lawson and then on to Brize Norton on 3rd July. AM 5 was ferried back to Farnborough on 1st October 1945 for display at the German Aircraft Exhibition, but was not flown again. It is believed to have been taken to the Miles Aircraft factory airfield at Woodley and scrapped there in 1948.

AM 6   Junkers Ju 290A-7   W Nr 110186

Surrendered at Flensburg, coded 'A3+OB' of III/KG 200. This was the first production Ju 290A-7, originally coded 'KR+LQ' while under works test by the manufacturer. AM 6 was flown at Schleswig by S/Ldr McCarthy on 22nd June 1945 and he completed a further air test from here on 28th June. It was ferried from Lübeck to Wormingford on 2nd July 1945, also by S/Ldr McCarthy. On the following day, it continued to Farnborough and then returned to Schleswig. Two further flights, Schleswig - Copenhagen and return, were made between the 7th and 10th July. On 13th July, AM 6 flew from Schleswig to Farnborough and was test flown there on 21st July and 8th August 1945. The aircraft was ferried from RAE to No. 6 MU, Brize Norton, on 17th August 1945 and remained in storage at that unit until SoC on 14th August 1947.

AM 7   Dornier Do 217M-9   W Nr 0040

Surrendered at Flensburg, coded 'KF+JN'. This was a non-standard aircraft fitted with a Do 317-type tail unit. It was not flown to the United Kingdom, possibly because one of its rudders was lost. Photographs taken at Flensburg show a rudder missing; this was consistent with initial Allied instructions for the immobilisation of Luftwaffe aircraft but problems may have arisen when the aircraft was to be restored to airworthiness. Any loss or damage to the non-standard rudders would have been difficult or impossible to rectify.

The unusual Do 217M-9, Air Min 7, with triangular Do 317-type fins, at Flensburg in June 1945. *B. Halgrimson, courtesy N. Malayney collection*

AM 8   Junkers Ju 352A-0   W Nr 100010

Surrendered at Flensburg, coded 'KT+VJ'. Probably the Ju 352 test-flown by S/Ldr King and by S/Ldr McCarthy at Flensburg on 19th June 1945. This aircraft was one of the most actively used 'Air Min'-numbered aircraft. Test-flown at Flensburg on 22nd June 1945 and ferried to Farnborough on the following day, by S/Ldr Joe McCarthy. Between 26th June 1945 and 10th May 1946 AM 8 made numerous trips to the Continent, to collect ex-RLM and Luftwaffe equipment for use at Farnborough and Cranfield. On 26th April 1946 the RAF serial number VP550 was allocated to this aircraft and its last flights are recorded in the RAE Flight Log under this identity, although it does not appear to have been worn on the aircraft. An almost complete log of flights by this aircraft is tabulated below:

26 Jun 45	Farnborough - Tangmere - Gilze-Rijen - Lübeck - Schleswig
27 Jun	Schleswig - Flensburg - Lübeck - Travemünde - Knokke
28 Jun	Knokke - Farnborough
30 Jun	Farnborough - Lübeck
1 Jul	Lübeck - Eindhoven - Farnborough
2 Jul	Farnborough - Gilze-Rijen - Schleswig
6 Jul	Schleswig - Farnborough
9 Jul	Farnborough - Schleswig
18 Jul	Schleswig - Farnborough
20 Jul	Farnborough - Lübeck
21 Jul	Lübeck - Gilze-Rijen - Farnborough
22 Jul	Farnborough - Travemünde - Lübeck - Gilze-Rijen - Lasham
23 Jul	Lasham - Farnborough - Lübeck
24 Jul	Schleswig - Travemünde - Lübeck - Gilze-Rijen - Farnborough
10 Aug	Farnborough - Knokke
11 Aug	Knokke - Bad Oeynhausen - Fassberg
12 Aug	Fassberg - Schleswig - Travemünde
13 Aug	Travemünde - Neumünster - Lübeck - Manston - Dunsfold
14 Aug	Dunsfold - Farnborough
30 Nov	Local air test at Farnborough after engineering survey
6 Dec	Local air test at Farnborough
7 Dec	Farnborough - Volkenrode
8 Dec	Volkenrode - Nürnburg
12 Dec	Nürnburg - Stuttgart
14 Dec	Stuttgart - Ansbach - Melsbroek - Farnborough

2 Jan 46	Farnborough - Volkenrode
3 Jan	Volkenrode - Hamburg
4 Jan	Hamburg - Ansbach - Schweinfurt
7 Jan	Schweinfurt - Farnborough
17 Jan	Farnborough - Witchford - Farnborough
4 Feb	Air test at Farnborough
5 Feb	Air test at Farnborough
7 Feb	Farnborough - Celle
11 Feb	Celle - Melsbroek
15 Feb	Melsbroek - Farnborough
8 Mar	Farnborough - Yeovilton - Farnborough
13 Mar	Farnborough - Melsbroek
14 Mar	Melsbroek - Volkenrode
19 Mar	Volkenrode - Coxyde - Cranfield - Farnborough
8 May	Air test at Farnborough, then to Volkenrode
10 May	Volkenrode - Cranfield - Farnborough
21 May	Farnborough - Fassberg - Volkenrode. Became unserviceable
28 Jun	Volkenrode - Manston - Farnborough

The aircraft was not flown again and was noted on the scrap area at Farnborough on 15th December 1946 still marked as 'Air Min 8'.

The RAF serial number VP550 has been attributed in other publications to another Ju 352 (AM 109) but official records definitely show AM 8 as being the aircraft involved and this is quite clearly confirmed by the activities of the two aircraft.

The frequent visits to Volkenrode highlight the importance of this RLM research centre, from which much equipment, including complete wind-tunnels, was transferred to the RAE, and the newly formed College of Aeronautics at Cranfield, in the immediate post-war period.

Opposite, top: **AM 10, the radar-equipped Fw 190A-6/R6 in Hyde Park, London in September 1945. This aircraft survives at the Museum of War History in Johannesburg. In the photograph the over-wing FuG 217 aerials are visible. False German marks have been re-applied over the British ones used for its ferry flight; also concealed are the code letters 'PN+LU' which appeared on the aircraft at Leck.** *R. S. Punnett collection*

Below: **The well-travelled Ju 352A AM 8, in Germany.** *Steve Coates collection.*

AM 9   Junkers Ju 88G-6   W Nr 621965

Surrendered at Leck, coded '4R+DR' of III/NJG 2 and initially chosen for investigation of its FuG 220 and FuG 350 radars. Ferried from Schleswig to Farnborough on 13th July 1945 by F/Lt Taylor. It was test-flown by F/Lt Dixon of the RAE Instrument Flight on 23rd July and then was delivered to No. 6 MU, Brize Norton, on 27th July by Lt/Cdr E. M. Brown. The '88 returned to the RAE on 30th August, by which time the RAF serial number VL991 had been allocated to it. On 10th, 23rd and 24th October, and again on 6th November 1945, it made test-flights under the identity VL991, but the tests were cancelled on 5th December 1945, possibly because of the accident to AM 37 on 30th November, which caused restrictions to be placed on the flying of ex-Luftwaffe aircraft at Farnborough. The trials related to the 'Kurskoppler', which was an early mechanical navigational computing device developed by the Luftwaffe. The trials were carried out by the RAE Instrument Flight but it had been intended that they would have been continued in conjunction with the Blind Landing Experimental Unit at Woodbridge. The 'Kurskoppler' was removed from VL991 and trials continued after it had been installed in the Mosquito FB VI HR210. VL991 remained on charge at the RAE, being recorded with it on 8th August 1946 and it was not recorded as 'sold for scrap' until 14th March 1950. In fact, the Ju 88 was transported to Shoeburyness, to be used for firing trials on 21st March 1950.

AM 10   Focke Wulf Fw 190A-6/R6   W Nr 550214

Surrendered at Leck, coded 'PN+LU', of III/NJG 11. This aircraft was a radar-equipped night fighter version. It was selected for trials of its FuG 217 radar installation, which of course was not normally fitted to a single-seat fighter; the radar aerials were fitted to the wing leading edges. The aircraft is presumed to have been on test with Staffel 7 of NJG 11, a Leck-based unit primarily equipped with Bf 109Gs in the night fighting role.

The aircraft was flown from Schleswig to Farnborough on 16th June 1945 by F/O Lawson and then onwards to No. 6 MU on 22nd June by F/Lt McGill without any flight tests being made. This aircraft was displayed statically in Hyde Park, London, from 16th September 1945 and then at White Waltham airfield on 29th September, for the Air Transport Auxiliary Benevolent Fund Pageant. It was later returned to No. 6 MU, being recorded there at the annual aircraft census on 21st March 1946.

The '190 was allocated to No. 47 MU, Sealand, on 1st May 1946, where it was packed for shipment to South Africa. It left Birkenhead aboard the SS *Perthshire* on 20th October 1946, arriving at Cape Town on 6th November. Later, this aircraft was at the SAAF Central Flying School at Dunnottar before going to No. 15 Air Depot, Snake Valley, in 1971 for preparation as an exhibit for the South African National Museum of Military History, Saxonwold, near Johannesburg where it has been on display since 1972.

AM 11   Focke Wulf Ta 152H-0   W Nr 150004

Surrendered at Leck, coded '6+ -' (possibly of JG 301). For reasons unknown, this aircraft was not brought to the UK and was replaced by the example described in the next entry. 150004 was transported by road from Leck to Schleswig on 22/23rd January 1946 'to await disposal'.

AM 11   Focke Wulf Ta 152H-1   W Nr 150168

Presumed also surrendered at Leck, although this has not been confirmed. Coded '9+ ' of Stab/JG 301. Flown from Schleswig to Farnborough on 3rd August 1945 by F/O Lawson. Ferried from RAE to No. 6 MU, Brize Norton, on 18th August by Lt/Cdr Eric Brown, returning to Farnborough on 22nd October. Statically displayed during the German Aircraft Exhibition from 29th October to 12th November 1945. Noted on the scrap area at Farnborough on 15th December 1946.

AM 12   Siebel Si 204D-3   W Nr 351547

Surrendered at Leck, no code recorded. Ferried from Schleswig to Farnborough on 23rd July 1945 by F/Lt Taylor and onwards to Brize Norton on 27th July. Still present there at the Census of Aircraft on 21st March 1946 and believed SoC from No. 6 MU on 14th August 1947.

AM 13   Siebel Si 204D-1   W Nr 251922

Surrendered at Leck, no code recorded. Flown from Tangmere to Farnborough on 7th July 1945 by F/Lt Roberts and from there to Brize Norton on 18th July. Allocated from No. 6 MU to RAF Cranwell on 11th October 1946, probably for the Station Museum, but was SoC at No. 58 MU, Newton, on 25th November 1947.

AM 14   Junkers Ju 88G-6   W Nr 620788

Surrendered at Eggebek, coded 'C9+AA' of NJG 5. Equipped with FuG 220 and FuG 350 radars. Ferried to Tangmere during June 1945 (possibly on 16th June) and flown there by the Night Fighter Development Wing of the Central Fighter Establishment until damaged beyond repair in a belly landing there after a hydraulic failure, on 18th July 1945, while being flown by F/O Hodgen.

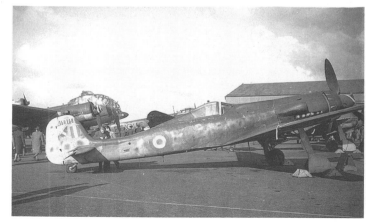

Right: **A shot of the second Air Min 11, Ta 152H-1 W Nr 150168, taken at Farnborough during the German Aircraft Exhibition.** *R. S. Punnett collection*

AM 15   Messerschmitt Bf 110 G-4/R8   W Nr 180560

Surrendered at Eggebek, coded '3C+BA' of NJG 4. Equipped with FuG 218 radar. Possibly flown from Eggebek to Schleswig on 14th June 1945 and believed to have left Schleswig for England on 23rd June. This aircraft was photographed at Knokke-Le Zoute in the course of its ferry flight. On charge with the Fighter Interception Development Squadron/Night Fighter Leader School of the Central Fighter Establishment, Tangmere. According to the Movement Card for this aircraft, it was at RAE Farnborough on 13th December 1945, but this has not been confirmed by any other source. AM 15 was SoC on 30th May 1946. It was not the aircraft of Major Schnaufer, Geschwader – Kommander of NJG 4, as has been reported elsewhere.

AM 16   Junkers Ju 88 G-6   W Nr 622311

Surrendered at Eggebek, coded '3C+DA' of NJG 4, and flown from there to Schleswig on 15th June 1945. Continued its ferry flight to Tangmere on 16th June, flown by F/Lt D. G. M. Gough. No further details are known except that the record of 'Air Min' numbers shows it as having FuG 220 radar. However there are photographs in existence of a Junkers Ju 88 G-6 with the code '3C' taken at Ford, the satellite airfield to Tangmere from which much of the test flying of ex-Luftwaffe aircraft was undertaken. The Ju 88 in question had a 'Morgenstern' (Morning Star) type aerial array associated with the FuG 218 rather than the FuG 220. The Field Intelligence report on Luftwaffe aircraft surrendered at Eggebek confirms that W Nr 622311 had the 'Morgenstern' type aerial array. AM 16 was flown from Tangmere to Ford on 3rd July 1945 by F/Lt R. T. H. Collis.

AM 17   Arado Ar 232 B-0   W Nr 305002

Surrendered at Eggebek, coded 'A3+RB' of III/KG 200. Flown Eggebek - Schleswig - Flensburg - Schleswig on 11th July 1945, by S/Ldr McCarthy, and then from Schleswig to Gilze-Rijen on 13th July 1945, where it force landed after loss of aileron control. Ferried from Gilze-Rijen to Farnborough on 14th July 1945, by S/Ldr McCarthy. Other flights are as tabulated below:

19 Jul 45	Local test flight from Farnborough
21 Jul	Two local test flights from Farnborough
25 Jul	Farnborough - Gilze-Rijen - Fassberg
26 Jul	Fassberg - Detmold - Knokke
27 Jul	Knokke - Farnborough
2 Aug	Local test flight at Farnborough
3 Aug	Local test flight at Farnborough
4 Aug	Farnborough - Melsbroek - Fassberg
6 Aug	Fassberg - Melsbroek
8 Aug	Melsbroek - Farnborough

Reports that this aircraft was used to air-freight dismantled Messerschmitt Me 163B airframes from Germany to Farnborough can be discounted – most of these aircraft had arrived at RAE by surface transport before the Ar 232 itself. AM 17 appeared in the static display during the German Aircraft Exhibition and was still at Farnborough in April 1946, although, at the time of the Home Census of Aircraft on 21st March, it was recorded as being on the books of No. 49 MU Colerne - this was only a paperwork transaction. During May 1946, the aircraft was selected for museum storage by the Air Ministry Air Historical Branch and was transferred to No. 47 MU, Sealand, on 19th September. Packing for museum storage was completed on 3rd April 1947, but in September AM 17 was on offer for disposal due to lack of storage space at Sealand or elsewhere (it occupied ten large crates) and is presumed to have been scrapped shortly thereafter, the last mention in No. 47 MU records being in November 1947.

AM 18   Junkers Ju 352 A-1   W Nr 100015

Surrendered at Eggebek, coded 'G6+WX' of V/TG 4. Flown Schleswig - Celle - Fassberg - Lübeck - Travemünde on 26th August 1945. Ferried Travemünde - Lübeck - Gilze-Rijen - Farnborough on 27th August, by S/Ldr Somerville. Further flights were as follows:

28 Aug 45	Local air test at Farnborough
29 Aug	Local air test at Farnborough
30 Aug	Farnborough - Gilze-Rijen
31 Aug	Gilze-Rijen - Schleswig
3 Sep	Schleswig - Lübeck - Gilze-Rijen - Farnborough
14 Sep	Farnborough - Gilze-Rijen - Volkenrode
17 Sep	Volkenrode - Munich
19 Sep	Munich - Ansbach - Kassel - Volkenrode
23 Sep	Volkenrode - Lübeck
26 Sep	Lübeck - Gilze-Rijen - Farnborough
28 Sep	Farnborough - Gilze-Rijen - Volkenrode
29 Sep	Volkenrode - Gilze-Rijen - Farnborough
2 Oct	Farnborough - Frankfurt - Munich - Salzburg - Klagenfurt
8 Oct	Salzburg - Volkenrode - Farnborough

This aircraft was recorded as 'G6+WX' in the official record of 'Air Min' numbers but photographs exist showing the last two code letters as 'CX'. Conceivably the 'C' may have been superimposed on the original Luftwaffe code after the surrender, but the official record may possibly be in error. AM 18 was noted in the scrap area at RAE in December 1946.

AM 19   Junkers Ju 352 A   W Nr unknown

Surrendered at Eggebek, coded 'G6+YX' of V/TG 4. Ferried from Eggebek to Farnborough on 23rd June 1945, by S/Ldr Somerville. Further flights are as recorded below:

26 Jun 45	Farnborough - Schleswig
30 Jun	Schleswig - Farnborough
1 Jul	Local air test at Farnborough
3 Jul	Farnborough - Twente
4 Jul	Twente - Lübeck
5 Jul	Lübeck - Farnborough
12 Jul	Local air test at Farnborough
13 Jul	Farnborough - Schleswig
14 Jul	Schleswig - Farnborough
25 Jul	Local air test at Farnborough
30 Jul	Farnborough - Fassberg
31 Jul	Schleswig - Farnborough - Knokke
6 Aug	Schleswig - Farnborough
7 Aug	Farnborough - Melsbroek
8 Aug	Melsbroek - Travemünde - Lübeck
9 Aug	Lübeck - Farnborough
10 Aug	Farnborough - Croydon (unserviceable en route to Fassberg)
23 Aug	Croydon - Farnborough
24 Aug	Farnborough - Schleswig

There is no further record of AM 19 and it is presumed to have been scrapped in Germany.

AM 20   Heinkel He 219 A-2   W Nr 290126

Coded 'D5+BL' of I/NJG 3. Surrendered in Denmark at Grove, which was renamed by the Royal Danish Air Force post-war and is now known as Karup. Equipped with FuG 220 radar. Air tested and then flown Grove - Schleswig on 1st August 1945 by S/Ldr Joe McCarthy. Ferried from Schleswig to Farnborough on 3rd August 1945, by S/Ldr Somerville.

Test-flown at Farnborough on 7th August and then ferried to No. 6 MU, Brize Norton, for storage on 21st August. SoC at No. 6 MU on 14th August 1947.

Above: **This shot, taken on 2nd October 1945 in front of 'A' Shed at the RAE, Farnborough, shows to advantage the Hirschgewihe aerials and the underwing fuel tanks of Bf 110G-4/R3, Air Ministry 30.** *IWM MH4904*

Right: **This photograph is a publicity shot taken at Grove, showing the 'Air Ministry' number being painted on Bf 110G AM 30.** *IWM CL3297*

Below left: **The two-seater Fw 190F-8/U1 AM 36 at Kastrup prior to the application of British markings.** *PRO AIR 40/2022*

Below right: **The CFE's Junkers Ju 88G-6 AM32 in a garden after overshooting Heston on landing on 15th October 1945.** *Ray Sturtivant collection*

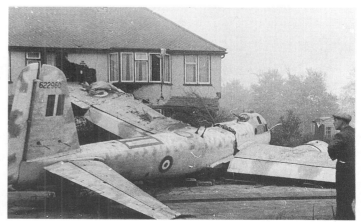

AM 41   Junkers Ju 88G-6   W Nr 622054
Surrendered at Copenhagen/Kastrup, coded '7J+OV' of NJG 102.
Equipped with FuG 220 radar. For reasons unknown, this aircraft
was not delivered to the UK, being replaced by the aircraft
described below:

AM41   Junkers Ju 88G-6   W Nr 622461
Surrendered at Copenhagen/Kastrup, coded '7J+CV' of NJG 102.
The serial number was painted on the aircraft as 'Air Min K41' (see
notes associated with AM 69 to 74 inclusive). Flown from Schles-
wig to Farnborough on 13th October 1945 by F/Lt Taylor. Flown in
the air display at the German Aircraft Exhibition on 4th
November. Ferried from RAE to Brize Norton for storage on 14th
November. SoC by No. 6 MU on 14th August 1947.

Below: **The Ju 88G-6 '7J+CV' W Nr 622461, the second 'Air Min K41', at the
RAE in November 1945. In the background to the left is a prototype Vickers-
Armstrongs Windsor heavy bomber.** *PRO, AIR 40/126*

Bottom: **The Si 204D 'Air Ministry K42' '7J+XL' at the RAE.** *PRO, AIR 40/128*

AM 42   Siebel Si 204D-1   W Nr 251147
Coded '7J+XL' of NJG 102. Surrendered at Copenhagen/Kastrup
and painted as 'Air Ministry K42' (see notes with entries for AM 69
to 74). Ferried from Schleswig to Melsbroek on 6th October 1945
and onwards to Manston and Farnborough on the following day.
Made further flights as follows:

25 Oct 45	Farnborough - Nordholz
27 Oct	Nordholz - Farnborough
8 Nov	Farnborough - Melsbroek
9 Nov	Melsbroek - Schleswig
10 Nov	Schleswig - Schiphol
11 Nov	Schiphol - Farnborough
14 Nov	Farnborough - Brize Norton - Farnborough - Biggin Hill - Farnborough
15 Nov	Local test flight from Farnborough
5 Dec	Farnborough - Manston - Farnborough
14 Dec	Left Farnborough for Schleswig but returned due to bad weather

Although officially recorded in the log of 'Air Min' numbers as
'7J+ZK' there is photographic evidence to show that this aircraft
was individually coded 'X' while the 'staffel' letter appears to be 'L'
– i.e., it was actually coded '7J+XL'. Although there is no record in
the RAE Flight Log, it appears that the aircraft was transferred to
Miles Aircraft for trials and was later scrapped at its airfield at
Woodley.

AM 43   Heinkel He 219A-2   W Nr *unknown*
This aircraft was surrendered at Sylt, no code recorded. The W Nr may have been 310215, which has been erroneously reported as applying to AM 44, but this is a speculative theory. This may be the He 219 with the code letter 'E' on its nose, shown in photographs taken at Ford in 1945. Until July 1945 Ford had been in use by the Night Fighter Development Wing (NFDW) of the CFE as a satellite airfield to the CFE's main base at Tangmere. The photograph referred to was taken about the time Ford was returned to the Fleet Air Arm in August 1945. See also text of AM 44 below.

AM 44   Heinkel He 219A-2   W Nr 310106
Surrendered at Sylt, no code recorded. May conceivably be the air-craft coded 'E' referred to under the entry for AM 43. One of the He 219 tested at CFE arrived at Ford from Germany, *en route* to Tangmere, on 24th June 1945. One He 219, probably this aircraft, was flown from Ford to Tangmere on 27th July 1945, following the transfer of the NFDW to the main CFE airfield at Tangmere on 16th July. AM 44 was flown from Tangmere to Brize Norton on 19th October 1945 by Lt/Cdr Brown, for storage at No. 6 MU and remained there until SoC on 14th August 1947.

AM 45   Junkers Ju 188A-2   W Nr 180485
Place of surrender not known but possibly Sylt, no code recorded. Flown from Schleswig to Farnborough on 13th July 1945 by F/Lt Edwards. Ferried onwards to Brize Norton on 18th July. Remained in store with No. 6 MU until SoC there on 14th August 1947.

AM 46   Siebel Si 204D-1   W Nr *unknown*
No confirmed details of this aircraft or code have been traced; W Nr 221558 has been reported but this W Nr is shown in the official record as belonging to AM 28. AM 46 was test-flown at Schles-wig on 14th June 1945 and ferried to Tangmere on the following day by G/Capt Hards, for use by the Fighter Interception Develop-ment Squadron and Night Fighter Leader School of the CFE. Based at Ford, Tangmere's satellite airfield, apart from a spell at RAE Farnborough from 21st to 27th June, until the FIDS/NFLS moved to Tangmere on 16th July. During July 1945, it was in fre-quent use both as a communications aircraft and for tests of its arti-ficial horizon, being flown on at least ten days of the month. Like the CFE's Bf 110 AM 15, its history card states it was at RAE on 13th December 1945 but the writer has been unable to confirm this from any other source. There is no further record of the aircraft until 23rd September 1948 when it appeared on the books of No. 6 MU, Brize Norton, where it remained until being sold as scrap to the Eyre Smelting Co on 16th December 1948. It is possible that in the 1945-1948 period this aircraft was in use at the CFE West Raynham, although no evidence has been found to support this theory.

AM 47   Junkers Ju 88G-6   W Nr 620968
Probably surrendered at Flensburg. Code not known. Ferried from Schleswig to Farnborough on 6th July 1945 by F/Lt Edwards and onwards to No. 6 MU, Brize Norton, on 17th July. Remained in store with this unit until SoC on 14th August 1947.

AM 48   Junkers Ju 88G-6   W Nr 622811
Surrendered at Flensburg, coded '3C+MN' of II/NJG 4. Equipped with FuG 240 centrimetric-band radar in an enclosed radome with-out external aerials. Had the individual code letter 'G' painted on the radome, which is consistent with reports that this aircraft had earlier been coded '3C+GB'. Flown from Schleswig to Farnborough on 22nd August 1945 by F/Lt Lawson and onwards

to No. 6 MU, Brize Norton, on 30th August. Has been erroneously reported as being W Nr 622838 (which was AM 3) but identities for both AM 3 and AM 48 are confirmed by photographic evidence. SoC at No. 6 MU on 14th August 1947.

AM 49   Siebel Si 204D-1   W Nr 251104
Surrendered at Lutjenholm, coded 'D5+OM' of II/NJG 3. Flown from Schleswig to Farnborough on 25th June 1945 by S/Ldr King. Ferried onwards to No. 6 MU, Brize Norton, on 3rd July. Still at No. 6 MU at the Home Census of Aircraft on 21st March 1946 and probably remained there until SoC on 14th August 1947.

AM 50   Messerschmitt Me 262B-1a/U1   W Nr 110305
Two-seat night fighter version of Me 262B trainer equipped with FuG 218 radar. Surrendered at Schleswig, coded 'Red 8' of IV/NJG 11. Flown from Schleswig to Gilze-Rijen on 18th May 1945 and onwards to Farnborough on the following day by W/Cdr R. J. Falk. Photographs of the aircraft do not show an 'Air Min' number and this was almost certainly a retrospective allocation as 'Air Min 1' was allocated on the same day as this aircraft left Schleswig for the UK. Flown from Farnborough to Ford on 6th July 1945 by W/Cdr Gonsalvez for use by the Fighter Interception Development Squadron of the CFE. Overshot the runway on land-ing at Ford at the end of the ferry flight, sustaining slight damage, but was repaired and returned to service. It is believed that this was the Me 262 which was allotted the RAF serial number VH519 on 14th June 1945, although this identity was not painted on the aircraft. The '262's active life ceased after the CFE moved to West Raynham in September 1945. In October 1946 110305 was trans-ported from Ford to Sealand by No. 71 MU and transferred to No. 47 MU charge on 8th November 1946. It was then packed for shipment to South Africa, leaving Birkenhead on 23rd February 1947 on board the SS *Clan McCree*, arriving at Cape Town on 17th March. After being held for some years at the SAAF Central Flying School, Dunnottar, AM 50 was transferred to No. 15 Air Depot, Snake Valley, in late 1971, for restoration to display standard. After work was complete 110305 was transferred to the South Afri-can National Museum of Military History, Saxonwold, Johannes-burg. It has been on display there since 1972.

The Ju 88G-6 AM 48 W Nr 622811 at Flensburg still in Luftwaffe marks.
B. Halgrimson, courtesy Norm Malayney collection

AM 51   Messerschmitt Me 262A-2a   W Nr 112372

Surrendered at Fassberg, coded 'Yellow 7' of I/JG 7. Taken over by No. 616 Squadron, RAF (see Chapter Ten), later becoming AM 51. It was ferried from Copenhagen/Kastrup to Farnborough on 23rd June 1945 by S/Ldr Moloney and initially used for an engineering assessment of the type by RAE Structures & Mechanical Engineering Flight. It was transferred to the Aero Flight on 27th July. It made its first test flight at RAE on 6th September 1945. By its next flight it had been allotted the RAF serial number VK893. Subsequent flights were made on 19th and 27th September, 11th and 16th October, 1st, 2nd, 6th, 7th, 8th, 19th, 27th and 29th November, totalling 8 hrs 15 mins flight time. Most of these flights were made by S/Ldr A. F. Martindale although F/Lt Foster and F/Lt R. A. Marks also flew the aircraft. By 1947, this aircraft was at Royal Air Force College, Cranwell, in the station museum. It remained there until the museum was dispersed in 1960, at which point it went to RAF Gaydon.

When Gaydon closed, the aircraft moved to Finningley, where it was allocated the RAF Ground Instructional serial number 8482M for book-keeping purposes. After appearing at the 'Wings of the Eagle' exhibition at the Royal Air Force Museum, Hendon, in 1976, AM 51 was transferred to RAF Cosford, where it remained on display in the Aerospace Museum until transferred to the Historic Aircraft Collection at RAF St Athan in December 1985. By 1991, it had returned to Cosford following the closure of the museum at St Athan.

Note: The reference in the writer's previous book *Air Min* to this aircraft having acquired the wings of W Nr 500200, another Me 262 flown at RAE, has been proved to be incorrect.

AM 52   Messerschmitt Me 262A-2a   W Nr 500210

Coded 'Yellow 17' of I/JG 7. Surrendered at Fassberg and taken over by No. 616 Squadron RAF. Flown by them to Lübeck on 29th May 1945, but then ferried to Schleswig and handed over to AI2(g) to become AM52. Flown from Schleswig to Farnborough, via Melsbroek and Manston, on 9th June 1945 by F/Lt Arend. Allocated RAF serial number VH509 on 14th June. Ferried from Farnborough to No. 6 MU, Brize Norton, on 29th June 1945 by S/Ldr Martindale.

It remained in storage there until allocated to No. 47 MU, Sealand, on 1st July 1946, although it has been reported that it made one test flight at Brize Norton, on an unknown date prior to moving to Sealand. It is believed that the test was made by the Chief Test Pilot of Bell Aircraft, Jack Woolams. The fuel for the flight was obtained by draining the tanks of the Arado Ar 234Bs in storage at the unit (jet fuel then being a rare commodity).

Shipped to Canada, leaving Ellesmere Port on board the SS *Manchester Shipper* on 23rd August 1946, arriving at Montreal on 1st September. AM 52 was sold to Cameron Logan of New Scotland, Ontario, in about 1947, with three-hundred other war-surplus RCAF aircraft, and was eventually scrapped by him at New Scotland.

Note 1: Many errors have been caused in the past due to confusion in official records between AM 52 (W Nr 500210) and AM 81 (W Nr 500200). The information shown in this book has been confirmed to be correct after detailed research.

Note 2: AM 52 has been reported widely in the past as being a Blöhm und Voss Bv 138. This was in fact 'Air Min S-2' – see entry under AM69 to AM71 inclusive.

AM 53   Bücker Bü 180   W Nr *unknown*

No details of this reported aircraft have been traced. It has always been reported as present at Farnborough during the German Aircraft Exhibition, but the writer has been unable to trace any reference to it in any official record, such as the RAE Flight Log, the inventory of German aircraft received at Farnborough, or the 'Enemy Aircraft' reports which summarised technical details of aircraft examined by the RAE.

The writer is somewhat sceptical about the existence of the aircraft. Any readers with details of such an aircraft are invited to write to the author of this book. It is possible that this AM number in reality belonged to an Me 262 or Ar 234 which had been surrendered at Schleswig. If this is the case, it is quite likely that the aircraft in question might be the Me 262B W Nr 111980, although no Air Min number was painted on that aircraft. (see Chapter 5.2 for details).

AM 54   Arado Ar 234B   W Nr 140113

Coded 'F1+AA' of KG 76. This Ar 234 was the aircraft of the commander of KG 76, Oberstleutnant Robert Kowalewski. It was surrendered at Schleswig and ferried from there to Tangmere on 5th June 1945.

It appeared at a private display of British and German aircraft held at Tangmere for the benefit of the CFE, before continuing to Farnborough on 12th June. On 19th June, this aircraft was allocated the RAF serial number VH530. It was ferried from Farnborough to No. 6 MU, Brize Norton, on 7th September 1945 by Lt/Cdr Brown and remained there until struck off charge on 1st October 1948.

AM 55   Siebel Si 204D-1   W Nr 321288

No code recorded. Ferried from Schleswig to Farnborough on 30th June 1945 by F/Lt Taylor, continuing to No. 6 MU, Brize Norton, on 3rd July. Believed to have been struck off charge at Brize Norton on 14th August 1947.

AM 56   Siebel Si 204D-1   W Nr 321308

(See also AM 56A). Coded ' +AP'. Has been reported as coded 'BU + AP', but this is an erroneous report. Ferried from Schleswig to Farnborough on 30th June 1945 by F/Lt Edwards. Made several flights from Farnborough as detailed below:

2 Jul 45	Farnborough - Halton and return, and local flight from Farnborough
26 Jul	Local test flight from Farnborough
31 Jul	Farnborough - Ford - Gosport - Farnborough - Boscombe Down - Thorney Island
2 Aug	Thorney Island - Farnborough
3 Aug	Farnborough - Ford - Farnborough
17 Aug	Farnborough - Munster
18 Aug	Munster - Detmold - Schleswig
27 Aug	Schleswig - Farnborough
31 Aug	Farnborough - Matching - Manston - Farnborough
6 Sep	Farnborough - Neubiburg
7 Sep	Neubiburg - Nürnberg - Neubiburg - Reims
8 Sep	Reims - Farnborough
13 Sep	Farnborough - Knokke - Schleswig
3 Oct	Schleswig - Teuge

AM 56 landed at Teuge in Holland on 3rd October due to fog developing while it was *en route* to the UK. Its undercarriage collapsed on landing, causing 'Category B' damage.

It was removed by road to Schleswig on 5th October but there is no further record of the aircraft and it was probably broken-up for spares.

AM 56A Siebel Si 204D   W Nr 251190

No code recorded. Presumed to be an unintended duplication of the original AM 56, probably surrendered at the same airfield. Flown from Schleswig to Farnborough on 23rd September 1945 by F/Lt Smith, returning to Schleswig on 3rd October. Since it was airborne at the same time as the original AM 56 was returning to Farnborough on this date, prior to its landing accident *en route*, there is no possibility that AM 56A did not exist! It is presumed that this aircraft was scrapped in Germany or possibly handed over to the Armée de l'Air.

AM 57 Junkers Ju 290A-2   W Nr 110157

Surrendered at Flensburg, coded '9V+BK' of 2/FAGr 5. Flown from Flensburg to Schleswig on 17th August 1945 by S/Ldr McCarthy. Ferried from Schleswig to Farnborough on 21st September 1945 by S/Ldr King. Not test flown at Farnborough but was statically displayed during the German Aircraft Exhibition. By 15th December 1946, it was in the scrap area at Farnborough although it was not actually scrapped until about 1950.

AM 58 Heinkel He 162A-2   W Nr 120221

Surrendered at Leck, JG 1 aircraft. Arrived at Farnborough via the 'Return Ferry Service' on 16th June 1945. It was allocated RAF serial VH526 on 19th June, but there is no record of this aircraft being flown at RAE. The aircraft was used as a source of spares for other flyable He 162s and was in the scrap area by 15th December 1946.

AM 59 Heinkel He 162A-2   W Nr 120076

Surrendered at Leck, coded 'Yellow 4' of JG1. Arrived at Farnborough by surface transport on 15th June 1945 and allocated the RAF serial VH523 on 19th June. Test flown locally from Farnborough on 29th June, 5th, 6th and 23rd July, making two flights on the latter date. The first three flights were made by W/Cdr Falk and the others were by S/Ldr Martindale and F/Lt Cleaver. The short range of the aircraft is emphasised by the fact that none of the flights exceeded 20 minutes and the total flight time added up to 1 hour 30 minutes. On 2nd August 1945, it made a further 15 minute flight to Brize Norton, flown by Bell Chief Test Pilot, Jack Woolams, where it went into storage with No. 6 MU. On 29th June 1946, AM 59 was handed over to No. 47 MU, Sealand, for despatch to Canada. It left Salford Docks on 26th August aboard SS *Manchester Commerce*, arriving at Montreal on 9th September 1946. It has been on display at the Canadian National Aeronautical Collection at Rockcliffe, near Ottawa, since 1964.

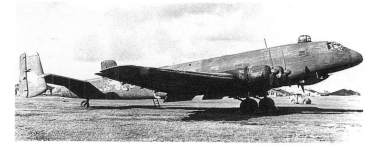

Top: **The Me 262A AM52, shown here as VH509, after arrival in Canada.** *Steve Coates collection*

Right: **The Junkers Ju 290A AM 57, photographed after arrival at Farnborough.** *MAP*

Below: **The Siebel Si 204D AM 56 at the RAE, Farnborough, on 27th August 1945.** *IWM, MH4911*

AM 60   Heinkel He 162A-2   W Nr 120074
Surrendered at Leck, coded 'White 11' of JG 1. Arrived at
Farnborough by surface transport on 10th August 1945 and
despatched by road to Brize Norton on the same day. Was in storage at No. 6 MU at the Home Census of Aircraft on 21st March
1946. Although it has been reported that this aircraft also went to
Canada, there is no evidence to support this and it is believed to
have been SoC by No. 6 MU on 14th August 1947.

AM 61   Heinkel He 162A-2   W Nr 120072
Surrendered at Leck, no code recorded; aircraft of JG 1. Arrived at
Farnborough by surface transport on 31st July 1945. Test flown at
RAE on 27th and 29th October by F/Lt Foster, and flown in the air
display at the German Aircraft Exhibition on 4th and 9th
November, by F/Lt R. A. Marks. It crashed on the latter date, killing Marks. The AIB Report (No. W2291) states that the accident
was caused by loss of control following an upward roll. During the
roll, excessive rudder yawed the aircraft sufficiently to initiate a
stall at too low a level to permit recovery. The total flight time of
this aircraft in the UK was 50 minutes.

AM 62   Heinkel He 162A-2   W Nr 120086
Surrendered at Leck, no code recorded; aircraft of JG 1. Arrived at
Farnborough by surface transport on 22nd August 1945 and
despatched by road to Brize Norton on the same day. Exhibited in
Hyde Park, London, from 16th September 1945 and again at White
Waltham airfield on 29th September. By the Census of 21st March
1946, AM 62 was back in store at No. 6 MU. Allocated to No. 47
MU, Sealand, on 29th May 1946 for packing and shipment to
Canada. Like AM 59, it left Salford on 26th August aboard the
Manchester Commerce, arriving at Montreal on 9th September. It
has been in store at Rockcliffe with the CNAC since about 1964.

AM 63   Heinkel He 162A-2   W Nr 120095
Surrendered at Leck, no code recorded; aircraft of JG 1. Arrived at
Farnborough and despatched to Brize Norton by surface transport
on 10th August 1945. AM 63 was used in travelling exhibitions as
a display item at a number of locations in the English Midlands for
some months, for example being shown at the Birmingham Civic
Centre in September 1945. With No. 6 MU at the Census of 21st
March 1946. AM 63 was not W Nr 120235 as has been reported
elsewhere. SoC by No. 6 MU on 14th August 1947.

AM 64   Heinkel He 162A-2   W Nr 120097
Surrendered at Leck, no code recorded; aircraft of JG 1. Arrived at
Farnborough by surface transport on 31st July 1945. Statically displayed in 'A' Shed during the German Aircraft Exhibition and allocated RAF serial VN153 on 8th November 1945. There is no record
of any flight being made by this aircraft at RAE, although its RAF
serial number was applied. AM 64 was recorded in the scrap area
on 15th December 1946.

AM 65   Heinkel He 162A-2   W Nr 120227
Surrendered at Leck, no code recorded; aircraft of JG 1. Arrived at
Farnborough by surface transport on 31st July 1945. Reports that
this aircraft became VH513 are in error (see AM 67), but it was allocated the RAF serial VN679, on 26th November 1945. However
this serial was not painted on the aircraft and there is no record of
it making any flights at RAE. This aircraft was in the scrap area at
Farnborough on 15th December 1946, but was rescued for use as a
display exhibit and appeared as such at the Blackpool Air Pageant
at Squires Gate in July 1947. By 1949, it was at the Central Gunnery
School, Leconfield. It is probable that the rescue from the scrap

heap was at the behest of the AHB but that the aircraft was later
deleted from its lists because of pressure on storage space at Sealand and Stanmore Park. By 1961, AM 65 was at RAF Colerne and
by 1964 it had become one of the first exhibits of the Station
Museum which grew until the closure of the station in 1975. At
this point AM 65 moved to St Athan where it was allocated the
maintenance serial number 8472M for accounting purposes. It
remained an exhibit of the St Athan Historic Aircraft Collection for
many years and was transferred to the RAF Museum, Hendon,
following the rundown of St Athan's role in aircraft preservation.

AM 66   Heinkel He 162A-2   W Nr 120091
Surrendered at Leck, no code recorded; aircraft of JG 1. Arrived at
Farnborough by surface transport on 31st July 1945. Statically displayed in partly sectioned condition in 'A' Shed during the German Aircraft Exhibition, and was later on display in the Science
Museum at South Kensington, from mid-February to mid-May
1946. Although most of the other exhibits in the Science Museum
display then seem to have gone to RAF South Cerney, there is no
record of the He 162 having done so and its final fate is not known.

AM 67   Heinkel He 162A-2   W Nr 120098
Surrendered at Leck, no code recorded; aircraft of JG 1. Arrived at
Farnborough by surface transport on 11th June 1945 and allocated
RAF serial VH513 on 14th June. Allocated to RAE Aero Flight on
18th July. Test flown from Farnborough on 3rd, 10th, 11th August,
7th, 18th, 21st, 27th & 28th September, 2nd, 5th, 7th, 8th, 9th,
10th, 11th, 19th, 29th, 30th & 31st October, and 29th & 30th
November 1945. On many occasions it flew more than once in a
day, and the total flight time came to 11 hours 40 minutes. Pilots
involved were Lt/Cdr Eric Brown, S/Ldr Tony Martindale, F/Lt
Foster and F/Lt R. A. Marks. This was a longer-range version than
the other '162s flown at RAE and made flights of up to 40 minutes
duration. In addition to the RAF roundels and serial number it
wore a yellow 'P' prototype marking. It was noted in wrecked condition on the scrap heap at Farnborough on 15th December 1946.

AM 68   Heinkel He 162A-2   W Nr *unknown*
Surrendered at Leck, no code recorded; aircraft of JG 1. It is probable that this reported allocation to an He 162 belonged to
W Nr 120235, although the inventory of German aircraft received
at RAE shows no 'Air Min' number against this aircraft. Some
records show a twelfth He 162 as being despatched to the UK,
therefore it cannot be conclusively stated that AM 68 was
W Nr 120235. 120235 was received at RAE on 10th August 1945 and
despatched onwards to No. 6 MU, Brize Norton, on the same day.
It was with No. 6 MU at the Census of 21st March 1946. By 1947
it was in the station museum at RAF Cranwell, where it remained
until at least March 1960, after which the museum was dispersed.
At this point, it went to the Imperial War Museum at Lambeth
where it was on display for many years until transferred to Duxford in 1986. By June 1989, the aircraft had returned to South
Lambeth where it remains at the time of writing.

AM 69 to AM 71 inclusive were at first allocated as AM S-1 to
AM S-3, but not in sequence. These aircraft are considered
together because their identities have not yet been completely
resolved. All three were Blöhm und Voss Bv 138 flying-boats surrendered at Kastrup-See and selected for evaluation by G/Capt
Hards on 9th June 1945. They were initially identified as 'Air Min
S-2' etc and the relationship between these identities and their true
Air Min numbers has not yet been traced, although it is clear that
they were not in sequence. Details of two follow:

AM 69   Blöhm und Voss Bv 138   W Nr *unknown*
One of the three Bv 138s identified as AM S-1 to AM S-3 as detailed on the previous page.

AM 70   Blöhm und Voss Bv 138C-1   W Nr 0310081
This aircraft of FA 125 was surrendered at Kastrup-See as described above and was delivered to MAEE Felixstowe on 15th December 1945. It was allotted the RAF serial number VN881 on 3rd January 1946 and was on charge with the MAEE from the following day for full armament trials. By 1st June 1946 it was awaiting disposal there because of lack of resources to maintain it. The RAF serial number was not painted on the aircraft. The history card for the aircraft shows that on 9th January 1947 it was reprieved from disposal – it was retained for training RAF marine

craft crews in the towing of flying-boats. It was collected by J. Dale & Co, after sale to them as scrap on 14th November 1947, although the date of sale is also recorded as 6th October 1948.

AM S-2   Blöhm und Voss Bv 138B-1   W Nr *unknown*
This aircraft, coded 'B', was flown from Kastrup-See to Kiel on 16th June 1945 and made a local test flight from Kiel on the same day. On 19th June, it flew from Kiel to Enkhuizen on the Zuider-Zee, where it made an unscheduled landing to pick up water supplies, flying onwards to Calshot on the following day. After minor repairs it was test flown from Calshot on 5th July prior to departing to MAEE Helensburgh on 7th July. All its flights up to 5th July had been made by G/Capt Hards. The '138 was allocated the RAF serial number VK895 on 26th July. The MAEE returned to its pre-war base at Felixstowe on 1st August 1945. VK895 was on MAEE strength at Felixstowe on 28th February 1946, but by 1st June 1946 was awaiting disposal due to lack of resources to maintain it. When observed in October 1946, it still wore both 'Air Min S-2' and VK895. It was still present in May 1947 and was SoC on 3rd January 1948. This aircraft must be AM 69 or AM 71.

AM 71   Blöhm und Voss Bv 138   W Nr *unknown*
One of the Bv 138's AMS-1 to AMS-3 as detailed on the previous page.

Below: **Heinkel He 162A Air Min 61 W Nr 120072 at the RAE on 11th September 1945.** *MAP*

Bottom: **He 162A W Nr 120235 in RAF marks at Leck.** *S. Kahlert collection*

AM 72 to AM 74 inclusive were at first allocated as AM V-1 to AM V-3, respectively.

AM 72   Messerschmitt Me 410A-1/U2   W Nr 420430

Code and unit not recorded. Surrendered at Vaerløse in Denmark and selected for evaluation on 9th June 1945 by G/Capt Hards. Initially painted as 'Air Min V-1'. Flown from Vaerløse to Kastrup on 20th August 1945 by S/Ldr Ian Somerville. It force-landed at Kastrup at the end of the ferry flight with one engine on fire after an oil tank burst. Repaired and flown again on 25th August. Kastrup - Schleswig on 3rd October 1945 by S/Ldr McCarthy. Ferried from Schleswig to Farnborough, via Gilze-Rijen, on 13th October 1945 by S/Ldr McCarthy. Flown from Farnborough to No. 6 MU, Brize Norton, on 28th December. Selected for preservation by the AHB in May 1946 and transferred to the charge of No. 76 MU, Wroughton, on 14th August 1946, for museum storage. Presumed to have been transferred to No. 47 MU, Sealand, on the closure of No. 76 MU. By 1949 AM 72 was in store at the GAFEC at No. 3 MU's Stanmore Park sub-site. By 1957, to No. 15 MU, Wroughton, and then to Fulbeck by January 1960. To Cosford in 1961 and remained there until moving to RAF St Athan in November 1985, apart from temporary moves to other stations for display (e.g. to Gaydon Battle of Britain displays in the 1960s). Allocated RAF Ground Instructional serial number 8483M at Cosford c 1975. It returned to Cosford, following the rundown of the St Athan collection, in late 1989. This aircraft is recorded as W Nr 410478 in the inventory of German aircraft received at RAE, but this is definitely in error. The W Nr 420430 was definitely painted on the aircraft and shown on its manufacturer's identity plate on the port side of the forward fuselage. The plate shows its type as a 'Krj 410 A-1/U2', indicating it to have been built by factory 'Krj', which was, in fact, the Messerschmitt factory at Augsburg. Since the engine serial numbers for the aircraft coincide with those shown for AM 72/'410478' in the inventory, it is almost certain that the incorrect W Nr recorded is a clerical error rather than a reference to a different aircraft. The aircraft, at one time, probably pre-delivery to the Luftwaffe, had the radio call-sign 'PD+VO'. This identity is still painted in its cockpit. The unit to which this aircraft belonged at its surrender has not been traced but paint-stripping carried out at Cosford showed evidence of the previous codes '3U+AK' and (earlier) '3U+CC'. These indicate that at one time the aircraft served with Zerstörer Geschwader (ZG) 26.

AM 73   Messerschmitt Me 410A-1   W Nr 130360

Code and unit not recorded. Surrendered at Vaerløse in Denmark and initially painted as 'Air Min V-2'. Flown Vaerløse - Kastrup 20th August 1945 by S/Ldr Somerville. Ferried from Schleswig to Farnborough on 11th November 1945 by S/Ldr Lancaster. Test flown locally from Farnborough on 14th December and then ferried from RAE to No. 6 MU, Brize Norton, on 21st December. SoC at No. 6 MU on 14th August 1947.

AM 74   Messerschmitt Me 410B-6   W Nr 410208

Code and unit not recorded. Surrendered at Vaerløse in Denmark and initially painted as 'Air Min V-3'. Flown Vaerløse - Kastrup 19th August 1945 by S/Ldr Somerville. Ferried from Gilze-Rijen to Farnborough on 17th September 1945 by F/Lt Lawson. It was an anti-shipping strike aircraft equipped with FuG 200 radar. On static display during the German Aircraft Exhibition. Fuselage noted in the Farnborough scrap area on 15th December 1946.

AM 75   Ju 88H/Fw 190A 'Mistel S 3B'
Composite aircraft, of IV/KG 200, comprising –
Ju 88H-1 (see note below AM 76)   W Nr unknown
Fw 190A-8/R6   W Nr 733682

Surrendered at Tirstrup in Denmark. This was a 'Mistel S 3B' trainer version using a Ju 88H-1 lower component. Ferried from Tirstrup to Schleswig on 30th July 1945 as a combination by a German pilot in formation with AM 76 and AM 77, under RAF fighter escort. At Schleswig, the composite aircraft was separated into its components for ferrying to the UK, but the Ju 88H was not delivered and is presumed to have been scrapped at Schleswig. Contrary to some published reports, the Fw 190 was not part of the 'Mistel' displayed at the German Aircraft Exhibition, since it did not arrive in England until after the Exhibition closed. (See AM 77.) The Fw 190 was ferried from Amsterdam/Schiphol to Farnborough on 11th November 1945 by S/Ldr Easby, continuing to No. 6 MU, Brize Norton, on 30th November. Allocated to RAF Cranwell on 18th September 1946 for the Station Museum, remaining there until 1960 when the Museum was dispersed. It then went to Bicester (noted there in April 1961) and Biggin Hill (noted there in September 1962), before being allocated to the Imperial War Museum at Lambeth where it was on display for many years until moving to Duxford in April 1986. In 1989, the '190 returned to Lambeth to be displayed in a flying attitude, suspended from the roof of the newly refurbished Museum building.

Below: **Me 410A AM 74, photographed at the RAE, Farnborough, during the German Aircraft Exhibition, wearing the number 'AIR MIN V-3'.** *Flight*

Bottom: **The Ju 88 lower components of three 'Mistel' composite aircraft pictured at Schleswig in August 1945. The aircraft on the left is the Ju 88A which came to Farnborough. The other two Junkers are the later Ju 88H version with the night fighter type square fin.** *PRO, AIR 40/126*

AM 109   Junkers Ju 352A   W Nr *unknown*

Surrendered at Eggebek, coded 'G6+RX' of V/TG 4. Flown from Schleswig to Farnborough on 31st August 1945 by S/Ldr King. Made one flight back to Schleswig on 3rd September, returning to RAE on 4th September 1945. Although this aircraft has been reported as receiving RAF serial VP550, this is definitely incorrect (VP550 was AM 8). AM 109 was noted in the scrap area at Farnborough on 15th December 1946.

AM 110   Junkers Ju 352A   W Nr *unknown*

Surrendered at Eggebek, coded 'G6+SX' of V/TG 4. Flown from Schleswig to Farnborough on 13th July 1945 by F/Lt Lawson, returning to Schleswig on 16th July. From Schleswig to Farnborough again on 28th July. On 31st July it took off from Farnborough *en route* to Schleswig.

S/Ldr Somerville's log shows that he flew AM110 from Schleswig to Kastrup and return on 4th August 1945. AM110 also flown by S/Ldr McCarthy 2nd & 12th August. The aircraft (or possibly AM 19) was later abandoned at Knokke after force landing there with engine trouble, then being offered to the Belgian government in lieu of one of a number of Junkers Ju 52/3ms which that government had requested. The offer was declined and the aircraft scrapped.

Opposite page, from the top: **This shot shows Ju 352A AM110 'G6+SX'.** *RAFM P11492*

After capture at Beldringe in Denmark, Do 217M AM 107 reached Farnborough on 13th October 1945. This shot was taken towards the end of the month at the RAE. *Flight 12098/16*

This shot of Ju 188A AM 108 was taken at the RAE, with the later Ju 388L in the background, towards the end of October 1945. *Flight 12098/6*

Right: **The anti-shipping strike variant of the Ju 88A, AM 112, seen at the RAE, Farnborough, prior to delivery to the ATDU, Gosport.** *MAP*

Below: **This photograph of the torpedo-bomber version of the Fw 190F AM 111 was taken at the RAE on 20th October 1945. Note the lengthened tailwheel to provide ground clearance for the torpedo.** *IWM MH4876*

AM 111   Focke Wulf Fw 190F-8/R15   W Nr *unknown*

Uncoded aircraft of TVA. Surrendered at Travemünde/Priwall and ferried from there to Schleswig on 9th July 1945 by S/Ldr McCarthy. It was an Fw 190F-8/R15 torpedo-carrying version, selected for investigation of the torpedo installation. Although usually reported as an aircraft of III/KG 200, a special duties unit which operated this variant of the Fw 190, it is much more likely that it belonged to the Luftwaffe Torpedowaffen Versuchsanstalt (TVA), which was based at Travemünde. This unit, the German equivalent of the Air Torpedo Development Unit, had moved to Travemünde from Gdynia in Poland in February 1945. AM 111 was flown from Schleswig to RAE on 19th July and onwards to No. 6 MU, Brize Norton, on 28th July 1945. Flown back from Brize Norton to Farnborough on 15th October 1945 to appear in the static display at the German Aircraft Exhibition. Later taken to the College of Aeronautics at Cranfield, for exhibition as part of its 'Library of Flight', for example being noted there in 1948.

AM 112   Junkers Ju 88A-6/U   W Nr 0660

Coded '1H+MN' of II/KG 26. Place of surrender was Lübeck. This was an anti-shipping strike aircraft, equipped with FuG 200 radar. It was ferried from Schleswig to Farnborough on 27th August 1945 by S/Ldr King. It was flown to Gosport on 18th December 1945 for torpedo dropping trials at the Air Torpedo Development Unit, and was allocated the RAF serial VN874 on 29th December. The Ju 88 remained at Gosport until collected by Enfield Rolling Mills, to whom it had been sold as scrap, on 10th November 1947. So far as is known, no flying trials were under-taken at Gosport.

AM 113   Junkers Ju 188A-2   W Nr 190327
Coded '1H+GT' of III/KG 26. The W Nr 5366 has also been
reported for this aircraft (both 5366 and 0327 were painted on its
fin). It was surrendered at Lübeck. It was an anti-shipping strike
aircraft. AM 113 was ferried from Lübeck to Schleswig on 8th
August 1945 by S/Ldr Joe McCarthy. It was flown from Schleswig
to Farnborough on 27th August 1945 by S/Ldr McCarthy, continuing to Gosport on 8th September for torpedo-dropping trials at the
Air Torpedo Development Unit. This aircraft was allocated the
RAF serial number VN143 on 30th October 1945. It remained at
Gosport until collected by Enfield Rolling Mills, to whom it had
been sold as scrap, on 10th November 1947. So far as is known, the
Ju 188 was not in fact flown at Gosport.

AM 114   Dornier Do 24T   W Nr 1135
Aircraft of SNG 81. Place of surrender was Guldborg in Denmark.
It was selected for evaluation of its Air-Sea Rescue equipment. The
Do 24 was ferried from Schleswig-See to Felixstowe on 6th
December 1945. The RAF serial number VN865 was allocated on
20th December and the Do 24 was on the strength of the Marine
Aircraft Experimental Establishment from 27th December for 'type
trials'. By 1st June 1946 it was awaiting disposal because of the lack
of resources to maintain it. It was still present at Felixstowe in
April 1947 and was collected by J. Dale & Co for reduction to scrap
on 14th November 1947.

AM 115   Dornier Do 24T-3   W Nr *unknown*
Aircraft of KG 200. This Do 24T may have been W Nr 3296, which
was test flown at Schleswig-See on 16th July 1945 by S/Ldr Ian
Somerville. This allocation has not been traced in any documented
record but it is reasonably certain that it was one of the three
Do 24Ts selected for evaluation of German ASR equipment at
MAEE. It was almost certainly the Do 24 which was flown from
Schleswig-See to Calshot on 21st August 1945 by G/Capt Alan
Hards. This aircraft made a local test flight at Calshot with an RAE
crew on 23rd August, prior to departing the same day to the MAEE
at Felixstowe. At the time, the MAEE was in the process of returning to Felixstowe from its wartime base at Helensburgh. It was
allocated the RAF serial VM483 on 2nd October 1945. VM483 sank
at Felixstowe on 24th October, when one of its pontoon floats was
punctured during a gale, and was written off as Category E.

AM 116   Dornier Do 24T   W Nr 3435
Aircraft of SNG 81. Surrendered at Guldborg in Denmark. Code
was 'VH+JM'. Ferried from Schleswig-See to Felixstowe on 6th
December 1945. Allocated the RAF serial number VN870 on 20th
December. On the strength of the MAEE for study of German ASR
equipment and methods from 27th December 1945, but was awaiting disposal by 1st June 1946, because of lack of servicing
resources.
    It was sold to J. Dale & Co as scrap and collected by them on 14th
November 1947. This aircraft has usually been reported in the past
as AM 118, but the number AM 116 is shown against its RAF serial
allocation in the official records.

AM 117   Focke Wulf Fw 58C-2/U6 Weihe   W Nr 2093
Surrendered at Fassberg, coded 'TE+BK' of Ekdo 40. This was an
insecticide sprayer and was initially selected for study of its spray-
ing system at the Chemical Warfare Establishment at Porton
Down. Later it was reallocated to the RAE for study. Ferried from
Schleswig to Farnborough on 18th January 1946 via Gütersloh and
Melsbroek. Made one test flight on 26th January. Was noted in the
scrap area at Farnborough on 15th December 1946.

AM 118   – allocation so far untraced
There are indications that this number was allotted to a Junkers
Ju 88 which was surrendered at Fassberg and selected for evaluation of chemical weapon delivery by the Chemical Warfare Establishment at Porton Down. There may be a connection with the Junkers aircraft mentioned in Chapter Six (Section 6.6) under the
Chemical Warfare Establishment, which were flown in chemical
weapon delivery trials from Fassberg by pilots of the A&AEE,
although none of these aircraft wore an 'Air Min' number. It is
equally possible that the number may have been allotted to a so far
untraced aircraft.

AM 119   Siebel (Halle) Fh 104A Hallore   W Nr *unknown*
Code and unit unknown. There are some indications that this
aircraft was surrendered at Husum, although the statistics of aircraft captured at this airfield do not show an Fh 104A. The aircraft
was ferried from Husum to Schleswig at the end of October 1945.
On 28th November 1945, AM 119 left Schleswig *en route* to the UK
but while it was over the North Sea the reduction gear failed on
one engine and the aircraft made a forced landing on the Goodwin
Sands. The crew was picked up safely, but the aircraft was written
off as Category E.

AM 120   Arado Ar 96B   W Nr *unknown*
Code and unit unknown. Believed to have been surrendered at
Husum. On 1st December 1945, AM 120 was at No. 435 DSRU
Schleswig, awaiting air test. By 28th February 1946, it was notified
as 'awaiting collection' at Schleswig. Its 'Movement Card' at AHB
2 has a reference to 'EFS', which may indicate that the EFS (or
ECFS - Empire Central Flying School) had a role in its selection. On
26th April 1946, AM 120 arrived at White Waltham, *en route* to
Woodley, flown by S/Ldr S. L. Hughes and on 3rd July it was noted
as being on the strength of the Woodley Station Flight. A photograph taken later in 1946 shows that it nosed-over, damaging its
propeller. AM 120 was SoC on 29th May 1947.

AM 121   Bücker Bü 181 Bestmann   W Nr *unknown*
Believed to have been surrendered at Husum, code and unit unknown. On 1st December 1945, AM 121 was at No. 435 DSRU Schleswig, awaiting air test. Like the Ar 96B AM 120, it was 'awaiting collection' at Schleswig on 28th February 1946. There is no record of this aircraft arriving at RAE, ECFS, or any other likely unit. However, the BAFO statistics of aircraft despatched to the UK do indicate that two Bü 181s were sent there and there is little doubt that this was the unmarked Bestmann which arrived at White Waltham on 22nd March 1946, *en route* to Woodley, having flown from Schleswig via Oldenburg, Twente and Manston. This flight took 9 hours and was made by F/O Osborne of No. 83 Group Communications Squadron. Reports that this AM number belonged to an Ar 96B seen at Woodley are in error but it is likely that the report arose from misidentification of the Bü 181, which was presumably identified with its 'AM' number after arrival there.

AM 122   Bücker Bü 181C-3 Bestmann   W Nr 120417
Believed to have been surrendered at Husum, code and unit unknown. This aircraft left Schleswig on 30th October 1945, flown by W/O Davies of No. 83 Group Communications Squadron. It arrived at Farnborough, via Hawkinge and Dunsfold, on 1st November 1945. It made four local test flights from Farnborough on 2nd November, piloted by G/Capt Hards and pilots named Martin, Parker and Hood. It flew to and from White Waltham on 3rd November and then flew in the German Aircraft Exhibition air display on 4th November. Made further local test flights on 8th and 19th November 1945 and on 16th January 1946. By 24th April 1947, AM 122 had been transported to No. 6 MU, Brize Norton. During June, it was re-classified from an 'ex-German' to a 'civilian' aircraft in No. 6 MU records, which may be connected with the reservation of the British civil registration marks G-AKAX for it on 10th July 1947 in the name of O. F. Maclaren Ltd of Heston Airport. On 22nd April 1948, the owner was changed to Owen Finlay Maclaren in the official record, but AM 122 remained on charge with No. 6 MU until 8th July 1948. It then appears to have gone to Heston for overhaul (possibly by Airwork Ltd), and was later to be

seen at Denham, where it was scrapped in about 1950. Although during the overhaul its British civil registration marks were painted on the aircraft, it appears that the authorities were unwilling to grant a Certificate of Airworthiness to the type. At that time, such matters were much more inflexibly controlled than they are today and obtaining a Type C of A would have been prohibitively expensive, even if the appropriate design data had been readily available. Its civilian registration was cancelled on 30th June 1950.

AM 123   Arado Ar 96B   W Nr *unknown*
Believed to have been surrendered at Husum, code and unit unknown. Test-flown at Husum on 23rd October 1945 by S/Ldr Joe McCarthy. Awaiting air test at Schleswig on 1st December 1945, and awaiting collection on 28th February 1946. AM 123 landed at White Waltham on 1st May 1946, *en route* to RAF Woodley. On charge with Woodley Station Flight on 3rd July 1946. SoC on 29th May 1947.

AM 124   Messerschmitt Bf 108   W Nr *unknown*
The Bf 108 '124' recorded in my previous book *Air Min* has now been proved not to have had an AM number. Further details of this aircraft are given in Chapter Six under RAF Cranwell.

AM GD 1   Junkers Ju 52/3m   W Nr 5375
A Ju 52/3m with this identity was in use by the RAE General Duties Flight for communications duties. A Ju 52/3m first visited the RAE from Schleswig on 22nd May 1945, returning to Schleswig on 24th May. On 25th May it flew back to the RAE, on 28th May returning to Schleswig via Grove, Kastrup and Leck. Various other flights took place up to 8th June involving Leck, Grove, Schleswig and Farnborough, but no identity is shown for the aircraft in the Flight Log. From 16th to 20th June, W Nr 5375 is recorded as making various flights, again involving Farnborough, Gilze-Rijen, Schleswig, Tangmere, Flensburg, Bremerhaven, Fassberg and Lübeck. The last record was a flight from Schleswig to Gilze-Rijen and return on 14th July 1945 by S/Ldr Somerville.

AM GD   Siebel Si 204D   W Nr *unknown*
Coded 'C'. This aircraft was also flown by the RAE General Duties Flight on communications work. In some Flight Log entries, it is shown as 'AM GD 1' which is the identity known from photographic evidence to have been painted on a Ju 52/3m. It is believed that the Si 204 was actually painted as 'AM GD', and it is shown as such in the RAE's inventory of German aircraft received at Farnborough. The Si 204 is first recorded as flown from Eggebek to Flensburg on 10th June by S/Ldr King, and Flensburg - Schleswig on 13th June by S/Ldr McCarthy. It also flew at Flensburg on 15th June 1945. Visited Farnborough from 22nd to 24th August 1945, arriving from and returning to Schleswig. Was at Farnborough again from 7th to 13th November, again arriving from and returning to Schleswig. Finally flown from Schleswig to Farnborough on 28th November 1945, there being no record of any further flights. Fate unknown.

AM K41	– see AM 41
AM K42	– see AM 42
AM S-1	– see AM 69 to 71
AM S-2	– see AM 69 to 71
AM S-3	– see AM 69 to 71
AM V-1	– see AM 72
AM V-2	– see AM 73
AM V-3	– see AM 74

Opposite page, top: **The Ju 188A AM 113 in a striking camouflage scheme at Lübeck in north Germany prior to its British markings being applied.** *Chris Thomas, courtesy Steve Coates collection*

Opposite page, bottom: **The Arado Ar 96B Air Min 120, photographed at Woodley in 1946, after nosing over and damaging its propeller.** *Flight 12205/4*

Below: **The Bücker Bü 181 AM 122, at Heston after painting in civilian markings G-AKAX.** *Steve Coates collection*

AM 138

Several published sources have attributed this identity to a Bv 138 or Bv 222 flying-boat. The source of this incorrect information is almost certainly an entry in the RAE Flight Log for 5th July 1945, which shows AM 138 as a Bv 138 making a test flight from Calshot on this date. This aircraft must have been 'Air Min S-2' which had arrived at Calshot a few days previously. It is clear from analysis of separate records originating from RAF Calshot and the RAE, that there was only one Bv 138 at Calshot at the time. The AM number entry is clearly a confusion with the type number of the aircraft. The Bv 222C-012 which later became VP501 could not have been involved either, since it was still at Trondheim in Norway on 5th July 1945.

AM 439

The RAE Flight Log also quotes this identity for an Arado Ar 234B. Analysis clearly shows that the aircraft in question was in fact WNr 140493 (see AM 227 to 229 entries below).

7.2 ALLOCATIONS MADE AT RAE FARNBOROUGH
(AM 200 onwards)

These numbers were allocated by G/Capt A. F. Hards to aircraft which, for a variety of reasons, had not received 'Air Min' numbers at their points of surrender. The allocations made to the Messerschmitt Me 163Bs cannot in all cases be related to specific aircraft because no complete documented record of the allocations is known to survive. However, it appears from tie-ups which are confirmed from other documentary records, that the AM numbers were allocated in the order in which these aircraft are listed in the inventory of German aircraft received at the RAE. With the exception of VF241, the first complete captured Me 163B, which arrived at Farnborough before hostilities ceased, the inventory contains a complete list of Me 163Bs received in the UK, although there may be clerical errors in some of the Werk Nummern listed. The numbers from AM 200 to AM 222 inclusive were all allotted to Messerschmitt Me 163Bs. The list below is based on the order shown in the inventory of aircraft as they were received at the RAE.

AM 200 Messerschmitt Me 163B WNr 191329

Aircraft of JG 400. Surrendered at Husum and shipped to RAE via the 'Return Ferry Service'. Despatched by road from Farnborough to No. 6 MU, Brize Norton, on 9th July 1945. Recorded at No. 6 MU at the Home Census of Aircraft on 21st March 1946, but there is no later record, and it is presumed that the aircraft was one of the nine Me 163Bs SoC as scrap at No. 6 MU on 14th August 1947.

AM 201 Messerschmitt Me 163B WNr 191330

Aircraft of JG 400. Surrendered at Husum and other details identical to WNr 191329 above, with the exception that it was not recorded in the 21st March 1946 Census.

AM 202 Messerschmitt Me 163B WNr 191915

Aircraft of JG 400. Details identical to WNr 191329, except that on 4th February 1946 it was returned to the RAE Farnborough by road. Not recorded in the 21st March 1946 Census.

AM 203 Messerschmitt Me 163B WNr 310061

Coded 'Yellow 13' of JG 400. Surrendered at Husum and shipped to the RAE. Despatched from Farnborough to No. 6 MU, Brize Norton, on 9th July 1945. To No. 76 MU, Wroughton, on 21st

December 1945, for packing, and officially transferred to the French Armée de l'Air on 6th March 1946. Despatched to Dieppe on the SS *Groningen* on 9th March, and handed over to the French authorities on the following day. Later history not known.

AM 204 Messerschmitt Me 163B WNr 191454

Coded 'Yellow 11' of JG 400. Surrendered at Husum and shipped to the RAE. Despatched from Farnborough to No. 6 MU, Brize Norton, on 12th July 1945 and used as a static exhibit in Hyde Park, London, during September 1945. Later returned to No. 6 MU, being recorded there at the Census on 21st March 1946. On 25th June 1946, transferred to No. 47 MU, Sealand, for packing and transfer to Canada. AM 204 left Salford Docks on 28th August 1946, aboard the SS *Manchester Commerce* and arrived at Montreal on 9th September. One of the record cards for this aircraft has been interpreted as reading 191452, but photographic and other documentary evidence supports the view that 191454 is the correct identity. This aircraft is believed to have been scrapped at Arnprior, Ontario, in about 1957.

AM 205 Messerschmitt Me 163B WNr 191905

Aircraft of JG 400. Surrendered at Husum and shipped to the RAE. Despatched from Farnborough to No. 6 MU, Brize Norton, on 21st July 1945. With No. 6 MU during the Census of 21st March 1946 and is presumed to be one of the nine Me 163Bs SoC as scrap at No. 6 MU on 14th August 1947.

AM 206 Messerschmitt Me 163B WNr 191902

Aircraft of JG 400. Surrendered at Husum and shipped to the RAE. Despatched from Farnborough to No. 6 MU, Brize Norton, on 21st July 1945. Comments as for WNr 191905 above.

AM 207 Messerschmitt Me 163B WNr 191461

Aircraft of JG 400. Surrendered at Husum and shipped to the RAE. Despatched from Farnborough to No. 6 MU, Brize Norton, on 21st July 1945. No further record. This may conceivably be the aircraft (reputedly WNr '191614') which was for many years at the Rocket Propulsion Establishment at Westcott and which in 1980 was transferred to the Aerospace Museum at RAF Cosford and is currently there as '191614' (8481M).

AM 208 Messerschmitt Me 163B WNr 191912

Aircraft of JG 400. Surrendered at Husum and shipped to the RAE. Despatched from Farnborough to No. 6 MU, Brize Norton, on 21st July 1945. Returned to Farnborough for static display in 'A' Shed during the German Aircraft Exhibition and subsequently displayed at the Science Museum, South Kensington, London, from February to May 1946. Subsequent fate unrecorded.

AM 209 Messerschmitt Me 163B WNr 191315

Aircraft of JG 400. Surrendered at Husum and shipped to the RAE. Despatched from Farnborough to No. 6 MU, Brize Norton, on 21st July 1945. Recorded with No. 6 MU at the Census of 21st March 1946. No further details and presumed to be one of the nine Me 163Bs SoC as scrap at No. 6 MU on 14th August 1947.

AM 210 Messerschmitt Me 163B WNr 191316

Coded 'Yellow 6' of JG 400. Surrendered at Husum and shipped to the RAE. Despatched from Farnborough to No. 6 MU, Brize Norton, on 21st July 1945. With No. 6 MU in the Home Census of Aircraft on 21st March 1946 and despatched to No. 47 MU, Sealand, on 17th June. By 1949, was with the GAFEC, No. 3 MU, Stanmore Park, remaining there until at least 1955.

Up to the time that BEA took over from RAS on 1st February 1947, the date on which all the surviving private airlines were nationalised, only three more Ju 52s had been delivered (G-AHOF, 'HOK and 'HOL), but the remainder followed within a few weeks. On 20th March 1947 twice-daily direct London-Belfast services were added to the Junkers' workload. At this point the Junkers were quite well regarded by BEA and it was intended to keep them in service until September 1948; maintenance contracts, chiefly with Fields for engine overhauls, were arranged accordingly. On 1st February 1947 the Ju 52s had entered service on the BEA Scottish Division routes, including Glasgow-Belfast, Prestwick-Belfast, Glasgow-Aberdeen-Orkney-Shetland, Glasgow-Stornoway-Inverness, and Glasgow-Inverness-Orkney-Shetland. During the severe 1947 winter one had even been employed to drop supplies to the keepers of the marooned Dubh Artach lighthouse. However, the poor quality of materials and workmanship of the wartime German production lines began to catch up with the outdated Junkers. Supplies of tyres had to be sought in places as far afield as Hungary; exhaust collector rings remained a problem and engine cylinder failures multipled. On the Scottish routes the type was unpopular because ground power units were required to start the Junkers' engines and these were only available at Glasgow. The Ju 52 was withdrawn from the London-Belfast services on 18th May 1947. G-AHOK, which had suffered a landing accident at Glasgow/Renfrew on 26th January, had been sent to Scottish Aviation at Prestwick for repair, but this work was cancelled and the aircraft was used for spares. A policy decision was taken by Philip Wills (the same Philip Wills as mentioned in Chapter Nine) the BEA Technical Director, to ground the Junkers fleet on 10th August 1947, retaining three aircraft in airworthy condition up to that date by cannibalisation. In fact, it seems that a few flights were made up to the end of August, the last flight being a non-scheduled one from Renfrew to Liverpool on 31st August. All aircraft had been withdrawn from use before their initial Certificates of Airworthiness had expired.

After lingering at Renfrew for some time, they were ferried to Manchester/Ringway, for storage pending disposal. By 1st January 1948 all but one of the surviving passenger aircraft had arrived there and the last one soon followed, all to be picketed out in open storage. The training aircraft, G-AHBP, went into storage at Birmingham/Elmdon. All were sold for scrap later in 1948. The conversion of the ten passenger aircraft had cost the MCA £155315, in addition to heavy maintenance costs. Critics pointed out that Dakota civilian conversions seldom cost more than £3000 per aircraft, and the AAJC's 'in-house' conversion of G-AHBP had cost a mere £2705. The financial settlement between BEA and the MCA valued the hire cost of each Junkers at a mere £20 per month! Enquiries of Junkers operators in France and Scandinavia produced similar tales of woe when Ju 52 operating costs were compared with those of other contemporary aircraft.

Details of the individual Ju 52/3ms are given below:

VM892   Junkers Ju 52/3m   W Nr *unknown*
Surrendered in north Germany. Serial allocated on 15th October 1945. With the EASSU Fühlsbuttel on 25th October 1945. No further details.

VM900 - VM932 and VM961 - VM987: these serial numbers were allocated to the EASSU on 26th October 1945 for local allottment to individual Ju 52/3m aircraft. The individual serial allocations appear to have been made on the date of arrival of each aircraft at Hamburg/Fühlsbuttel.

VM900   Ju 52/3m ge   W Nr 5232
Ex- Transport Gruppe (TGr) 20. Surrendered at Kristiansand/Kjevik. Ferried to EASSU on 8th October 1945. Left EASSU for No. 6 MU on 17th November 1945 and was at Brize Norton by 19th November. Sold as scrap to J. Dale & Co Ltd on 11th March 1948.

VM901   Ju 52/3m g4e   W Nr 6064
Ex- TGr 20. Surrendered at Kristiansand/Kjevik. Arrived at EASSU on 8th October 1945 and was at No. 6 MU on 15th January 1946. Sold to Short Bros on 7th March 1946.

VM902   Ju 52/3m g4e   W Nr 6724
Ex- 2/TGr 20, coded '7U+CK'. Surrendered at Oslo/Fornebu. Arrived at EASSU on 8th October 1945 and at No. 6 MU on 20th December 1945. Sold to Short Bros on 21st March 1946.

VM903   Ju 52/3m g14e   W Nr 640758
Ex- TGr 20. Surrendered at Eggemoen. Arrived at EASSU on 16th October 1945 and at No. 6 MU on 29th May 1946. Sold as scrap to J. Dale & Co Ltd on 11th March 1948.

VM904   Ju 52/3m g4e   W Nr 6294
Ex-TGr 20. Surrendered at Kristiansand/Kjevik. Arrived at EASSU on 8th October 1945. SoC on 16th July 1946 'for destruction' at Fühlsbuttel and destroyed on the following day by No. 8401 Air Disarmament Wing (ADW).

VM905   Ju 52/3m g8e (MS)   W Nr 3448
Ex- Teilkdo 2/Minensuchsgruppe 1, coded '3K+KK'. A minesweeping aircraft, with a ring for generating magnetic fields to explode magnetic mines. Surrendered at Oslo/ Fornebu. Arrived at EASSU on 8th October 1945 and at No. 6 MU on 27th November 1945. Sold as scrap to J. Dale & Co Ltd on 11th March 1948.

VM906   Ju 52/3m g14e   W Nr 640066
Ex- 2/TGr 20, coded '7U+AK'. Surrendered at Oslo/Fornebu. Arrived at EASSU on 16th October 1945 and at No. 6 MU by 27th November. Sold to Short Bros on 21st March 1946.

VM907   Ju 52/3m
W Nr quoted in EASSU records as '729' and delivered to this unit on 12th October 1945. Place of surrender not yet traced. Ferried from Fühlsbuttel to Eindhoven on 17th November and damaged at Eindhoven on 25th November. This aircraft was SoC on 28th February 1946 and was handed over to the Netherlands government as a source of spares for other flyable Ju 52/3ms transferred to Holland.

VM908   Ju 52/3m   W Nr 6750
Ex D-APZX of Deutsche Luft Hansa, named *Raoul Stoisvljevic*. Believed to have been surrendered at Oslo. Arrived at EASSU on 18th October 1945. Ferried from Fühlsbuttel to Liverpool/Speke on 10th January 1946 for use by Railway Air Services as a crew training aircraft. After overhaul at the AAJC maintenance facility at Speke it was painted in Railway Air Services (RAS) colours and registered to RAS as G-AHBP on 20th August 1946. A restricted C of A was issued on 7th October 1946 allowing its use for purposes other than passenger carrying. G-AHBP was subsequently taken over by the BEAC on 1st February 1947. After cancellation from the register on 2nd February 1948, it was stored at Birmingham/Elmdon until it was sold for scrap. It was taken to the yard of Minworth Metals Ltd at Castle Bromwich on 7th July 1948. It was eventually scrapped after being used as a tea-room by the yard workers.

VM909   Ju 52/3m g14e   W Nr 640994
Ex- TGr 20. Surrendered at Eggemoen. Arrived at EASSU on 16th October 1945. SoC at Fuhlbuttel on 16th July 1946 and handed over to No. 8401 ADW on the following day, for destruction.

VM910   Ju 52/3m g8e (MS)   W Nr 3443
Coded '3K+BK' of Teilkdo 2/Minensuchsgruppe 1 at Oslo/Fornebu. Arrived at EASSU on 8th October 1945. Despatched from Fühlsbuttel to No. 6 MU on 31st May 1946 but suffered damage while running up at Manston on the following day and was SoC on 6th June 1946.

VM911   Ju 52/3m g8e   W Nr 130740
Ex- TGr 20. Surrendered at Kristiansand/Kjevik. Arrived at EASSU on 16th October 1945. SoC on 16th July 1946 and handed over to No. 8401 ADW on the following day, for destruction.

VM912   Ju 52/3m g6e   W Nr 3003
Ex- TGr 20. Surrendered at Kristiansand/Kjevik. Arrived at EASSU on 8th October 1945 and at No. 6 MU Brize Norton on 14th June 1946. Sold as scrap to J. Dale & Co Ltd on 11th March 1948.

VM913   Ju 52/3m g14e   W Nr 640604
Ex- TGr 20. Surrendered at Eggemoen. Arrived at EASSU on 16th October 1945 and at No. 6 MU on 14th June 1946. Sold as scrap to J. Dale & Co Ltd on 11th March 1948.

VM914   Ju 52/3m ge   W Nr 5810
Ex- TGr 20. Surrendered at Kristiansand/Kjevik. Arrived at EASSU on 28th October 1945 and despatched to No. 6 MU on 17th November. Sold as scrap to J. Dale & Co Ltd on 11th March 1948.

VM915   Ju 52/3m g8e   W Nr 501195
Ex- Jagdführer (Jafu) Norwegen. Surrendered at Kristiansand/Kjevik. Arrived at EASSU on 28th October 1945 and at No. 6 MU on 9th January 1946. Sold to Shorts Bros on 21st March 1946 but not delivered until 24th April 1946, having force-landed at Little Rissington on its initial delivery flight and been repaired by a working party from No. 10 MU, Hullavington.

VM916   Ju 52/3m g4e   W Nr 6069
Ex- 4/TGr 20, coded '7U+EM'. Surrendered at Oslo/Fornebu. Arrived at EASSU on 28th October 1945 and at No. 6 MU on 5th February 1946. Sold to Short Bros on 26th June 1946.

VM917   Ju 52/3m g8e   W Nr 7339
Ex- TGr 20. Surrendered at Bardufoss. Arrived at EASSU on 28th October 1945 and at No. 6 MU on 27th November. Sold as scrap to J. Dale & Co Ltd on 11th March 1948.

VM918   Ju 52/3m g8e   W Nr 501367
Unit and place of surrender unknown. (As with many other Ju 52/3m, EASSU records show its source as 'Norway' but this is disproved by the surviving detailed records of Luftwaffe aircraft in Norway on the date of surrender. It is probable that the aircraft actually came from Denmark*.) Arrived at EASSU on 5th November 1945. Left EASSU for Leck (en route to the French Armée de l'Air) on 27th April 1946.

*similar comments apply to VM919 to 932 and VM962 to 968 inclusive.

VM919   Ju 52/3m g8e   W Nr 3366
Arrived at EASSU on 5th November 1945 and despatched to Leck on 9th May 1946 for transfer to the French Armée de l'Air via No. 8302 ADW.

VM920   Ju 52/3m g8e   W Nr 501167
Arrived at EASSU on 5th November 1945. Despatched to No. 8302 ADW, Leck on 27th May 1946, for transfer to the French Armée de l'Air.

VM921   Ju 52/3m g8e   W Nr 501148
Arrived at EASSU on 5th November 1945 and at No. 6 MU on 20th December 1945. Sold as scrap to J. Dale & Co Ltd on 11th March 1948.

Junkers Ju 52/3m G-AHOC in British European Airways colours at Croyden, at the inauguration of the London-Liverpool-Belfast service on 18th November 1946. *MAP*

VM922   Ju 52/3m   W Nr 3433
Arrived at EASSU on 12th November 1945 and at No. 6 MU on 9th December 1945. Sold as scrap to J. Dale & Co Ltd on 11th March 1948.

VM923   Ju 52/3m g8e   W Nr 501441
Arrived at EASSU on 12th November 1945 and at No. 6 MU on 12th February 1946. Sold to Shorts on 28th February and, after conversion under Short Bros works number SH16C, became G-AHOC of BEAC as the first of its *Jupiter* Class. It was registered to the Ministry of Civil Aviation on 21st May 1946 and transferred to BEAC on 1st October prior to its C of A issue on 5th November 1946. After withdrawal from service G-AHOC was ferried from Renfrew to Manchester/Ringway on 9th September 1947 and was scrapped at the British Aluminium Co Ltd at Latchford, Warrington, in February 1948. It was officially cancelled from the UK register on 2nd February 1948.

VM924   Ju 52/3m   W Nr 3436
Arrived at EASSU on 12th November 1945 and at No. 6 MU on 5th February 1946. Sold as scrap to J. Dale & Co Ltd on 11th March 1948.

VM925   Ju 52/3m   W Nr 3345
Arrived at EASSU on 12th November 1945. Transferred to No. 8302 ADW, Leck, on 10th July 1946 for transfer to the French Armée de l'Air.

VM926   Ju 52/3m   W Nr 3298
Arrived at EASSU on 12th November 1945 and at No. 6 MU on 8th January 1946. Sold to Short Bros on 21st March 1946.

VM927   Ju 52/3m   W Nr 3428
Arrived at EASSU on 16th November 1945. On 2nd April 1946 transferred to the charge of No. 131 (P) Squadron and delivered to Ahlhorn for handover to the Netherlands government. Became PH-UBB *Ome Keesje* of the Rijks Luchtvaart School (RLS) in July 1946 and remained active until scrapped in September 1949.

VM928   Ju 52/3m   W Nr 3376
Arrived at EASSU on 16th November 1945. Transferred to No. 8302 ADW at Leck on 3rd May 1946 for transfer to the French Air Force.

VM929   Ju 52/3m   W Nr 3452
Arrived at EASSU on 16th November 1945 and at No. 6 MU on 20th June 1946. Sold as scrap to J. Dale & Co Ltd on 11th March 1948.

VM930   Ju 52/3m   W Nr 3341
Arrived at EASSU on 16th November 1945. On 24th April 1946 flew to Gutersloh and was handed over to No. 2002 Wing. The aircraft delivered to Gutersloh were handed over to the Belgian Government; used for spares (registration OO-SNC not taken up).

VM931   Ju 52/3m   W Nr 501220
Arrived at EASSU on 16th November 1945. On 15th April 1946 VM931 flew to Fassberg and was transferred to No. 8301 ADW for handover to the Czech Government.

VM932   Ju 52/3m   W Nr 3412
Arrived at EASSU on 16th November 1945. On 3rd May 1946, VM932 flew to Leck to be handed over to the French Air Force via No. 8302 ADW.

VM961   Ju 52/3m   W Nr 641007
Ex- T Gr 20. Surrendered at Oslo/Fornebu. Arrived at EASSU on 21st November 1945 and at No. 6 MU on 15th January 1946. Sold as scrap to J. Dale & Co Ltd on 11th March 1948.

VM962   Ju 52/3m   W Nr 641051
Arrived at EASSU from Aalborg in Denmark on 23rd November 1945. Ferried to No. 6 MU on 20th December 1945. Sold as scrap to J. Dale & Co Ltd on 11th March 1948.

VM963   Ju 52/3m   W Nr 052/0097
Arrived at EASSU from Aalborg in Denmark on 23rd November 1945. SoC at Fühlsbuttel on 16th July 1946 and handed over to No. 8401 ADW on the following day, for destruction.

VM964   Ju 52/3m   W Nr 3353
Arrived at EASSU on 21st November 1945 and No. 6 MU on 20th December 1945. Sold as scrap to J. Dale & Co Ltd on 11th March 1948.

VM965   Ju 52/3m   W Nr 501207
Arrived at EASSU on 21st November 1945, possibly from No. 409 Repair & Salvage Unit (which is mentioned on its record card). SoC at EASSU on 16th July 1946 and handed over to No. 8401 ADW on the following day, for destruction.

VM966   Ju 52/3m   W Nr 3422
Arrived at EASSU on 21st November 1945 and No. 6 MU on 5th June 1946. Sold as scrap to J. Dale & Co Ltd on 11th March 1948.

VM967   Ju 52/3m   W Nr 3453
Arrived at EASSU on 21st November 1945 and No. 6 MU on 20th December 1945. Sold as scrap to J. Dale & Co Ltd on 11th March 1948.

VM968   Ju 52/3m   W Nr 500350
Arrived at EASSU on 21st November 1945 and at No. 6 MU on 9th January 1946. Sold to Short Bros on 21st March 1946.

VM969   Ju 52/3m g8e   W Nr 7334
Ex- TGr 20. Surrendered at Kristiansand/Kjevik. Arrived at EASSU by 22nd November 1945 and at No. 6 MU on 20th December 1945. Sold as scrap to J. Dale & Co Ltd on 11th March 1948.

VM970   Ju 52/3m g4e   W Nr 5096
Coded 'RK+AV' of unknown unit. Surrendered at Oslo/Fornebu. Arrived at EASSU by 22nd November 1945 and was delivered from Fühlsbuttel to Short Bros at Sydenham on 10th January 1946. This aircraft was used for a detailed engineering assessment of the type, including the structural testing of components, as part of the acceptance of these Ju 52/3ms by the airworthiness authority in the UK (then the Air Registration Board).

VM971   Ju 52/3m g8e (MS)   W Nr 3401
Code '3K+MK' of Teilkommando 2/Minensuchsgruppe 1, surrendered at Oslo/Fornebu. Arrived at EASSU by 22nd November 1945 and at No. 6 MU on 15th January 1946. Sold to Short Bros on 3rd April 1946.

VM972   Ju 52/3m g4e   W Nr 6780
Ex- TGr 20. Surrendered at Kristiansand/Kjevik. Arrived at EASSU by 22nd November 1945. Left Fühlsbuttel on 7th

December 1945 for No. 6 MU, but was damaged at Brussels en route and returned to EASSU.

It was delivered from Fühlsbuttel to Leck on 13th July 1946 for transfer to the French Armée de l'Air, being the 89th and last airworthy Ju 52 to leave EASSU.

VM973   Ju 52/3m   W Nr 3372
At EASSU by 22nd November 1945. Ferried to Leck on 12th July 1945 for transfer to the French Armée de l'Air via No. 8302 ADW at Leck.

VM974   Ju 52/3m
W Nr reported as 3433 (which is the same as VM922). At EASSU by 22nd November 1945. Transferred to No. 6 MU on 23rd April 1946 and sold as scrap to J. Dale & Co Ltd on 11th March 1948.

VM975   Ju 52/3m   W Nr 3420
At EASSU by 22nd November 1945. SoC at Fühlsbuttel on 16th July 1945 and handed over to No. 8401 ADW on the following day, for destruction.

VM976   Ju 52/3m   W Nr 3424
Arrived at EASSU about 22nd November 1945. SoC at Fühlsbuttel on 16th July 1946 and handed over to No. 8401 ADW, for destruction.

VM977   Ju 52/3m   W Nr 3309
Arrived at EASSU about 22nd November 1945 and despatched to No. 6 MU on 9th May 1946. Sold as scrap to J. Dale & Co Ltd on 11th March 1948.

VM978   Ju 52/3m   W Nr 500136
Arrived at EASSU on 22nd November 1945. Despatched to Leck on 10th July 1946 for transfer to the French Armée de l'Air via No. 8302 ADW.

VM979   Ju 52/3m g3e   W Nr 3317
Arrived at EASSU on 27th November 1945 from Schleswig. Sold to Shorts on 28th February 1946 and flown from Fühlsbuttel to Sydenham on the same day. Converted to BEA 'Jupiter'-class under Shorts & Harland works number SH17C and became G-AHOG.

Registered on 21st May 1946 to the UK Ministry of Civil Aviation and transferred to BEA on 22nd October prior to issue of its C of A on 5th November 1946. After withdrawal from service G-AHOG was flown from Renfrew to Manchester/Ringway on 4th September 1947 prior to its C of A expiry in November 1947. G-AHOG was sold to the British Aluminium Co Ltd and scrapped at its Latchford, Warrington, works in February 1948. Its registration was cancelled on 2nd February 1948.

VM980   Ju 52/3m   W Nr 5984
This aircraft had been SX-ACF of Hellenic Airways until it was taken over by the Luftwaffe following the invasion of Greece in April 1941.

Ferried from Schleswig to Fühlsbuttel for EASSU on 27th November 1945. Left Fühlsbuttel en route for No. 6 MU on 17th February 1946. Sold to Short Bros on 7th March 1946.

VM981   Ju 52/3m   W Nr 5024
Ferried from Schleswig to Fühlsbuttel on 27th November 1945 for EASSU. Delivered to No. 6 MU, via Gütersloh, on 3rd May 1946. Sold as scrap to J. Dale & Co Ltd on 11th March 1948.

VM982   Ju 52/3m   W Nr 6466
Ferried from Schleswig to Fühlsbuttel for EASSU on 27th November 1945. Left EASSU for No. 6 MU on 20th December 1945 but suffered engine trouble en route at Brussels and did not finally arrive at Brize Norton until 21st May 1946, having in the meantime been on the books of the EASSU, No. 151 Repair Unit and No. 49 MU. Sold as scrap to J. Dale & Co Ltd on 11th March 1948.

VM983   Ju 52/3m   W Nr 3429
Arrived at EASSU on 6th December 1945. Flown to Leck on 4th July 1946 for transfer to the French Armée de l'Air via No. 8302 ADW.

VM984   Ju 52/3m   W Nr 3460
Arrived at EASSU on 6th December 1945. SoC at Fühlsbuttel on 16th July 1946 and handed over to No. 8401 ADW, for destruction.

VM985   Ju 52/3m   W Nr 5715
Arrived at EASSU on 7th December 1945. Flown to Ahlhorn on 2nd April 1946 for transfer to the Netherlands government, via No. 131 (P) Squadron. Became PH-UBA *Opa* of the Rijks Luchtvaart School (RLS) in June 1946 and remained in service until 1950, when it was briefly transferred to Avio-Diepen NV for use as a static exhibit and then scrapped in January 1951.

VM986   Ju 52/3m   W Nr 3413
Arrived at EASSU on 11th December 1945. Ferried to No. 6 MU on 5th June 1946. Sold as scrap to J. Dale & Co Ltd on 11th March 1948.

VM987   Ju 52/3m   W Nr 3380
Arrived at EASSU on 14th December 1945. SoC at Fühlsbuttel on 16th July 1946 and handed over to No. 8401 ADW, for destruction.

VN124   This serial number has been reported as allotted late in October 1945 to a Ju 52/3m surrendered in Germany. See entry in Chapter Ten for the Siebel Si 204 with this RAF serial number.

VN176   Ju 52/3m   W Nr *unknown*
This serial number was allotted on 13th November 1945 for use on a Bücker Bestmann. When the Bestmann allocations were cancelled, this number was reallotted to a Ju 52/3m. The aircraft was surrendered at Travemünde/Priwall. It was flown from there to Fühlsbuttel on 9th May 1946, for the EASSU. Ferried to No. 6 MU on 15th May 1946. Believed sold as scrap to J. Dale & Co Ltd on 11th March 1948.

VN177   This serial number has been reported as a Ju 52/3m but no record has been traced. This serial was originally allocated for a Bücker Bü 181 Bestmann but later cancelled. The serial number was possibly reused, as in the case of VN176 above.

VN709 - VN731 and VN740 - VN756:   further serial allocations made on 30th November 1945 for local assignment to individual aircraft at EASSU.

VN709   Ju 52/3m   W Nr *unknown*
Probably arrived at EASSU on 14th December 1945. Despatched to No. 6 MU on 4th May 1946. Sold as scrap to J. Dale & Co Ltd on 11th March 1948.

VN710   Ju 52/3m   W Nr *unknown*
Probably arrived at EASSU on 14th December 1945. Despatched to Leck on 8th July 1946 for transfer to the French Armée de l'Air, via No. 8302 ADW.

Chapter Nine

Gliders and Sailplanes in the United Kingdom

This Chapter covers:
- pre-war sailplanes of German origin which were impressed for British military service.
- sailplanes recovered in Denmark and Germany in 1945 which were brought to the UK for service with the Air Training Corps (ATC), the RAE, the Royal Air Force, the Royal Navy, or the British Gliding Association.
- post-war British production of German-designed sailplanes.

Sailplanes taken over in Germany and used by British service gliding clubs in Germany itself are briefly covered in Chapter Ten.

9.1 PRE-WAR SAILPLANES IMPRESSED INTO MILITARY SERVICE

Prior to the Second World War, a large number of German-designed sailplanes were imported to the UK, while a substantial number of others of German design had been licence-built by individuals or firms in the UK. After the outbreak of war many sailplanes were impressed for war service, initially as 'targets' for radar development, and later as trainers for the Airborne Forces and the Air Training Corps. It should be noted that, prior to the aircraft census of 19th March 1947, there appears to have been no central record of Air Training Corps gliders kept by the Air Ministry, so that it is almost impossible to trace the history of gliders prior to that time.

BGA 320   Dittmar Condor II   **W Nr** *unknown*

Owned by G. D. Smith & A. L. Slater. The sole example of its type in the UK in 1939, the Condor was impressed in January 1941, arriving at Ringway on 6th January for use by the Development Unit of the Central Landing Establishment, which was a training and development centre for the Airborne Forces. Its fate is not known, although it may have been the example flown post-war as VW918, which was first recorded on 19th March 1947 when it was at No. 185 ATC Gliding School at Manchester/Barton. It was despatched to Slingsby Sailplanes on 5th February 1948 for 'Repair in Works' and was SoC on 8th April 1948 as Category E1.

BGA 338   Göppingen Gö III Minimoa   W Nr 158

Owned by P. A. Wills. This was at first used by the Special Duties Flight at Christchurch as a radar target in June 1940. It is then believed to have been the Minimoa taken from Dunstable to Ringway on 10th October 1940 for use by the Development Unit of the Central Landing Establishment. In August 1941, it was delivered to No. 1 Glider Training School when this unit split off from the CLE and moved to Thame. This sailplane was later allocated to No. 159 Squadron, Air Training Corps, at Weston-super-Mare County Grammar School on 3rd February 1943 with the ground instructional serial number 3544M.

On 26th October 1943, the RAF serial number RN224 was allotted on its transfer from the Controller of Research & Development

to the Air Training Corps. It is possible that it served at a test establishment (A&AEE ?) prior to use by the ATC. The serial number was later cancelled. In 1944, Philip Wills' Minimoa was sold to F/Lt J. S. Sproule by the Ministry of Aircraft Production, after being damaged in an accident. John Sproule repaired the sailplane, which was flown post-war as BGA338 by Lawrence Wright. Later registered as G-ALLZ and then sold to Iceland as TF-SOM.

HM536   Kassel Zögling

At least one of the German-built Zöglings in the UK in 1939 was impressed – on 31st March 1942. This was the type on which the British-built 'Dagling' was based.

HM538   Kassel Prüfling

Again, at least one example of the German-built Prüflings in the UK in 1939 was impressed on 31st March 1942. It was SoC on 1st September 1942.

HM586   Kassel Sailplane

One example of an unknown Kassel type was impressed on 31st March 1942.

Schleicher Rhonbussard

At the outbreak of war there were four Schleicher Rhonbussards in the UK. These were: BGA 145 W Nr 99 owned by the Robinson syndicate at Great Hucklow; BGA 335 W Nr 486 owned by the London Gliding Club at Dunstable; BGA 337 W Nr 620 owned by Cooper & Baker, and BGA 395 W Nr 485 owned by R. Pasold. All of these were flown again post-war.

BGA 145   Schleicher Rhonbussard   W Nr 99

Owned by the Robinson syndicate at Great Hucklow. This sailplane was impressed on 9th August 1940 for use by the CLE at Ringway. Late in 1941, it was taken to No. 37 MU Burtonwood for storage and its subsequent fate is not recorded.

TK710   Schleicher Rhonbussard   W Nr *unknown*

Early history not known. This example was allotted from the Air Training Corps to RAE Farnborough on 7th July 1944. It made its first recorded flight at Farnborough on 19th August 1944. It was used to give test pilots sailplane experience, until replaced in 1945 by ex-Luftwaffe sailplanes. Its last recorded flight at RAE was on 6th August 1945.

VD216   Schleicher Rhonbussard   W Nr *unknown*

Early history not known. This example was on charge with No. 44 Elementary Gliding School, Desford, on 7th October 1946. By the census of 19th March 1947, it was with the Empire Central Flying School at Hullavington. On 23rd July 1948 it passed to Slingsby Sailplanes for repair before despatch to No. 146 GS, Hornchurch, on 30th September 1948. On 1st July 1949 it was transferred to the Central Gliding Instructors School at Detling. VD216 suffered a flying accident on 23rd July 1950 and was re-categorised as Category 5 (scrap) on 7th September 1950. Although it is remotely possible that this sailplane was acquired in Germany in 1945 it is far more probable that it was one of the impressed civilian examples. Since BGA 337 and BGA 395 had been restored to the BGA Register during the known history of VD216, it follows that it must have been ex-BGA 145 or BGA 335.

Schneider Grunau Baby
Many of these had been built in the UK by individuals and by glider manufacturers such as Slingsby Sailplanes. No German-built examples are, in fact, known to have been imported to the UK pre-war.

Weltensegler Hols-der-Teufel
Three German-built examples were in England in 1939, together with three examples built by Slingsby under licence. From this total, two were impressed on 31st March 1942, as HM572 and HM577.

9.2 GLIDERS AND SAILPLANES ACQUIRED BY THE UK POST-WAR

Both the Air Training Corps, and the Ministry of Civil Aviation (the latter on behalf of the British Gliding Association (BGA)), put in claims for, respectively, 212 and 100 sailplanes for their use. These claims were made rather late in the day, when all the 291 gliders found in areas under British control in Germany and Denmark had been allocated as Category One or had been taken into use by gliding clubs started by the British forces in Germany for recreational purposes. The Air Training Corps' needs were advised to the US authorities, who were able to find a number of Grunau Babys in the US Zone of Germany. These sailplanes were brought to England and refurbished by Slingsby Sailplanes for ATC use. The original ATC claim comprised 200 Grunau Babys, 6 Olympia-Meise and 6 Kranich two-seaters.

Note: The BGA is the representative organisation for all civilian glider clubs in the UK. It was formed in 1930 and has since then been the organisation with delegated authority to set airworthiness standards for gliders and sailplanes in the UK. Certificated sailplanes therefore have Certificates of Airworthiness issued by the BGA.

The RAE selected sixteen 'Category One' sailplanes for evaluation. However the Horten Ho IV, which was not on the Category One list, was flown more extensively than any of these. Most of the selected examples were of standard types, which were generally used to provide sailplane experience to RAE test pilots, rather than for the study of particular technical features. A further six sailplanes were placed in 'Category One' at the instigation of Lt/Cdr J.S.Sproule and were used to form the basis of the Royal Naval Gliding and Soaring Association. The Farnborough and Royal Navy sailplanes are shown in statistical records, produced in 1947, as being:

	RAE	RN		RAE	RN
Grunau	6	3	SG 38	2	–
Hannover	1	–	Minimoa	–	1
Olympia	2	1	Mu 13	1	–
DFS 108-43	1	–	Reiher	1	–
Kranich	2	1	Totals	16	6

The majority of the sailplanes for RAE came from the Luftwaffe airfield at Vaerløse in Denmark, where they were selected by G/C Alan F. Hards on 9th June 1945. These included an Olympia, two Kranichs, two SG38s and six Grunau Babys. They were flown in German markings for several months until Air Ministry numbers were allotted in 1946. Since some Grunaus sent to Canada seem to have come from the same source as aircraft at RAE, some further Grunaus may have been collected from elsewhere. (See Chapter Twenty-One)

The 'Hannover' shown under RAE is almost certainly the prototype Akaflieg Hannover AFH-10 D-9-826. The 'DFS 108-43' is a mystery; undoubtedly there would have been a sailplane with this designation but it cannot be traced to any known type. It is possible that the recorded 108-43 may be a clerical error for the DFS 108-49 Grunau Baby, or (more probably in the author's view), the DFS 108-53 Habicht. The Habicht was a small aerobatic sailplane which was used in some of its versions for training Me 163 pilots; there have been unconfirmed reports of a Habicht at RAE in 1945, which would be consistent with this theory. No Minimoas are actually known to have been brought to the UK in 1945, but possibly there was an as-yet-untraced example. The Mü 13 was in fact an RN rather than RAE, aircraft. Missing entirely from the above is the Horten Ho IV which definitely did arrive at RAE. So far as is known, this type was not the DFS 108-43 – it had a powered aircraft Reich Luft Ministerium designation (8-251) and being a Horten design should not have also had a DFS type number.

Note: All RLM equipment designations had a classification number as a prefix – '8' indicated powered aircraft, '108' indicated sailplane – thus a Messerschmitt Bf 109 would in fact be an '8-109'. Many aircraft and glider dataplates quoted these prefices.

In addition to the Horten Ho IV, a DFS 108-68 Weihe was at RAE in 1946, and a Schleicher Rhonbussard was present in 1945. The Rhonbussard had the serial TK710 allocated on 7th July 1944, and was probably one of the four of the type imported into the UK before September 1939. For details of the Weihe, see under 'Aircraft recovered by P. A. Wills' below.

The BGA had become aware of the numerous gliding clubs started by military personnel serving in Germany and had approached the Ministry of Civil Aviation for assistance in obtaining surplus gliders from German sources. Its bid arrived too late to produce any result since all the gliders had been taken into use by the Service gliding clubs. Eventually, it was agreed that the BGA could take over, on loan, seven sailplanes held at RAE Farnborough, on condition that they were used 'for research purposes'. During May 1946, six sailplanes were taken by road to Marshalls of Cambridge Ltd at Cambridge Airport for survey and return to flying condition. (The promised seventh example, a Kranich, did not materialise). The aircraft were repaired and overhauled and were handed over to some of the major gliding clubs which were corporate members of the BGA.

The sailplanes comprised two Grunau Babys, two Olympias, one Weihe and one Kranich. The Kranich, for which some new parts had to be made, was assigned to the Cambridge Gliding Club, the Weihe to Surrey GC, the Grunaus to the Bristol GC and the Derby & Lancs GC, and one Olympia to the Newcastle GC. The second Olympia, originally allocated to the Derby & Lancs GC, is believed to have been found to be beyond repair. The detailed history of these aircraft is given in the following section detailing aircraft brought to England by the RAE or by Philip Wills who recovered examples of some other sailplanes which are discussed separately.

9.3   AIR TRAINING CORPS AIRCRAFT

The Air Training Corps is a youth organisation, originally formed in 1938 by the Air League of the British Empire as the Air Defence Cadet Corps. In 1941 it was reorganised as the Air Training Corps and came under the sponsorship of the Air Ministry. It is still in existence today under Ministry of Defence sponsorship. Its aims are to promote interest in aviation among boys, and more recently girls of from 14 to 18 years of age, by involvement in various activities, including visits to RAF installations and training in piloting gliders at a number of Gliding Schools run by members of the RAF Volunteer Reserve.

As noted above the Air Training Corps had requested an allocation of ex-German gliders which was obtained largely from sources in the US Zone of Occupation in Germany. F/Lt C. A. Narbeth of the Directorate-General, Air Training Corps, visited the Wasserkuppe gliding site and the nearby Alexander Schleicher works at Poppenhausen on 15th June 1945 to select suitable gliders. Five complete Grunau Baby IIB gliders and sixteen fuselages were found at Poppenhausen and one Kranich II, a further Grunau Baby, and a supply of Grunau Baby wings at the Wasserkuppe. The gliders were shipped to Slingsby Sailplanes for reconditioning. It is presumed that the SG 38s were found at the same locations. A Meise selected for the ATC at the Wasserkuppe may have gone to the RAE instead.

VT886 to VT898 inclusive (13 aircraft). These serial numbers were shown as allocated to 'Reconditioned SG 38 gliders'. The serial numbers were allotted on 25th January 1947 and cancelled on 16th July 1947, before the reconditioning of any examples could be completed. Any further information on these aircraft would be received with interest. These aircraft were in a damaged condition when received at Slingsby Sailplanes Kirkbymoorside works. The ATC requirement was cancelled and one glider, W Nr 061404, was rebuilt as BGA 613. It is believed that the remaining SG 38s were burned.

BGA 613   DFS 108-14 Schulgleiter 38   W Nr 061404
Refurbished by Slingsby Sailplanes as BGA 613 and sold to the Derby & Lancs GC in August 1948. Registered as G-ALKR in 1949. Final fate unconfirmed, but is believed to have been damaged beyond repair in an accident.

VT916 to VT928 inclusive (13 aircraft). These serial numbers were allocated to 'Reconditioned Grunau Baby gliders' on 25th January 1947. Of these, the first ten were rebuilt by Slingsby Sailplanes Ltd at Kirkbymoorside and are detailed below. The remaining serial numbers were cancelled on 16th July 1947. It is interesting to note that Aircraft Movement Cards exist for three Grunaus for which complete or partial German Werk Nummern are given – possibly these may have been intended as the remainder of the batch. However, there is no direct evidence of this. All aircraft in this batch are DFS 108-49 Grunau Baby IIBs. Only the W Nr of one aircraft is known. (See VT921)

VT916   DFS 108-49 Grunau Baby IIB   W Nr *unknown*
First recorded on 7th October 1947 at No. 127 Gliding School, Panshanger. On 14th May 1948 to No. 106 GS, Henlow. To No. 168 GS, Detling, on 11th March 1949, and then to No. 143 GS, Kenley, on 8th August 1949. On 1st April 1954, this aircraft was SoC as Category 5 (components), indicating that it may have been repairable by another owner.

VT917   DFS 108-49 Grunau Baby IIB   W Nr *unknown*
First recorded on 7th October 1947 at No. 94 GS, Yate, moving to No. 95 GS, St Eval, on 31st December 1947. To No. 89 GS, Christchurch, on 11th March 1949. Still with this unit when it suffered a flying accident on 16th March 1950 and was categorised as scrap.

VT918   DFS 108-49 Grunau Baby IIB   W Nr *unknown*
First recorded on 9th October 1947 at No. 6 GS, Turnhouse. To Slingsby Sailplanes for repair on 18th March 1949 and reallotted to No. 2 GS, Grangemouth, on 22nd July 1949. Returned to Slingsby Sailplanes on 20th October 1949 for repair after an accident and re-categorised as scrap on 24th November 1949.

VT919   DFS 108-49 Grunau Baby IIB   W Nr *unknown*
First recorded on 23rd September 1947 at No. 186 GS, Hooton Park. This GS moved to Woodvale in December 1947 taking VT919 with it. On 30th April 1948, VT919 was transferred to No. 192 GS, Sealand, reverting to No. 186 GS at Woodvale on 12th March 1949. VT919 was SoC as 'Category 5 (components)' on 7th February 1952.

VT920   DFS 108-49 Grunau Baby IIB   W Nr *unknown*
First recorded on 23rd September 1947 at No. 130 GS, Abingdon, moving to No. 163 GS at Gosport on 3rd December 1947. It was allotted to Slingsby Sailplanes on 16th December 1947, on CS(A) charge, for flight trials in connection with the structural testing of the type and it arrived at Slingsby Sailplanes on 16th January 1948 for these tests, which were carried out in conjunction with those on VT762 (see RAE Grunau Baby list). On the completion of the trials, VT920 was despatched by road to the Reserve Command Communications Squadron at White Waltham, on 21st June 1948. Returned to Slingsby on 10th June 1949 for a Category B repair, after which it was transferred to the Central Gliding Instructor School at Detling, on 10th August 1949. Remained with this unit until SoC as Category 5 (scrap), on 16th August 1954.

This photograph of Grunau Baby VT920 was taken at the Central Gliding Instructor School at RAF Detling in June 1950. *Peter Green collection*

VT921   DFS 108-49 Grunau Baby IIB   W Nr 030795
This Flugzeubau Petera-built example was first recorded on 23rd September 1947 at No. 167 GS, Fairoaks, and transferred to No. 104 GS at Ipswich or Martlesham Heath on 3rd December 1947. On 6th May 1949 transferred to No. 102 GS at Horsham St Faith (Norwich) and then on 28th February 1951 returned to No. 104 GS, Martlesham Heath. SoC as Category 5 (scrap) on 26th January 1957. The 'scrap' parts were sold to the Royal Air Force Gliding & Soaring Association and rebuilt as RAFGSA 226. After some years, the Grunau was disposed of to the Midlands Aircraft Preservation Society. The Society passed the Grunau to an Air Training Corps unit in Shrewsbury, to be rebuilt on its behalf, after which the Grunau disappeared.

It is not known whether the glider was scrapped, or if it was acquired by a sailplane enthusiast to be returned to flying condition under a new identity.

VT922   DFS 108-49 Grunau Baby IIB   W Nr *unknown*
First recorded on 13th November 1947 with No. 143 GS, Kenley. On 11th December 1948, VT922 was allocated to Slingsby Sailplanes for Category B repair, but returned to No. 143 GS on 15th February 1949. VT922 was reallotted to No. 106 GS, Henlow, on 8th August 1949, No. 104 GS at Martlesham Heath on 25th June 1950, and No. 102 GS, Horsham St Faith, on 25th February 1951. On 11th May 1952 it was SoC as Category 5 (components) after a flying accident.

VT923   DFS 108-49 Grunau Baby IIB   W Nr *unknown*
First recorded on 19th November 1947 with No. 162 GS, Biggin Hill. On 4th October 1948, VT923 was allotted to Slingsby Sailplanes for repair, being re-allocated to No. 105 GS, Cambridge, on 22nd November 1948 after repairs were complete. On 1st June 1953, VT923 was recorded as being Category 4R (indicating it was awaiting major repair after an accident) but was re-assessed as Category 5 (scrap) on 26th June 1953 and SoC.

VT924   DFS 108-49 Grunau Baby IIB   W Nr *unknown*
First recorded on 19th November 1947 at No. 1 GS, Dungarrel. On 24th August 1949, VT924 was at Slingsbys as Category B, being re-assessed as Category E on the same date. (Category E was the original designation for what is now Category 5 - i.e., a 'write-off').

VT925   DFS 108-49 Grunau Baby IIB   W Nr *unknown*
First recorded on 4th December 1947 at No. 42 GS, Bramcote. On 24th February 1949, VT925 was allotted to Slingsby Sailplanes for repair. After repairs were complete, it was transferred to No. 146 GS at Hornchurch.

On 20th June 1950, VT925 suffered a Category 4R flying accident. There is no further record of VT925, until it was SoC at No. 614 GS, Hornchurch, on 4th February 1956. (No. 614 GS was the same unit as No. 146 GS, renumbered in 1955).

VT926 to VT928 inclusive. These numbers were allocated to Grunau Babys but cancelled on 16th July 1947.

VW908   DFS 108-49 Grunau Baby II   W Nr *unknown*
This may have come from a German source. First recorded on 19th March 1947 at No. 161 GS, Ford. On 25th March 1948, VW908 was transferred to Airwork General Trading Ltd for major repair, but then went to Slingsbys on 21st April where the repair work was actually done. Returned to No. 161 GS at Tangmere, on 7th July 1948. VW908 was categorised as scrap on 14th June 1950 and burned on site on 18th July.

—   DFS 108-49 Grunau Baby II   W Nr *unknown*
First recorded on the same date as the above aircraft, 19th March 1947, at No. 50 GS, Pershore. It was SoC at Slingsby Sailplanes on 12th September 1947.

Another sailplane of German origin was the DFS 108-30 Kranich II VD224. The gliders in the 'VD' serial block were generally for Air Training Corps use and the batch of serial numbers was allotted to the ATC HQ at White Waltham for allocation to individual aircraft. Many of these had previously received other serial numbers and it is often difficult to trace the histories of particular aircraft because the detailed records have not been found. All the other known gliders with VD serial numbers were of British design or were German gliders known to have been imported into the UK before 1939. The Kranich, in fact, received the last allocated serial number of the sixty to be allotted and was recovered from the Wasserkuppe gliding site in the US Zone of Germany at the same time as the ATC Grunau Babys.

VD224   DFS 108-30 Kranich II   W Nr *unknown*
Code unknown. First recorded on 4th December 1948 at Slingsby Sailplanes where it received Category B repairs. On 14th December 1948 to Station Flight, Halton. To RAF College, Cranwell on an unspecified date after 30th September 1952. SoC as Category 5 (components) at No. 54 MU, Hucknall, on 28th May 1956, probably after an accident, since No. 54 MU was responsible for the salvage of damaged aircraft.

9.4   **ROYAL AIRCRAFT ESTABLISHMENT AIRCRAFT**

VP587   DFS 108-49 Grunau Baby IIB   W Nr *unknown*
Coded 'LH+FT', arrived at RAE in July 1945. Became VP587 on 26th April 1946. On the strength of RAE for training test pilots in glider handling. VP587 was delivered to the RNGSA Portsmouth Naval Gliding Club on 15th June 1954 and was formally sold to that organisation during the following month. Its subsequent fate has not been traced.

VT762   DFS 108-49 Grunau Baby IIB   W Nr *unknown*
Coded 'LN+SS', also ex D-IX-46. Arrived at RAE in July 1945. Was flown at RAE in German markings in 1945/6. This aircraft was later with the AFEE at Beaulieu, where it was allocated the serial VT762 on 12th November 1946. VT762 arrived at Slingsby Sailplanes on 2nd February 1947 by road from Beaulieu, for structural analysis work to be carried out in connection with the certification of other Grunau Babys built by RNAS Fleetlands for the RNGSA. After refurbishment by Slingsby Sailplanes, commencing on 1st April 1948, VT762 was declared surplus to CS(A) requirements on 10th June 1948 and was allocated for use by the Air Training Corps. VT762 was allocated to the No. 26 ATC Gliding School detachment at Sutton Bank, on 16th June 1948. On 30th June 1949 VT762 was transferred to No. 26 Gliding School's main base at Rufforth, and was damaged in an accident on 22nd August 1952, later being categorised as Cat 5 (c) and SoC.

The Grunau Baby VN148 'LN+ST' at Farnborough early in 1946.
Joe McCarthy collection

9.8 BRITISH PRODUCTION OF GERMAN SAILPLANES

In 1945 Chilton Aircraft Ltd of Hungerford built an example of the DFS 108-70 Olympia-Meise. This was built to the order of the well-known British glider pilot, Dudley Hiscox. Chilton built the fuselage but sub-contracted the manufacture of the wings to Elliotts of Newbury Ltd. Elliotts was a long-established furniture manufacturer in the neighbouring town to Chilton's works, and had been a major production facility for the Airspeed Horsa troop-carrying glider during the Second World War. It was this connection which encouraged the managing director of Elliotts, Horace Buckingham, to continue the company's involvement with gliders after the war.

Under the conditions prevailing in 1945, Elliotts was unable to resume its traditional furniture manufacture because of government controls and turned instead to the production of sailplanes. After the death of Mr A. Dalrymple of Chilton Aircraft in the crash of a Fieseler Storch on Christmas Day 1945, Elliotts purchased the Olympia fuselage jigs from Chilton and went into large-scale production of the type. The Elliotts version differed in some small details from the DFS original, in particular being strengthened to meet British Civil Airworthiness Requirements.

The first Elliott-built Olympia, BGA 501, made its first flight at White Waltham on 17th January 1947. A batch of 100 was built initially although only the first fifty or so had been sold by May 1948. The remainder were stored in the works and were sold gradually in the years up to 1956. When the stock had been sold a further fifty were built and sold between 1958 and 1963.

Although many of the original one hundred aircraft were sold in the home market, numerous others were exported to countries such as Argentina, Belgium, Denmark, Egypt, India and Pakistan. Second-hand examples eventually reached Australia, Canada, New Zealand, South Africa and the USA.

Following the initial venture with the Olympia, Elliotts took on the development of British versions of the DFS 108-14 Schulgleiter (SG) 38 and DFS 108-49 Grunau Baby IIB as the EoN Primary and EoN Baby, respectively.

As with the Olympia, a batch of 100 EoN Primaries was manufactured, although only sixty-three were sold. The first Primary made its maiden flight in February 1948. By the time the Primary appeared on the market, training policies were tending to favour dual-control training rather than solo work on primary types, and only twenty or so examples were sold to civilian customers in the UK, with another ten going to the RAF for Air Cadet use in 1951. Twenty-four were exported to Pakistan, five to India and two to Ceylon. Some of the unassembled airframes were transferred to Slingsby Sailplanes Ltd, when Elliotts sold its glider interests to Slingsby in 1966, following the death of Horace Buckingham. At least four of the Primaries perished in the major fire which destroyed Slingsby's factory in November 1968.

The EoN Baby was built in smaller numbers than the other types. The first example received its Certificate of Airworthiness on 7th October 1948, although it probably made its first flight in April or May of that year. Most examples were exported, at least thirteen going to India, nineteen to Pakistan, and others to Norway, Malaya, New Zealand and Portugal. A total of forty-seven was completed, the fuselage of the forty-eighth example being later used to repair an earlier example after an accident.

Below: **The Surrey & Hants Gliding Club DFS Weihe BGA 448 photographed at Lasham on 17th June 1962.** *P. H. Butler collection*

Bottom: **Philip Wills' DFS Weihe G-ALKG/BGA 433, photographed at Camphill in Derbyshire during a competition in July 1951.** *Peter Green collection*

Chapter Ten

Aircraft used by the British Air Forces
of Occupation in Germany

These aircraft were almost all communications types, predominantly the Bücker Bestmann, Fieseler Storch, Messerschmitt 108 and Siebel 204. They were pressed into service in large numbers from May 1945 onwards, but were all officially grounded in April 1946. By then it was realised that the effort expended on their maintenance was unduly high due to lack of spares and other difficulties. It was pointed out that Maintenance Units in the UK held large stocks of suitable communications aircraft for which spares were readily available. Only a very few aircraft used by senior officers survived this edict, although many of the aircraft were handed over to the French Armée de l'Air, which had access to production lines - and therefore spare parts - of the identical aircraft, built in France while it was occupied by the Germans and production of which had continued to meet French post-war requirements.

The British Air Forces of Occupation comprised the former RAF 2nd Tactical Air Force, or at least those elements of the 2nd TAF which were not immediately disbanded with the end of the war. The 2nd TAF comprised four RAF Groups, No. 2 and Nos 83, 84 and 85. No. 2 Group had originally been formed in RAF Bomber Command to be the controlling organisation for light bombers within that Command. Nos 83 and 84 Groups were 'composite' organisations of fighter, fighter-bomber, reconnaissance and air observation Squadrons. No. 85 Group, which was disbanded soon after VE-Day, comprised day and night-fighter units for air defence duties. Each of the Groups had a number of Wings of three or four operational Squadrons. In addition, each Group had its own Communications squadron equipped with single- and twin-engined liaison and transport aircraft for logistic support. The composition of the Groups is tabulated below:

No. 2 Group: Nos 137, 138, 139 and 140 Wings
No. 83 Group: Nos 39, 121, 122, 124, 125, 126, 127, 129, 143 & 144 Wings
No. 84 Group: Nos 35, 123, 131, 132, 133, 134, 135, 136, 145 & 146 Wings

Within the above, Nos 35 and 39 Wings held the Reconnaissance role. All the Wings listed were of RAF Squadrons, except Nos 39, 126, 127, 143 and 144, which comprised Royal Canadian Air Force units.

The operational Squadrons, which were highly mobile to enable them to keep pace with the Army, had an effective maintenance back-up organisation. Unlike fixed-base Squadrons, the units of a Tactical Air Force did not have their own maintenance staff. First-line maintenance was performed by servicing echelons attached to the parent Wing, rather than to the Squadron. Second-line maintenance and repair was carried out by Repair Units, or Repair and Salvage Units. In the text below, the main Repair Unit to be mentioned is No. 151 RU, based at Lüneburg. This unit, post-war, assumed the responsibility for collecting, maintaining and storing the ex-German light aircraft types which were originally intended to be used by the BAFO organisation for liaison and communications duties.

The Bestmanns and other aircraft allotted to Group Communications Squadrons were in many cases dispersed to individual

units within the Group, i.e. individual aircraft would be delivered to Squadrons or other sub-units which came under the command of the Group. These might be operational squadrons such as those listed above, or Repair Units, or Air Disarmament Wings operating under the control of the Group. There were also many cases where aircraft were moved from unit to unit without proper records being passed back to the Air Ministry in England. For example, the Bestmann VM215 of No. 83 Group Communications Squadron is known to have served with No. 8401 Air Disarmament Wing as one of its liaison aircraft, and the Bestmanns VM162 and VM181 allotted to No. 2 Group Communications Squadron are known to have been delivered to No. 8303 Air Disarmament Wing at Bad Godesburg for its use. No. 8303 and No. 8401 Air Disarmament Wings were, by definition, units of No. 83 and 84 Groups, respectively.

The Communications Squadrons attached to the 2nd TAF/ BAFO Headquarters and the constituent 2nd TAF Groups were the major users of German aircraft such as the Bf 108, Bü 181 and Fi 156. The unit for which the best documented records survive is No. 83 Group Communications Squadron (GCS), some extracts from which are quoted below. The Squadron comprised a Flight of Avro Ansons, together with a few Percival Proctors, which were used for longer-range flights – the Ansons, for example, made daily flights to the UK. A second Flight, equipped with Taylorcraft Austers, made purely local flights within the No. 83 Group geographical area, in the main distributing mail to the local RAF and British Army units. No. 83 GCS arrived at its first post-war base, B156 Lüneburg, on 6th May 1945. Its first German aircraft was a Junkers Ju 52/3m, which was collected from Flensburg on 15th May by the Squadron CO, S/Ldr C. F. Babbage DFM. A further Ju 52 was collected from Schleswig on the following day. The Ju 52s were used for a number of flights within Germany during May, but are scarcely mentioned after the Squadron moved to B164 Schleswig on 10th June. It is probable that the '52s found their way to the EASSU at Fühlsbuttel to be serviced and passed on to other users. On 21st August, No. 83 GCS commenced the task of ferrying Fi 156 Storch aircraft to a 'pool' at Schleswig, and three days later collection of Bücker Bü 181s commenced. It seems that the Fi 156s were to be used by the various Communications units and the Bü 181s were to be dispersed to the Air Disarmament Wings, also for use as communications aircraft. Those aircraft not immediately required were to be ferried to No. 151 Repair Unit at Lüneburg, where servicing would be carried out and reserve aircraft held. By 7th September Messerschmitt Bf 108s had been added to the ferrying task. By October an Enemy Aircraft Flight had been added to the Squadron. This was equipped with Bf 108, Fi 156 and Bü 181 aircraft and carried out many of the short-range tasks within the Group area. These aircraft were still in use in April 1946 when the record ceases, but were almost certainly retired at the end of that month in line with the general policy, to stop using German aircraft, which came into force at that time. The records make occasional mention of flights being made by Ju 52/3m or

Siebel Si 204 aircraft, but it seems that these were being flown on an *ad hoc* basis, while being ferried from one place to another. The unit did fly the two Bücker Bü 181s, Air Min 121 and 122, from Germany to England, as described in Chapter Seven. No. 84 GCS, based at B118 Celle, makes mention in its Operational Record Book of two Fi 156 and seven Bü 181 being allotted to the unit during September and October 1945, but there is no mention of them making any flights. The Fi 156s were certainly used for towing sailplanes of the 84 Group Gliding Club at Salzgitter. In the period from December 1945 to March 1946 there is frequent reference to the Savoia Marchetti SM 82 (VN163) being used.

A summary of the aircraft allotted to Communications Squadrons of the 2nd TAF is given below:

BAFO Communications Squadron (later Wing)
Bf 108   VM495, VM502, VM508
Bü 181   VM771
DC-2   VP102
Fi 156   VH751 to VH753, VM472, VN266
Si 204   VM466, VN136

No. 2 Group Communications Squadron
Bf 108   VH762
Bü 181   VM143/148/151/157/162/169/174/181/188/193, VM769/777/780/
         789/794, VN169 to VN171, VN175, GA201/202/203
Fi 156   VN267

No. 83 Group Communications Squadron, Lüneberg
Bf 108   VM856, VM859
Bü 181   VM199/206/215/220/227/231/238/243, VM770, VM783 to VM787,
         VM790 to VM793, VM795 to VM797, VN172, VN783 to VN787,
         GA831 to GA838
Fi 156   VM291 to VM296, VM824 to VM829, VM832 to VM835

No. 84 Group Communications Squadron, Celle
Bü 181   VM252/259/263/269/274/278, VM776/779/781/879, VN173/174
Fi 156   VM831/873/874/897
SM 82   VN158, VN163

As described in Chapter Eight, an entirely new unit, the Enemy Aircraft Servicing and Storage Unit (EASSU), was set up at Hamburg/Fühlsbuttel to service Ju 52/3m aircraft which were to be sent to the UK for possible civilian use. The Unit also serviced Siebel Si 204s. After work on the Ju 52/3ms was completed, the Si 204 task was handed over to No. 151 Repair Unit, Lüneburg.

The immediate Air Disarmament task was carried out by specially formed Air Disarmament Wings (ADW), operating under each of the 2nd TAF Groups. Each Wing covered part of the geographical area of its parent Group. The Wings in turn each had a number of Squadrons whose duty was to look after disarmament tasks at a main airfield together with its satellite and subsidiary installations. Each identified 'target' was visited by a reconnaissance team and its existence confirmed or otherwise. (The 'targets' had largely been identified previously by photo-reconnaissance or other intelligence sources). The military hardware at each site was then catalogued, categorised (e.g. for shipment to the UK for intelligence investigation, for use by British or other Allied forces, for use by the military government to fulfil civilian needs, or for disposal), and moved to a storage depot where it could be more easily guarded.

Apart from the small proportion of aircraft and weapons required for Allied intelligence investigation, all the remaining military hardware had to be physically destroyed, initially by explosive charge, before removal as scrap. Equipment requiring servicing for future use was sent to the RAF Repair Unit or Repair & Salvage Unit responsible, although the initial work to (say) make an aircraft serviceable for a ferry flight would be done by the Air

Disarmament team on site, with assistance from ex-Luftwaffe personnel as required. In addition to these tasks, almost one million Luftwaffe personnel had to be demobilised in an orderly manner, no small task. At the end of the activity, more than 4,800 aircraft had been 'neutralised', 12,800 spare engines disposed of and 222,000 tons of ammunition destroyed. To assist in carrying out all the work involved, those Luftwaffe personnel not immediately required to be released for work in civilian jobs – i.e. those other than farm workers or miners – were formed into German Air Force Disarmament Labour Corps – 'Deutsche Arbeitskorps (Luft)' – (DAKL). These units were still commanded by German officers but wore a new uniform, with the objective of making them as non-military as possible. After a time the units came to be called 'Dienstgruppen' (Service Groups). As well as assisting with disarmament tasks, these units were involved in restoring airfield facilities required for use by the British Air Forces of Occupation.

Those aircraft officially recognised as being required by the BAFO were allotted RAF serial numbers by BAFO Headquarters. The aircraft, listed in the section below, were initially employed in all areas under British control, which included most of the area allocated as the British Zone of Occupation in Northern Germany, and some other areas later handed over to the Russians and the French. The area also included the whole of Denmark, pending the completion of the Air Disarmament task in that country, which was ended on 31st December 1945.

10.1   AIRCRAFT SERIAL NUMBER ALLOCATIONS TO BAFO

VH751   **Fieseler Fi 156**   **W Nr** *unknown*
Serial allotted 2nd July 1945. Operated by 2nd Tactical Air Force Communications Squadron (later the BAFO Communications Squadron). Transferred to the French Armée de l'Air in April 1946.

VH752   **Fieseler Fi 156**   **W Nr** *unknown*
Serial allotted 2nd July 1945. Operated by 2nd Tactical Air Force Communications Squadron (later the BAFO Communications Squadron).

VH753   **Fieseler Fi 156**   **W Nr** *unknown*
Serial allotted 2nd July 1945. Operated by the 2nd Tactical Air Force Communications Squadron (later the BAFO Communications Squadron). Sustained gale damage at Hannover/Langenhagen on 29th December 1945 and was SoC on 3rd January 1946.

VH754   **Fieseler Fi 156**   **W Nr** *unknown*
Serial allotted 2nd July 1945. Served with the RAF Denmark Communications Flight.

VH755   **Fieseler Fi 156**   **W Nr** *unknown*
Serial allotted 2nd July 1945. Served with the RAF Denmark Communications Flight.

VH756   **Fieseler Fi 156**   **W Nr** *unknown*
Serial allotted 2nd July 1945. Served with the RAF Denmark Communications Flight.

VH762   **Messerschmitt Bf 108B**   **W Nr** *unknown*
Serial allotted 2nd July 1945. Operated by No. 2 Group Communications Squadron. Transferred to the French Armée de l'Air in April 1946.

VM143   Bücker Bü 181 Bestmann   W Nr *unknown*
Serial allotted 11th September 1945. Allocated to No. 2 Group Communications Squadron. SoC by 30th May 1946. Transferred to French Armée de l'Air.

VM148   Bücker Bü 181 Bestmann   W Nr *unknown*
Serial allotted 11th September 1945. Allocated to No. 2 Group Communications Squadron. SoC by 30th May 1946.

VM151   Bücker Bü 181 Bestmann   W Nr 110207
Serial allotted 11th September 1945. Allocated to No. 2 Group Communications Squadron. SoC by 30th May 1946.

VM157   Bücker Bü 181 Bestmann   W Nr *unknown*
Serial allotted 11th September 1945. Allocated to No. 2 Group Communications Squadron. SoC by 30th May 1946.

VM162   Bücker Bü 181 Bestmann   W Nr *unknown*
Serial allotted 11th September 1945. Allocated to No. 2 Group Communications Squadron and delivered to No. 8303 Disarmament Wing at Bad Godesburg. SoC by 30th May 1946.

VM169   Bücker Bü 181 Bestmann   W Nr *unknown*
Serial allotted 11th September 1945. Allocated to No. 2 Group Communications Squadron. SoC by 30th May 1946.

VM174   Bücker Bü 181 Bestmann   W Nr *unknown*
Serial allotted 11th September 1945. Allocated to No. 2 Group Communications Squadron. SoC by 30th May 1946. Transferred to French Armée de l'Air.

VM181   Bücker Bü 181 Bestmann   W Nr *unknown*
Serial allotted 11th September 1945. Allocated to No. 2 Group Communications Squadron and delivered to No. 8303 Disarmament Wing at Bad Godesburg. SoC by 30th May 1946. Transferred to French Armée de l'Air.

VM188   Bücker Bü 181 Bestmann   W Nr *unknown*
Serial allotted 11th September 1945. Allocated to No. 2 Group Communications Squadron. SoC by 30th May 1946. Transferred to French Armée de l'Air.

VM193   Bücker Bü 181 Bestmann   W Nr *unknown*
Serial allotted 11th September 1945. Allocated to No. 2 Group Communications Squadron. SoC by 30th May 1946.

VM199   Bücker Bü 181 Bestmann   W Nr 502083
Serial allotted 11th September 1945; to No. 83 Group Communications Squadron. SoC by 30th May 1946. Transferred to French Armée de l'Air.

VM206   Bücker Bü 181 Bestmann   W Nr 501990
Serial allotted 11th September 1945. Allocated to No. 83 Group Communications Squadron. SoC by 30th May 1946. Transferred to French Armée de l'Air.

VM215   Bücker Bü 181 Bestmann   W Nr 4022
Serial allotted 11th September 1945. Allocated to No. 83 Group Communications Squadron and operated by No. 8401 Air Disarmament Wing for a time. SoC by 30th May 1946. Transferred to French Armée de l'Air, photographed in airworthy condition at Buc, in July 1946.

VM220   Bücker Bü 181 Bestmann   W Nr 502087
Serial allotted 11th September 1945. Allocated to No. 83 Group Communications Squadron. SoC by 30th May 1946.

VM227   Bücker Bü 181 Bestmann   W Nr 120502
Serial allotted 11th September 1945. Allocated to No. 83 Group Communications Squadron. SoC by 30th May 1946. Transferred to French Armée de l'Air.

VM231   Bücker Bü 181 Bestmann   W Nr 120222
Serial allotted 11th September 1945. Allocated to No. 83 Group Communications Squadron. SoC by 30th May 1946. Transferred to French Armée de l'Air.

VM238   Bücker Bü 181 Bestmann   W Nr 331331
Serial allotted 11th September 1945. Allocated to No. 83 Group Communications Squadron. SoC by 30th May 1946. Transferred to French Armée de l'Air.

VM243   Bücker Bü 181 Bestmann   W Nr 120508
Serial allotted 11th September 1945. Allocated to No. 83 Group Communications Squadron. SoC by 30th May 1946. Transferred to French Armée de l'Air.

VM252   Bücker Bü 181 Bestmann   W Nr 501997
Serial allotted 11th September 1945. Allocated to No. 84 Group Communications Squadron. SoC by 30th May 1946. Transferred to French Armée de l'Air.

Left: **The Bücker Bestmann VM215 in French Armée de l'Air service. Believed to have been photographed at Buc in 1946.** *J. Mutin collection*

Right top: **This Fieseler Storch, seen here at Lübeck early in 1946, has its serial number painted as 'YM489' in lieu of the correct VM489.** *A. Herbert courtesy I. Simpson collection*

Right: **This Siebel Si 204A is believed to be an example allocated for the use of Prince Bernhard of the Netherlands.** *IWM, CL3539*

VM259 Bücker Bü 181 Bestmann W Nr 110248
Serial allotted 11th September 1945. Allocated to No. 84 Group Communications Squadron. SoC by 30th May 1946. Transferred to French Armée de l'Air.

VM263 Bücker Bü 181 Bestmann W Nr 110800
Serial allotted 11th September 1945. Allocated to No. 84 Group Communications Squadron. SoC by 30th May 1946.

VM269 Bücker Bü 181 Bestmann W Nr 110947
Serial allotted 11th September 1945. Allocated to No. 84 Group Communications Squadron. SoC by 30th May 1946. Transferred to French Armée de l'Air.

VM274 Bücker Bü 181 Bestmann W Nr 110426
Serial allotted 11th September 1945. Allocated to No. 84 Group Communications Squadron. SoC by 30th May 1946. Transferred to French Armée de l'Air.

VM278 Bücker Bü 181 Bestmann W Nr 110764
Serial allotted 11th September 1945. Allocated to No. 84 Group Communications Squadron. SoC by 30th May 1946. Transferred to French Armée de l'Air.

VM291 Fieseler Fi 156 W Nr 779
Serial allotted 17th September 1945. Allocated to No. 83 Group Communications Squadron. Transferred to French Armée de l'Air in April 1946.

VM292 Fieseler Fi 156 W Nr 1576
Serial allotted 17th September 1945. Allocated to No. 83 Group Communications Squadron. Transferred to French Armée de l'Air in April 1946.

VM293 Fieseler Fi 156 W Nr 2010
Serial allotted 17th September 1945. Allocated to No. 83 Group Communications Squadron. Transferred to French Armée de l'Air in April 1946.

VM294 Fieseler Fi 156 W Nr 1665
Serial allotted 17th September 1945. Allocated to No. 83 Group Communications Squadron. Transferred to French Armée de l'Air in April 1946.

VM295 Fieseler Fi 156 W Nr 5746
Serial allotted 17th September 1945. Allocated to No. 83 Group Communications Squadron. Transferred to French Armée de l'Air in April 1946.

VM296 Fieseler Fi 156 W Nr 2547
Serial allotted 17th September 1945. Allocated to No. 83 Group Communications Squadron. Transferred to French Armée de l'Air in April 1946.

VM466 Siebel Si 204 W Nr _unknown_
Serial allotted 20th September 1945. Allocated to the BAFO Communications Wing for the use of Prince Bernhard of the Netherlands. It was later handed over to the Netherlands government.

VM472 Fieseler Fi 156 W Nr 5656
Serial allotted 20th September 1945. Allocated to the BAFO Communications Wing for the use of the General Officer Commanding 21st Army Group (General Sir Bernard Montgomery). It is believed that the serial number was applied as 'YM472'. Transferred to the French Armée de l'Air in April 1946.

VM489 Fieseler Fi 156 W Nr _unknown_
Serial allotted 2nd October 1945. Allocated to No. 26 Squadron at Lübeck. The serial number – as in the case of several of these aircraft – was wrongly applied as 'YM489'. SoC on 1st May 1946.

VM495 Messerschmitt Bf 108 W Nr 3010
Serial allotted 2nd October 1945. Allocated to the BAFO Communications Wing.

VM502 Messerschmitt Bf 108 W Nr 3076
Serial allotted 2nd October 1945. Allocated to the BAFO Communications Wing. Transferred to the French Armée de l'Air in April 1946.

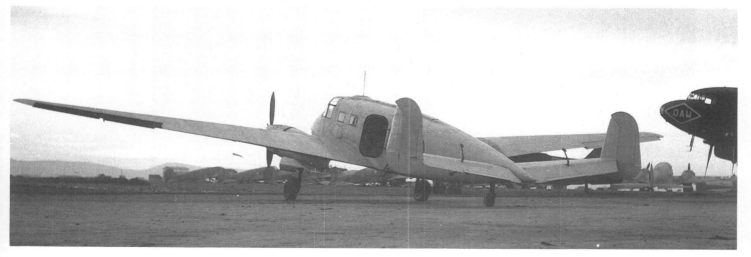

VM508   Messerschmitt Bf108   WNr 1105
Serial allotted 2nd October 1945. Allocated to the BAFO Communications Wing.

VM768   Bücker Bü 181 Bestmann   WNr 330750
Serial allotted 12th October 1945 at No. 151 Repair Unit. Transferred to the French Armée de l'Air in April 1946.

VM769   Bücker Bü 181 Bestmann   WNr 331337
Serial allotted 12th October 1945 at No. 151 Repair Unit. Allocated to No. 2 Group Communications Squadron. SoC (destroyed) on 25th May 1946.

VM770   Bücker Bü 181 Bestmann   WNr 218
Serial allotted 12th October 1945 at No. 151 Repair Unit. Allocated to No. 83 Group Communications Squadron. Transferred to the French Armée de l'Air in April 1946.

VM771   Bücker Bü 181 Bestmann   WNr 210208
Serial allotted 12th October 1945 at No. 151 Repair Unit. Allocated to BAFO Communications Wing, 31st December 1945. No further record.

VM772   Bücker Bü 181 Bestmann   WNr 120518
Serial allotted 12th October 1945 at No. 151 Repair Unit. Transferred to the French Armée de l'Air in April 1946.

VM773   Bücker Bü 181 Bestmann   WNr 331345
Serial allotted 12th October 1945 at No. 151 Repair Unit. Transferred to the French Armée de l'Air in April 1946.

VM774   Bücker Bü 181 Bestmann   WNr 110208
Serial allotted 12th October 1945 at No. 151 Repair Unit. Transferred to the French Armée de l'Air in April 1946.

VM775   Bücker Bü 181 Bestmann   WNr 120046
Serial allotted 12th October 1945 at No. 151 Repair Unit. Transferred to the French Armée de l'Air in April 1946.

VM776   Bücker Bü 181 Bestmann   WNr 210178
Serial allotted 12th October 1945 at No. 151 Repair Unit. Allocated to No. 84 Group Communications Squadron. Transferred to the French Armée de l'Air in April 1946.

VM777   Bücker Bü 181 Bestmann   WNr 110222
Serial allotted 12th October 1945 at No. 151 Repair Unit. Allocated to No. 2 Group Communications Squadron. Transferred to the French Armée de l'Air in April 1946.

VM778   Bücker Bü 181 Bestmann   WNr 331330
Serial allotted 12th October 1945 at No. 151 Repair Unit. Transferred to the French Armée de l'Air in April 1946.

VM779   Bücker Bü 181 Bestmann   WNr 331358
Serial allotted 12th October 1945 at No. 151 Repair Unit. Allocated to No. 84 Group Communications Squadron. Transferred to the French Armée de l'Air in April 1946.

VM780   Bücker Bü 181 Bestmann   WNr 8074
Serial allotted 12th October 1945 at No. 151 Repair Unit. Allocated to No. 2 Group Communications Squadron. Transferred to the French Armée de l'Air in April 1946.

VM781   Bücker Bü 181 Bestmann   WNr 331328
Serial allotted 12th October 1945 at No. 151 Repair Unit. Allocated to No. 84 Group Communications Squadron. Transferred to the French Armée de l'Air in April 1946.

VM782   Bücker Bü 181 Bestmann   WNr 330207
Serial allotted 12th October 1945 at No. 151 Repair Unit. Transferred to the French Armée de l'Air in April 1946.

VM783   Bücker Bü 181 Bestmann   WNr 501335
Serial allotted 12th October 1945 at No. 151 Repair Unit. Allocated to No. 83 Group Communications Squadron. Transferred to the French Armée de l'Air in April 1946.

VM784   Bücker Bü 181 Bestmann   WNr 501608
Serial allotted 12th October 1945 at No. 151 Repair Unit. Allocated to No. 83 Group Communications Squadron. Transferred to the French Armée de l'Air in April 1946.

VM785   Bücker Bü 181 Bestmann   WNr 501606
Serial allotted 12th October 1945 at No. 151 Repair Unit. Allocated to No. 83 Group Communications Squadron. Transferred to the French Armée de l'Air in April 1946.

VM786   Bücker Bü 181 Bestmann   WNr 502061
Serial allotted 12th October 1945 at No. 151 Repair Unit. Allocated to No. 83 Group Communications Squadron. Transferred to the French Armée de l'Air in April 1946.

VM787   Bücker Bü 181 Bestmann   WNr 2087
Serial allotted 12th October 1945 at No. 151 Repair Unit. Allocated to No. 83 Group Communications Squadron. Transferred to the French Armée de l'Air in April 1946.

VM788   Bücker Bü 181 Bestmann   WNr 120520
Serial allotted 12th October 1945 at No. 151 Repair Unit. Transferred to the French Armée de l'Air in April 1946.

VM789   Bücker Bü 181 Bestmann   WNr 331563
Serial allotted 12th October 1945 at No. 151 Repair Unit. Allocated to No. 2 Group Communications Squadron. Transferred to the French Armée de l'Air in April 1946.

VM790   Bücker Bü 181 Bestmann   WNr 120071
Serial allotted 12th October 1945 at No. 151 Repair Unit. Allocated to No. 83 Group Communications Squadron. Transferred to the French Armée de l'Air in April 1946.

VM791   Bücker Bü 181 Bestmann   WNr 331319
Serial allotted 12th October 1945 at No. 151 Repair Unit. Allocated to No. 83 Group Communications Squadron. Transferred to the French Armée de l'Air in April 1946.

VM792   Bücker Bü 181 Bestmann   WNr 111192
Serial allotted 12th October 1945 at No. 151 Repair Unit. Allocated to No. 83 Group Communications Squadron, then to 84 Group Communications Squadron by 15th November 1945. Transferred to the French Armée de l'Air in April 1946.

VM793   Bücker Bü 181 Bestmann   WNr 501338
Serial allotted 12th October 1945 at No. 151 Repair Unit. Allocated to No. 83 Group Communications Squadron. Transferred to the French Armée de l'Air in April 1946.

VM794 Bücker Bü 181 Bestmann W Nr 233562
Serial allotted 12th October 1945 at No. 151 Repair Unit. Allocated to No. 2 Group Communications Squadron.

VM795 Bücker Bü 181 Bestmann W Nr 16106
Serial allotted 12th October 1945 at No. 151 Repair Unit. Allocated to No. 83 Group Communications Squadron. Transferred to the French Armée de l'Air in April 1946.

VM796 Bücker Bü 181 Bestmann W Nr 110402
Serial allotted 12th October 1945 at No. 151 Repair Unit. Allocated to No. 83 Group Communications Squadron. Transferred to the French Armée de l'Air in April 1946.

VM797 Bücker Bü 181 Bestmann W Nr 110759
Serial allotted 12th October 1945 at No. 151 Repair Unit. Allocated to No. 83 Group Communications Squadron.

VM824 Fieseler Fi 156 Storch W Nr 1733
Serial allotted 12th October 1945 at No. 151 Repair Unit, Lüneburg. Allocated to No. 83 Group Communications Squadron. Transferred to the French Armée de l'Air in April 1946.

VM825 Fieseler Fi 156 Storch W Nr 5195
Serial allotted 12th October 1945 at No. 151 Repair Unit, Lüneburg. Allocated to No. 83 Group Communications Squadron. Transferred to the French Armée de l'Air in April 1946.

VM826 Fieseler Fi 156 Storch W Nr 110396
Serial allotted 12th October 1945 at No. 151 Repair Unit, Lüneburg. Allocated to No. 83 Group Communications Squadron. Transferred to the French Armée de l'Air in April 1946.

VM827 Fieseler Fi 156 Storch W Nr 110325
Aircraft surrendered at Lutjenholm, which was a satellite of Leck. Coded 'F3+AB'. Serial allotted 12th October 1945 at No. 151 Repair Unit, Lüneburg. Allocated to No. 83 Group Communications Squadron. Transferred to the French Armée de l'Air in April 1946.

VM828 Fieseler Fi 156 Storch W Nr 1557
Serial allotted 12th October 1945 at No. 151 Repair Unit, Lüneburg. Allocated to No. 83 Group Communications Squadron. Transferred to the French Armée de l'Air in April 1946.

VM829 Fieseler Fi 156 Storch W Nr 1431
Serial allotted 12th October 1945 at No. 151 Repair Unit, Lüneburg. Allocated to No. 83 Group Communications Squadron. Transferred to the French Armée de l'Air in April 1946.

VM830 Fieseler Fi 156 Storch W Nr 1753
Serial allotted 12th October 1945 at No. 151 Repair Unit, Lüneburg. Allocated to No. 122 Wing.

VM831 Fieseler Fi 156 Storch W Nr 5322
Serial allotted 12th October 1945 at No. 151 Repair Unit, Lüneburg. Allocated to No. 84 Group Communications Squadron. Transferred to the French Armée de l'Air in April 1946.

VM832 Fieseler Fi 156 Storch W Nr 1159
Serial allotted 12th October 1945 at No. 151 Repair Unit, Lüneburg. Allocated to No. 83 Group Communications Squadron. Transferred to the French Armée de l'Air in April 1946.

VM833 Fieseler Fi 156 Storch W Nr 24266
Serial allotted 12th October 1945 at No. 151 Repair Unit, Lüneburg. Allocated to No. 83 Group Communications Squadron. Transferred to the French Armée de l'Air in April 1946.

VM834 Fieseler Fi 156 Storch W Nr 5825
Serial allotted 12th October 1945 at No. 151 Repair Unit, Lüneburg. Allocated to No. 83 Group Communications Squadron.

VM835 Fieseler Fi 156 Storch W Nr 775
Serial allotted 12th October 1945 at No. 151 Repair Unit, Lüneburg. Allocated to No. 83 Group Communications Squadron. Transferred to the French Armée de l'Air in April 1946.

VM836 Fieseler Fi 156 Storch W Nr 5799
Serial allotted 12th October 1945 at No. 151 Repair Unit, Lüneburg. Transferred to the French Armée de l'Air in April 1946.

VM837 Fieseler Fi 156 Storch W Nr 4256
Serial allotted 12th October 1945 at No. 151 Repair Unit, Lüneburg. Transferred to the French Armée de l'Air in April 1946.

VM838 Fieseler Fi 156 Storch W Nr 1655
Serial allotted 12th October 1945 at No. 151 Repair Unit, Lüneburg. Transferred to the French Armée de l'Air in April 1946.

VM839 Fieseler Fi 156 Storch W Nr 1033
Serial allotted 12th October 1945 at No. 151 Repair Unit, Lüneburg. Transferred to the French Armée de l'Air in April 1946.

VM840 Fieseler Fi 156 Storch W Nr 1044
Serial allotted 12th October 1945 at No. 151 Repair Unit, Lüneburg.

VM841 Fieseler Fi 156 Storch W Nr 5712
Serial allotted 12th October 1945 at No. 151 Repair Unit, Lüneburg.

VM842 Fieseler Fi 156 Storch W Nr 4277
This example was surrendered at Beldringe in Denmark and was ferried from there to Lüneberg on 2nd October 1945. Serial allotted 12th October 1945 at No. 151 Repair Unit, Lüneburg. Transferred to the French Armée de l'Air in April 1946.

VM843 Fieseler Fi 156 Storch W Nr 789
Serial allotted 12th October 1945 at No. 151 Repair Unit, Lüneburg.

VM844 Fieseler Fi 156 Storch W Nr 1623
Serial allotted 12th October 1945 at No. 151 Repair Unit, Lüneburg. Allocated to No. 151 Repair Unit. SoC after a forced landing at Ochitmissen on 12th November 1945.

VM845 Fieseler Fi 156 Storch W Nr 5103
Serial allotted 12th October 1945 at No. 151 Repair Unit, Lüneburg.

VM846 Fieseler Fi 156 Storch W Nr 4335
Serial allotted 12th October 1945 at No. 151 Repair Unit, Lüneburg.

VM851 Messerschmitt Bf 108 W Nr 5121
Serial allotted 12th October 1945 at No. 151 Repair Unit, Lüneburg. Transferred to the French Armée de l'Air in April 1946.

VM852 Messerschmitt Bf 108 W Nr 2142
Serial allotted 12th October 1945 at No. 151 Repair Unit, Lüneburg. Transferred to the French Armée de l'Air in April 1946.

VM853   Messerschmitt Bf 108   W Nr 1082
Serial allotted 12th October 1945 at No. 151 Repair Unit, Lüneburg. Transferred to the French Armée de l'Air in April 1946.

VM854   Messerschmitt Bf 108   W Nr 858
Serial allotted 12th October 1945 at No. 151 Repair Unit, Lüneburg. Transferred to the French Armée de l'Air in April 1946.

VM855   Messerschmitt Bf 108   W Nr 5039
Serial allotted 12th October 1945 at No. 151 Repair Unit, Lüneburg. Allocated to No. 122 Wing. Transferred to the French Armée de l'Air in April 1946.

VM856   Messerschmitt Bf 108   W Nr 2007
Serial allotted 12th October 1945 at No. 151 Repair Unit, Lüneburg. Allocated to No. 83 Group Communications Squadron. Transferred to the French Armée de l'Air in April 1946.

VM857   Messerschmitt Bf 108   W Nr 5035
Serial allotted 12th October 1945 at No. 151 Repair Unit, Lüneburg. Transferred to the French Armée de l'Air in April 1946.

VM858   Messerschmitt Bf 108   W Nr *unknown*
Serial allotted 12th October 1945 at No. 151 Repair Unit, Lüneburg. Allocated to No. 151 Repair Unit. Transferred to the French Armée de l'Air in April 1946.

VM859   Messerschmitt Bf 108   W Nr 2214
Serial allotted 12th October 1945 at No. 151 Repair Unit, Lüneburg. Allocated to No. 83 Group Communications Squadron. Transferred to the French Armée de l'Air in April 1946.

VM860   Messerschmitt Bf 108   W Nr 5005
Serial allotted 12th October 1945 at No. 151 Repair Unit, Lüneburg.

VM861   Messerschmitt Bf 108   W Nr 5168
Serial allotted 12th October 1945 at No. 151 Repair Unit, Lüneburg.

VM862   Messerschmitt Bf 108   W Nr 2057
Serial allotted 12th October 1945 at No. 151 Repair unit, Lüneburg. Allocated to No. 124 Wing.

VM873   Fieseler Fi 156 Storch   W Nr *unknown*
Serial allotted 15th October 1945. Allocated to No. 84 Group Communications Squadron. Handed over to the French Armée de l'Air in April 1946.

VM874   Fieseler Fi 156 Storch   W Nr *unknown*
Serial allotted 15th October 1945. Allocated to No. 84 Group Communications Squadron.

VM879   Bücker Bü 181 Bestmann   W Nr *unknown*
Serial allotted 15th October 1945. Allocated to No. 84 Group Communications Squadron. Transferred to the French Armée de l'Air in April 1946.

VM885   Siebel Si 204A   W Nr 110 (?)
Serial allotted 1st October 1945. Not recorded at EASSU. This aircraft was allocated to No. 151 Repair Unit and later went to the Netherlands as PH-NAV.

VM886   Siebel Si 204D   W Nr *unknown*
Serial allotted 15th October 1945. Allocated to the EASSU at Hamburg/Fühlsbuttel.

VM887   Siebel Si 204D   W Nr *unknown*
Serial allotted 15th October 1945. Allocated to the EASSU at Hamburg/Fühlsbuttel.

Note: Three Si 204s recorded at EASSU in October or November (W Nr 1079, 252029 and 251834) may conceivably be connected with VM885/6/7 above.

VM897   Fieseler Fi 156 Storch   W Nr *unknown*
Serial allotted 22nd October 1945. Allocated to No. 84 Group Communications Squadron, although later temporarily to No. 652 Squadron before returning to No. 84 Group. Handed over to the French Armée de l'Air in April 1946.

This Siebel Si 204 wearing the RAF serial number VN112 is believed to have been photographed at Hamburg/Fühlsbuttel. *Richard King collection*

Above: **This Dornier Do 24T in RAF marks at Flensburg is believed to be one of those flown by Luftwaffe crews on air-sea-rescue or radio calibration duties in 1945/6.** *RAFM P19856*

Top left: **A Junkers W 34 wearing RAF markings and the code letters 'PGJ' photographed in Germany in 1945.** *Steve Coates collection*

Left: **This photograph shows the No. 616 Squadron Me 262A 'Yellow 7' at Lübeck following its landing accident, which took place on 29 May 1945.** *Len Smithies collection*

Bottom left: **This shot shows the Messerschmitt Me 262A '17' which had been flown by the Meteor pilots of No. 616 Squadron at Fassberg and Lübeck. It then flew to Schleswig, where this photograph was taken, and became Air Min 52.** *Steve Coates collection*

Messerschmitt Me 262A W Nr 112372

Surrendered at Fassberg. Code ' Yellow 7'. Flown to Lübeck on 29th May 1945 by W/Cdr W. E. Schrader of No. 616 Squadron, the first RAF jet fighter squadron. It suffered a nosewheel collapse on landing at Lübeck and was seriously damaged. Nevertheless it was quickly repaired and on 23rd June was flown from Lübeck to Farnborough. (See AM 51 in Chapter Seven).

Messerschmitt Me 262A-2a W Nr 500210

Surrendered at Fassberg. Code 'Yellow 17'. Flown to Lübeck on 29th May 1945 by F/Lt R. C. Gosling of No. 616 Squadron, which had been equipped with Gloster Meteors since the previous year. It is believed to have been flown at Lübeck by other No. 616 Squadron pilots. No RAF serial number allotted, although RAF markings were applied. Transferred to Schleswig and became AM52 (which see, Chapter Seven).

* * *

In addition to the aircraft flown by RAF units, a number of Dornier Do 24T flying boats were operated with German crews but in RAF markings. These were operated on Air-Sea Rescue duties, in support of the ferry operation to move ex-Luftwaffe aircraft from Norway to Germany for re-allocation. These are detailed in Chapter Twenty-One under 'Norway'.

Further Dornier Do 24Ts were flown from German bases, again in RAF markings but flown by German crews. These were used to calibrate German marine radio navigation beacons which continued in use by the Allies in the months after the war. The Do 24s continued to fly on these duties until early 1946.

Above: **Messerschmitt Bf 108 and Fieseler Fi 156: photographed in the hands of a Canadian Wing of the RAF's BAFO at Flensburg in July 1945, this pair was typical of many ex-Luftwaffe aircraft flown in RAF markings prior to the allocation of RAF serial numbers.** *A. H. Fraser courtesy Chris Thomas collection*

Above and below: **A Junkers Ju 88A and two different Junkers Ju 188As in RAF markings, believed to have been taken at Celle in 1945. The Ju 88 was previously 'IH+FF' of KG26. Any reader with information about their RAF use is invited to contact the author.** *Graham Skillen collection*

10.3   SAILPLANES

In addition to the powered aircraft, a large number of sailplanes surrendered in Denmark and the British Zone of Germany was taken into use by gliding clubs set up by the British Forces to provide recreation for service personnel, their families, and UK civilian employees. These clubs formed the basis for the later development of the Royal Air Force Gliding and Soaring Association. The RAFGSA was eventually formed in 1949. The section of the RAFGSA based in West Germany later separated to become the RAFGGA (Royal Air Force Germany Gliding Association). The main Service Gliding Clubs, which later became the basis of the RAFGSA and RAFGGA, included the following organisations:

- Air Division Gliding Club, Barntrup
- Air Headquarters BAFO Gliding Club, Minderheide and Scharfoldendorff
- Fassberg Gliding Club, Fassberg
- Hamburg District Gliding Club
- Lübeck Gliding Club, Lübeck
- Lüneburg Gliding Club, Lüneburg
- Uetersen & District Gliding Club, Uetersen
- Wahn Gliding Club, Wahn
- No. 2 Group Gliding Club, Oerlinghausen
- 4th Armoured Brigade Gliding Club
- 22nd Armoured Brigade Gliding Club
- No. 84 Group Gliding Club, Salzgitter.

Typical of these was the No. 2 Group Club, based at a former National Sozialistiche Flieger Korps (NSFK) gliding site at Oerlinghausen. Operations commenced in October 1945, after twenty-five RAF pilots had been trained as gliding instructors by a former Luftwaffe gliding instructor. By early 1946, membership was open to RAF personnel of No. 2 Group HQ and No. 140 Wing and to local British Army units. The Club operated six days-per-week, with over 1,000 glider launches being made every month. During 1946 the types of glider in use included the SG 38 (both with and without a cockpit nacelle), Grunau Baby, Olympia-Meise, Kranich, Minimoa, Weihe, München Mü 13 and Mü 17.

The Air Division GC joined forces with the AHQ BAFO GC during 1946 and the No. 84 Group GC amalgamated with the No. 2 Group GC at Oerlinghausen in 1947.

The sailplanes flown by the gliding clubs were generally flown with RAF roundels and with an identity which included the initial letter of the airfield at which it was based – e.g., 'S-46' for a München Mü 13D-3 flown by the club at Scharfoldendorff.

The initial fleet of these clubs was drawn from the following sailplanes surrendered in Denmark and northern Germany. Undoubtedly in later years some further sailplanes of Luftwaffe origin were found and added to the numbers.

DFS 108-49 Grunau Baby	101		
DFS 108-70 Olympia-Meise	7		
DFS 108-30 Kranich	17		
DFS 108-14 SG 38	97		
DFS 108-68 Weihe	6		
Göppingen Gö 1 Wolf	1		
Göppingen Gö III Minimoa	1		
München Mü 13	2	plus	
Schweyer Rhonsperber	1	Unidentified types	33
Schleicher Rhonadler	2		
Schleicher Rhonbussard	1	Total	269

Among the unidentified types (or possibly an example found after the statistics were compiled) was a Horten Ho IV tailless sailplane. This was discovered minus its wing-tips but was repaired and was flown by the BAFO Gliding Club at Scharfoldendorff. This was W Nr 26, ex D-10-1452 and 'LA-AD'. It was seriously damaged in a landing accident at Scharfoldendorff in about 1950. However, the sailplane survived this accident, and is now in the reserve collection of the Deutsches Museum at Munich.

The post-war use of German aircraft by units in Italy and Austria is covered in Chapter Four.

Opposite page, top far left: **The Kranich 'D4' being launched at Oerlinghausen. The '140W' legend refers to No. 140 Wing, RAF, one of the participating organisations in the BAFO Gliding Club at Oerlinghausen.** *Chris Wills collection*

Top left: **The Grunau Baby 'B2'at Oerlinghausen.** *Chris Wills collection*

Left: **The Göppingen Minimoa 'S-42' at its home base of Scharfoldendorff.** *Chris Wills collection*

Bottom left: **DFS Weihe '84G-1' of No. 84 Group GC, photographed at RNAS Bramcote while attending at inter-service gliding competition in 1947** *Charles E. Brown courtesy Chris Wills collection*

Top right: **The Grunau Baby 'LJ-WG' being launched at Salzgitter in 1946.** *Chris Wills collection*

Right: **A scene in the Fassberg Gliding Club hangar, showing Weihe 'F6' together with SG 38s 'F1' and 'F2' and the Minimoa 'S-42' from Salzgitter.** *Brennig James courtesy Chris Wills collection*

Chapter Eleven

British Activities
in the Far East

**ALLIED TECHNICAL AIR INTELLIGENCE UNIT
SOUTH-EAST ASIA**

The ATAIU-SEA was formed at Calcutta in India in 1943. It was composed of British and American personnel and was similar in concept to the Technical Air Intelligence Units organised in other areas where the war was being pursued against the Japanese. These other units are described in more detail in Chapter Eighteen.

The ATAIU-SEA started its life, as did all other similar units operating in the Far East and Pacific war zones, as an intelligence gathering organisation. A number of badly damaged aircraft were brought back to the Unit's headquarters for examination, but none of them was in a fit state to be flown, or even for repairs to be contemplated. The Unit was based at Maidan airfield (otherwise 'Red Road' or 'Angel'), which was located on a wide, straight, red-surfaced road in the centre of Calcutta. Among the relatively complete aircraft received at Maidan were examples of the Mitsubishi Ki-21 'Sally', Nakajima Ki-43 'Oscar', Mitsubishi Ki-46 'Dinah', and Kawasaki Ki-48 'Lily'. For most of its time at Calcutta, the ATAIU was commanded by F/Lt, later S/Ldr, Chris Glover, RAAF.

In September 1945, Operation *Zipper* was planned to take place. This was the invasion of Malaya and Singapore by British Commonwealth forces. The plan was delayed because of the impending Japanese surrender following the dropping of atom bombs on the cities of Hiroshima and Nagasaki. After the invasion fleet had sailed around in the Indian Ocean for some days while negotiations proceeded, the troops landed on Singapore Island and on the west coast of Malaya, without opposition. Many Japanese Army and Navy aircraft were found at Singapore, and at least one Nakajima Ki-44 'Tojo' was made airworthy for the benefit of the RAF Commanding Officer of Kallang, one of the Singapore airfields.

After a short time, the US members of the ATAIU were withdrawn and flown to Japan to assist with the Disarmament and Air Intelligence tasks in the Japanese home islands. The rest of the Unit, about fifteen-strong under the command of F/Lt Jim Reason, an RAF Engineer Officer, continued with the Air Intelligence tasks in Singapore. Items of equipment were sent to the UK for examination at Farnborough and elsewhere, although at first the only complete aircraft was a Kugisho Ohka, which was found at Seletar. The Ohka was shipped to the UK aboard the escort carrier HMS *Speaker* in April 1946. It seems likely that this was the Ohka examined at the RAE, resulting in the issue of Report EA272/1 by the Structures and Mechanical Engineering Department, in May 1946.

Towards the end of 1945, a number of Japanese aircraft were brought together at a former Imperial Japanese Navy (IJN) airstrip at Tebrau on the Malayan mainland. This strip was just across the Johore Straits from Singapore. The nucleus of the aircraft were IJN types which had been based at Tebrau, supplemented by IJAAF

aircraft flown in from elsewhere. The aircraft were flown, by Japanese pilots, with British nationality markings and with the acronym 'ATAIU-SEA' painted on them. It seems that examples of marine aircraft were flown under a similar arrangement from RAF Seletar on Singapore Island itself. It is not known specifically why the flights were made by Japanese aircrew. Most of the flights were for the benefit of the press or visiting VIPs and there is no evidence that any performance measurements or equipment evaluations were made.

It seems probable that the flights were intended to confirm the airworthiness of individual aircraft prior to their shipment to the UK for further testing at Farnborough. Records show that the British Ministry of Aircraft Production and Air Intelligence 2(g) selected sixty-four Japanese aircraft for shipment to the UK. In the event this plan was abandoned due to lack of available shipping space, which was mainly being targeted on repatriating British military personnel to Britain for demobilisation. Even if these aircraft had arrived, it seems unlikely that any would have been flown, since by 1946 flights by German aircraft at the RAE had been severely restricted.

Permission was given for four, of the intended sixty-four, Japanese aircraft to be shipped to England for museum purposes. Hence four such aircraft arrived at Portsmouth on a Royal Navy vessel in August 1946 and were then despatched to No. 47 MU, Sealand, for crating. These aircraft included the Mitsubishi A6M 'Zeke' whose cockpit is now with the Imperial War Museum, the Mitsubishi Ki 46 'Dinah' at RAF Cosford and a Kyushu K9W1 'Cypress'. The last of these three was held at RAF Wroughton until 1957, when it was scrapped after accidental fire damage. The fourth aircraft is believed to have been the Kawasaki Ki 100 displayed at Cosford, although this has not been totally confirmed. The selection of the four museum examples seems to have been on the basis of immediate availability rather than historic value. Although the 'Zeke' and 'Dinah' were undoubtedly of historic value, it would seem difficult to justify selection of the 'Cypress' – a licence-built Bücker Jungmann of little historic worth in the context of the Japanese aircraft industry. It might be that the museum selection was based on which of the sixty-four original aircraft selected had been crated at the time the selection was made. Nevertheless, the survival of three of the four aircraft to this day relies entirely on the deliberate effort made by HQ ACSEA to secure them for museum purposes. The selection of the aircraft was made on 25th March 1946 at Tebrau by S/Ldr Prosho.

The Ki 100 was, of course, one of the best Japanese fighters of the war and was entirely unknown to the Allies until after the surrender of Japan. The presence of a Ki 100 at Singapore would have been surprising, since the type was entirely employed by home-defence fighter units in Japan. It may be that it was brought to Singapore by the RAF, or the US authorities, after the Japanese surrender. No information has been found on this topic, despite extensive research. Nevertheless, it is possible that the Japanese military intended to reinforce Singapore with the latest equipment

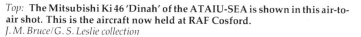

Top: **The Mitsubishi Ki 46 'Dinah' of the ATAIU-SEA is shown in this air-to-air shot. This is the aircraft now held at RAF Cosford.** *J. M. Bruce/G. S. Leslie collection*

Above: **A Kyushu K9W1 'Cypress' (licence-built Jungmann) 'B2-20' of the Imperial Japanese Navy at Tebrau in Malaya in 1946. At least one of these was later flown in RAF markings.** *Jim Reason collection*

Top: **A Nakjima A6M2-N 'Rufe' floatplane version of the Mitsubishi 'Zeke', photographed at Seletar in RAF markings with the 'ATAIU' title on its fin.** *USAF Museum*

Above: **The 'Cypress' of the RAF Air Historical Branch, derelict at RAF Wroughton in 1957 after being damaged by fire.** *MAP*

Below: **An air-to-air photo of two Mitsubishi J2M 'Jacks', BI-01 and BI-02, flying near Tebrau in 1946.** *MAP*

– the known presence of a Kugisho Ohka, and of a Mitsubishi G4M 'Betty' capable of air-launching the suicide aircraft, would tend to support this theory.

The types flown at Tebrau included:
Mitsubishi A6M3 and A6M5 'Zeke' fighters (codes BI-05, -12, -21)
Mitsubishi J2M 'Jack' fighters (codes BI-01 and BI-02)
Mitsubishi G4M 'Betty' bomber (code FI-11)
Kyushu K9W1 'Cypress' primary trainer (codes B2-20 and B2-21)
Mitsubishi Ki 46 'Dinah' reconnaissance aircraft (c/n 5439). This aircraft formerly belonged to the 3rd Chutai of the 81st Sentai, IJAAF.

At Seletar, the Unit flew at least one Nakajima A6M2-N 'Rufe' floatplane fighter. The ATAIU also flew one Kawanishi H6K 'Mavis' four-engined flying-boat. This was found at Sourabaya in Java and was made airworthy by the local RAF No. 3210 Servicing Commando. When captured, this aircraft had been marked with the colours of the Indonesian rebels, who were at the time resisting the re-establishment of Dutch rule in the Netherlands East Indies. When serviceable, the 'Mavis' was flown to RAF Seletar by an RAF crew. This aircraft survived for some time at Seletar, where its hull was later used as a floating headquarters by the local RAF sailing club.

11.2   **GREMLIN TASK FORCE – SAIGON, FRENCH INDO-CHINA**

The 'Gremlin Task Force' was a unit of ex-Japanese military aircraft flown on transport and reconnaissance duties in French Indo-China. The aircraft were flown by Japanese crews in green-cross surrender markings or RAF SEAC roundels. Although most flights were undertaken to repatriate Japanese prisoners to ports

of embarkation to be returned by sea to Japan, or to fly food and other supplies within Indo-China, some flights were made to drop pamphlets to 'Annamite' rebels (the origins of the Viet-Minh or Viet-Cong) who were contesting the return of the French to Indo-China. The RAF and British Army were in Indo-China, in advance of the arrival of French forces, to disarm the surrendering Japanese forces. Whenever the 'Gremlin Task Force' aircraft flew reconnaissance or leaflet-dropping operations, the Japanese crews were accompanied by RAF aircrew, from the local Air Intelligence Unit, or from No. 273 Squadron under the command of S/Ldr W. J. Hibbert at Tan Son Nhut.

The name 'Gremlin Task Force' derived from the 'Gremlins' in the RAF wartime flight safety publications. The 'Gremlins' were mischievous cartoon characters who would appear from nowhere and cause mishaps which might have been avoided if the aircrew concerned had taken care to follow their training and instructions. Other characters who appeared in the cartoons and comic strips were various, usually careless, individuals, such as P/O Percy Prune, F/Lt Lyne-Shute, G/Capt Booste, AC Plonk, WAAF Winsum, and Binder the Dog. All of these names were used on individual GTF aircraft.

Aircraft used by the 'Gremlin Task Force' were surrendered at Saigon/Tan Son Nhut or at other points in southern Indo-China. They included examples of the following:
Mitsubishi Ki-21 'Sally' twin-engined bomber
Tachikawa Ki-36/Ki-55 'Ida' army co-operation/trainer
Mitsubishi Ki-46 'Dinah' twin-engined reconnaissance aircraft
Kawasaki Ki-48 'Lily' twin-engined bomber
Tachikawa Ki-54 'Hickory' twin-engined light transport
Mitsubishi Ki-57 'Topsy' twin-engined transport
Kawasaki Ki-61 'Tony' single-engined fighter
Mitsubishi Ki-67 'Peggy' twin-engined bomber
Nakajima L2D 'Tabby' twin-engined transport

Left: **The radar-equipped Mitsubishi G4M 'Betty' bomber coded 'FI-11' of the IJN, flying from Tebrau in Malaya in 'ATAIU-SEA' markings.** *Jim Reason collection*

Top right: **'Zeke' BI-12 in 'ATAIU-SEA' markings on a flight from Tebrau.** *J. M. Bruce/G. S. Leslie collection*

Right: **'Zeke' BI-21 in 'ATAIU-SEA' markings at Tebrau in 1946.** *RAF Museum P12181*

Below: **The 'Zekes' BI-05 and BI-12 in formation over Malaya. BI-05 came to England and its cockpit is in the Imperial War Museum; BI-12 was allotted to Australia, although it is believed it did not arrive there.** *Jim Reason collection*

The unit records also show the Douglas DC-2 as a type used – this reference is a mis-report of Nakajima L2D 'Tabby' transports, which were developments of the DC-3 for which the Japanese held a production licence.

Known details of 'Gremlin Task Force' aircraft are:

No. 1	Mitsubishi Ki-57-II 'Topsy'	*WAAF Winsum*
No. 2	Mitsubishi Ki-57-II 'Topsy'	*F/Lt Barrel Foulynge*
No. 3	Mitsubishi Ki-57-II 'Topsy'	*P/O Prune*
No. 10	Mitsubishi Ki-21 'Sally'	*F/Lt Lyne-Shute*
No. 11	Tachikawa Ki-54 'Hickory'	No name
No. 14	Mitsubishi Ki-21-I 'Sally'	No name
No. 17	Mitsubishi Ki-21-II 'Sally'	*Happy*
No. 18	Kawasaki Ki-48-II 'Lily'	*Sneezy*
No. 19	Mitsubishi Ki-21-II 'Sally'	*Doc*
No. 22	Mitsubishi Ki-57-II 'Topsy'	*Bashful*
No. 26	Nakajima L2D3 'Tabby'	*Sub/Lt Swingit*
No. 27	Nakajima L2D3 'Tabby'	*Fanny's Frolic*

The South-East Asia Command newspaper, *SEAC*, noted the names *G/Capt Booste*, *AC Plonk* and *Binder the Dog* for other GTF aircraft, of which details have not been traced. Presumably, the remaining 'Seven Dwarfs' also appeared, in addition to *Happy*, *Sneezy*, *Doc* and *Bashful*. All the listed examples wore the *SEAC*-type RAF roundels – i.e. without the red centre spot. Most, if not all, examples had previously been flown in the Japanese surrender markings – white overall, with green crosses in place of nationality markings.

One 'Dinah' operated by the 'GTF' crashed and was written-off at Pakse, in October 1945, after a tyre burst on landing. Another Japanese aircraft of the 'GTF' was burned-out after being sabotaged by the Annamite rebels on 5th November.

The unit operated under the control of the RAF Element, Saigon Control Commission. The prime role of the unit was transport within Indo-China, although freight flights were also made to Thailand. A secondary role was Army reconnaissance, leaflet-dropping and other support duties, where these tasks were beyond the range of the locally-based Spitfires of No. 273 Squadron, RAF. The CO of the 'GTF' was S/Ldr H. F. McNab. He was assisted by F/O A. E. Bell, who acted as interpreter, and by W/Cdr G. R. Nottage and S/Ldr Hibbert, who were both involved in vetting the flying abilities of the Japanese aircrew. Another officer involved was F/O E. G. W. Collyer, who kindly provided many of the details of this unit. Eddy Collyer made flights in a Ki 57 'Topsy' of the 'GTF' in September and October 1945, piloted by S/Ldr Hibbert.

During November 1945, six reconnaissance flights were made by 'Hickorys' and one message-dropping flight was made by an 'Ida', while in December 37 sorties were made by 'Dinah', 'Ida' and 'Hickory' aircraft, on supply dropping and photo-reconnaissance duties. These flights were in addition to transport missions. The record for January 1946 shows the total of 810 flying hours accumulated in 408 sorties. Duties during January included flying food from Phnom-Penh to Saigon and taking the ground equipment of No. 684 Squadron, RAF, from Saigon to Bangkok. In all, the 'GTF' carried over 2,200 passengers and 228 tons of freight during its short existence.

The unit was disbanded when the French Armée de l'Air arrived in Indo-China in sufficient strength to take-over from the RAF, in February 1946. It seems that a number of the 'GTF' aircraft then continued to fly under French control. The 'Hickory' marked '11' was certainly later noted in French national markings.

The main French unit to operate them was Escadrille Aérienne de Liaison 99. French records also show 'Hickorys' numbered '8', '9' and '10'. Although '10' conflicts with the list of 'GTF' aircraft in this Chapter, the other numbers at least may fill spaces in the list. (See Chapter Twenty). It is conceivable that the 'Dinah' flown at Tebrau may have come from the 'GTF'.

Bottom left: **This ex-Imperial Japanese Navy H6K 'Mavis' was photographed at Sourabaya in Java. Traces of the Japanese green-cross surrender markings can be seen on the fuselage. Indonesian red-and-white rebel markings have been added, those on the fuselage having a blue band added to convert them to Dutch colours! The Mavis was painted in British markings after servicing and was then flown to Singapore.** *IWM, CF1074*

Inset: **The same aircraft as earlier photographed at Sourabaya after arrival at Seletar in 'ATAIU-SEA' markings.** *Peter Green collection*

Below: **This photograph shows the Mitsubishi Ki-57-II 'Topsy' named *P/O Prune* of the Gremlin Task Force, at Seletar, Singapore.** *S/Ldr E. B. G. Goldsmith courtesy Bruce Robertson collection*

Bottom: **Another aircraft photographed in ATAIU hands is this Tachikawa Ki 54 'Hickory'. No records have survived to show whether it was flown in RAF markings, but others of the type were flown by the Gremlin Task Force.** *Jim Reason collection*

11.3   USE OF EX-LUFTWAFFE AIRCRAFT IN SOUTH-EAST ASIA

As explained in Chapter Six, it was proposed that should sufficient examples of the Messerschmitt Me 323 Gigant six-engined transport be captured in areas under British control in Europe, the type would have been introduced to RAF service in South-East Asia for the transport of bulldozers and similar items of heavy equipment. The powered version of the General Aircraft Hamilcar transport glider (the Hamilcar Mark X) was under development for similar duties but availability of ready-made Me 323s would have rendered the Hamilcar X unnecessary. In the event, no Me 323s were found in areas under British control so the plan never became a realistic proposition.

The joint RAF/Army Specifications A 2/45 and A 4/45, calling for the production of liaison aircraft of greater capability than the Taylorcraft Auster were no doubt influenced by requirements for operation in South-East Asia, amongst other areas. Both Specifications were influenced to a degree by experience in operating captured Fieseler Fi 156 Storch aircraft. Perhaps as part of the build-up to the development of these Specifications, six Fieseler Storches were shipped from England to Air Command South-East Asia in December 1945. These were presumably from stocks of aircraft held in Germany following the surrender of the Luftwaffe in May 1945. The writer has been unable to trace whether any subsequent use was made of the Storch by the RAF in the Far East.

Chapter Twelve

Museum Aircraft
in the United Kingdom

It is appropriate here to mention the background to the preservation of the aircraft surviving in the United Kingdom.

It was recognised during the Second World War that some aircraft should be retained for museum purposes and as early as 1943 the Fiat CR 42 BT474 and Messerschmitt Bf 109E DG200 had been set aside for storage at No. 16 MU, Stafford, with this need in mind. Later in the war, these aircraft were transferred to No. 52 MU, Cardiff, together with the remains of Rudolf Hess's Bf 110E W Nr 3869 'VJ+OQ', which crashed in Scotland on 10th May 1941. (These remains are now with the Imperial War Museum).

When ex-Luftwaffe aircraft were being selected for transfer to the UK for evaluation, a number of 'museum' aircraft were added to the list, including the Ju 87 now at Hendon and a Bf 109G-14 now in Australia. These aircraft, together with the Cardiff examples and, later, a selection of surplus airworthy aircraft from Farnborough and Tangmere, were concentrated at No. 47 MU, Sealand. The reason for the use of this unit was its expertise in crating aircraft for shipment and storage. No. 47 MU improvised many of the storage crates from standard types in use for the shipment of Avro Ansons and Waco CG-4 Hadrian troop-carrying gliders. The aircraft remained at Sealand, although No. 47 MU was not an Aircraft Storage Unit as such, and had no space allocation for the long-term storage of aircraft. When pressure on space at Sealand became a problem towards the end of 1947, many 'museum' aircraft began to be moved to the 'German Air Force Equipment Centre' at RAF Stanmore Park. This had earlier been set up in an MU near London for storing small items of captured equipment used for travelling exhibitions. The GAFEC was transferred to the control of No. 3 MU, Milton, when it began to add complete aircraft to its inventory. The Centre remained on its own sub-site at Stanmore Park in hangars which had been built to house part of

London's balloon barrage defences. Almost all of the Axis aircraft had arrived at Stanmore Park by the end of 1948 and they remained there until 1955/6, with the exception of the Bf 110G AM 34, which went to RAF Andover in about 1949. In 1955 and '56 some of the museum aircraft were disposed of and the remainder moved to No. 15 MU, Wroughton, during 1956. In about mid-1958 they moved again to RAF Fulbeck in Lincolnshire; Fulbeck was a satellite airfield of RAF Cranwell, which was used for circuits and landings by aircraft based at the RAF College. Fulbeck airfield was manned as required by personnel from Cranwell. It had no permanent staff and no buildings except a control tower and one 'T2' hangar where the historic aircraft were stored, most in crates.

The move to Fulbeck was associated with the small museum on Cranwell's North airfield, which had been established in 1946. This contained an Me 262, Me 163, He 162, Fw 190, a Kugisho MXY7 Ohka, and some German missiles and weapons. Further details of this pioneer museum are given in Chapter Six. The move was also influenced by the presence on the staff of the RAF College of Dr John Tanner, later to become Director of the RAF Museum at Hendon.

In 1961, the Cranwell Museum closed because its building was required for other purposes. Its aircraft and those from Fulbeck moved to Biggin Hill, or were dispersed to other museums, such as the Imperial War Museum. During later years, they moved to Finningley, Gaydon, Cosford or St Athan, which were RAF Stations tasked to preserve the collection of aircraft being built up for display in the eventual RAF Museum at Hendon. Of these, Cosford still plays an important role in displaying the RAF Museum Reserve Collection in the Cosford Aerospace Museum.

Other aircraft from the original Air Historical Branch (AHB) collection were transferred to other museums, including the Imperial War Museum at Duxford in Cambridgeshire and the Science Museum at South Kensington, London.

12.1   THE MUSEUM AIRCRAFT

This Section describes the ex-Axis aircraft which were deliberately chosen to be brought back to the UK as Museum exhibits. Nine of the twelve aircraft still exist today. The first four aircraft were added to the list of aircraft to be sought by the Air Ministry intelligence teams in Germany but for historical rather than technical intelligence purposes. They were selected at Eggebek airfield in Schleswig-Holstein and left there by surface transport on 4th September 1945. They did not receive 'Air Min' numbers because they were to be retained in their original markings for display.

Top left: **The Air Historical Branch's Heinkel He 111H during one of its regular appearances at Horse Guards Parade in London during Battle of Britain week, 12th September 1955.** *P. H. Butler collection*

Left: **The Heinkel He 162A W Nr 120235 in the original RAF College Museum at RAF Cranwell North.** *Neville Franklin collection*

—   Messerschmitt Bf 110G   W Nr 180850

WNr 180850 was at the GAFEC, Stanmore Park, in 1949. It had arrived at No. 47, MU Sealand, by January 1946, later being transferred to Stanmore with the other AHB aircraft. This aircraft was scrapped after use in ground shots for the film *Angels One Five*, which was made at RAF Kenley in 1952.

—   Junkers Ju 87D-5   W Nr 494083

Coded 'RI+JK', this aircraft arrived at No. 47 MU, Sealand, by January 1946. Later moved to Stanmore Park, Wroughton, Fulbeck, Biggin Hill, St Athan, Henlow (in 1968 for the film *Battle of Britain*), St Athan, Hendon (in 1976 for the 'Wings of the Eagle' exhibition), St Athan, and then the Battle of Britain Museum at Hendon from 1980. It was allotted the RAF ground instructional serial number 8474M during its later days at St Athan. WNr 2883 has been reported for this aircraft but this is almost certainly in error; WNr 494083 was visible on the aircraft while it was at Stanmore Park in 1949, although the data plate has since disappeared.

—   Messerschmitt Bf 109G-14   W Nr 464863

This aircraft, coded '863' had arrived at No. 47 MU, Sealand, by 9th October 1945, which was the date it was crated there for museum storage. Probably the other three aircraft had also arrived by this time, although the unit records do not show them until a little later. By 1948, this Bf 109 was at Stanmore Park but it had arrived at RAF Wittering by October the following year. It was still at Wittering in February 1950 but its fate thereafter is not known.

—   Messerschmitt Bf 109G-14   W Nr 163824

This Bf 109G departed from Eggebek on 4th September 1945 with the other three aircraft but was not recorded at Sealand until January 1946. It is believed to have left Sealand in June 1946 for shipment to Australia. After storage for some years at No. 1 Aircraft Depot, RAAF Laverton, it was sold because of lack of available space at the Australian War Memorial, its intended final resting place. It was for many years in the Marshall Airways' hangar at Bankstown, near Sydney, New South Wales. It was acquired in 1979 for shipment to the UK by Doug Arnold, but the transaction was blocked by the authorities and the aircraft is still in Australia. The British civilian registration G-SMIT was allocated to the aircraft on 10th December 1979, but this has not been used because of the non-issue of an export licence from Australia. The aircraft was for some time at No. 2 Stores Depot, RAAF Base Villawood, e.g. in 1986. By 1988, the '109 was in the Mitchell Annex of the Australian War Memorial, near Canberra, Australian Capital Territory.

The remaining aircraft are of Japanese origin. The conventional aircraft were originally among the sixty-four Japanese aircraft selected by Air Ministry Intelligence and the Ministry of Aircraft Production for evaluation in Britain. When shipping space for these aircraft was refused a concession was allowed to permit four examples to be brought to Britain for museum purposes.

Three of the aircraft definitely came from the Allied Technical Air Intelligence Unit, South-East Asia (ATAIU-SEA). This Unit had been formed at Calcutta in India to investigate crashed and captured Japanese aircraft and was a joint British and American unit. The Unit had moved from India to Tebrau in Johore State, Malaya, following the re-occupation of Singapore in September 1945. The aircraft were selected for shipment at Tebrau in April 1946 and packed into crates on site by Japanese personnel under the supervision of No. 390 MU, Seletar, during June. They were loaded aboard a so far unidentified RN vessel at Singapore and arrived at Portsmouth on or about 24th August 1946, where they were unloaded for transport to No. 47 MU, Sealand. These three aircraft were as follows:

—   Mitsubishi A6M5 Navy Fighter Type 0
**   Model 52 'Zeke'**

Constructor's number unknown. This aircraft was painted with British national markings superimposed over its original colour scheme, together with the acronym 'ATAIU-SEA'. It also retained its original Imperial Japanese Navy unit code 'BI-05' on its fin, indicating it to be aircraft '05' of the second aircraft carrier of the Second Koku Sentai. By January 1948, this aircraft had been transferred from Sealand to the GAFEC at Stanmore Park, where it remained until 1955. At that time it was agreed that it would be transferred to the Imperial War Museum at South Lambeth, but because of space limitations in the museum it was only possible to display the cockpit section. The remainder of the aircraft was

Top right: **WNr 163824 was one of the Bf 109s taken over at Eggebek as a museum exhibit in 1945; this aircraft later went to Australia where it still exists.** *MAP*

Right: **The Ju 87 'RI+JK' and Bf 109G '863' at Eggebek in 1945. The Stuka is the example now in the Battle of Britain Museum at Hendon; the Bf 109G was brought to England for preservation but was last heard of in about 1950. The Bf 110G in the background is WNr 180850 which was also selected at Eggebek for preservation.** *PRO, AIR 37/1442*

therefore sold as scrap and was to be seen in the scrapyard of the British Aluminium Co Ltd at Latchford, Warrington, in early 1956. The cockpit section remained on display with the Imperial War Museum at South Lambeth for many years but by February 1986 was at the IWM's facility at Duxford. By June 1989, the cockpit had returned to Lambeth.

— Mitsubishi Ki-46-III Army Type 100 Command Reconnaissance Plane Model 3 'Dinah'

Constructor's number 5439. This IJAAF aircraft came from Tebrau as described above and was crated at Sealand on 26th January 1947. It is reported to have been coded '29', but this could not have been an Empire Test Pilot School code marking as has been reported elsewhere! Some IJAAF aircraft used for communications duties by the RAF in Indo-China in 1945/6 had two-digit number codes and it is conceivable that the 'Dinah' may have been one of these aircraft prior to being transferred to the ATAIU-SEA at Tebrau. (See Chapter Eleven for details of the 'Gremlin Task Force'). The ATAIU 'Dinah' arrived at Tebrau from Kuala Lumpur, flown by an RAF pilot.

The acronym 'ATAIU-SEA' was painted on this aircraft, confirming its use by the Unit prior to its crating for shipment at Tebrau. The Ki-46 was at Stanmore Park by January 1948, and later at Wroughton, Fulbeck and Biggin Hill, before transfer to St Athan. After arrival at St Athan, it was allotted the Ground Instructional serial number 8484M for book-keeping purposes. During refurbishing at St Athan, markings of the 3rd Chutai of the 81st Sentai were discovered on this aircraft. In 1989 the 'Dinah' moved to the Aerospace Museum at Cosford, for future display there, following the rundown of the St Athan Collection.

— Kyushu K9W1 Navy Type 2 Primary Trainer 'Cypress' (licence-built Bü 131)

This was a Japanese-built Bücker Jungmann. When seen by the writer at Stanmore Park in September 1955, this had an overall canary-yellow colour scheme with red Hinomaru national markings and had no unit markings or traces of British marks. There was no evidence of a maker's data plate to confirm its origin as a Kyushu-built aircraft. It is usually reported as an Army Type 4 Primary Trainer, the Kokusai Ki-86, but photographs of aircraft at Tebrau were almost all of naval aircraft and included at least two K9W1s, coded 'B2-20' and 'B2-21'. The former is stated by the CO of the Unit to have been the example flown later in British markings.

The aircraft was crated at No. 47 MU, Sealand, on 3rd April 1947, but had arrived at Stanmore Park by 1949. During 1956, it was transferred to No. 15 MU, Wroughton, with the other Air Historical Branch aircraft. It is believed to have been damaged by an accidental fire while in store at Wroughton where it was noted in derelict condition in April 1957, in one of the MU's dispersed storage fields.

— Kawasaki Ki-100-1b Army Type 5 Fighter

The origin of this aircraft is less certain than the other three, in that it is not certain that it came from Tebrau or that it arrived in England on the same ship or at the same time as the other three aircraft. This aircraft did not have an Allied code name (such as 'Dinah' or 'Zeke') because the type originated in 1945 as a stop-gap modification of the existing Ki-61, and was unknown to Allied intelligence until after the Japanese surrender. It is possible that this aircraft was surrendered in mainland Japan and later taken to the ATAIU at Tebrau, although this has yet to be confirmed. The Ki-100 is not known to have been deployed outside Japan and it is known that the US military authorities allocated a number of air-

craft surrendered in Japan for RAF use in October/November 1945. So far as is known the RAF did not test any such aircraft in Japan.

It is almost certain that this aircraft was the 'Oscar II' recorded at No. 47 MU, Sealand, in February 1947, and crated for storage there on 15th April 1947. The code name 'Oscar' rightly belonged to another type of Japanese fighter, the Nakajima Ki-43, which was of fairly similar layout. By January 1948, the 'Oscar II' was at Stanmore Park and it later moved to Wroughton, Fulbeck, Biggin Hill and Cosford. In the course of these moves, it received the RAF Ground Instructional serial number 8476M for book-keeping purposes. In November 1985, it was moved to St Athan to join all the other ex-Axis aircraft in the RAF Museum reserve collection. With the later rundown of the St Athan Collection, the aircraft had returned to the Cosford Aerospace Museum by June 1989.

— Kugisho MXY7 Navy Suicide Attacker Ohka Model 11

The Ohka was the ultimate suicide attack weapon designed to be flown against invasion forces threatening the Japanese homeland. Four examples (at least) were brought to Britain for museum purposes.

One is on display at the Fleet Air Arm Museum at Yeovilton; this aircraft was previously at the Science Museum at South Kensington, London, usually reported as serial number 15-1585.

The second was for many years on display at the station museum at Royal Air Force College, Cranwell. When this museum was closed in 1961, the Ohka went to Cottesmore and then to Henlow and finally to the Greater Manchester Air and Space Museum (now incorporated into the Manchester Museum of Science and Industry); this aircraft has the serial number 997. It is identified as 8485M for book-keeping purposes.

A third example was for many years at the Rocket Propulsion Establishment at Westcott in Buckinghamshire; this later went to RAF Cosford where it is on display. It received the number 8486M for book-keeping purposes.

A fourth is at the Defence Explosive Ordnance School at Chattenden in Kent and has been there for many years.

At least one example was found at RAF Seletar, Singapore, in 1945. This was shipped to the UK and was examined at the RAE, Farnborough. This may be one of the examples listed above. The origins of the other examples are uncertain.

12.2 THE DEVELOPMENT OF AVIATION MUSEUMS IN THE UK

The first museums to include aircraft among their exhibits were the Science Museum at South Kensington and the Imperial War Museum (IWM) at South Lambeth. The Science Museum received its first complete aircraft in 1913, while the IWM obtained its first aircraft exhibits immediately after the First World War.

The Science Museum

The Science Museum opened its first exhibition to include Second World War German aircraft in February 1946. Most of the exhibits from this event were returned to the RAF when the exhibition closed in May of the same year. The Museum retained a Focke-Achgelis Fa 330 rotor-kite and later obtained an example of the Me 163B rocket fighter from the RAF. Exhibit details:

Fieseler Fi 103		
(FZG-76 or V-1)	W Nr 442795	S. Kensington
Focke-Achgelis Fa 330A	W Nr 100509	Wroughton
Messerschmitt Me 163B	W Nr 191316	S. Kensington

Right: **Heinkel He 219A W Nr 210903 (later to become USA 8 and FE-612) at Grove (Karup) in Denmark in June 1945 before being painted in US markings.** *Mrs J. Woolams collection*

Below right: **Messerschmitt Me 262A '777' *Jabo Bait* of Watson's Whizzers at Newark AAF, New Jersey on 24th August 1945.** *Mrs J. Woolams collection*

Below: **Henschel Hs 129B FE-4600 and Heinkel He 111H FE-1600 at Freeman Field during September 1945.**
H. Ray White courtesy Lou Thole collection

Bottom: **Macchi MC202 Folgore FE-300, Mitsubishi A6M5 'Zeke' TAIC 7/FE-130 and Supermarine Spitfire VII EN474/FE-400 lined up at Freeman Field in September 1945.**
H. Ray White courtesy Lou Thole collection

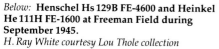

Above: **Messerschmitt Me 262B FE-610** photographed at Freeman Field in 1945. The fin swastika and fuselage cross are non-authentic, painted after arrival in the US to cover earlier British and USAAF markings.
Norm Malayney collection

Left: **The rarely photographed Junkers Ju 88A FE-1599** *The Comanche*, showing the 86th Fighter Squadron Comanche badge on its nose and pilot Capt H. Ray White on the left in the foreground. The photograph was taken at Kansas City, Mo, in April 1945. *H. Ray White courtesy Lou Thole collection*

Below: **The Focke Wulf Fw 190F FE-116** at Freeman Field in September 1945. *H. Ray White courtesy Lou Thole collection*

Above: **Arado Ar 234B FE-1010 at Freeman Field in September 1945; as with other ex-Luftwaffe aircraft the fin swastika and fuselage cross are non-authentic additions made in the USA to cover US 'stars and bars'.**
H. Ray White courtesy Lou Thole collection

Right: **The Messerschmitt Bf 108 FE-4610 wearing a striking (but non-authentic) colour scheme at Freeman Field in September 1945. The Focke Wulf Fw 190 FE-116 and Heinkel He 162A FE-489 are in the background.**
H. Ray White courtesy Lou Thole collection

Below: **The Heinkel He 162A T2-489 at Ed Maloney's 'Planes of Fame' museum in 1970. The colour scheme is original with the exception of the fuselage cross and fin swastika.**
Dick Phillips collection

Above: **Messerschmitt Me 410A FE-499 'F6+WK' at Freeman Field in 1945.** *Norm Malayney collection*

Right: **Messerschmitt Me 163B FE-500 and Flettner Fl 282B helicopter FE-4613 at Freeman Field in September 1945.**
H. Ray White courtesy Lou Thole collection

Below: **A French built Nord 1000 (Messerschmitt Bf 108) of the Armée de l'Air believed to have been photographed in Italy in 1945, in a contemporary camouflage scheme.**
J. Michaels courtesy Norm Malayney collection

Chapter Thirteen

United States' Army Air Force Wright Field 1941-1945

The USAAF Air Intelligence organisation was built up from a very small nucleus in the days immediately before and after the entry of the United States into the Second World War on the 'Day of Infamy', 7th December 1941. From small beginnings, and to some extent building on the experience of the Royal Air Force which had been studied in detail by USAAC personnel, a complex organisation developed, to be centred at Wright Field, Ohio.

The organisation drew on the existing laboratory expertise at Wright Field in the same way that the Royal Aircraft Establishment at Farnborough in the UK obtained the back-up of many specialists in a multitude of departments. The Technical Intelligence organisation was initially set up under the Engineering Branch of the USAAC Materiel Division. The Materiel Division was an Air Corps organisation which was responsible both for experimental engineering and for the Air Corps equipment procurement functions; it had its Headquarters at Wright Field until 1939. In October 1939 the Chief of the Materiel Division moved to Washington, DC, to be located with the Chief of the Air Corps, with his Assistant Chief remaining at Wright Field in charge of day-to-day Division activities.

In the years from 1939 a considerable expansion and re-organisation of the Air Corps took place. On 15th March 1941 a Maintenance Command was set up to take over the Materiel Division's procurement activities and also the eight main Air Corps Depots. Initially it had its headquarters at Patterson Field. In October this organisation was renamed Air Service Command, to better reflect the fact that its logistics role included procurement as well as maintenance. Meanwhile, the US Army Air Corps, effective from 20th June 1941, became the United States Army Air Forces. The former Air Corps Chief, Major-General Henry H. Arnold, then became the Chief of the Army Air Forces and was given responsibility for establishing policies and plans for all Army aviation activities.

On 9th March 1942 the former Materiel Division, which remained in charge of Wright Field experimental activities, became Materiel Command. At the same time the Wright Field experimental establishment was redesignated the Materiel Center.

Finally, on 1st April 1943, the functions of the former Materiel Division came together once more when Air Service Command and Materiel Command were merged into Air Technical Service Command with its headquarters at Patterson Field.

When the Materiel Division was up-graded to Command status, it became responsible for two major Divisions, namely Engineering and Production. The Engineering Division was responsible for many hundreds of research and development projects spread across its various Laboratories, varying from windtunnel tests of new aircraft configurations to the development of materials, aircraft ancilliary equipment and airfield equipment. Within the Laboratories were various Branches and Sections – for example the Aircraft Laboratory had a Glider Branch which carried out trials of troop-carrying gliders and their equipment.

Foreign Equipment was at first evaluated by the Foreign Equipment Unit of the Technical Staff within the Engineering Division. Later, after the formation of the Technical Data Laboratory in December 1942, came the Evaluation Branch of the Technical Data Laboratory, giving rise to the 'EB-' series of numbers. The Foreign Equipment Unit then became part of the Evaluation Branch, which was in turn one of the six branches of the Technical Data Laboratory. The Technical Data Laboratory's tasks included 'Procurement, evaluation and dissemination of technical information on foreign aircraft and aeronautical equipment, particularly enemy aircraft and equipment, of technical or military interest to the Engineering Division and American manufacturers producing AAF materiel'. Later the Evaluation Branch identities were changed to 'FE-' for 'Foreign Equipment', presaging the formation of a Foreign Equipment Branch in April 1945 as one of Evaluation Branch's successor organisations (the Flight Data Branch being the other). Finally, in July 1945, came a re-organisation in which the Technical Data Laboratory became part of 'T-2 Intelligence' within the organisational structure, with other 'T' designators indicating Personnel, Engineering, Administration and other functions. By November 1945, 'T-2' was transferred to a new Collection Division, under the command of Harold Watson, charged with the collection and assessment of equipment and technical information recovered from Germany, Japan and other sources. This Division remained in being until its task was completed in April 1947.

Although Wright Field was the centre for operations, the size of the Materiel Center and its successors greatly exceeded the capacity of the base. Because of this, several nearby bases were used to cater for the overflow. These included Patterson Field, Clinton County Army Air Field (AAF) and Dayton AAF. At its peak, the Center employed 50,000 civilian and military personnel. In 1943, personnel from Wright Field set up a further subsidiary unit at Rogers Lake, Muroc, California, known as the Materiel Command Flight Test Base, Muroc. This site is now known as Edwards AFB. In January 1948, Wright Field (originally named for Wilbur Wright) and Patterson Field were amalgamated to form Wright-Patterson AFB. The Collection Division was responsible for the operation of Freeman Field, where its Technical Operations Section looked after Restoration, Maintenance and Flight Research Branches as described in Chapter Seventeen.

The first Axis aircraft to be flown at Wright Field was the Messerschmitt Bf 109E AE479, an example previously flown by the Luftwaffe, and then by the French Armée de l'Air and the British Royal Air Force. This aircraft was shipped to the USA, arriving at Wright Field on 14th May 1942. Subsequent Axis aircraft were identified by the EB-, FE- or T2- numbers, but AE479 continued to be identified by its RAF serial number.

Later Axis aircraft were in the most part shipped in from the Middle East and Italy. In two cases Junkers Ju 88s were flown from the Middle East to the USA via the South Atlantic route.

In 1944, Col Harold E. Watson was attached to the USAAF in Europe and was responsible for the despatch of further aircraft captured by US forces on the continent of Europe, culminating in the post-surrender shipment aboard HMS *Reaper* in July 1945. Aircraft were painted in US national markings at their point of surrender and flown to a suitable port for onward shipment to the USA, or, in exceptional cases, air-ferried or air-freighted to the US.

After receipt at Wright Field, identities incorporating the letters 'EB-' (Evaluation Branch), 'FE-' (Foreign Equipment) or 'T2-' (for the T-2 Office of Air Force Intelligence) were painted on the aircraft. The identity numbers were unique to the aircraft and were rarely duplicated, although the prefixes EB-, FE- and T2- were valid on the same airframe at different times, as the intelligence organisation underwent changes. It was usual for the prefix to be changed if the aircraft remained on charge after one of the organisational changes – thus several 'EB-' aircraft changed to 'FE-' and later 'FE-' aircraft became 'T2-'. In fact the vast majority of 'FE-' numbered aircraft had their prefix overpainted as 'T2-'. The 'T2-' identities survived into the post-Second World War period, being used again for North Korean aircraft captured during the Korean War (such as the Yak-9P T2-3002).

After the end of the war in Europe, Freeman Field, Seymour, Indiana, was transferred to the control of Wright Field for use as a subsidiary centre where many of the prizes received from Europe were re-assembled. The aircraft were flown from Freeman Field to Wright Field for evaluation testing to be carried out, since Freeman Field did not have equipment to support all flight tests under properly-controlled conditions. At this time, Freeman Field was called the Foreign Aircraft Evaluation Center. With the end of the war against Japan, the priority for assessment of German aircraft disappeared, since its main thrust was to ensure that any developments which might have been transferred from Germany to Japan were fully understood before they were met in combat during an invasion of the Japanese home islands. Freeman Field was soon closed and the Axis aircraft dispersed to Wright Field, or to storage at Davis-Monthan Field in Arizona, or to No. 803 Special Depot in the former Douglas C-54 factory at Park Ridge, Illinois (today's Chicago O'Hare Airport). A list of available Axis aircraft and equipment was published and the listed items released for study by approved US industrial organisations. The survivors were scrapped or moved to the Smithsonian Institution store at Silver Hill, Maryland, when the Park Ridge store was required for other purposes at the time of the Korean War.

13.1   GERMAN AIRCRAFT

EB-1   Messerschmitt Bf 109F-4
(It is believed that this aircraft later became EB-100)

EB-100   Messerschmitt Bf 109F-4   W Nr 7640
At Wright Field on 1st March 1943, this aircraft came from the USSR to the USA having been presented by the Soviet government as a goodwill gesture during a visit to Moscow by the US Secretary of State, Wendell Wilkie, in November 1942. To Eglin AFB, Florida, on 21st March 1944, at which point it had 13 hours flight time. Among the pilots who flew this aircraft at Wright Field was Ralph C. Hoewing, who made four flights in this '109 in November 1943 and February 1944, a total of 1 hr 35 mins. The final fate of this aircraft is not known.

EB-101   Focke Wulf Fw 190A-3
This Fw 190 was at Wright Field on 20th August 1943 after shipment from North Africa. It was assigned for flight tests to be carried out, to determine speed versus altitude curves for the type, climb rates and stalling speeds in various configurations. The '190 was captured in North Africa. EB-101 made its first test flight after overhaul in February 1944. It was flown to Eglin Field, Florida, on 7th March 1944, for armament trials. Its place in the programme to evaluate Fw 190 performance was taken over by EB-104. As at 1st April 1944, EB-101 was awaiting replacement of its propeller at Eglin. No further details have been traced, but it is possible that this aircraft later became FE-497.

Above: **This Bf 109F EB-100 is the same aircraft as 'EB-1' after renumbering.** *NASM*

Opposite: **The ex-Soviet Bf 109F photographed after arrival at Wright Field and repainting with the first 'Evaluation Branch-' serial number EB-1.** *USAF Museum*

EB-102   Messerschmitt Bf 109G-6/trop   W Nr 16416
Coded 'White 9'. At Wright Field on 14th July 1943 after shipment
from North Africa. To Eglin Field on 21st March 1944. On 1st September 1944, this aircraft was severely damaged in a landing accident at Wright Field and is presumed not to have been repaired. At
the time of the accident, the '109 was landing after a 10-minute
local flight, flown by Major Coleman D. Kuhn. By this point, the
aircraft had flown 29 hours in US hands.

The aircraft swung off the runway due to the wheel brakes being
unevenly adjusted and was then deliberately ground-looped to
avoid a Lockheed P-38 which had previously suffered a tyre blow-
out and was waiting to be towed away from the grass at the edge
of the runway. The undercarriage of EB-102 was torn off in the
accident and its propeller and wings were damaged. By 24th
October 1944, the '109 had been assigned to 'salvage'.

EB-103   Messerschmitt Me 410A-2/U1   W Nr 10018
This aircraft arrived at Wright Field during January 1944. On 1st
April 1944 it was still being re-assembled in Hangar 3 at Wright
Field. This is the same aircraft as FE-499 (see Chapter Seventeen)
which still exists in store at Silver Hill, Md.

EB-104   Focke Wulf Fw 190G-3   W Nr 160016
This aircraft, coded 'DN+FP', was recorded as being at Wright
Field on 20th August 1943. However, it has also been reported as
being captured at Monte Corvino airfield in southern Italy, following the Allied landings at Salerno, on September 9th 1943.

EB-104 made its first flight at Wright Field, after overhaul, on
26th February 1944. This was a 50-minute trip made by Capt Wal-
lace A. Lien. Further flights were conducted, mainly by Major
Gustav E. Lundquist, although it was also flown by Capt Kenneth
Chilstrom and by Ralph C. Hoewing.

Below left: **An air-to-air photograph of the Fw 190A EB-101.** *USAF Museum*

Below right: **The Fw 190G EB-104 on display at Wright Field after the war; this aircraft became T2-125 but that number may not have been painted on the aircraft.** *NASM*

Bottom: **The Bf 109G EB-102 after its landing accident which resulted in the aircraft being scrapped.** *USAF Museum*

Left: **The ex-Rumanian Junkers Ju 88D, later to be identified as FE-1598, in flight near Wright Field.** *USAF Museum*

Opposite top: **The first USAAF Zeke EB-2 rebuilt from parts at Kunming in China, after arrival in the United States – the background (probably a scene at Wright Field) has been blacked out by the wartime censor.** *USAF Museum*

Opposite bottom: **The Gotha Go 242B FE-2700 transport glider picketed out, possibly at Freeman Field.** *Edgar Deigan courtesy Norm Malayney collection*

These flights commenced in earnest on 14th March with the start of instrument calibration. The test series continued with the establishment of speed performance at various altitudes, climb rates, etc. By 13th April 1944, EB-104 had flown 17.5 hours. The results of these tests were published in Report No. ENG-47-1743-A, dated 26th May 1944 and approved by Lt Col Harney Estes Jr, Chief of Fighter Flight Test Branch.

It was concluded that the Fw 190 compared favourably with existing USAAF fighter types in manoeuvrability, speed and climb at heights below 28,000 feet. The maximum speed was assessed as being 415 mph at 22,000 feet, with a maximum rate of climb of 4,000 ft/min. Vision from the cockpit was considered good, except forward vision during take-off and in the climb. The extremely high rate of roll in manoeuvres was considered outstanding, but the turning radius was thought to be poor. The cockpit layout was considered to be good. Ground handling, take-off and landing characteristics were all commented on in favourable terms.

This aircraft was displayed at Wright Field after the war and during this period was renumbered as FE-125/T2-125. On 1st August 1946 it was still at Wright Field, being used as part of a mobile display; it is presumed to have been scrapped soon afterwards.

EB-105   Henschel Hs 129B-1/R2   WNr *unknown*
This aircraft was recorded as being at Wright Field from 20th August 1943. It seems likely that it was captured in North Africa. It is known to have been shipped from Wright Field to Tulsa, Oklahoma, for reassembly and restoration to flying condition on 27th March 1944. To FE-4600 (which see, Chapter Seventeen).

This series of numbers continued with the prefix changed - i.e., from FE-106 – see Chapter Seventeen.

(FE-1598) Junkers Ju 88D-1/Trop   WNr 430650
This aircraft was ex HK959 of RAF Middle East. It was originally flown to Limassol in Cyprus by a defecting Rumanian pilot on 22nd July 1943 and was later flown to Heliopolis in Egypt, where it was serviced by the British Airways' Repair Unit and received RAF markings. The serial number HK959 was allocated but it is not known if this was painted on the aircraft. It was handed over to the USAAF intelligence organisation in Cairo and was ferried across the South Atlantic to be tested at Wright Field, arriving there on 14th October 1943. The crew comprised Maj Warner E. Newby and Lt G. W. Cook.

Its route included Wadi Halfa in Egypt, Freetown in Sierra Leone, Ascension Island, Natal in Brazil, Georgetown in British Guiana, Puerto Rico, Morrison Field in Florida, and Memphis, before arriving at Wright Field. It received the name *Baksheesh*. By 15th March 1944 it had flown 156 flying hours, including 36 hours of trials at Wright Field between 9th November 1943 and 9th March 1944. It then departed to Eglin Field, Florida, for further trials. Up to this point it was identified by its German WNr 430650. The main Wright Field trials were flown by Maj Gustav E. Lundquist and Capts E. W. Leach, W. A. Lien, F. C. Bretcher and Ralph C. Hoewing.

It was at Freeman Field in September 1945, by now identified as FE-1598, taking part in displays for the aviation press and remained there in flyable condition until allotted to Davis-Monthan AFB, Arizona, in August 1946. It was eventually handed over to the Air Force Museum at Wright-Patterson AFB, Ohio, in January 1966. It remains on display there. Its flight trials at Wright Field are described in report ENG-47-1727A.
(See also entry in Chapter Four under HK959).

(FE-1599) Junkers Ju 88A-4   WNr '4300227'?
This Junkers 88 was captured at Foggia No. 3 (Salsola) airstrip in Italy. It was rebuilt by members of the 86th Fighter Squadron of the 79th Fighter Group as its 'Junk Heap 88' for use as a Squadron 'hack' aircraft. It was identified with the 86th FS badge which included a picture of a Comanche warrior, which remained on the aircraft in the USA. This aircraft was on occasion referred to as *The Comanche* because of this badge. Before the Junkers could be used by the 86th Squadron, it was re-assigned for transfer to Wright Field, and left Salsola for the USA on 19th October 1943. It was piloted by Major Frederic A Borsodi, the former Commander of the 86th FS, who was returning to the US on completion of his tour of duty. The Ju 88 arrived at Wright Field on 5th November 1943. It left Wright Field on 6th February 1944 for de-icing trials at the Materiel Command Ice Research Base, Ladd Field, Minneapolis, Minn. Up to this point it was identified by its reported WNr '4300227'. Later it returned to Wright Field and was then loaned out on War Bond exhibitions. For one such event it was flown to Mines Field, Los Angeles, Ca, and then towed into the city, where it had the misfortune to be hit by a street car, suffering wing and propeller damage. After this event in April 1945 it was ferried back to Wright Field by Captain H. Ray White via Victorville AAF, Albuquerque, NM, and Kansas City, Mo.

By May 1946 it was in store at Freeman Field and was being used as a source of spare parts to service the flyable FE-1598. It was 'awaiting disposition' at Freeman Field on 15th August of the same year. Fate unknown.

FE-2700) Gotha Go 242B-4   **W Nr** *unknown*

This cargo glider was captured in Italy and was repaired by US Forces using components from other Go 242s. It was shipped to the USA and is believed to have been the example received at Wright Field on 27th March 1944. It was shipped to Clinton County Army Air Field for reassembly on 1st April 1944. Clinton County AAF was the satellite base to Wright Field which conducted all test work with troop-carrying gliders. Photographs show that it was named *The Fabric Fortress*. Up to this point, no 'FE-' number was allotted. This aircraft was at Freeman Field on 17th May 1946, by now identified as FE-2700, under restoration for further flight tests. It was transferred to Wright Field in flyable condition during July 1946. Its record card is endorsed 'required for museum 25th September 1946' and it is believed to have been taken to Park Ridge for storage, but its fate is not known.

3.2   JAPANESE AIRCRAFT

**EB-2   Mitsubishi A6M2 'Zeke' Navy Type 0
Carrier Fighter Model 22**

This has been erroneously reported as the original 'Zeke' which was recovered by the US Navy from its crash site on Akutan Island in the Aleutians. (See details in Chapter Seventeen).

However, 'EB-2' was an example, coded 'V-173' of the Tainan Naval Air Corps which force-landed near Teitsan airfield on 17th February 1941. It was made airworthy at Kunming by American engineers under Gerhard Neumann and flown in Chinese markings with the number 'P-5016'. Later in 1941 it was flown to Ran-

goon but returned to Kunming when the RAF was unwilling to assist in shipping the aircraft to the UK or USA. Finally in 1943 it was flown to Karachi for shipment to Wright Field.

EB-2 was with the USAAF at Wright Field, from 13th July 1943, later (by 1st April 1944) becoming EB-200. On 8th October 1943 it was flown to Eglin Field, Florida, for further trials, being flown for 4 hours 50 minutes between its arrival and 11th February 1944, when it was placed in temporary storage. By 1st April 1944, it had flown a total of 31 hours and had returned to Wright Field. It was noted in the list of aircraft available for release to the industry on 10th March 1946, shown as 'EB-2' once more. It is believed that its 'EB-200' identity was never painted on the aircraft.

This aircraft has been reported as on display with the United States' Marine Corps Museum at MCAS Quantico, Virginia, but this is an erroneous report – the aircraft in question is a rebuild of a wrecked 'Zeke' recovered from a Pacific island long after the war.

EB-21   Mitsubishi A6M5 'Zeke' Navy Type 0 Carrier Fighter
This reported allocation may be erroneous.

**(FE-130)   Mitsubishi A6M5 'Zeke' Navy Type 0 Carrier Fighter
(T2-130)   Model 52**
This example was captured at Aslito airfield on the island of Saipan on 18th June 1944 where it had served with the 153rd Naval Air Corps, IJN. The aircraft was shipped to the USA with twelve other 'Zekes' aboard the US escort carrier *Copahee* (CVE-12) in July and sent to NAS Anacostia, which was the base of the main Technical Air Intelligence Center for the evaluation of Japanese aircraft. This example was constructor's number 4340. It was identified as 'TAIC 7' at Anacostia and named *Tokyo Rose*. The 'Zeke' made its first flight at NAS Anacostia on 14th December 1944, flown by Major Farrier (who had earlier flown the A6M3 with the TAIU in Australia). After one further test flight on 21st December, the aircraft was handed over to the USAAF.

The aircraft was flown to Eglin Field, Florida, on 2nd January 1945. The flight was made by Lt Campbell, and the aircraft was to undertake armament tests. The trials involved weapons firing and altogether eighteen flights were made, totalling 32.5 flying hours.

On completion of the trials it was ferried to Dayton AAF (a satellite of Wright Field and now Dayton Municipal Airport). After some further flying at Wright Field and Freeman Field, which increased its flight time to 105 hrs 40 mins, the aircraft was retired on 15th February 1946, when one of its undercarriage legs was noted to be out of alignment.

The 'Zeke' was prepared for storage in March 1946 and by June had been transferred to Park Ridge, Illinois, whence it eventually came to Silver Hill and is now on display in the NASM in Washington, DC. Although the identity 'FE-130' was allocated, it seems that it was never painted on the aircraft.

EB-200   Mitsubishi A6M2 'Zeke' Navy Type 0 Carrier Fighter Model 22   (See EB-2).

EB-201   Mitsubishi A6M3 'Zeke/Hamp' Navy Type 0 Carrier Fighter Model 32

This aircraft was captured at Buna in New Guinea and was restored to flying condition at Eagle Farm, Brisbane, by the TAIU-SWPA. After flight tests by RAAF and USAAF pilots in Australia, as described in Chapter Fourteen, it was shipped to the USA aboard the escort carrier USS *Copahee* (CVE-12), leaving Townsville at the end of September 1943. After maintenance at Oakland, the Hamp was flown to Wright Field by Col J. M. Hayward, Chief of the Technical Data Laboratory.

It was at Wright Field from 1st November 1943. Note - the code name 'Hamp' was later changed to 'Zeke 32'. By March 1944 it had flown 95 hours; including its flights in Australia and a series of seven performance and handling tests carried out by Ralph C. Hoewing in February/March 1944 (totalling 10 hrs 50 mins).

On 10th March, '201 departed to Eglin Field, Florida, for further trials. The results of the trials carried out in Australia and at Wright Field were published in Materiel Command 'AAF Technical Report No. 5115' on 12th June 1944. The data included maximum power performance curves, determined at Brisbane, and normal power curves, measured at Wright Field.

Ralph Hoewing remembers that he really loved to fly this aircraft, once he had squeezed into the rather tight cockpit, and that it was the most manoeuvrable fighter he ever flew, apart from the Lockheed F-80. It performed well at altitudes up to 30,000 feet and had an excellent rate of climb. Its limitations included lack of speed in the dive and lack of manoeuvrability at high speed. It was also lightly constructed and therefore did not stand up well to the impact of .50 calibre bullets. The light construction was evidenced by the progressive wrinkling of the wing skin in a tight turn or in a pull-out from a dive.

The Air Museum at Chino holds parts of a 'Zeke' painted up in the original markings worn by this aircraft at the time of its capture. It is not known if the aircraft is connected with EB-201.

?   Nakajima Ki-43 'Oscar' Army Type 1 Fighter Hayabusa
An example of this type was received at Wright Field on 21st July 1943 from India. It was recorded as 'Inactive' in outdoor storage with the Technical Data Laboratory on 1st April 1944. No 'EB-' or 'FE-' number is shown for this aircraft in the records.

13.3   ITALIAN AIRCRAFT

**EB-300/   Macchi MC 202 Folgore
FE-300**

These allocations are presumed to be the same aircraft; EB-300 is shown as being at Wright Field on 20th August 1943. On 27th March 1944, it was shipped to ASC Tulsa, Oklahoma, for re-assembly and restoration to flying condition. Believed to have returned to Wright Field by 15th May 1944 as FE-300. This aircraft became FE-498. (see Chapter Seventeen).

13.4   OTHER AIRCRAFT

These include aircraft used for museum purposes or for test work which did not involve flight testing.

—   Junkers Ju 87B-2/Trop   W Nr 5954
Coded 'A5+HL' of I/St G1. This Ju 87 was captured in North Africa and was taken to the USA during the war. It is now on display in the Museum of Science and Industry in Chicago. Although in the custody of this Museum, the aircraft was in the 1970s loaned to the Experimental Aircraft Association Museum, Hales Corners, Wisconsin. This Ju 87 was not flown by the USAAF because of engine damage and was almost certainly taken to the United States solely to be displayed as a static exhibit.

Below: **The Zeke 32 EB-201, captured at Buna in New Guinea, pictured in the snow at Wright Field in the winter of 1943/44.** *USAF Museum*

Opposite: **The Macchi MC 202 Folgore EB-300 parked in the static display at Freeman Field during September 1945. This Macchi is the one now on display in the Air and Space Museum in downtown Washington, DC.** *MAP/Real Photos*

— **Messerschmitt Bf 109E-3**   **W Nr 1190**

This Bf 109E, coded 'White 4' of II/JG 26, was shot down at East Dean in Sussex on 30th September 1940. It was sent to Canada, and later the USA, to be displayed in its damaged condition at events which were to raise welfare donations for the civilian population in Britain. Some time after the war, the '109 was held at the Arnprior Research Establishment in Canada. After being examined by the Canadian War Museum and considered to be beyond repair, it was bought by British enthusiasts in 1961 and returned to England. Since then it has gradually been restored, using parts from crash sites and elsewhere, and it still exists in the area of Bournemouth, Dorset, England.

— **Messerschmitt Bf 109E**   **W Nr 36313**

This '109 was recorded with some other examples of the type at No. 13 MU, RAF Henlow, in December 1940. All were presumed to have been shot down in England during the Battle of Britain. This example was delivered to Wright Field USA at the same time as the flyable AE479, presumably to act as a source of spares.

— **Messerschmitt Bf 109G-2/R2**   **W Nr 14329 or 14629**

One Bf 109G shot down in Libya by British forces and later made airworthy by 79th Fighter Group, USAAF, was taken to Wright Field for structural testing. It was in use in the Static Test Building at Wright Field on 1st April 1944. This '109G was named *Irmgard*. It was shot down by machine-gun fire from infantry of the Gordon Highlanders, serving with General Montgomery's British 8th Army, near Zarzis in Tunisia, on 1st March 1943. The aircraft was 'Black 14' of 2 (H)/14, an Army Co-operation Reconnaissance Gruppe. It was being flown by Hauptmann Ehlers, the unit's Staffelkapitan, who was wounded but managed to evade capture and to return to his unit after force-landing in Allied territory.

It was returned to flying condition by personnel of 87th Fighter Squadron, USAAF, which belonged to 79th Fighter Group. The 79th FG squadrons were collectively the most ardent restorers of ex-enemy equipment of all USAAF units in the MTO. After restoration, the '109 wore a British fin flash, American stars on its fuselage and wings, and the individual code 'X8-7'. The unit was based in March 1943 at Causeway Landing Ground, not far from Zarzis.

After a wheels-up landing, the '109 was taken over by the 86th FS (another 79th Group squadron), and acquired its 'Comanche' badge. The aircraft was later ferried to Deversoir in the Suez Canal Zone by Major Frederic Borsodi for onward shipment to the USA. *Irmgard* arrived in the Static Test Building at Wright Field on 1st November 1943. Structural testing began on 27th January 1944 and the final test took place on 13th May 1944. During the tests many components were loaded to destruction and the '109 was no doubt of nothing but scrap value when they were completed.

— **Messerschmitt Bf 110**   **W Nr 3341**

Coded 'S9+CK' of SKG 210. Shipped to the USA in 1941 and sent to Vultee Aircraft for engineering analysis. This aircraft was shot down in England on 15th August, 1940. Fate unknown.

— **Macchi MC 200 Saetta**   **ex MM8146**

The remains of a Macchi MC 200 were owned by the New England Air Museum at Bradley International Airport, Windsor Locks, Connecticut, (Hartford/Springfield Airport). The aircraft was in storage for many years. It came to the USA during the Second World War period, as an exhibition item. It has since been rebuilt to static exhibition standard by Aermacchi in Italy, and returned to the USA for display at the USAF Museum, at Dayton, Ohio.

— **Savoia Marchetti SM 82**   **MM60317**

This three-engined transport aircraft of the Regia Aeronautica was recorded in non-flyable condition at Patterson Field during 1944. It is noted as having been sold as scrap to the Reconstruction Finance Corporation, the US government agency responsible for disposing of war-surplus material, on 26th October 1944. The records also show a Savoia Marchetti SM 72 in non-flyable condition at Patterson Field. This record must be in error, since the SM 72 was an obsolete design produced for China in 1935. Whatever type was involved, there is no evidence that it was flown. The records show a serial number of 32049 for the latter aircraft, which seems not to have been an Italian Air Force 'Matricola Militare' (serial number), although it may well have been the manufacturer's serial number. The aircraft was later recorded at Dallas, Love Field. It was sold as scrap to the Reconstruction Finance Corporation.

Chapter Fourteen

Technical Air Intelligence Units

The United States Navy (USN) bore the brunt of the air war in the Pacific because its aircraft carriers were the main means of bringing the Japanese air forces to combat. It was therefore natural that the USN made a major contribution to the Technical Air Intelligence Centers which were the major evaluation units concerned with flying Japanese aircraft in the USA. The first captured Japanese 'Zero' was flown at NAS North Island, San Diego, and later at other Naval Air Stations, under the aegis of the Air Intelligence organisation at NAS Anacostia. Thereafter it was agreed between the USAAF and USN that the Navy would take the lead in Intelligence relating to aircraft, by heading up the joint intelligence organisation, which also included Allied representation (primarily from the RAF and Royal Navy).

The first Technical Air Intelligence Unit was formed in Australia as a joint USAAF/USN/RAAF organisation. Many of the lessons learned by this Unit enabled the development of a more comprehensive TAI organisation, which was set up in 1944. The staff of the TAIU in Australia was withdrawn to NAS Anacostia, near Washington, DC, to become the 'Technical Air Intelligence Center'. New TAI Units were then set up, covering geographical areas of activity. The sections below start by describing the first TAIU and follow with the TAIC and then the various later TAIUs.

Associated with the TAIUs were the Air Technical Intelligence (ATI) personnel known as 'Crash Intelligence Officers'. Typical of these was Garland Horne, who was one of the first to attend the USAAF intelligence school at Harrisburg, Pa. From there he went to Wright Field for further training, attending lectures and demonstrations in various laboratories relating to airframes, engines, radio, electronics, armaments etc for both US and foreign aircraft. The sessions included examination of a Messerschmitt Bf 109 looking for 'clues' such as airframe and equipment data plates and other information relevant to the task.

After 'graduating' Garland Horne went to England, assigned to the 9th AAF and received further training at RAE Farnborough and 'on the job' with his British counterparts in the Air Ministry's AI2(g) section. In July 1944 he went to France as a member of one of the crash intelligence teams attached to the US 3rd Army. In Europe there were no TAIUs as such – the ATI personnel reported to central points and all equipment of interest was shipped to the RAE at Farnborough for evaluation in preference to going to the USA.

14.1   **TECHNICAL AIR INTELLIGENCE IN AUSTRALIA 1942-1944**

The Technical Air Intelligence Unit (TAIU) South-West Pacific Area was formed at Melbourne in Australia, later moving to Brisbane. It was an Allied unit, staffed by personnel from the US 5th AAF, the US Navy and the Royal Australian Air Force, and commanded by Capt Frank T. McCoy of the USAAF.

At Brisbane the Unit started to rebuild captured Japanese aircraft in Hangar 7 at Eagle Farm airfield (now Brisbane Airport). These aircraft were identified with numbers 'XJ 001' onwards (XJ – Experimental Japanese).

This unit was the first TAIU and many of its staff were withdrawn to the USA to form the TAIC at NAS Anacostia in 1944. In the meantime, the staff in Australia had pioneered many Technical Intelligence activities and learned many lessons which were applied to the whole Air Intelligence effort. The best-remembered of the pioneer initiatives is the Allied Code Name System, originally known as the MacArthur South-West Pacific Code Name System, by which we still recognise Japanese Second World War aircraft today. This system, invented in July 1942 by T/Sgt Francis Williams of the USAAF, provided easily-remembered nicknames for aircraft types identified in combat or from reconnaissance photographs. These names provided a ready means of transmitting information on Japanese aircraft, even if their true designations were unknown to the Allies. The same concept is used by NATO today in identifying aircraft of the former Warsaw Pact.

Thus, 'Zeke' and 'Dinah' owe their nicknames to the TAIU. Under the system, male first names were given to fighters, female first names to bombers, flying-boats and reconnaissance types. Transport types had names beginning with the letter 'T', while trainers were named after trees, and gliders after birds. The 'hillbilly' names, such as 'Zeke', 'Rufe', 'Nate' and so on, derived from the Tennessee background of the Unit CO, Capt Frank McCoy. When the TAIC was formed at Anacostia, control of the system was transferred to this new unit.

The Code Name System was combined with a 'Field Name' System, which had previously been used by the RAF in Europe. Once a new aircraft type was identified (or suspected) on the basis of reconnaissance photographs, it was allotted a provisional name, e.g. 'Omura Field 31', based on the location where the photograph was taken plus the estimated wing span of the aircraft (in feet). Once the photographs, and silhouettes prepared from them, could be related to captured documents, aircraft, components, or other data which confirmed the identity of the type, a 'Code Name' was allocated.

Note: Strictly speaking, the Allied code-name system was invented by T/Sgt Williams, Capt McCoy and Corporal Joseph Grattan when they were members of the Directorate of Intelligence, HQ Allied Air Forces, some time before the TAIU was set up. All three men later transferred to the TAIU.

Opposite top: **The Junkers Ju 87B Stuka in the EAA Museum, Hales Corners, Wisconsin in July 1974. This aircraft has now returned to the Museum of Science and Industry in Chicago.** *P. H. Butler collection*

Opposite: **Evidence that not all captured aircraft were flown is this photograph of Bf 109G 'Irmgard' in a structural test rig at Wright Field.** *USAF Museum* (see Chapter Fifteen for detailed history)

Known identity numbers used by the TAIC in Australia are:

XJ 001   Mitsubishi A6M3 'Zeke' Navy Type 0
Carrier Fighter Model 32 C/n 3030

This number was retrospectively allocated to the first aircraft flown by the unit (although it was never painted on the aircraft). The 'Zeke' was rebuilt using parts of five different aircraft captured at Buna in New Guinea on 27th December 1942 and these items were shipped to Brisbane, arriving there on 19th February. The aircraft, when captured, had the tail code 'V-190' and the number '874' on the rear fuselage.

The aircraft belonged to the Tainan Naval Air Corps and the rear fuselage number '874' related to its presentation to the IJN by fund raisers in Japan (other examples captured at the same airfield were similarly numbered '872' and '873').

The rebuilt aircraft used the fuselage of construction number 3030 with some items from number 3032. The first test flight after repair was made at Eagle Farm on 20th July 1943. Some of the first flights on this aircraft were carried out at RAAF Base Laverton by S/Ldr D. R. Cuming of the RAAF Special Duties and Performance Flight. Some difficulties were experienced due to unserviceable wheel brakes: because of this all taxying was done at slow speeds with the aid of ground handling staff, and all landings were done 'tail-up' to maintain rudder control. On 14th, 17th and 18th August 1943, the trials included mock combats between the 'Zeke' and a Spitfire Vc, flown by S/Ldr Les Jackson and F/Lt C. R. Wawn of the RAAF, respectively. These flights were made at Eagle Farm and they concluded that the 'Zeke' was superior to the Spitfire V below 20,000 feet and that the Spitfire must maintain a minimum speed of 250 mph to keep its manoeuvrability advantage.

Extensive reports of the tests carried out were published in October 1943, while a detailed report on the recovery and reconstruction of the aircraft, Technical Intelligence Report No. 163, was issued on 16th September 1943. In the meantime the 'Zeke' had been shipped from Townsville to the USA aboard the escort carrier USS *Copahee* (CVE-12). Upon arrival in the USA it went to Wright Field and was flown there with the identity EB-201 (which see in Chapter Thirteen).

XJ 002   Nakajima Ki-43-I 'Oscar' Army Type 1
Fighter Model 1 Hayabusa

This 'Oscar' was captured at Lae in New Guinea on 16th September 1943. It was shipped to Brisbane, arriving on 4th November 1943, and made its first flight at Eagle Farm on 17th March 1944, piloted by Capt William O. Farrior, USAAF. The initial performance test flights, totalling 5 hrs 30 minutes, were carried out by S/Ldr D. R. Cuming of No. 1 Aircraft Performance Unit from RAAF Laverton. The results of the tests were recorded in a report dated 3rd April 1944. A further series of flights was then made to compare the 'Oscar' in combat with various Allied fighter types, these tests being completed by 27th April 1944.

Technical Intelligence Report No. 221 of 27th April 1944 described the recovery and reconstruction of this aircraft.

XJ 003   Kawasaki Ki-61-Ia 'Tony' Army Type 3 Fighter Hien

This 'Tony' was captured at Cape Gloucester in New Britain. Three flights were made at Eagle Farm by S/Ldr D. R. Cuming from No. 1 Aircraft Performance Unit, based at RAAF Laverton. It had been intended to carry out tactical trials against the P-38, P-40, P-47 and Spitfire VIII, but the series of flights was terminated after bearing metal was found in the engine oil filter following the third flight. The test results were recorded in a test report dated 10th July 1944.

This example was later shipped to NAS Anacostia. It was later the example identified as 'TAIC 9' at Anacostia. This aircraft, when captured, was identified by the number '263' on its fin and this number, believed to have been the manufacturer's construction number, was painted on 'TAIC 9', which see, below.

XJ 004   *unknown*

(Possibly the 'Dinah' captured at Hollandia which later became 'TAIC 10').

XJ 005   Nakajima Ki-43-II 'Oscar' Army Type 1
Fighter Model 2 Hayabusa

This example was captured at Hollandia in New Guinea in May 1944 and was test flown in Australia. Fate unknown, but it may be the example which still exists in Australia (see Chapter Twenty One).

In June 1944 this unit was transferred to NAS Anacostia, where its personnel became the cadre for the TAIC.

14.2   **TECHNICAL AIR INTELLIGENCE CENTER (TAIC) NAS ANACOSTIA**

The TAIC was set up at NAS Anacostia with the aim of combining the expertise of the original Australian-based TAIU members with more immediate access to the intelligence resources concentrated around the US government centers in Washington, DC. The Center was a centralised joint services organisation, under the US Division of Naval Intelligence, but incorporating USAAF and Allied personnel. The TAIC included a 'Captured Enemy Aircraft Unit' (CEAU) which was concerned with rebuilding and maintaining German and Japanese aircraft selected for evaluation at US Navy establishments.

The functions of the TAIC were:

1   To receive, evaluate and analyse all intelligence reports, despatches, photographs, etc., relating to enemy air equipment.
2   To determine Japanese airplane and engine performance data.
3   To prepare master drawings, silhouettes, sketches and models for use in recognition training, and in the development of performance data.
4   To receive, catalogue, examine, overhaul, and rebuild captured airplanes, engines, and air equipment as necessary, and to arrange for or conduct required tests.
5   To produce and issue timely and useful technical air intelligence summaries and reports for dissemination to the Allied military services and government agencies.

In practice, many of the tests were delegated to NAS Patuxent River in nearby Maryland, which was the central site for test and evaluation of new Navy aircraft and equipment. NAS Patuxent River was a new Naval Air Station whose construction began on 4th April 1942. It was commissioned on 1st April 1943 as a central site for Navy test and evaluation work. Initially the Station included Flight Test, Radio Test and Aircraft Armament Divisions, with the addition of the Aircraft Experimental Development Squadron (AEDS) transferred from NAS Anacostia.

In March 1944 the AEDS was decommissioned and its personnel re-assigned to become the Tactical Test Division under Cdr Jay Anderson as director. Under the director were a number of project officers, including Lt Clyde C. Andrews who looked after fighter projects and Lt/Cdr 'Bert' Earnest who was responsible for torpedo aircraft.

During the war, Tactical Test was responsible for the comparative evaluations of Navy aircraft against captured enemy aircraft. After hostilities ceased, what flying was done of ex-enemy aircraft was carried out by the Flight Test Division. Some ex-enemy aircraft were held by the Tactical Test Division after the war but they were used for ground-based evaluations rather than flight.

Post-war a batch of German aircraft evaluated by the USN at NAS Patuxent River was allotted USN Bureau of Aeronautics' serial numbers but none of the other aircraft evaluated received official 'BuAer' numbers. However, often the manufacturer's construction numbers were recorded in pilots' log books and in official reports in lieu of 'BuAer' serial numbers.

Aircraft flown by the TAIC were identified by 'tail numbers' prefixed by the unit's title, as indicated below:

TAIC 1   Mitsubishi A6M2 'Zeke' Navy Type 0
Carrier Fighter Model 21   C/n 4593

This was the Mitsubishi A6M2 'Zeke' which force-landed on Akutan Island in the Aleutians on 4th June 1942. It had been taking part in a Japanese attack on the US base at Dutch Harbor, carried out by aircraft from the carrier *Ryujo*. The aircraft received battle-damage and made a forced-landing, the pilot being killed when the aircraft overturned in soft ground. On 10th July 1942 the 'Zeke' was sighted by a USN Consolidated PBY reconnaissance flying boat and plans for its salvage were set in train. The aircraft, serial number 4593, was coded 'DI-108', indicating an aircraft of the first aircraft-carrier of the Fourth Koku Sentai. This particular 'Zeke' had been accepted for IJN service on 19th February 1942.

The aircraft was shipped to Dutch Harbor and then to San Diego, California, where it was received on 12th August 1942. It was re-assembled and repaired at NAS North Island, where it made its first flight on 26th September 1942. During September and October 1942, twenty flights were made to establish its performance figures and to compare its dogfighting characteristics with the Grumman F4F and Chance-Vought F4U. In addition, USAAF pilots from the Proving Ground Group at Eglin Field, Florida, were involved in the North Island trials, flying P-38F, P-39D, P-40F and P-51 aircraft. The USN trials were conducted by Lt/Cdr E. R. Sanders, under the cognisance of the Test Section of NAS Anacostia. The section at Anacostia became the basis of the USN (and later Joint Service) Air Technical Intelligence organisation. This aircraft was later identified as 'TAIC 1' on its fin, following the formation of the TAIC in 1944.

Although it has been reported that this aircraft was later transferred to the USAAF and became 'EB-2' at Wright Field, there were detailed differences between these two aircraft, and their subsequent histories are not consistent with this report. (See 'EB-2' in Chapter 13).

After its initial trials at NAS North Island, the 'Zeke' was ferried to NAS Anacostia. It was test flown there for a period, by Lt/Cdr Charles 'Tommy' Booth, Chief of the Test Section prior to the TAIC being set up, until damaged in a landing accident at Greensville, NC, on 5th January 1943.

No further record has been found for No. 4593 until a flight made by Lt Clyde C. Andrews from Anacostia to Andrews AFB on 23rd August 1944. This had been intended as a delivery flight to Patuxent River, but the pilot was forced to make a dead-stick landing at Andrews after engine failure. No. 4593 was flown onwards to Patuxent River on 24th August, and two further test flights were made at Patuxent River on 28th and 29th August.

By 14th September 1944, No. 4593 was at NAS North Island, San Diego, when it was flown by W. N. Leonard, who was Carrier Fighter Training Officer there. Leonard made six flights in the aircraft in the period to 25th October, after which he was posted to join Task Force 38 in the Pacific. His flights included a test against an F6F on 19th September and a dogfight with a Grumman FM-2 on 21st October. On about 10th February 1945, No. 4593 was being taxied at NAS North Island by Cdr Richard Crommelin when it was in collision with a Curtiss SB2C Helldiver. The SB2C suffered from very poor forward visibility on the ground and its pilot failed to see the 'Zeke' until his propeller chopped pieces off its fuselage. The 'Zeke' was damaged beyond repair and was subsequently scrapped, apart from a wing-tip and some instruments which are now in the Navy Museum at the Washington Navy Yard, Washington, DC.

TAIC 2   Aircraft with these numbers have not been traced, but
TAIC 3   it is probable that one was the Focke Wulf Fw 190
TAIC 4   detailed at the end of the section, and that the others
were an Aichi E13A 'Jake' Navy Type 0 Reconnaissance Seaplane and Nakajima A6M2-N 'Rufe' Navy Type 2 Fighter Seaplane known to have been at Anacostia. The 'Jake' is believed to have been a Watanabe-built example, c/no 3167, found in wrecked condition at Chichagof Harbor, Attu, in the Aleutian Islands in June 1943.

TAIC 5   Mitsubishi A6M5 'Zeke' Navy Type 0
Carrier Fighter Model 52   C/n 5357

This example was one of those captured on Saipan on June 18th, 1944. It was coded '61-120', indicating it to be an aircraft of 261st Naval Air Corps, one of the two Saipan-based IJN fighter units. It was shipped to the USA aboard the USS *Copahee* (CVE-12), arriving at San Diego on July 16th, 1944. It was made airworthy at NAS North Island and made its first flight in the United States on 5th August. On 22nd August, it was ferried to NAS Anacostia, and on the following day it was flown to NAS Patuxent River by Cdr Fitzhugh L. Palmer, the project pilot. At this point it was identified as 'TAIC 5'.

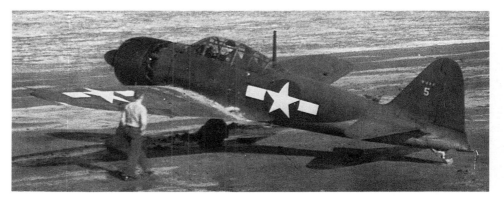

This photograph of 'Zeke' TAIC 5 is believed to have been taken at Anacostia.
John Underwood collection

On 6th September 1944 it was flown by Clyde C. Andrews. During September and October 1944, No. 5357 was flown on seventeen occasions by Andrews, totalling 21.5 flying hours. He then flew the Supermarine Seafire, Lockheed P-38, Bell P-63, N A P-51, Republic P-47, Grumman F7F and Chance-Vought F4U to compare them with the 'Zeke'. On 23rd October 1944, Andrews checked out Charles Lindbergh in the 'Zeke 52' and he continued the test programme. Later the 'Zeke' was flown by many other pilots, including C. L. Sharp and R. H. Burroughs (Chance-Vought test pilots), Jack Woolams (Bell test pilot), C. H. Meyers (Grumman test pilot) and others. Military pilots involved included Lts Herbert Jay and J. Michael Kirchberg, USNR, and Maj F. E. 'Al' Hollar, USMC.

After the completion of trials, No. 5357 was ferried back to NAS Anacostia on 30th November 1944. On 6th December, it was flown to NAS North Island, to be used in the training of USN fighter pilots about to be posted to the Pacific war zone. It was flown there by William N. Leonard on 19th February 1945 and again on 19th and 20th March 1945. On the latter dates affiliation exercises were flown against a USN Convair PB4Y-2. By the end of September 1945, No. 5357 had logged over 190 hours. It was flown to NAS Alameda on 30th September 1945 and was declared surplus to requirements not long thereafter.

It was eventually purchased by Ed Maloney and became one of the exhibits of his Air Museum. In 1973 work commenced to make the 'Zeke' airworthy once more and this eventually resulted in the first flight after restoration being made on 28th June 1978. No. 5357 is still in the Air Museum, now at Chino airfield, California, and is still owned by Ed Maloney. It is in flying condition and has the US civil registration marks NX46770.

TAIC 6   Nakajima B5N2 'Kate' Navy Type 97
Carrier Attack Bomber Model 12   C/n 2194

This 'Kate' was captured on Saipan in June 1944 and taken to the USA aboard the USS *Copahee*. This example was manufactured in December 1943. It was equipped with ASV radar. The first test flight after overhaul was made on 16th November 1944. The early test flights were aimed at evaluating the performance of the radar equipment. This was done by flight tests with US Naval vessels off the Delaware coastline, to determine its range and effectiveness, with the equipment being operated by an experienced radar technician from the Naval Radio Laboratory. These tests were so

urgent that they commenced on 16th November 1944, on the same day as the airworthiness test of the aircraft. After this test series was completed, comparative flying trials were made with the Grumman TBM-1c and TBM-3 Avenger and the Curtiss SB2C-4 Helldiver and the aircraft was flown in mock combat against current USN fighter aircraft. Most of the flights on this aircraft were made from NAS Patuxent River by Lt/Cdr A. K. 'Bert' Earnest. 23.5 hours were flown on radar trials from Anacostia during November 1944, following which the 'Kate' was delivered to Patuxent River on 13th December. A further 12.4 flying hours were accumulated by 'Bert' Earnest between December 1944 and April 1945 with the Tactical Test Division during the comparative trials, before the aircraft flew back to Anacostia on 27th April 1945.

In October 1945, the 'Kate', and a 'Zeke 52' also from the TAIC at Anacostia, were attached to a group known as 'The Navy's Flying Might'. This unit, under the command of Lt/Cdr Willard E. Elder, was set up as a travelling display to take part in nationwide Victory Loan promotions across the USA. The 'Kate' was flown to NAS Wildwood to join this unit and it took part in a number of displays at various locations across the USA. Thereafter, the history of the 'Kate' becomes obscure, although it is believed to be the aircraft which appeared on static display during an Air Fair at Omaha in July 1946.

TAIC 7   Mitsubishi A6M5 'Zeke' Navy Type 0
Carrier Fighter Model 52   C/n 4340

Captured on Saipan (see FE/T2-130 in Chapter Eighteen). It was being made airworthy at NAS Anacostia during December 1944 and later flew with the USAAF at Wright Field. It was named *Tokyo Rose*. It is the example now in the NASM at Washington, DC.

TAIC 8   Mitsubishi A6M5 'Zeke' Navy Type 0
Carrier Fighter Model 52   C/n 2193

Captured on Saipan. In use during April 1945, allotted to 412th Fighter Group US 4th AAF, based at Bakersfield Municipal Airport, Ca., the training and trials Group for the Bell P-59 Airacomet and Lockheed P-80 Shooting Star jet fighters.

TAIC 9   Kawasaki Ki-61-1a 'Tony' Army Type 3 Fighter Hien
C/n 263

For details see 'XJ-003', above. After shipment from Australia, this aircraft was made airworthy again at NAS Anacostia. The Project Pilot for this aircraft was Lt John A. Thomas. Lt/Cdr 'Bert' Earnest flew this aircraft at NAS Patuxent River on 1st June 1945. On 2nd July 1945 the engine failed during a ferry flight with Lt Thomas as the pilot, and the aircraft was written off in the subsequent belly landing at Yanceyville, NC, *en route* from Patuxent to Eglin.

TAIC 10   Mitsubishi Ki-46-II 'Dinah' Army Type 100
Command Reconnaissance Plane   C/n 2846

Captured at Hollandia, New Guinea, and made airworthy in September 1944. This aircraft was made airworthy by personnel of 13th Bomb Squadron, 3rd Bomb Group, which brought its Douglas A-20s to Hollandia on 12th May 1944. The aircraft was later flown at NAS Anacostia, NAS Patuxent River and at Eglin Field in Florida on armament trials with the USAAF Proving Ground Command. It was at Eglin during April 1945.

TAIC 11   Mitsubishi A6M5 'Zeke' Navy Type 0
Carrier Fighter Model 52   C/n 1303

Painted silver overall, with British national markings, this was one of the Saipan aircraft. It was restored to flying condition at Anacostia and by April 1945 had been allotted to the ATAIU in India.

The Nakajima B5N2 'Kate' TAIC 6 at NAS Anacostia. The Japanese 'meatball' insignia has been reapplied over the US national markings for recognition photographs to be taken. *US National Archives*

The Kawasaki Ki-61-1a 'Tony' TAIC 9, captured at Cape Gloucester and flown in Australia before arriving at NAS Anacostia where this photograph was taken. *US National Archives, 80G-126187*

The 'Zeke 52' TAIC 7 *Tokyo Rose*. The Japanese insignia has been applied for recognition photographs to be taken and the constructor's number '4340' appears on the fuselage. *US National Archives*

The 'Zeke 52' TAIC 11 photographed at the end of the war in a line-up of Japanese and American aircraft. The British markings are unusual for a TAIC aircraft but emphasise Allied participation in the Center – the legend 'A I 2G' (the British Air Ministry section responsible for German and Japanese Air Intelligence) appears below the cockpit. This Zeke was due to be transferred to the ATAIU operated by the RAF in India. *US National Archives, 80G-192152*

Aircraft for which the TAIC identity is untraced:

—   **Focke Wulf Fw 190A-4**   **W Nr 160057**

Also referred to as 'CEE No. 2900'. This example was one of two captured at Gerbini in Sicily by the 85th Fighter Squadron of the 79th Fighter Group, USAAF, in September 1943. On 19th November 1943 it was flown from Foggia No. 3/Salsola to Bari for shipment to NAS Anacostia where it arrived on 24th January 1944. Repairs were completed on 22nd February 1944 and the aircraft was flown to NAS Patuxent River (a flight of 1 hour) by Lt C. C. Andrews, USN, on 25th February. Here it was flown by the Tactical Test Division in comparative trials with the Chance-Vought F4U-1 Corsair and Grumman F6F-3 Hellcat. Flights from Patuxent River by Lt (later Rear Admiral) Andrews totalled 9.7 hours and the aircraft was also flown by other pilots, under Project no. PTR-1107.

The results of the tests were recorded in Captured Aircraft Equipment Report No. 14, published in April 1944. The Project Pilots were Lt Andrews, Lt H. M. Jay and Lt/Cdr F. L. Palmer. The report recorded exhaustive tests on the Focke Wulf, including comparative rates of climb, speeds, accelerations, rates of roll, turning circles, manoeuvrability, stability and control in dives, control forces, cockpit visibility, etc. The report concluded by suggesting tactics to be used by F6F and F4U pilots in combat with the Fw 190. It was suggested that, if attacked by a '190, the F6F and F4U could evade by use of tight turns, followed by tight loops.

There are a number of other aircraft known to be operated by the TAIC for which no 'tailnumbers' are known. They include a 'Zeke 52' identified by the number '29' which appeared in publicity photographs in early 1945 (This may be TAIC 8, after transfer to the USAAF).

Another example is a 'Zeke 52' which was transferred from the TAIC to a group called 'The Navy's Flying Might' at NAS Wildwood in October 1945. This unit was concerned with providing air shows at locations across America in aid of Victory Loan promotions. The 'Zeke' assigned to this unit suffered a ground-loop while landing at NAS Atlanta, Ga. The remains of this aircraft survived for many years at an antiques' business in Peachtree Street, Atlanta, Ga. Since sold to R. D. Wittington, Ft Lauderdale, Fl; it may be C/n 5356 (see next paragraph).

In April 1945 work was still proceeding on an old Zeke Model 21 (C/n 2284) and a newer Model 52 (C/n 4523) to make them airworthy at Anacostia. In addition to the TAIC aircraft which were test flown, several non-repairable Zekes had been allocated to other uses. C/n 5356 had been allotted for shipment to England; C/n 8221 had gone to Wright Field for structural tests; C/n 2183 had been sent to the Douglas Aircraft Company Inc. for structural analysis. C/ns 4388 and 4437 had gone to the Ford Motor Company, probably for analysis of production engineering aspects. A further seven Zeke Model 52s were on hand to provide spares or to use for exhibiting in 'War Bond Drives' and recruiting displays.

Finally Zeke C/n 4361, the first Saipan capture to be made airworthy, was written-off when it ground looped at El Paso, Tx, on 10th August 1944 while *en route* to Anacostia.

Above: **The so-far unidentified 'Zeke 52' marked as '29', during the production of aircraft recognition photographs early in 1945. The US star on the fuselage and a TAIC serial number on its fin have been overpainted for the occasion. This aircraft may be TAIC 8.** *US National Archives, 80G-248975*

Opposite: **The US Navy's Focke Wulf Fw 190A W Nr 160057 photographed on a flight near NAS Anacostia.** *US National Archives, 80G-105758*

14.3   **THE LATER TAIUs**

Technical Air Intelligence Units, as finally constituted, were the working field arms of the TAIC described above. The TAIUs were formed in each theatre of war, with the following functions:
1   To take possession, control, examine, and make interim reports on all Japanese Air Force equipment (except bombs, mines and torpedoes).
2   To arrange for packing and shipment of such material to interested agencies as required.
3   To be responsible, within their theatre of operations, for collection and dissemination of all technical intelligence on the Japanese Air Forces.

Field TAI Units were headed by trained TAI officers and included aviation mechanics, photographers, radio and ordnance specialists and Japanese translators. They were equipped to travel into any kind of territory and make use of all available types of transportation and native help.

The biggest obstacle to obtaining complete intelligence information was 'souveniring' by the troops finding crashed or captured aircraft. It was therefore the responsibility of local Commanding Officers and their own non-specialist intelligence officers to notify their TAIU of crash locations as soon as possible and to post guards on any material found. To promote the co-operation of the

troops, instructions were given for 'souvenir' material to be returned to the 'finder' after its use by the TAIU had been completed. It was found that the guards placed on aircraft were often the main culprits when it came to 'souveniring', and disciplinary action often ensued.

The instructions to Intelligence officers included as the first priorities the taking of a comprehensive set of photographs of any material found, followed by the removal of any makers' plates. The plates were to be identified with the location on the aircraft from which they were taken, the type and serial number of the aircraft and the date and place of crash or capture. Most of the intelligence effort was of course expended during the fighting in picking up clues from crashed aircraft to determine unit strengths, production figures and the technical features of new types of aircraft, or of new equipment fitted to familiar types.

There were four TAIUs, as follows:

ATAIU-SEA: Allied TAIU, South-East Asia.
An RAF/USAAF unit covering India, Burma, Malaya, Singapore, etc, formed at Calcutta in 1943. This unit moved to Singapore in September 1945 and shortly afterwards established a flying unit at Tebrau in Malaya to evaluate captured aircraft, which were flown in RAF markings. (See Chapter Eleven for details).

TAIU-SWPA: TAIU-South-West Pacific Area.
Originally formed in Australia in 1943. Personnel of this Unit started the Allied Code Name system for the identification of Japanese aircraft, which later became standardised across all Allied commands - i.e., the series of names, such as 'Zeke' for the Mitsubishi Type 0. The members of this unit rebuilt aircraft captured in New Guinea at Brisbane in Australia and carried out flight tests. The US personnel of this Unit were withdrawn to NAS Anacostia in July 1944 to become the TAIC. A reformed TAIU-SWPA operated thereafter and was flown to the Philippines after US forces landed there in 1945. This unit established a flight test section at Clark Field, Manila, which operated until the surrender of Japan.

Above: **Zekes on the flight deck of USS *Copahee*.**
US National Archives, 80G-276964

Right: **Captured aircraft at Clark Field. Amongst the wreckage and cannibalised parts are four Japanese aircraft wearing US markings.**
USAF Museum, Brundage collection

TAIU-POA: TAIU-Pacific Ocean Area.

This was the Unit responsible for work on the never-ending succession of Pacific Islands captured by US forces. So far as is known, this Unit never flew any Japanese aircraft on its own account.

The TAIU-POA's main claim to fame was the recovery of the first 'Zeke 52' and the first 'Kate' to be captured. These achievements took place with the capture of Aslito airfield on Saipan, one of the Mariana Islands, on 18th June 1944.

These aircraft were shipped to the USA aboard the escort carrier USS *Copahee*, which left the Garapan anchorage off Saipan on 8th July, and unloaded its cargo of fourteen Japanese aircraft and thirty-seven engines at NAS North Island, San Diego, on 28th July. The aircraft were thirteen 'Zekes', in various states of disrepair, and the 'Kate'. The aircraft were then taken to NAS Anacostia, where a number were restored to flying condition by the TAIC, as described above.

TAIU-CHINA:

Operated in areas of China under the control of the Nationalist Chinese regime of General Chiang Kai-Shek. So far as is known, the only aircraft found in China flown by the Air Intelligence organisation was the Mitsubishi A6M2 'Zeke' rebuilt at Kunming and later shipped to Wright Field (see history of 'EB-2' in Chapter Thirteen). This took place some time before TAIU-China was formed as a separate organisation.

Technical Air Intelligence teams operating in the field often consisted of three to four men living very closely with the front-line troops and linked by radio to their headquarters.

The experiences of Lt/Col Harry B. Smith of Rogers, Arkansas, a former TAI officer with ATAIU-SEA, are probably typical:

'I was a TAI Officer with the ATAIU in South-East Asia from the summer of 1944 to the end of the war, and then with the aircraft collection team in Japan from September to November 1945.'

'The Unit in South-East Asia was made up of RAF, USN and USAAF personnel. Our commander was Squadron Leader Chris Glover, RAAF, (although he was a New Zealander by nationality). We were directly subordinate to the Head of Intelligence for the South-East Asia Command. In field operations we were generally divided into units of three-to-four, in each case trying to get an even mix of the services involved. All team commanders carried a pass signed personally by Mountbatten, requiring co-operation and logistic support wherever we went. In fact it was seldom necessary to use it; I don't recall using mine.

'For my own part, I started out with the US 10th Air Force HQ in Kanjikoah, Upper Assam, India. After a few weeks, I was transferred to Myitkyina in Burma to get closer to the action whereby some Japanese equipment might come into our possession.

'This proved ineffective so shortly our team moved south to Bhamo. From here I was recalled to Calcutta to make a new team to accompany the Indian 14th Army advance into central Burma. We attached ourselves to Nos 34 and 113 Squadrons of the RAF for rations and support. I have very fond memories of those few weeks, though I pale at the thought of bully-beef and cheese for Christmas Dinner 1944, at Yazagyo, Burma.

'The situation unfolded more rapidly than expected and we soon had to leave to stay in close contact with the advancing Indian troops. We had long ago learned that captured enemy equipment would be stripped almost literally overnight by souvenir hunters, be they British, American or Indian. It was heavy going over the Naga hills, the only road was a slash made by tank dozers through the jungle. On one occasion, for example, it took twenty-six continuous hours of brutal effort for us to advance seventy-five miles. The road was nothing but mud. Our procedure, in large part, was to start sliding down a hill with all brakes set. Finally, bumping to a stop at the bottom, we would run out the winch cable to the top of the next hill, loop it around a handy tree, and winch ourselves to the top, only to repeat it all over again at the next hill. We finally emerged at Shwebo on the plains before Mandalay. From Shwebo, I returned to Calcutta escorting a Japanese engine in fair condition aboard a combat-cargo C-47.

'It was a quick turn around and back to Bhamo with a new team. We attached ourselves to the Chinese 1st Army under General Sun-Li-Jen and advanced south. Our team this time was only me and an RAF NCO, Bob Ramsey from Dundee. We stayed with the Chinese, depending on the American Mars Task Force for support, until we reached Maymyo. At that point, the Chinese were held up by diplomatic agreement and withdrew back to China.

'In the meantime the 14th Army had captured Mandalay and proceeded south towards Rangoon. We went with them, using the west road along the Irrawaddy through Yenan-gyaung and Prome. The Japanese drifted eastwards towards the Shan states and Thailand. Meanwhile the paratroop drop and seaborne assault on Rangoon outflanked them. The road seemed open for us to proceed and join up with our teams in Rangoon. After a wild drive we eventually met up with a group of grim-faced Indian sol-

diers, all training their weapons on us, on the outskirts of the city.

'After one more fruitless trip into Burma, on VJ-Day we were in the assembly area in Rangoon waiting to board transports in the harbour for the invasion of Malaya. We clambered aboard the transports from lighters and departed for Singapore. When we eventually landed in Singapore the Japanese were still fully under arms and were surly and belligerent.

'We made our centre of operations in the terminal of the International Airport (Kallang). We were able to present to the RAF Group Captain commanding the field a brand-new 'Tojo' fighter of his very own. He had great fun flying it as long as they let him have it! I only spent a week and a half in Singapore before I was ordered back to Calcutta to fly to Japan and take part in the collection programme planned for there.

'We were formed into teams now consisting only of USAAF and USN personnel, each assigned to a specific geographic area. My team had eastern Honshu from about Mito to Tsu, south of Nagoya. Each team had a Japanese Air Force liaison officer and a Nisei American as interpreter. We were to select and escort four first-class examples of every known Japanese aircraft – singles where they were experimental – to Yokosuka for loading on the carriers. We had many interesting experiences, some hard to believe.

'In November 1945 I was assigned as an escort officer for the second carrier load to be returned to the United States. Our ship was the USS *Core*; all the planes on the *Core* were consigned to Freeman Field for flight testing. As I understand it, the programme petered out early in 1946 and only some planes were test flown.'

14.4   **TECHNICAL AIR INTELLIGENCE UNIT
        IN THE PHILIPPENES – 1945**

TAIU-SWPA:

By February 1945 the reformed TAIU South-West Pacific Area was operating at Clark Field, north of Manila in the Philippines. Aircraft tested by this unit were identified with the legend 'Tech Air Intel S W P A' and in many cases had an identity consisting of the letter 'S' followed by a number. Known examples are listed below. Although the unit operated in the Philippines, several of the aircraft were later taken to the USA. This unit was commanded by Capt Theodore T. Brundage, USAAF.

Known examples are:

7   **Kawanishi N1K1-J 'George'
        Navy Interceptor Fighter Shiden Model 11**

This aircraft, coded '23' of the 341st Kokutai, was abandoned by the Japanese at Clark Field and taken over by the TAIU/SWPA. It was probably the example flown once by the TAIU and damaged beyond repair on its first landing by a collapse of its main undercarriage. This problem was endemic to the N1K1-J design, arising from the addition of a conventional land undercarriage on an aircraft originally designed as a float-seaplane.

S9   **Kawanishi N1K1-J 'George'
        Navy Interceptor Fighter Shiden Model 11**

No details known, except that the aircraft was flown at Clark Field.

S10   **Nakajima Ki-84 'Frank' Army Type 4 Fighter Hayate**

This aircraft was captured at Clark Field and later crashed there following a test flight.

S11   **Nakajima Ki-44-II 'Tojo' Army Type 2
        Single-seat Fighter Shoki**

The constructor's number of this aircraft was 2068. Believed to have crashed at Clark Field during June 1945.

Top: **The Kawanishi N1K1-J 'George' marked as '7' at Clark Field. The prefix 'S' was added to later numbers in the series of identities.** *NASM*

Above: **The Nakajima Ki-84 'Frank' 'S10' at Clark Field.** *USAF Museum*

Below: **The Nakajima Ki-44-II 'Tojo' 'S11' at Clark Field.** *USAF Museum*

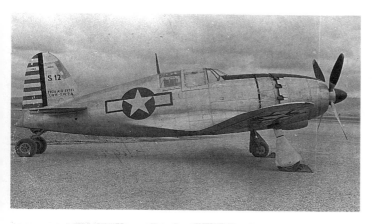

Top: **The Mitsubishi J2M3 'Jack' 'S12' at Clark Field.** *USAF Museum*

Above: **The Kawasaki Ki-45-KAI 'Nick' 'S14' at Clark Field.** *USAF Museum*

Below: **The Nakajima Ki-84 'Frank' 'S17' on board the escort-carrier USS *Long Island* en route to the USA.** *US National Archives, 80G-413478*

S12   Mitsubishi J2M3 'Jack'
Navy Interceptor Fighter Raiden Model 21
The C/n of this aircraft was 3008. It was captured in Dewey Boulevard, Manila, which was being used as an emergency airstrip by the Japanese, and taken to Clark Field. It made two test flights totalling 3 hours 20 minutes from there. On its second flight the main oil delivery hose failed, causing the engine to seize.

S14   Kawasaki Ki-45 KAIc 'Nick' Army Type 2
Two-seat Fighter Toryu Model C
The C/n of this aircraft was 3303. This aircraft was shipped to the USA after being test flown at Clark Field.

S15   Showa L2D3 'Tabby' Navy Type 0
Transport Model 22
This was a Japanese-built Douglas DC-3. Believed to have been captured at Zamboanga, Mindanao, on 3rd May 1945 and taken to Clark Field.

S16   Yokosuka D4Y3 'Judy'
Navy Carrier Bomber Suisei Model 33
Flown at Clark Field. No other details known.

S17   Nakajima Ki-84 'Frank' Army Type 4 Fighter Hayate
This aircraft was C/n 1446 and was captured at Clark Field. After tests there, it was shipped to the USA aboard the USS *Long Island* (CVE-1). It was received at Park Ridge from NAS Anacostia on 22nd July 1946 for storage for the proposed National Air Museum.

In 1952 it was declared surplus and sold to the Ontario Air Museum at Claremont, California, being delivered to the Museum in September 1952. In July 1954 the aircraft was used in the film *Never So Few* and was repainted in Japanese markings. It was restored to taxiing condition for this film and returned to the Museum for further display until 1963. In April 1963 the Ki-84 was taken to AiResearch Aircraft Co at Los Angeles Airport for rebuild to flying condition. The first test flight of the Ki-84 after rebuild took place in June. For the flights after overhaul it was marked as N3385G and remained with the Museum, which later moved to Chino, California, and is now known as the Air Museum. Sold to the Kyoto-Arashiyama Museum in Japan.

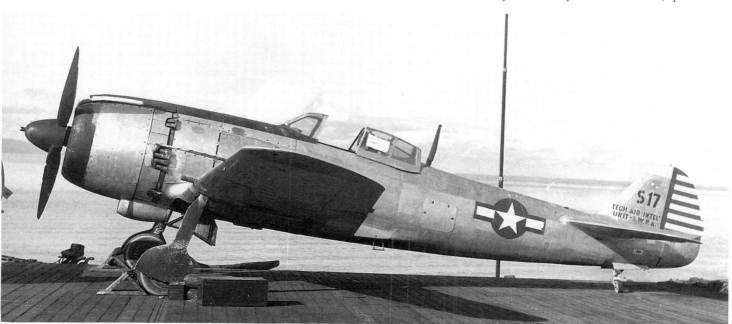

**S18   Nakajima Ki-44-II 'Tojo' Army Type 2
        Single-seat Fighter Shoki**
At Clark Field. Photographs show ground shots only. No other
details known.

**S19   Nakajima B6N2 'Jill' Navy Carrier
        Attack Bomber Tenzan Model 12**
No details known, except that the aircraft was flown at Clark Field.

**S22   Kawasaki Ki-45 KAI 'Nick' Army Type 2
        Twin-engined Fighter Toryu**
No details known, except that the aircraft was flown at Clark Field.

*   *   *

The unit also flew a Mitsubishi G4M2 'Betty' (previously coded
'762-12') and a Tachikawa Ki-54c 'Hickory' for which no 'S' numbers are known. The 'Nick' S14, the 'Frank' S17, 'Hickory', and
possibly the 'Betty', were shipped to the USA. It was also intended
to fly a Mitsubishi Ki-46 'Dinah' at Clark Field, but this was damaged in a ground accident before it could be flown. The 'Hickory',
which was named *Lemon*, was later at Wright Field. The TAIU also
assisted in the rebuild of a Mitsubishi A6M5 'Zeke' Model 52
which was taken over by the Royal Australian Air Force Detachment at Clark Field. The 'Zeke' was handed over to No. 457 Squadron RAAF and flown by them on familiarisation exercises. This aircraft was silver overall with 'SEAC'-type roundels - i.e. without a
red centre spot.

A possible additional aircraft was a Ki-45 'Nick', captured on the
island of Palawan in the western Philippines. Photographs show
this aircraft, with US stars applied, after nosing over on the
ground. It is not known if any test flights had been made before
this incident.

After the surrender of Japan the personnel of this Unit flew to
Japan to assist in the evaluation of aircraft found there. With the
exception of the aircraft mentioned in the preceding paragraph
and one Ki-43 which was mounted on a pole at the entrance to the
base at Clark Field for some years, all the aircraft tested by the Unit
at Clark Field were scrapped there following the move of the TAIU
to Japan.

Opposite top: **The Nakajima 'Frank' 'S17' in formation with a Royal Navy
Seafire, USN F6F & USAAF P-51D.** *Bruce Robertson collection*

Opposite bottom: **The Nakajima B6N2 'Jill' 'S19' in flight near Manila in the
hands of the TAIU-SWPA.** *USAF Museum*

Below: **The Nakajima Ki-44-II-'Tojo' 'S18' on display in the Philippines.**
USAF Museum

Top: **The Kawasaki Ki-45-KAI 'Nick' 'S22' in flight over the Philippines.**
USAF Museum

Above centre: **The TAIU-SWPA Mitsubishi G4M2 'Betty', after falling off its
jacks during refurbishing; the aircraft was repaired and flown after this
incident.** *USAF Museum*

Above: **The Tachikawa Ki-54c 'Hickory' of the TAIU-SWPA, named *Lemon*,
at Wright Field in 1946.** *Howard Levy collection*

Below: **The Ki-45 'Nick' in US marks, photographed on Palawan Island in the
western Philippines.** *USAFM*

Chapter Fifteen

Aircraft Flown by the USAAF in the ETO and MTO

15.1   **EUROPEAN THEATER OF OPERATIONS (ETO)**

—   **Heinkel He 177A-5**   **W Nr 550256**

This aircraft, call sign 'GP+RZ', was surrendered to forces of the French Resistance at Toulouse-Blagnac in September 1944. After overhaul by the SNCASE facility there it was test flown by Colonel Harold E. Watson on 28th November 1944 and ferried to Villacoublay on the same day. Here American radio equipment was fitted and other servicing undertaken by 10th Depot Repair Squadron. It was the aircraft which later arrived at RAE Farnborough from Villacoublay on 14th January 1945, flown by S/Ldr Randrup of the RAF. On 19th January 1945 the Heinkel was flown to Bovingdon by Lt Col Robert J. Koster. On 2nd February an operations order was issued for the ferrying of the aircraft to Wright Field and on 3rd February the Heinkel made flights totalling 2 hours 30 minutes from Bovingdon. On 9th February Lt Col Koster flew the He 177 to Paris-Orly on the first leg of its intended delivery flight. Engine trouble (a common problem with the coupled engine installations of the '177) was encountered and the aircraft remained at Orly while an engine change was carried out. Besides Lt Col Koster the crew consisted of Lt Col Charles F. Maas (navigator), M/Sgt Joseph Callichio (flight engineer) and T/Sgt Arthur B. Anderson (radio operator).

On 28th February 1945 the Heinkel attempted to take-off from Orly *en route* to the USA but the aircraft burst a tyre during the take-off run and was damaged beyond repair during the ensuing ground-loop. Its fuselage was broken in two and the aircraft was abandoned as beyond repair. The cause of the accident was that the '177 had remained standing in one position during the whole period of its engine change. The synthetic rubber tyres had 'set' out of symmetrical shape because of being in one position under the weight of the aircraft. This caused too great a stress on the tyres during take-off, causing one of them to lose its tread.

In its place, the USAAF received the RAF Heinkel He 177 TS439 which was shipped to the USA to become FE-2100.

—   **Fieseler Fi 156 Storch**   **W Nr** *unknown*

There are reports of Fieseler Storches being used by the Allied forces in Europe in 1944/45. No specific reports have been found of the use of this type by the USAAF. However, one Morane Saulnier-built example (designation MS 500) was presented to General Dwight D. Eisenhower, the Supreme Commander of the Allied Expeditionary Forces, for his own use, after the French Fieseler Storch production line at Puteaux, near Paris, was liberated in 1944. This example was painted with US stars and black-and-white 'invasion stripes'. The final fate of this aircraft is not known, but an example of the Fieseler Fi 156 was at Andrews AFB, Md. in 1946, and conceivably could have been this aircraft.

Many ex-Luftwaffe aircraft were flown in US markings in Europe, especially after the German capitulation. E.g:

—   **Focke Wulf Fw 190F-9/R1**   **W Nr 347763**

This aircraft was flown from Germany to Boxted in England in May 1945 and flown for about ten flying hours by USAAF pilots of the 56th Fighter Group based at that airfield. It was withdrawn from use after the engine seized.

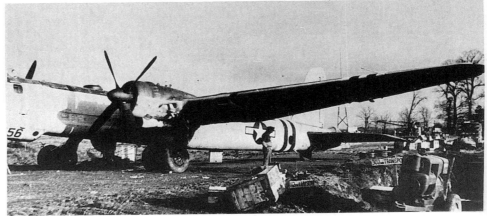

Top right: **Focke Wulf Fw 190F W Nr 347763 at Boxted, home of the 56th Fighter Group, after being ferried to England.** *Steve Coates collection*

Right: **The Heinkel He 177A '56', possibly at Bovingdon in England.** *NASM*

— Focke Wulf Fw 190F   W Nr *unknown*

This aircraft was captured following the Luftwaffe 'Operation Bodenplatte' – the last major offensive operation by the Luftwaffe in the West. This took place on New Year's Day 1945. A large number of Luftwaffe aircraft carried out surprise bombing and strafing attacks on Allied airfields, causing considerable damage but losing many aircraft in the process.

The Fw 190 concerned wore the marks '1-1-45' on its fin and rudder after capture, commemorating that event. The aircraft concerned force-landed on the airfield at St Trond in Belgium, the base of 404th Fighter Group, US 9th AAF, during the operation. Photographs of this aircraft were taken at St Trond on 18th March 1945, after the '190 had been repaired and painted bright red overall. In addition to the US 'Stars and Bars', the aircraft wore the code

letters of one of the 404th FG's squadrons and the individual code letter 'L'. At the time, 404 FG, a P-47 unit, comprised the 506th, 507th and 508th Fighter Squadrons.

— Focke Wulf Fw 190A-8   W Nr *unknown*

This Fw 190 belonged to SG 4. It was taken over by the 356th FS of the 354th FG, a unit of the US 9th AAF. The '190 was flown during the period that the Group was equipped with Republic P-47s (November 1944 to February 1945). Photographs of this aircraft were allegedly taken at St Trond in Belgium, although the 354th FG was not recorded as being based at that airfield. The '190 has perhaps been confused with the one recorded above. The 354th FG was, in fact, based in the Meurthe-et-Moselle region of France during the period that the '190 was operated.

Above: **The Focke Wulf Fw 190F marked '1-1-45' at St Trond in Belgium. The tail marking refers to the date (January 1, 1945) of the last major Luftwaffe offensive operation against the Allied air forces, possibly the date of capture of the aircraft. Photograph dated 18th March 1945.** *USAF Museum*

Right: **The Focke Wulf Fw 190A of 356th Fighter Squadron, 354th Fighter Group.** *USAF Museum*

— Messerschmitt Bf 108 Taifun
One Messerschmitt Bf 108 was overhauled at Villacoublay for the Air Intelligence organisation before the end of hostilities. This aircraft is recorded as being flyable by 23rd March 1945 and was identified as 'GA-2'. This is believed to be the aircraft which later became 'FE-4610'. (See Chapters Sixteen and Seventeen).

USAAF historical records show brief details of the following aircraft, most of which seem to have been flown by units of the US 8th and 9th AAFs immediately after the German surrender in May 1945. Recorded details are:

Fieseler Fi 156 – examples identified as:
C92   Fieseler Fi 156   W Nr *unknown*
Recorded on 31st May 1945.

C903   Fieseler Fi 156   W Nr *unknown*
Recorded as 'condemned as salvage' 9th August 1945.

C5904   Fieseler Fi 156   W Nr *unknown*
Recorded as 'excluded from inventory' 31st December 1945.

C5905   Fieseler Fi 156   W Nr *unknown*
Recorded as 'excluded from inventory' 31st December 1945.

Focke Wulf Fw 190 – examples identified as:
CA3   Focke Wulf Fw 190   W Nr *unknown*
Recorded as 'written off' 1st November 1945.

CA11   Focke Wulf Fw 190   W Nr *unknown*
Recorded as 'condemned as salvage' 16th July 1945.

CA45   Focke Wulf Fw 190   W Nr *unknown*
Recorded as 'condemned as salvage' 16th July 1945.

C901   Klemm Kl 35   W Nr *unknown*
Recorded as 'condemned as salvage' 14th April 1945.

The bulk of ex-Luftwaffe aircraft flown by the USAAF were those taken over by 'Watson's Whizzers' as described in Chapter Sixteen.
One of them also deserves mention here, since it was also later flown by the 56th Fighter Group of the 8th AAF.

— Heinkel He 111H-20   W Nr 701152
This aircraft had been acquired by Col. Watson and had been intended for shipment to the USA. When it became known that there was insufficient space on HMS *Reaper* for the Heinkel to be shipped with the other aircraft, it was flown to Boxted in England by members of the 56th Fighter Group who had been assisting Col. Watson's Intelligence team. The He 111 arrived at Boxted on 2nd July 1945. It was repainted in 56th FG colours after arrival, including the code letters 'HV' of the Group's 61st Fighter Squadron. Instead of an individual aircraft letter, there was a device adjacent to the 'HV' code, comprising a 'W' inside a 'C' inside an 'O'. These letters were for the initials of Major J. Carter of 61st FS, Major Williamson of 62nd FS and Captain Ordway, who was the Engineering Officer of 61st FS. On 12th September 1945, with the impending return of 56th FG personnel to the USA, the Heinkel was flown to the RAF airfield of North Weald. Its last flight was made on 3rd November 1945, from Heston to Farnborough to appear in the German Aircraft Exhibition at the Royal Aircraft Establishment. By this time, RAF roundels had been painted over the US stars. This aircraft is now in the RAF Museum at Hendon. (See Chapter Five).

15.2   **MEDITERRANEAN THEATER OF OPERATIONS (MTO)**

The first Axis aircraft flown by US forces in the MTO, were those taken over by USAAF squadrons serving with the Desert Air Force in North Africa, part of Royal Air Force Middle East. The timescale for the campaigns in which these forces were involved is shown in Chapter Four.

79th Fighter Group
Typical of these aircraft were those flown by the Squadrons of the 79th Fighter Group, which seems to have been the most energetic unit in restoring Axis war trophies to airworthiness. The Group consisted of 85th, 86th and 87th Fighter Squadrons. Their prizes included:

— Messerschmitt Bf 109G-2/R2
This was *Irmgard*, shot down by British troops on 1st March 1943, near Zarzis in Tunisia. It was originally coded '14' of 2 (H)/14, a reconnaissance unit, and was an Erla-built aircraft with a W Nr of 14329 or 14629. It was removed to Causeway Landing Ground by 79th Fighter Group. It was repainted as 'X8-7' of that Group's 87th Fighter Squadron. After a belly-landing, the '109 was taken over by 86th Squadron and received its badge after repair.
It was eventually shipped to the USA and taken to Wright Field. The Messerschmitt was not flown at Wright Field, but was used for structural tests between January and May 1944, before being scrapped. (See further details in Chapter Thirteen).

— Fiat G 50
This example was captured by the RAF and handed over to 87th FS at Castel Benito in February 1943. While this aircraft was having engine runs on the ground, it ran away and hit a parked Curtiss P-40 belonging to the Squadron. The Fiat was not repaired after this incident and was never flown by the Group.

— Focke Wulf Fw 190
Two examples of the type were captured at Gerbini in Sicily in August 1943 and made airworthy by 85th Fighter Squadron. They followed the unit to Italy and remained with the Squadron until November 1943. On 20th November the two Fw 190s were flown from the Group base at Foggia No. 3/Salsola to Bari for shipment to the USA, the pilots being Lts Clark and Martin. It is believed that one of these aircraft was W Nr 160057, which was taken to NAS Anacostia and flown by the US Navy. The other Fw 190 was W Nr 181550.

The Bf 109G 'X8-7' *Irmgard* **of 87th Fighter Squadron, 79th Fighter Group, photographed in Tunisia before transfer to Wright Field.** *USAF Museum*

— Savoia Marchetti SM 79   ex MM 21750

This example was also captured at Gerbini in Sicily. On 10th September 1943, this aircraft was flown from Gerbini to the Group's new base at Palagonia by Col Grogan, the 79th Group's Operations Officer. The aircraft was flown for some time on communications duties in support of the Group and its Squadrons.

— Junkers Ju 88A-4   W Nr 4300227?

This aircraft was found at Foggia No. 3/Salsola and made airworthy by the 86th Fighter Squadron, as its 'Junk Heap 88'. It was intended for use as a communications aircraft for the Squadron. However, before use could be made of the Junkers, orders were received to transfer the aircraft to the USA. On 19th October 1943, the Ju 88 left Foggia No. 3 for the USA. It was piloted by Major Frederic A. Borsodi, former Commanding Officer of the 86th Fighter Squadron, who was returning to the USA at the end of his tour of duty. It arrived at Wright Field on 5th November 1943. (See entry for 'FE-1599' in Chapter Thirteen).

12th Bombardment Group

— Messerschmitt Me 410A   W Nr 263

One example, coded '2N+HT' of ZG 76, which had previously been taken over by No. 601 Squadron, RAF, was handed over to the USAAF 12th Bombardment Group at Gerbini in Sicily in September 1943. It was painted in RAF markings. The aircraft was destroyed on 1st October 1943, while attempting to take off on its first flight with the 12th BG. Its pilot, Lt Col G. E. Hall, 12BG Operations Officer, was killed.

12th Air Force Fighter Training School Constantine, Algeria
This unit, which gave operational training to pilots who had gained their 'wings' in the USA, had a number of German aircraft on its strength to give realistic combat training. During 1943 these aircraft included at least two Focke Wulf Fw 190s (one ex 79th FG), and one Messerschmitt Bf 110D. The Bf 110 carried the 'wasp' markings of ZG 1, the 'Wespen Geschwader'.

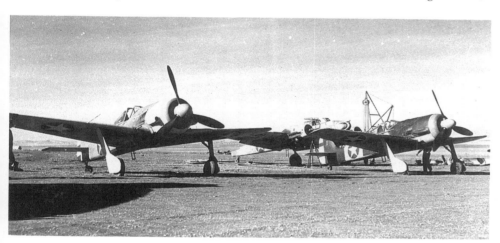

Left: **Two Fw 190 aircraft at Constantine, Algeria, with the Bf 110D in the background. US markings.** *Hugh Morgan collection*

Below: **Photographed at the 12th Air Force Fighter Training School, near Constantine in Algeria, after a belly-landing, Bf 110D wears US national markings and the unit markings of the Luftwaffe's ZG 1.** *Hugh Morgan collection*

15.3   OTHER MISCELLANEOUS AIRCRAFT

— **Bücker Bü Bestmann**   **W Nr** *unknown*
US unit unknown.

— **Junkers Ju 87B**   **W Nr** *unknown*
US unit unknown, photographed at Castel Benito.

— **Junkers Ju 188A**   **W Nr 0590**
Coded 'F8+CM' of KG 40, captured at Bolzano. This aircraft was in the hands of the Air Intelligence organisation in May 1945, and was flown from its point of capture to Florence for intended despatch to Wright Field.

— **Messerschmitt Bf 108B**   **W Nr 2246**
This liaison aircraft, was flown as a communications aircraft by US Navy Squadron VS-8. It was later taken to the USA and became NX54208. It was still extant in the USA as N108HP as compilation of this material for publication was reaching completion. Further details are given in Chapter Seventeen.

— **Messerschmitt Bf 109G-6**   **W Nr 166133**
This Rumanian Air Force example was painted in US markings and flown from Rumania to Italy by Capt Cantacuzino at the time Rumania renounced the Axis Treaty and came over to the Allies. He flew with Lt Col James A. Gunn as a passenger (in place of the radio behind the cockpit) – Gunn had been a Prisoner of War (PoW) and came to Italy to make arrangements for the repatriation of US prisoners from Rumania. The '109 carried US stars above the wings and a large 'Stars and Stripes' on each side of the fuselage. It is not known whether it was later flown by US forces in Italy, although it seems possible that it was.

— **Saiman 200**   **C/n** *unknown*
This biplane trainer was marked '51-224' on the fin. US unit unknown.

Top: **The former US Navy Messerschmitt Bf 108B N54208 photographed at Burlington, West Virginia.** *NASM*

Above left: **A Stuka Ju 87B in US markings at Castel Benito, Tripoli, in Libya.** *Howard Levy collection*

Left: **This Bücker Bü 181 is shown in US markings, probably photographed in North Africa.** *J. Mutin collection*

Bottom: **A Saiman 200 biplane, named *Patches* with US markings and the numbers '51-224' on its fin, photographed at Ponte Olivio, Sicily, on 19th August 1943.** *Howard Levy collection*

Chapter Sixteen

Watson's Whizzers

'Watson's Whizzers' was the popular name of a group of pilots, engineers and maintenance men who worked under Colonel Harold E. Watson to execute Project 'Lusty', the retrieval of German aircraft, engines and aviation equipment for study at Wright Field and other Centers in the USA.

Col Watson was seconded to Air Technical Intelligence at the end of the war, to achieve these objectives. He had previously served at Wright Field, although he had actually gone to Europe as Director of Maintenance in the 9th Air Force Service Command, an organisation tasked among other things with the maintenance of American aircraft in service with the French Air Force, and the training of French servicing personnel.

The intelligence task was to recover, for investigation, items of equipment named on a list compiled by experts at Wright Field. This list was later combined with a similar list compiled by British intelligence, to eliminate duplication of effort between the Allies.

Watson's group had two sections, one under Lt Bob Strobell, which was concerned with the acquisition of jet aircraft, and a second under Capt Fred McIntosh which was assigned to collect piston-engined aircraft. The overall title of 'Watson's Whizzers' related to the higher profile of these tasks, the collection of the jets. The jet pilots removed the propeller blades from their standard USAAF insignia to underline the point that they had no need of these out-dated appendages.

The pilots selected to support Watson were all experienced fighter pilots, many of them with an engineering background and/or rated flight instructors. The jet pilots were transferred to Lechfeld in southern Germany, where a number of Messerschmitt Me 262 jet fighters had been found, and the initial efforts of the group were concentrated at this airfield. A number of Me 262s were selected for repair and work was started on these by the 54th Air Disarmament Squadron (ADS). More than thirty Me 262s were found on the field but many of these had been damaged before the arrival of the Air Intelligence personnel, some being bulldozed to scrap areas by the US troops clearing the site for Allied use. The 54th ADS set about to build up ten flyable aircraft from the wreckage. The individual aircraft were given names by the 54th ADS mechanics, names such as *Wilma Jeanne* and *Doris*, which were painted on the port side of the aircraft nose. M/Sgt Eugene E. Freiburger was assigned to the 54th ADS, in charge of Platoon 1. The squadron arrived at Augsberg on 1st May 1945, moving to nearby Lechfeld a few days later. One intact Me 262A (the one now in the NASM) landed at Lechfeld after the ADS arrived there, but all the other 'Whizzers' were built up by cannibalising wrecked '262s. The intact '262 was named *Dennis* after Freiburger's son, while *Wilma Jeanne* and *Vera* were named after his wife and his sister-in-law. *Connie the Sharp Article* was named by M/Sgt H. W. Preston of Platoon 2, after his wife. Other key members of the "Feudin' 54th" were T/Sgts P. S. Dutcher and L. B. Fielder – the nickname being coined by a Sgt Brown after he analysed the disputes and discussions amongst the ADS personnel, who came from many different previous units and backgrounds. "Feudin'

54th" was also painted on several '262 noses. Its job done, 54th ADS moved from Lechfeld on 2nd June 1945 and the Me 262s were taken over by Watson's ATI personnel. After the aircraft flew away to Melun in France, *en route* to Cherbourg, the original names were painted out and new ones applied by Watson's pilots. Thus *Wilma Jeanne* became *Happy Hunter II* after Harold Watson's son, Hunter, and each of the other aircraft had a name personal to its USAAF pilot.

While work proceeded on the Messerschmitts at Lechfeld, the Air Intelligence teams were scouring the rest of liberated Europe for other prizes. The American teams were based at three points in Germany - Stuttgart, Merseburg and Nuremberg. The Merseburg team was later moved to Kassel and then briefly to Munich, returning later to Kassel. Selected items were flown or trucked to the three collection points for onward transmission to the USA. By arrangement with the British, Watson's teams also flew to North Germany, Denmark and Norway (areas under British control) to review items reported by British intelligence teams. Under reciprocal arrangements, British intelligence officers visited the US Zone of Germany, for example to select Dornier Do 335 fighters found at the Dornier works at Oberpfaffenhofen.

The order establishing these arrangements was published on 29th April 1945. The initial list of personnel involved with the Me 262s included Captains Kenneth E. Dahlstrom, Henry A. Nolte and Fred L. Hillis, and 1st Lieutenants Robert J. Anspach, William V. Haynes, Horace D. McCord, Roy W. Brown, James K. Holt and Robert C. Strobell. In the event, because of an administrative problem, McCord and Nolte were delayed in joining the group and did not take an active part in the operation. The list also included Technical Sergeants Noel D. Moon, Edward J. Thompson and Ernest C. Parker and Staff Sergeants John G. Gilson, Donald J. Wilcoxen, Archie E. Bloomer, Everett T. Box, Charles L. Taylor, Robert H. Moore and Charles A. Barr. A number of Messerschmitt personnel were also found at Lechfeld and elsewhere, including test pilots Karl Baur, Ludwig 'Willie' Hofmann and Hermann Kersting, and engineering superintendent Gerhard Caroli. Strobell was in charge of the '262 refurbishment and recovery, while Hillis was the unit Operations Officer.

The officers looking after the retrieval of the piston-engined types under Captain Fred B. McIntosh, as Operations Officer included Captain Edwin D. Maxfield (the Engineering Officer of 56th Fighter Group). Fred McIntosh had himself come from 56th FG, having been the wing-man for Col David Schilling who was CO of the 56th FG from August 1944 to January 1945. McIntosh had been a flight instructor in the US, prior to coming to England with a group of four-hundred 'replacement' pilots a little before 'D-Day' (6th June 1944) and also took a personal interest in the engineering aspects. By the time of the surrender, David Schilling was an assistant to the Director of Intelligence of the US 8th AAF, and his influence enabled both McIntosh and Maxfield (and, on an unofficial basis, several more 56th FG pilots and engineers) to become involved in Project 'Lusty'. One other official member of the team from 56th FG was S/Sgt Edmund R. Namowicz, a mechanic who spoke German, Russian and Polish. The three men from 56th FG were flown from Boxted (their base in England) to Merseburg in April 1945. They were later joined by other USAAF and ex-Luftwaffe mechanics at Merseburg and used this as a base to investigate reports of 'listed' aircraft throughout the area covering Merseburg, Dresden, Halle, Dessau and almost to Berlin. This was an area occupied by the US Army, but which was to be handed over to the Russians. Maxfield recalls that the Germans were keen to hand over their latest equipment lest it fall into Soviet hands. The group's work was not confined to the aircraft industry – they also searched for cryogenic and heavy-water laboratories, visited the Carl Zeiss optical equipment works at Jena, and went to Linz in Austria to a facility building the Heinkel He S 011 advanced turbo-jet engine, as part of a hectic schedule. The small team had the use of jeeps, a Stinson L-5 and later five captured Fieseler Storchs, which were all used to travel through the area. The Storchs were captured in the Halle area and flown to Merseburg. They were flown by Capt Horne and Lt Haskell ('Horne-Haskell Airlines') and used for communications trips and for giving recreation flights to released Allied Prisoners of War. A Bücker Bü 181 was also used until it was flown into a power line south of Munich, while a Messerschmitt Bf 108 found at Merseburg was also flown. 'Horne-Haskell Airlines' also attempted to acquire a Siebel Si 204 twin-engined light transport but this was sabotaged before it could be flown back to their base. On 1st June, the group moved to Munich because its original area of operation was to be handed over to Soviet control.

The group's main prize was the Junkers Ju 388L captured at Merseburg itself, although other examples were a Horten flying-wing from near Leipzig and Heinkel He 162s from near Halle. The Ju 388 was test flown at Merseburg prior to being ferried to Kassel on 20th May 1945. By 24th May, Maxfield and McIntosh were confident enough to propose ferrying the '388 to the USA via the northern Atlantic route (via Prestwick, Iceland and Greenland) but in the event this aircraft was shipped on board the *Reaper*. At Munich the group was joined by Jack Woolams and by Heinz Braun (who had been the Luftwaffe pilot of the Ju 290 captured by Watson at Munich-Riem). Aircraft from the Munich area were then ferried to Paris and Cherbourg by Braun, Woolams, McIntosh, another German pilot (Hauptmann Hans Padell of E-Stelle Rechlin) and by pilots from the 'jet' group. The Fw 190F versions to be taken to the US were captured at Neubiberg, south of Munich with the Bf 109s possibly from the same place. The Bf 109s were test flown locally by the Americans, but were then sent to Cherbourg by road because of their generally poor condition. The Do 335s were captured at the Dornier factory at Oberpfaffenhofen, to the west of Munich, while one of the Heinkel He 111s captured was also from an airfield in the Munich area. Finally, most of Watson's group, whether jet or piston dedicated, were involved in retrieving aircraft from areas under British control. These included Arado Ar 234s from Stavanger in Norway and Grove in Denmark, Messerschmitt Me 262s from Schleswig in North Germany, Heinkel He 219 night fighters from Grove and a Focke Wulf Ta 152 from Aalborg in Denmark.

Fred McIntosh recalls that the retrieval exercises were not safe and simple matters. When work commenced at an airfield near Munich on some Focke Wulf Fw 190Fs, the first was found to be booby-trapped. When this Fw 190 was put up on jacks for an undercarriage retraction test, its port wing was blown off by an explosive charge in the wing root. As the gear came up the charge was detonated by a wire linked to the retraction mechanism, which had been put in place by the last pilot to fly it. Similarly, a

Junkers Ju 87 was found with bombs still in place under its wings, set to explode when interfered with by any crew disarming the aircraft. Despite these difficulties, only one prize (an Me 262 which suffered engine failure) was lost during flights in Europe by the Air Intelligence teams.

Robert Strobell was assigned to Air Technical Intelligence on 20th May 1945, having previously been a P-47 pilot with 63rd Fighter Wing of the 12th AAF. He arrived at Lechfeld on 27th May, to take charge of the '262 Project. His orders were: to prepare as many '262s as possible for ferrying to Cherbourg; to train USAAF pilots to fly them; to train crew chiefs to maintain them; and finally to ferry the aircraft to Cherbourg. He was in charge of six USAAF pilots, ten crew chiefs, and twenty-eight Messerschmitt mechanics and test pilots.

Roy W. Brown and Ken Holt had flown P-47s with 86th FG of the 12th AAF, part of the 1st Tactical Air Force. They both arrived at Lechfeld on 3rd June 1945 and took part in ferrying the Me 262s to Melun and Cherbourg. Brown remembers that his first jet flights were a 'real thrill' by comparison with a year flying P-47s and that the '262 was a pilot's airplane, responsive, fast and smooth. Brown left Watson's group soon after arriving at New York aboard the *Reaper*. Holt, on the other hand, took part in the ferrying of the German aircraft to Freeman Field, and was then based at Freeman for several months, carrying out tests of four flyable USAAF '262s in accordance with test instructions transmitted from Wright Field. Holt also flew '262s to air displays, such as the one held at Omaha in July 1946.

The first airworthy '262 (*Dennis*) was test flown by Karl Baur, the Messerschmitt Chief Experimental Test Pilot, on 12th May, followed by *Wilma Jeane* on 14th May. On 16th May Baur flew *Beverley Ann* from Munich-Riem to Lechfeld. On 30th May, following the arrival of the Whizzers' pilots, Baur started making flights with the two-seater *Vera* at Lechfeld, checking out Watson, Strobell, Hillis, Anspach, Dahlstrom, Holt and Brown on the type.

After the jets had been delivered to Cherbourg, the '262 pilots were flown to Munich to assist with the recovery of other piston-engined aircraft. While there, they were joined by Jack Woolams, Chief Test Pilot of Bell Aircraft. He had been sent to Europe, partly because of the Bell Company's interest in the Messerschmitt Me 163B. At that time, Bell was designing and building the Bell XS-1 rocket-powered research aircraft and Woolams was eager to study the '163 and if possible to fly one. Harold Watson had previously been acquainted with Larry Bell, the founder of Bell Aircraft, from association with the P-59 jet project at Wright Field. Woolams made a proposal to assemble two Me 163Bs at Lechfeld under the guidance of Dr Alexander Lippisch and to fly them there, but this proposal was vetoed in favour of trials in the US.

Woolams had entered the USAAC in 1937 and had trained as a fighter pilot, flying the Curtiss P-36 at Barksdale Field. He then returned to college to complete his education, but continued Flight Instructor courses at government expense at the same time. After graduating, he joined Bell Aircraft as a production test pilot, flying Bell P-39s as they came off the Niagara Falls production lines. He soon aspired to become an Experimental Test Pilot, and after a number of assignments he was sent to Muroc to take charge of the flight test development of the Bell P-59 Airacomet, the first jet aircraft to be built in the USA.

Woolams helped to fly some of the piston-engined aircraft to Cherbourg, including Fw 190s, and in July visited the Royal Aircraft Establishment at Farnborough. Here he flew a Messerschmitt Bf 110 night-fighter and the Heinkel He 162 and Messerschmitt Me 262 jet fighters, before returning to the USA. He then went to Newark, to assist in the test-flying and ferrying of aircraft which had arrived there aboard HMS *Reaper*. This included a test flight in a Dornier Do 335 during which the rear engine of the '335 overheated, resulting in a hasty circuit and return to the airfield.

Bob Anspach arrived to join 'Watson's Whizzers' after being a P-47D pilot with 358th FG, 365th Fighter Squadron. Both Anspach and Hillis (who came from another Squadron in the same Fighter Group), had amongst the greatest number of flying hours in their units, and were both ex flying instructors. Anspach was checked out in a '262 on 9th June 1945 at Lechfeld and on the following day he flew one of the nine '262s ferried from Lechfeld to St Dizier and Melun.

It had originally been proposed to fly the Messerschmitt from Melun to Speke via Woodbridge, to join the *Reaper* at Liverpool, but the plan was changed and the port of departure became Cherbourg in France, with the aircraft being flown from Melun to Cherbourg/Querqueville. The transatlantic shipment became Project Seahorse, involving HMS *Reaper*, the Liberty ship *Richard J. Gatling*, and some other merchant vessels. The project name was an anagram of Lt Col Malcolm Seashore, the officer in charge.

After the demonstration to General Spaatz at Melun on 27th June, the main batch of '262s was flown onwards to Cherbourg on 30th June. Due to overcast weather, Bob Anspach missed Cherbourg and made a precautionary landing on the island of Jersey. The team's support C-47 brought supplies of fuel from Cherbourg and the aircraft was safely flown out to its destination on 1st July.

It was during this part of the operation that the cannon-equipped Me 262 '000' *Happy Hunter II* was lost, while being piloted by 'Willie' Hofmann. One engine shed some turbine blades, causing uncontrollable vibration. Hofmann successfully baled out but the aircraft was a total loss. On 6th July, Bob Anspach flew a second '262 from Melun to Cherbourg, this time a two-seater, (No. 555 *Willie*). When he selected his landing gear down as he started his approach, there was no indication that the nose wheel had extended. In the absence of a red light from the ground (the '262s had no US radio equipment fitted), he presumed that the wheel at least appeared to be locked down. After the aircraft rolled about one-third of the runway length, the nose dropped and it slid straight ahead for another thousand feet, causing minor damage to the nose section and engine nacelles.

Anspach and most of the other members of the team sailed to New York aboard HMS *Reaper* and joined in the operation at Newark AAF to ferry or ship the aircraft to Wright Field, Freeman Field or NAS Patuxent River. This required removal of the protective coatings which had been applied to the aircraft to protect them during the voyage, and other maintenance work.

Another significant area of interest to the Air Technical Intelligence (ATI) teams was the study of helicopters. Here the USAAF was lucky to receive examples of the Focke-Achgelis Fa 223E and Flettner Fl 282 helicopters, which were handed over to them at Ainring by members of the Luftwaffe's first helicopter squadron,

Transport Staffel (TS) 40. These aircraft comprised the Fa 223E (V-14), Fa 223E W Nr 0051, and one of the two Fl 282s which later came to the USA. The Fa 223V-14 was handed over to the British due to lack of shipping space on HMS *Reaper*. The other Fa 223, Nr 0051, suffered a technical failure on 23rd May during its ferry flight from Nellingen to Kassel and could no longer be flown. It force landed near Heilbronn with a rotor problem and was later dismantled. Nr 0051 was shipped to Wright Field aboard a merchant ship. It was not flown in the USA but components were evaluated by Prewitt Aircraft. A second Fl 282 was handed over by its designer, Anton Flettner, at Bad Tolz, whence the Flettner company had been evacuated shortly before the end of the war.

The flights of these helicopters were generally made by German pilots, such as Hans-Helmut Gerstenhauer, since the ATI organisation had no immediate access to Allied pilots with rotary-wing experience. Other pilots were Otto Dumke of E-Stelle Rechlin, together with Hans Fuisting and Ernst Reimann of the Fletfner company.

16.1   THE 'USA' NUMBERS

The 'USA' numbers were allotted by RAF Intelligence teams to aircraft selected by them in Denmark or North Germany which appeared on the list of US intelligence requirements. Their details were forwarded to Colonel Harold E. Watson and in many cases – if no aircraft of the type had already been logged by USAAF teams operating elsewhere in Germany – the aircraft were then handed over to the USAAF.

Note: For further details of references in this Chapter to FE- and T2- numbers, please see Chapter Seventeen

USA 1   Messerschmitt Me 262A   W Nr 500443
Coded 'Yellow 5'. Surrendered at Fassberg. It was not required by the USAAF because a number of single-seat Me 262 variants had been found at Lechfeld. The aircraft was therefore shipped to the UK and later taken to South Africa. For further details see Chapter Five.

USA 2   Messerschmitt Me 262B-1a/U1   W Nr 110306
Coded 'Red 6' of IV/NJG 11. Surrendered at Schleswig. This was a night-fighter version converted from an Me 262B two-seat trainer. Handed over to Col Watson on 19th June 1945 and flown via Twente and Beauvechain/Le Culot to Melun-Villaroche. Here it was numbered '999' in the 'Watson's Whizzers' series and received the name *Ole Fruit Cake*. It was ferried from Melun to Cherbourg on about 3rd July 1945 prior to shipment to the USA aboard HMS *Reaper*. For later history, see FE-610 in Chapter Seventeen.

The Me 262B night-fighter 'USA 2'. *NASM*

USA 3   Messerschmitt Me 262B-1a   W Nr 110165
Surrendered at Schleswig. This was an Me 262B two-seat trainer
version. Transferred to Col Watson on 19th June 1945 and flown to
Melun. Named *What Was It ?* It was number '101' in the 'Watson's
Whizzers' series. This aircraft was taken to the USA aboard HMS
Reaper. It was then transferred to the US Navy as BuAer
No. 121441.

USA 4   Messerschmitt Me 262B-1a/U1   W Nr 110635
Coded 'Red 10' of IV/NJG 11. Surrendered at Schleswig. Not
handed over to Colonel Watson.

USA 5   Arado Ar 234B   W Nr 140489
Surrendered at Grove. Handed over to Col Watson and flown
from Grove to Le Culot and then Melun by Watson on 24th June
1945. This aircraft became either '202' or '303' as described later
and was handed over to the US Navy after transfer to the USA
aboard HMS *Reaper*.

USA 6   Arado Ar 234B   W Nr unknown
Surrendered at Grove.

USA 7   Arado Ar 234B   W Nr unknown
Surrendered at Grove.

It is almost certain that the second US Navy aircraft was USA 6 or
USA 7 from Grove. Possible W Nrn for these two aircraft are
140467 and 140486 (but these identities are not confirmed).

USA 8   Heinkel He 219A-0   W Nr 210903
Coded 'SP+CR'. Surrendered at Grove. Handed over to Col Watson on 26th June 1945 and then flown to Cherbourg by Capt Fred
McIntosh. Taken to the USA aboard HMS *Reaper*. Subsequently
became 'FE-612', which see in Chapter Seventeen.

USA 9   Heinkel He 219A-2   W Nr 290060
Coded 'CS+QG'. Surrendered at Grove. Handed over to Col Watson on 26th June 1945. Flown to Cherbourg by Capt Fred McIntosh
and taken to the USA aboard HMS *Reaper*. Subsequently became
'FE-613', which see in Chapter Seventeen.

USA 10   Heinkel He 219A   W Nr 290202
Surrendered at Grove. Flown to Cherbourg, probably by Heinz
Braun on 27th June 1945, and taken to the USA aboard HMS
Reaper. Subsequently 'FE-614', preserved at Silver Hill, which see
in Chapter Seventeen.

USA 11   Focke Wulf Ta 152H-0   W Nr 150003
It was surrendered at Tirstrup in Denmark. It was taken from there

Right: **The He 219A 'USA 9' believed to have been
photographed at Freeman Field.** *NASM*

Below: **The Fw 190D-9 'USA 13' at Newark on 4th
September 1945.** *Fred McIntosh collection*

to Aalborg West by the RAF for servicing prior to handover to Col Watson. Flown to Cherbourg by Capt Fred McIntosh. Transported to the USA aboard HMS *Reaper*. To 'FE-112'. Flown from Newark to Freeman Field during September 1945. This aircraft is now in the Silver Hill facility of the National Air and Space Museum.

USA 12   Focke Wulf Fw 190D-9   W Nr *unknown*
Surrendered at Flensburg. Became 'FE-119' or 'FE-120' (which see in Chapter Seventeen). These two Fw 190Ds had the W Nrn 211016 and 601088, one being USA 12, the other USA 15.

USA 13   Focke Wulf Fw 190D-9   W Nr 401392
Coded 'Black 5' of JG 26. Surrendered at Flensburg. Became 'FE-121' (which see in Chapter Seventeen).

USA 14   Focke Wulf Fw 190D-13   W Nr 836017
Coded 'Yellow 10' of JG 26. Surrendered at Flensburg. Became 'FE-118' (which see in Chapter Seventeen). Currently with The Fighter Museum at Mesa, Arizona.

Above: **The Me 262B 'USA 4', photographed at Schleswig.** *NASM*

Below: **The Fw 190D-13 'USA 14' at Gilze Rijen, while en route from Flensburg to Cherbourg.** *Ross Finlayson courtesy N. Malayney*

Bottom: **The Focke Wulf Ta 152H W Nr 150003 photographed at Newark on 4th September 1945, while awaiting delivery to Freeman Field. Its Foreign Evaluation number, FE-112, appears on its fin.** *Ed Maxfield collection*

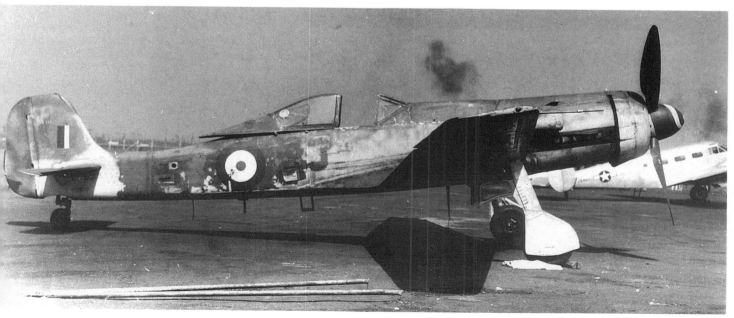

USA 15   Focke Wulf Fw 190D-9   W Nr *unknown*
Surrendered at Flensburg. Became 'FE-120' or 'FE-119' (see 'USA 12' above and Chapter Seventeen).

USA 16   These numbers are believed to have been allocated to
USA 17   Messerschmitt Me 410s surrendered at Sylt/Westerland.
USA 18   none of them was required by Col Watson.
USA 19

USA 20   *Untraced*

USA 21   Junkers Ju 88G-6   W Nr *unknown*
This example was surrendered at Grove in Denmark, and was handed over to Col Watson. After being test flown at Grove on 28th June 1945, it was flown to Cherbourg and taken to the USA aboard HMS *Reaper*. Flown from Newark to Freeman Field and became 'FE-611' (see Chapter Seventeen).

USA 022   Junkers Ju 290A-4   W Nr 110196
Coded 'P1+PS'. This aircraft was surrendered to US Forces immediately after Col Watson had been advised of the first batch of aircraft available to him in areas under British control; it was therefore given the next number in sequence. See under 'FE-3400' in Chapter Seventeen for further details.

USA 22: This number may also have been applied by the RAF to an aircraft surrendered in an area under British control.

USA 23 to USA 39 are untraced.

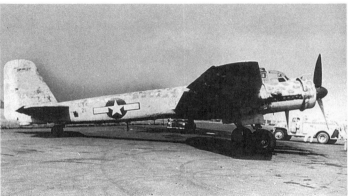

USA 40   Arado Ar 234B-2   W Nr 140311

Surrendered to the RAF at Stavanger in Norway. This aircraft belonged to II/KG 76 based at Grove in Denmark but had flown to Stavanger on 5th May 1945, which was the day German forces in Denmark surrendered. It was handed over to Col Watson and became 'Watson's Whizzers' No. 404. Became 'FE-1011' after shipment to the USA aboard HMS *Reaper* (see Chapter Seventeen).

USA 41 to USA 49 are untraced.

USA 50   Arado Ar 234B-2   W Nr 140312

Surrendered to the RAF at Stavanger. As with 'USA 40' above, this aircraft belonged to II/KG 76 based at Grove in Denmark and was flown to Norway with many other Luftwaffe aircraft on 5th May 1945 to avoid surrender to British forces in Denmark. The Ar 234 was handed over to Col Watson. Became 'FE-1010' after shipment to the USA aboard HMS *Reaper*' (see Chapter Seventeen).

The other aircraft to which USA numbers were allocated have not been specifically traced, but they almost certainly included the Bv 222V-2 from Trondheim, three Bv 138s surrendered at Kastrup-See, up to twelve He 162s from Leck, possibly two Me 262s and a Ju 86P at Fassberg, up to thirteen Me 163Bs from Husum, five Si 204s at Flensburg, a further Do 217M at Kastrup, an Ar 234 at Flensburg, three Heinkel He 219s and three Ju 188s at Sylt/Westerland, three Fw 190F-8/U1 two-seaters at Kastrup and a Ju 52/3m with magnetic mine-detonation ring at Schleswig.

Top left: **The Arado Ar 234B 'USA 50' (FE-/T2-1010), believed photographed at Freeman Field in 1946.** *NASM*

Centre left: **The Junkers Ju 88G-6 'USA 21' at Newark on 25th August 1945.** *Fred McIntosh collection*

Bottom left: **The Arado Ar 234B 'USA 40' (FE-/T2-1011) photographed at Wright Field.** *NASM*

It is possible that the numbers 'USA 40' and 'USA 50' were corruptions of 'Watson's Whizzers' numbers '404' and '505' and that not all the intervening USA numbers following on from 'USA 022' were actually allocated to aircraft. It is known that all the aircraft listed in the previous paragraph were allotted to Harold Watson for his use, should he have decided that they were required. In practice only some of the He 162s and Me 163s were taken over.

16.2   **'WATSON'S WHIZZERS' NUMBERS**

After servicing by the 54th ADS the Me 262s were ferried to Melun and renamed by the Watson's Whizzers pilots. They were also given identity numbers in the series '000', '111', '222' etc. After '999' had been reached a new series of numbers commenced at '101' and was used on the later Me 262 and Ar 234 jet aircraft. Not all the identity tie-ups between numbers, 54th ADS names and 'Watson's Whizzers' names are confirmed – the writers best estimate is given below and in the data table at the end of the chapter.

000   Me 262A-1a/U4   W Nr 170083 (V-083)

Trials aircraft for 50-mm cannon installation, named *Wilma Jeanne* and then *Happy Hunter II*. (Named after Col Watson's son, Hunter). Flown from Lechfeld to St Dizier and then to Melun on 10th June 1945. Crashed *en route* from Melun to Cherbourg, not delivered to the USA.

Top right: **Me 262A 000 *Wilma Jeanne*, photographed at Lechfeld.** *NASM courtesy Jeff Ethell collection*

Bottom right: **Me 262A 000 *Happy Hunter*, the renamed *Wilma Jeanne*, photographed at Melun.** *NASM courtesy Jeff Ethell collection*

111   Me 262A-1a   W Nr *unknown*
Fighter named *Beverley Anne* and then *Screamin' Meemie*. Aircraft of
Lt Robert Strobell. To the USA aboard HMS *Reaper*. To US Navy as
BuAer No. 121442. Now at the USAF Museum, Wright-Patterson
AFB.

222   Me 262A-1a/U3   W Nr *unknown*
Photo-reconnaissance variant named *Marge* then *Lady Jess IV*. Aircraft of Capt Kenneth Dahlstrom. To US Navy as 121443.

333   Me 262A-1a   W Nr *unknown*
Fighter, initially titled *Feudin 54th A.D. Sq* but also named *Pauline*.
Later renamed *Deelovely*. Aircraft of Lt Robert Anspach. Landed
on Jersey on 30th June 1945, but then to Cherbourg and thence to
the USA aboard HMS *Reaper*. To US Navy as 121444.

Above: **Me 262A 222 Lady Jess IV**, at Melun in June 1945. *NASM courtesy Jeff Ethell collection*

Below: **Me 262A 444 Connie the Sharp Article**, at Lechfeld in June 1945. *NASM*

Top: **Me 262A 111 Screamin' Meemie**, photographed at Melun in June 1945 *USAF Museum*

Above: **Me 262A 444 Pick II**, at Melun on 28th June 1945. *NASM*

Above: **Me 262A 555 *Vera*, at Lechfeld on 10th June 1945, awaiting delivery to Melun.** *NASM*

Right: **Me 262A 555 *Willie*, in the line-up at Melun, awaiting review by Carl Spaatz.** *NASM*

Below: **Me 262A 555 *Willie*, on fire at Cherbourg on 6th July 1945. It was repaired and is the aircraft now at NAS Willow Grove.**
Will Riepl collection courtesy Frederick A. Johnsen

444   Me 262A-1a/U3   W Nr *unknown*

Photo-reconnaissance variant, named *Connie the Sharp Article* and then *Pick II*. Aircraft of Lt Roy W. Brown. To the USA aboard HMS *Reaper*. Ferried from Newark to Pittsburgh and Freeman Field on 19th August 1945 by Col Harold Watson. Became 'FE-4012'. This aircraft had a fighter nose substituted for the bulged reconnaissance version after arrival in the US. It is now at the Planes of Fame Museum at Chino in California wearing the incorrect W Nr 111617.

555   Me 262B-1a   W Nr 110639

Two-seat trainer, named *Vera* and later *Willie* (for Willie Hoffman, the Messerschmitt pilot who checked out the USAAF pilots on the '262). Suffered a nosewheel collapse on landing at Cherbourg/Querqueville on 6th July 1945 and damaged. Repaired, with parts salvaged from Lechfeld and taken to the USA aboard HMS *Reaper*. This aircraft is the example currently at NAS Willow Grove.

666   Me 262A-1a/U3   W Nr 500098
Photo-reconnaissance variant, named *Joanne* then *Cookie VII*. Air-craft of Capt Fred Hillis. To the USA aboard HMS *Reaper*. Allotted an untraced 'FE-' number while at Newark, probably 'FE-4011'. Crashed at Pittsburgh Airport while *en route* from Newark to Freeman Field on 19th August 1945 and written off when it over ran the runway and caught fire on landing, flown by Lt Ken Holt.

777   Me 262A-1a   W Nr *unknown*
Fighter, initially named *Doris* and then *Jabo Bait*. Aircraft of Lt William V. Haynes. To the USA aboard HMS *Reaper*. Became 'FE-110' after arrival in the USA.

888   Me 262A-1a   W Nr 500491
Fighter, coded 'Yellow 7' of IV/JG 7. Named *Dennis* then *Ginny H.* Aircraft of Lt James K. Holt, named for his fiancée. After arrival in the USA aboard HMS *Reaper*, became 'FE-111'. Now with the National Air and Space Museum, Washington, DC.

999   Me 262B-1a/U1   W Nr 110306
Two-seat night-fighter, coded 'Red 6' of IV/NJG 11. Surrendered to the RAF at Schleswig and became 'USA 2'. Named *Ole Fruit Cake* after handover to Col Watson. To the USA aboard HMS *Reaper* and to 'FE-610' after arrival there. Last seen at Cornell University in the early 1950s. (See 'USA 2' for further details also).

Me 262A 666 *Cookie VII*, at Cherbourg in July 1945. *Charles A. Barr*

Cookie VII after its landing accident at Pittsburgh on 19th August 1945. *Robert J. Craver collection*

Above: **Me 262A 777 *Jabo Bait*, at Newark on 24th August 1945.** *Ed Maxfield collection*

Right: **Me 262B 999 *Ole Fruit Cake* at Melun.** *ASM*

Below: **Me 262A *Dennis* at Lechfeld. This was later '88' and named *Ginny H*, the aircraft is in the ASM, Washington, DC.** *Eugene Freiburger collection*

101   Me 262B-1a   W Nr 110165

Two-seat trainer. Surrendered to the RAF at Schleswig and became 'USA 3'. 101 was named *What Was It ?*. Although this aircraft has been reported as being the example now at NAS Willow Grove this is incorrect. Nevertheless, it seems certain that this aircraft was taken to the US aboard HMS *Reaper*. It is believed that it was the US Navy aircraft BuAer 121441, last heard of at the Naval Research Laboratory, NAS Anacostia, on the scrap pile, in November 1946.

Top: **Me 262B 101 in British markings at Schleswig.** *NASM*

Above: **Me 262B 101 *What Was It?* at Melun.** *NASM*

202 **Arado Ar 234B** **W Nr** *unknown*
Named *Jane I*. To US Navy as BuAer No. 121445. To the USA aboard HMS *Reaper*. Flown to NAS Patuxent River and scrapped there. (See note below regarding probable origin).

303 **Arado Ar 234B** **W Nr** *unknown*
Named *Snafu I*. To the USA aboard HMS *Reaper* and then to the US Navy as BuAer No. 121446. Flown to NAS Patuxent River and scrapped there.

404 **Arado Ar 234B** **W Nr 140311**
Surrendered to the RAF at Stavanger in Norway and identified as 'USA 40'. To USAAF as 'FE-1011' after arrival in the USA.

Top: **Ar 234B 202 after arrival at NATC Patuxent River.** *US National Archives 80G-408622*

Above: **Ar 234B 303 *Snafu I* at Melun in June 1945. *Snafu* is an acronym for 'situation normal, all fouled up'.** *Robert Anspach collection*

505 **Arado Ar 234B** **W Nr 140312**
Surrendered to the RAF at Stavanger in Norway and identified as 'USA 50'. To the USAAF as FE-1010 after arrival in the USA.

Above: **L to R: Brigadier George Macdonald, Colonel Watson, General Spaatz, Lt Dahlstrom, 27th June 1945, taken on the occasion General Spaatz reviewed 'Watson's Whizzers' at Melun.**
Roy Brown collection

Right: **Maxfield, McIntosh, Ordway, Braun, Namowicz, Woolams etc., taken in front of the C-47 used by Watson's Whizzers'.**
Fred McIntosh collection

'Watson's 'Whizzers' Data Matrix

Whizzers No.	Type	Captured	W Nr (Code)	54th ADS Name	Whizzers Name	Reaper No.	Service	Serial No. in US	Fate
000	Me 262A-1a/U4	Lechfeld	170083 (V-083)	Wilma Jeanne	Happy Hunter	–	–	–	Crashed in France
111	Me 262A-1a	Lechfeld	?	Beverley Anne	Screemin' Meemie	20	US Navy	121442	USAF Museum
222	Me 262A-1a/U3	Lechfeld	– (30)	Marge	Lady Jess IV	–	US Navy	121443	Crashed at Patuxent 7.11.45
333	Me 262A-1a	Lechfeld	–	Pauline	Deelovely	–	US Navy	121444	Displayed at NAS Anacostia, scrapped.
444	Me 262A-1a/U3	Lechfeld	? † (25)	Connie the Sharp Article	Pick II	19	USAAF	FE-4012	Air Museum, Chino, California
555	Me 262B-1a	Lechfeld	110639 (35)	Vera	Willie	–	US Navy	121448	NAS Willow Grove
666	Me 262A-1a/U3	Lechfeld	500098 (27)	Joanne	Cookie VII	–	USAAF	FE-4011	Crashed at Pittsburgh 19.8.45
777	Me 262A-1a	Lechfeld	? (L)	Doris	Jabo Bait	14	USAAF	FE-110	Not known
888	Me 262A-1a	Lechfeld	500491 (Yellow 7)	Dennis	Ginny H	29	USAAF	FE-111	NASM, Washington D.C.
999	Me 262B-1a/U1	Schleswig	110306 (Red 6)	–/USA 2	Ole' Fruit Cake	–	USAAF	FE-610	Last noted at Comell University
101	Me 262B-1a	Schleswig	110165	–/USA 3	What Was It?	–	US Navy	121441	Scrapped at NAS Anacostia
202	Ar 234B	Grove	? *	–	Jane I	11	US Navy	121445	Scrapped at NAS Patuxent
303	Ar 234B	Grove	? *	–	Snafu I ‡	13	US Navy	121446	Scrapped at NAS Patuxent
404	Ar 234B	Stavanger	140311 (H)	–/USA 40	–	28	USAAF	FE-1011	Scrapped at Freeman Field
505	Ar 234B	Stavanger	140312	–/USA 50	–	27	USAAF	FE-1010	NASM, Silver Hill, Maryland

* one of these was 140489, ex 'USA 5'.   † is now marked as 111617, which is incorrect.   ‡ Snafu is an acronym for 'Situation normal, all fouled up'.

Chapter Seventeen

German and Italian Aircraft in the USA Post-war

The USAAF Disarmament organisation set up Centers at Stuttgart, Nuremberg and Munich to which aircraft selected in the US Zone of Occupation were initially sent. 'Flyables' were ferried from these Centers or from their place of surrender to Paris (either Melun/Villaroche or Villacoublay/Velizy) and then to Cherbourg. At Cherbourg the aircraft were covered in preservative and tarpaulins and taken by road to the port where they were loaded on board the Royal Navy escort carrier HMS *Reaper*. The carrier made one trip carrying forty-one complete aircraft, leaving Cherbourg on 19th July 1945 and arriving at Pier 14, New York, on 31st July 1945. The aircraft were taken to Newark, New Jersey, and flown onwards to Patuxent River, Maryland, (US Navy aircraft). or to Wright Field, Ohio or Freeman Field, Indiana (USAAF aircraft). Other aircraft, including an engineless Me 262A, a Focke Wulf Ta 154A night fighter, two Me 163B and five sailplanes, were shipped from Cherbourg on board the Liberty ship *Richard J. Gatling*, also during July 1945.

One aircraft, the Junkers Ju 290A 'USA 022' *Alles Kaputt*, made the transatlantic flight under its own power while a few other examples were shipped on merchant vessels, in some cases after engineering evaluation in the UK prior to shipment to their final destination.

17.1   **FREEMAN FIELD**

In early June 1945, Air Technical Service Command was aware that it would receive an influx of captured German material, too large to be handled at Wright Field. A search then began for a nearby installation which would have the room to handle these aircraft. Clinton County Army Air Field was at first considered, but was dismissed because it had insufficient hangarage.

The choice fell on Freeman Field, Seymour, Indiana, one hour's flight away from Wright Field in the neighbouring state to Ohio. Freeman Field was transferred to ATSC from the 1st Air Force, to be used as a captured equipment centre, the handover taking place on 15th June 1945. The official title of Freeman Field was the 'Foreign Aircraft Evaluation Center'. The Center provided storage and engineering overhaul facilities. Once aircraft were restored to airworthiness, they either flew to Wright Field for detailed evaluation, or test flights were made from Freeman Field under specific detailed instruction from Wright Field. Freeman Field itself lacked the necessary equipment and personnel to analyse and evaluate the test results.

This method of working was inefficient and at the end of 1945 it was decided to re-allocate the overhaul engineering task to one of the existing Air Materiel Areas (AMAs) of Air Technical Service Command. (The AMA was a unit of the USAAF/USAF, akin to an RAF Maintenance Unit, capable of carrying out 'Depot Level' maintenance on various selected aircraft types). The task was then handed over to the Middletown AMA, Olmsted Field.

By the time this decision was taken, almost all the German aircraft selected for evaluation by Col Watson's 'Whizzers' had been received at Wright or Freeman Fields. Freeman Field personnel who had travelled to Langley Field in Virginia to service Japanese aircraft shipped from Japan were recalled to Freeman Field and the aircraft were moved by road and rail to Middletown, as described in Chapter Eighteen.

The sign at the Freeman Field gate – inscribed on a Focke Wulf Fw 190 wing.
Ken Hammer courtesy Norm Malayney collection

However, in addition to its role in the reconditioning and flight test of enemy aircraft, Freeman Field had been given the task of preserving examples of enemy aircraft and equipment for museum purposes. This task had been extended to include important types of US aircraft. While the testing and rebuilding work diminished, efforts were directed to carefully dismantle and crate both US and Axis aircraft for use in a future museum. These aircraft were then almost all shipped by road or rail to No. 803 Special Depot, Orchard Place, Park Ridge, Illinois, where they were placed in long-term storage. A few examples which were already in an airworthy state were ferried to Orchard Place, which was at the time an aircraft factory recently used by Douglas Aircraft to build C-54 Skymasters. The Orchard Place site is now the main international airport for Chicago. Its 'Orchard Place' origin is enshrined in the IATA three-letter designator for Chicago/O'Hare IAP, which is 'ORD'. This designator appears on such things as baggage labels on items consigned to Chicago.

<hr />

17.2 UNITED STATES ARMY AIR FORCE AIRCRAFT ALLOCATED FE-/T2- NUMBERS

As described in Chapter Thirteen, these markings were used to identify Axis aircraft evaluated by the USAAF at Wright Field and other Air Force test establishments. The logic behind the allocation of the individual aircraft identity numbers is not known. It is evident that the first main series, starting at 100, applied to single-seater fighter types and that a certain commonality of type or aircraft duty applied to other series of numbers. However, neither the basic logic nor a complete list of allocations has been traced in documented form. The most complete source of the numbers is the list of 'German Aircraft available for study by Industry' origi-

nally published on 10th March 1946, together with its various updates. A reasonably comprehensive but not complete list appears below. German aircraft are listed first, followed by Italian types. (British aircraft are included for completeness). Japanese types follow in Chapter Eighteen.

FE-1/T2-1   Bachem Ba 349B Natter
Believed to have been surrendered to US Forces at the DFS establishment at St Leonards, near Salzberg in Austria. Shipped to the USA but not flown. Taken to Freeman Field and prepared for static display by May 1946. In June 1946 taken to Park Ridge and is currently on display with the National Air and Space Museum, Silver Hill, Md.

FE-7/T2-7   Horten Ho IIIh (See FE/T2-5039, '5041)
This flying-wing sailplane was at Freeman Field by 16th May 1946. At that point it was awaiting 600-man hours of repair effort prior to being made flyable and was assigned for display purposes. By 1st August 1946 it had been re-assigned to the proposed Air Museum and was subsequently taken to Park Ridge for storage. It is currently in storage at the National Air and Space Museum Paul E. Garber facility at Silver Hill, Md. This is one of the series of flying-wing sailplanes built by the brothers Horten; this example was built in 1944.

Although 'FE-7' is recorded as a Horten III, it is possible that it might have been the Horten Ho II described at the end of this Chapter, for which no 'FE-' number has been traced.

The Bachem Ba 349B T2-1 on display at Freeman Field in September 1945. *USAF Museum*

FE-106   Junkers Ju 88
This number has been reported as a Ju 88. It may have been allocated to one of two Ju 88s which became FE-1598 and FE-1599.

FE-107/T2-107   Messerschmitt Me 262A-1a
At Wright Field from 21st May 1945. This must be one of two Me 262A shipped from Rouen early in May. One of these was the Hans Fay aircraft detailed under T2-711, while the other was an engineless example captured at Giebelstadt. The latter was not returned to airworthy status. The number may equally have been allotted to W Nr 111711, which is usually referred to as T2-711. 'T2-711' used the last three numbers of the aircraft Werk Nummer and was not an official Air Intelligence identity number.

FE-108   Messerschmitt Me 262
Allocation only. The status board at Wright Field showed these marks as allotted to one of the 'Watson's Whizzers' Me 262 aircraft brought to the USA aboard HMS *Reaper*. The entry states that the aircraft was delivered instead to the US Navy at NAS Patuxent.

FE-109   Messerschmitt Me 262
Comments as for FE-108 – i.e. marks not used, aircraft recorded as being assigned to the USN instead of the USAAF.

FE-110/T2-110   Messerschmitt Me 262A-1a
Recorded at Wright Field from 1st August 1945 although on that date it was still en route from Newark after shipment aboard HMS *Reaper*.

Previously '777' with 'Watson's Whizzers'. It was flown from Newark to Freeman Field on 28th September 1945 and was flown by Col Watson at Freeman Field during a display for the Institute of Aeronautical Sciences there on the following day. On 16th May 1946, it was still at Freeman Field on re-work after a series of test flights; by 19th June it was on the strength of Wright Field and was in use as a mobile display exhibit. No further record. It is possibly the aircraft which was displayed as a static exhibit at Bolling AFB, Washington, DC, for some years after the war. The Bolling Field aircraft has been reported as W Nr 113367, although this is not confirmed.

Right: **A ground to air shot of Me 262A FE-110 taken at Freeman Field on 29th September 1945.** *NASM*

Below **Me 262A T2-110 at Freeman Field.**
Edgar Deigan courtesy Norm Malayney collection

Above: **Heinkel He 162A T2-489 landing at Muroc, after its flight by Bob Hoover.** *USAF Museum*

Right: **The Gotha Go 229V-3 T2-490 in store at Silver Hill in 1988. It is to be hoped that this aircraft will be restored for display.** *Alan Curry collection*

Left: **Bf 109G T2-123 on display at an unknown location.** *Edgar Deigan courtesy N. Malayney collection*

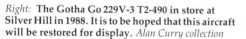

FE-490/T2-490   Horten Ho 229V-3 (Go 229V-3)   W Nr *unknown*

Surrendered in April 1945 in incomplete condition at a Gotha dispersal factory at Fredrichsroda known as Ortlepp Mobel Fabrik. Shipped to the USA. By 16th May 1946 FE-490 was in storage at Freeman Field; it was estimated that 15,000 man hours would be required to make the aircraft flyable. By August 1946 the Horten was being restored to display condition prior to transfer to Park Ridge for the Museum. It is currently stored with the Paul E. Garber facility of the National Air and Space Museum, Silver Hill, Maryland. This aircraft has never flown.

FE-493/T2-493   Heinkel He 162A-1   W Nr *unknown*

Although the USAAF captured He 162s in the Halle area, these seem to have been incomplete aircraft and it is believed that those intended for flight probably came from Leck, where large numbers of serviceable examples had been surrendered to the RAF. This aircraft may be W Nr 120067 'White 7', which was a '162 known to have been at Wright Field.

Transferred from Freeman Field to No. 803 Special Depot, Park Ridge, on 31st May 1946 for Museum storage. No further record has been found for this aircraft.

FE-494/T2-494   Heinkel He 162A-2   W Nr 120017
This Heinkel was recorded in storage at Freeman Field on 1st
August 1946. Believed to be 'Yellow 6' of JG1. It had been used as
a source of spare parts to service T2-489. No further record.

FE-495/T2-495   Messerschmitt Me 163B-1a   W Nr *unknown*
This aircraft (and the other Me 163Bs taken to the US) has been
reported as being surrendered at Rendsburg in the British Zone of
Occupation. It was taken by road to Cherbourg and shipped to the
US. This Me 163B was recorded at Wright Field on 1st August
1946, in use as a mobile display exhibit. It is believed to have been
scrapped in about 1950, after use in USAF recruitment displays up
to that time.

FE-496/T2-496   Messerschmitt Bf 109G-6   W Nr 160163
Origin unknown, but possibly captured in Italy in July 1944. At
Freeman Field, 17th May 1946. To No.803 Special Depot, Park
Ridge, on 31st May 1946 for Museum storage. It is currently with

the National Air and Space Museum, on display in the main
museum in Washington, DC, having been restored to display condition between 1972 and '74.

FE-497/T2-497   Focke Wulf Fw 190A-3   W Nr *unknown*
This example was recorded as in storage in incomplete condition
at Freeman Field on 1st August 1946. Nothing is known of its origin, but it may be the example previously identified as EB-101.

FE-498/T2-498   Macchi MC 202   C/n *unknown*
Possibly ex MM 9476. (See EB-300/FE-300 in Chapter Thirteen for
initial history). This aircraft was in flyable condition at Freeman
Field, as FE-300, in September 1945. By April 1946 it had been
renumbered as T2-498 and was assigned for display purposes.
During August 1946 it was crated and despatched to Park Ridge
for Museum storage.

It is now on display in the National Air and Space Museum at
Washington, DC.

Far right top: **FE-496 as it is today in the NASM in
Washington, DC.** *Alan Curry collection*

Far right bottom: **The MC 202 FE-498 (formerly
FE-300) at Silver Hill in July 1972.** *P. H. Butler
collection*

Right: **The Bf 109G FE-496 at Freeman Field.**
USAF Museum

Below: **Me 163B FE-495 at a USAF recruiting
display after the war.** *NASM photo*

Above: **The Me 410A FE-499 at Wright Field.**
P. M. Bowers

Right: **The Me 410A T2-499 in 'deep store' at Silver Hill.** *Alan Curry collection*

FE-499/T2-499   Messerschmitt Me 410A-2/U1   W Nr 10018
This aircraft, coded 'F6+WK' of 2(F)/122, was found in undamaged condition at Trapani, Sicily, in August 1943, its capture being recorded in RAF AI.2(g) Intelligence Report No. 204 of 12th August. Its radio call-sign was 'DI+NN' and it was built by Messerschmitt at Augsburg. It was shipped to the USA and was at Wright Field by 7th October 1944. It was originally identified as EB-103 but then renumbered as FE-499. It was recorded at Freeman Field on 17th May 1946 and was still there on 1st August 1946, by which time it had been assigned for display duty. It must subsequently have been transferred to Museum storage at Park Ridge. It is now with the National Air and Space Museum in storage at Silver Hill, Md. (See also entry for EB-103, Chapter Thirteen).

FE-500/T2-500   Messerschmitt Me 163B-1a   W Nr 191301
It is possible that this Me 163B was the example air-freighted from Europe to the USA aboard a Douglas C-54, immediately after handover to Col Watson. After arriving at Freeman Field and being refurbished there, this aircraft was air-freighted to Muroc (now known as Edwards Air Force Base), California, in a Fairchild C-82 Packet on 12th April 1946.

The first attempted flight trial was made on 3rd May 1946, in the presence of Dr A. Lippisch, the designer of the aircraft, but this was not successful because the towrope from the towing Boeing B-29 accidentally released. The Me 163 was towed to altitude by a Boeing B-29 and then released at 30-35,000 feet for a gliding descent. These trials were mostly flown by Gustav E. Lundquist, who had previously been a test pilot at Wright Field. Some details of the tests are given in a series of reports, reference F-IM-112-ND.

Although rocket fuel was obtained to enable powered flights to be made, flying trials were abandoned when delamination of the wooden wing structure was found. The '163 then went to Norton AFB, Ca, where it was stored until being transferred to Silver Hill in 1954. After years of storage, this aircraft is now on display with the National Air and Space Museum at the Silver Hill facility.

FE-501/T2-501   Messerschmitt Me 163B-1a   W Nr unknown
At Freeman Field on 17th May 1946. Recorded as 'to be scrapped for spare parts' on 25th September 1946 – previously parts of this aircraft had been used to service T2-500.

FE-502/T2-502   Messerschmitt Me 163B-1a   W Nr unknown
At Freeman Field on 17th May 1946. Recorded as 'to be scrapped for spare parts' on 25th September 1946 – as with FE-501, parts of this aircraft had been used in the refurbishment of T2-500.

FE-503/T2-503   Messerschmitt Me 163B-1a   W Nr unknown
This Me 163B was recorded as under restoration at Freeman Field on 1st August 1946, pending delivery to the Bell Aircraft Corporation at Buffalo, NY. Jack Woolams, the Chief Test Pilot of Bell Aircraft, had previously made requests to carry out test flights of the Me 163B, in connection with the Bell company's work on the experimental Bell XS-1 rocket-powered aircraft then under development. With Woolams' death in a flying accident on 30th August 1946 it is probable that the intended Bell test programme of the Me 163 was cancelled. There is no further record of this Me 163.

Note: One of the above Me 163B (FE-495, -501, 502, -503) had the W Nr 191190.

FE-504/T2-504   Heinkel He 162A-2   W Nr 120230
This aircraft was at Freeman Field on 1st August 1946, assigned to the Display Branch. It had been assembled with the tail unit of another He 162 captured in Europe, W Nr 120222, and had been coded 'White 23' of JG 1. This aircraft is at present with the National Air and Space Museum, Silver Hill, Maryland.

Below: **Me 163B T2-500 at Silver Hill 1988.** *Alan Curry collection*

FE-505/T2-505   Blöhm und Voss Bv 155B (V2)   W Nr *unknown*
Surrendered to British forces at the Blöhm u Voss Finkenwerder works in incomplete condition. Shipped to the UK and taken to Farnborough by 20th October 1945 to appear in the static display at the German Aircraft Exhibition there from 29th October to 9th November 1945. Transferred to No. 47 MU, Sealand, on 26th November 1945 and shipped to New York aboard the SS *Port Fairy* on 27th January 1946. It was then taken to Freeman Field, Indiana, and later went from Freeman to Park Ridge for storage with the other Museum aircraft, arriving there on 21st August 1946. It is currently stored for the National Air and Space Museum. This aircraft had never flown. Reports of it having the RAF serial 'PN820' are erroneous. There is still controversy about whether this aircraft was the Bv 155V2 or V3; the writer believes only one aircraft, the V2, was involved. Certainly the aircraft at Farnborough, Freeman Field and at Silver Hill was one and the same, since its engine serial number is the same.

FE-610/T2-610   Messerschmitt Me 262B-1a/U1   W Nr 110306
This aircraft was surrendered to the RAF at Schleswig in May 1945 and was initially identified as 'USA 2'. It was a two-seat night-fighter variant of the Me 262B two-seat trainer. 110306 was handed over to the USAAF in Europe and flown to Melun/Villaroche on 19th June 1945.

It was identified with the 'Watson's Whizzers' number '999' and the name *Ole Fruit Cake*. It was flown to Cherbourg prior to shipment to New York aboard the escort carrier HMS *Reaper* in July 1945. It became FE-610 upon arrival in the USA and is believed to have been ferried from Newark to Freeman Field on 28th September 1945. FE-610 was at Freeman Field on 17th May 1946. As at 1st August 1946 it was recorded as in flyable condition at Washington, DC, where it was taking part in a static display organised for the US Secretary of War. It was later scrapped, last being heard of at Cornell University in about 1950. Reports that this is the aircraft at NAS Willow Grove are incorrect – the latter aircraft is an Me 262B trainer version.

FE-611/T2-611   Junkers Ju 88G-6   W Nr *unknown*
This was 'USA 21', an aircraft surrendered to the RAF at Grove in Denmark and later handed over to Col Watson. To the USA aboard HMS *Reaper*. This aircraft was in storage at Freeman Field on 1st August 1946. Its final fate is unknown. Although the USAF Museum aircraft has been recorded as a Ju 88G-6 in various references, it is, in fact, a Ju 88D bomber version, not a Ju 88G night-fighter, and therefore is not FE-611.

FE-612/T2-612   Heinkel He 219A-0   W Nr 210903
This aircraft was surrendered to the RAF at Grove in Denmark and was initially identified as 'USA 8' originally having the Luftwaffe call-sign SP+CR. It was handed over to Col Watson and was shipped to the USA aboard HMS *Reaper*. It was at Freeman Field on 17th May 1946; although at first it was allotted for storage at Park Ridge, Illinois, that allotment was cancelled, and FE-614 was substituted for it. FE-612 was then assigned to the Display Branch and was later scrapped.

FE-613/T2-613   Heinkel He 219A   W Nr 290060
Call-sign 'CS+QG'. Details of origin are generally as for FE-612. It was 'USA 9' at Grove before handover by the RAF to Col Watson. This He 219 was used as a source of spares to service T2-614. On 1st August 1946 it was in storage at Freeman Field; it is presumed to have been scrapped later.

FE-614/T2-614   Heinkel He 219A   W Nr 290202
Details generally as FE-612. It was 'USA 10' at Grove before handover by the RAF to Col Watson. It was at Freeman Field in May 1946 and was under restoration to fly – on 1st August 1946 its restoration was logged as '90% complete'. Due to policy changes it was re-assigned for Museum storage and was shipped from Freeman Field to No. 803 Special Depot, Park Ridge, Illinois, on 17th September 1946. It is currently in storage at the Silver Hill facility of the National Air and Space Museum.

T2-711   Messerschmitt Me 262A-1a   W Nr 111711
So far as is known 111711 did not wear an 'FE-' or 'T2-' number but it is referred to in some documents as 'T2-711'. 111711 was surrendered at Frankfurt/Rhein-Main by defecting Messerschmitt test pilot Hans Fay, on 31st March 1945. The Me 262 was on its first test flight from Hessental where it had been built by the Messerschmitt-controlled company, Autobedarf Schwabisch Hall. It was examined on site by the USAAF Air Intelligence organisation and then shipped onwards from Rouen, France to the USA by a fast merchant ship, the *Manawska Victory*.

After re-assembly at Wright Field, it was test flown by Russ Schleeh on 29th August 1945, wearing its German Werk Nummer 111711, and was generally referred to as '711' or 'T2-711'. After 12 flights at Wright Field, totalling 10 hours 40 minutes, the aircraft suffered an engine fire and was abandoned by its pilot and crashed on 20th August 1946 at Xenia, Ohio. Its first two flights by Russ Schleeh on 29th August and 12th September 1945 totalled 1 hour 45 minutes. Later flights were by Major Walter J. McAuley. Details of the tests of this aircraft were given in Technical Report F-TR-1133-ND, published in 1947. The report summarised Project No. NAD 29, 'Evaluation of the Me 262'.

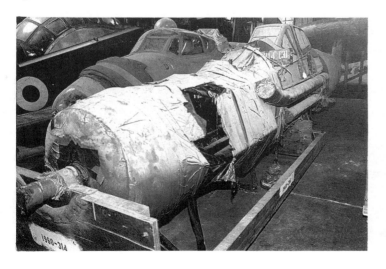

It was concluded that the '262 suffered from some poor features, including poor brakes (which were criticised on almost all German and Japanese aircraft tested by the Allies). During the course of the tests, '711 required five engine changes, which merely confirmed the early stage of development of the jet engine, and the difficulties of the German war machine in obtaining suitable high-temperature materials. Although the handling characteristics of the '262 were considered poor, this was blamed on the fact that those flown had their aileron and elevator servo-tabs disconnected.

The overall conclusion was that 'T2-711' was superior to the average Lockheed P-80A in acceleration and speed, and comparable in climb performance, despite a weight penalty of 2,000 lbs. A maximum True Air Speed of 568 mph was measured at a pressure altitude of 20,200 feet.

Far left: **The Blöhm und Voss Bv 155B in store at Silver Hill in 1988.** *Alan Curry collection*

Left: **Ar 234B T2-1010 at Freeman Field.** *NASM*

Right: **The He 219A FE-612 at Freeman Field.** *NASM*

Below: **Me 262A 'Old 711' on an early test flight from Wright Field.** *USAF Museum*

FE-1010/T2-1010   Arado Ar 234B-2   W Nr 140312

Surrendered to the RAF at Stavanger in Norway and handed over to Col Watson. Flown to Melun and then to Cherbourg for onward shipment to the USA aboard HMS *Reaper*. It was recorded as under restoration at Freeman Field on 16th May 1946, with the work '98% complete'. By 1st August it was 'flyable' at Wright Field, assigned to the Flight Test Unit (Bomber Test).

More than twenty hours of test flying were completed on this aircraft at Wright Field. The tests were reported in Report F-TR-1139-ND released in February 1947. Shortly after the flight tests were completed, the aircraft was flown to Park Ridge for Museum storage, by Lt Col Fred J. Ascani who was one of the pilots involved in tests of this aircraft and was the Chief of Bomber Test at the Flight Test Division at the time. Other flights of the '234

were made by Maj C. Cardenas, Capt James M. Little and Lt Charles J. Clemence Jr.

This aircraft is currently in the Silver Hill facility of the National Air and Space Museum and its restoration to display condition was completed early in 1989. It is believed that this aircraft will be transferred to the main Air and Space Museum in downtown Washington. As restored, the '234 is painted in the markings of an aircraft of KG76, coded as 'F1+GS'; these markings were not found on the aircraft during its restoration, but were selected as being suitably representative markings.

FE-1011/T2-1011   Arado Ar 234B-2   W Nr 140311
This Ar 234B was 'USA 40', also surrendered to the RAF at Stavanger in Norway and turned over to Col Watson. T2-1011 was at Freeman Field in May 1946, where it was in storage after providing parts for the restoration of T2-1010. By 15th August 1946 it was still at Freeman but was 'recommended for salvage'.

FE-1012/T2-1012   Dornier Do 335A-0   W Nr 240101
Surrendered to US Forces at the Dornier works at Oberpfaffenhofen and ferried from there to Neubiberg and then via Roth to Cherbourg for transport to the USA on board HMS *Reaper*. One of the Do 335s, almost certainly this aircraft, arrived at Cherbourg on 17th June 1945, piloted by Flugkapitan Padell. At Freeman Field on 17th May 1946 by which date its restoration was 75% complete; it was at Freeman Field still on 15th August, still awaiting the delivery of its engines from overhaul. Subsequent history is untraced.

FE-1597/T2-1597   Junkers Ju 188D-2   W Nr 150245
Surrendered to the RAF at Grove in Denmark and later flown from Schleswig to RAE Farnborough on 6th July 1945 as 'Air Min 35'. After storage at No. 6 MU, Brize Norton, from 18th July to 20th December 1945 'AM 35' was flown back to the RAE and thence to the USAAF Base Air Depot at Burtonwood on 2nd January 1946. It was later packed for shipment to the USA at No. 47 MU, Sealand, and left Liverpool (reportedly on 22nd May 1946), *en route* to Freeman Field. It was recorded at Freeman Field on 16th May 1946 and was taken to No. 803 Special Depot, Park Ridge, Illinois, where it was received on 22nd July 1946. Its final fate has not yet been traced.

FE-1598   See entries in
FE-1599   Chapter Thirteen

FE-1600/T2-1600   Heinkel He 111H-16   W Nr 8433
Coded '2B+DC' and 'Red 4'. Call-sign 'BT+KV'. Flown to San Severo north of Foggia, Italy, by an Hungarian pilot on 14th December 1944. This aircraft is believed to have been flown to Wright Field during January 1945, or possibly to have been shipped there at a slightly later date. The He 111 was at Freeman Field by 16th May 1946, assigned to the Display Branch, but by 15th August was still there 'awaiting disposition'.

FE-1948   Arado Ar 234B
No further details - almost certainly an erroneous report.

Top right: **The USAAF Dornier Do 335, later to be FE-1012, photographed at Roth bei Nurnburg in June 1945. The pilot standing by the aircraft is Flugkapitan Hans Padell.** *Ed Maxfield collection*

Centre right: **The Heinkel He 111H FE-1600 at Freeman Field.**
Edgar Deigan courtesy Norm Malayney collection

Below right: **The Ju 88A FE-1599** *The Comanche* **at Freeman Field in 1945.** *H. G. Martin photo from Robert J. Pickett collection courtesy Kansas Aeronautical Historical Society*

Below left: **The Ar 234B T2-1010 in the final stages of its magnificent restoration in the workshops at Silver Hill in 1988.** *Alan Curry collection*

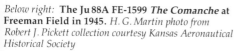

FE-2000/T2-2000   Dornier Do 17Z   **W Nr** *unknown*

Origin and details unknown. This aircraft was in storage in incomplete condition at Freeman Field on 17th May 1946 and was 'salvaged' (US terminology for scrapped) on 25th September 1946. An example of the Dornier Do 217 twin-engined bomber (a later development of the Do 17) was shipped from the Middle East to the USA in August 1944 aboard the US escort carrier *Shamrock Bay* (CVE-84). The carrier left Casablanca, with the Dornier aboard, on 21st August and had off-loaded it at New York by 1st September. It is possible that aircraft was the one reported as 'FE-2000', although it is also possible the Do 217 was used for structural tests. Photographs exist of a Do 17E or 'F in US markings with the name *Axis Sally*. This aircraft may be FE-2000, rather than a Do 17Z.

FE-2100/T2-2100   Heinkel He 177A-5   **W Nr 550062**

This was the ex-RAF Heinkel He 177 with the serial TS439, which was handed over to the USAAF following the accident to the USAAF's own He 177 at Orly late in February 1945.

It became 'FE-2100' on arrival in the USA and was at Freeman Field in crated storage by 16th May 1946 and was recorded as arriving at No. 803 Special Depot at Park Ridge on 4th October 1946 for Museum storage. Its fate is unknown.

FE-2600/T2-2600   DFS 108-49 Grunau Baby   **W Nr 031016**

This sailplane was at Freeman Field by 16th May 1946, assigned for display use and was still there in August 1946. This aircraft is currently on display at the Silver Hill facility of the National Air and Space Museum. The aircraft was built by Flugzeugbau Petera and is coded 'LZ-NC'.

FE-2601/T2-2601   'Secondary Glider'

This was also possibly a Grunau Baby. It was in crated storage at Freeman Field in May 1946 and by August had been assigned for transfer to Wright Field.

A possible candidate for the identity of this aircraft is the Flugzeugbau Petera-built Grunau Baby IIB W Nr 030240. This was registered on 24th September 1949 to the Soaring Society of Dayton, Ohio, as N69720. The registration documents show that this glider had been purchased as 'Air Force Surplus', probably from the nearby Wright Field. In 1983 this glider was still registered, although apparently inactive, with its owner shown as Walter G. Peterson of Madison, Wisconsin.

The USAAF retrieved further examples of the Grunau Baby from Germany. These included the Flugzeugbau Petera-built Grunau Baby W Nr 031014, which later appeared on the United States Civil Aircraft Register as N9070H. This example was damaged during shipment to the USA but was rebuilt after sale to a civilian owner. It was first registered as N9070H to the Pennsylvania Glider Council in about 1953, although it did not fly in the United States until its rebuild was completed in the hands of James C. Reilly at Davis-Edwards Airport, Long Island, on 12th July 1957. This Grunau was still registered, to its tenth American owner, Donald P. Hickman, in 1982.

FE-2700/T2-2700   Gotha Go 242B-4
(See entry in Chapter Thirteen)

FE-3400/T2-3400   Junkers Ju 290A-4   **W Nr 110165**

This aircraft, coded 'A3+HB' of KG 200, was surrendered to US Forces near Munich, probably at Riem, on 6th May 1945 and was initially identified as 'USA 022'. This number followed on from the first batch of identity numbers given by the RAF to aircraft surrendered in the British Zone of Occupation. The Ju 290 was flown from Munich to Roth bei Nürnberg later in the day of its surrender, 6th May 1945, and remained there until 9th July when it was flown to Beauvechain/Le Culot for installation of American-type radio equipment. The aircraft was named *Alles Kaputt* by Col Watson. On 19th July it flew from Le Culot to Orly and made a further test flight at Orly on 26th July. It then made its transatlantic delivery flight to Wright Field, as follows:

28 July	Paris/Orly – Lajes/Azores	9 hrs 10 mins flight time
30 July	Lajes – Kindley Field/Bermuda	12 hrs 15 mins
31 July	Bermuda – Patterson Field	6 hrs 30 mins
1 August	Patterson – Freeman Field	1 hr 30 mins

The crew for this flight included Col Watson, Capt McIntosh, Capt Maxfield and several other members of Watson's team. The Ju 290 distinguished itself by taking off from Lajes after President Truman's Douglas C-54 and arriving at Bermuda one hour ahead of the President's aircraft – quite a feat, bearing in mind that the C-54 (DC-4) was considered one of the leading transport aircraft of the day.

Patterson Field was adjacent to Wright Field and in the post-war era the two airfields became one base - i.e. Wright-Patterson AFB. The Ju 290 became FE-3400 upon arrival in the USA. It was

Far right top: **Junkers Ju 290A *Alles Kaputt* FE-3400 at Paris-Orly at the start of its record-breaking transatlantic delivery flight to Wright Field.** *NASM*

Right: **An early version Dornier Do 17 named *Axis Sally*, possibly photographed at Wright Field. Although FE-2000 has been reported as a Do 17Z, this example is an earlier variant, (Do 17E or 'F). It may nevertheless be the aircraft reported as FE-2000.** *USAF Museum*

Far right: **Grunau Baby FE-2600 (LZ-NC) at Freeman Field in 1945, with an SG.38 primary glider, Heinkel He 162A, Flettner Fl 282 helicopter and a Horten sailplane also visible.** *US National Archives 80G-420983*

Right: **The Me 262A T2-4012 at Wright Field.**
Edgar Deigan courtesy N. Malayney collection

Far right: **Junkers Ju 388L FE-4010 at Freeman Field.** *H. G. Martin photograph from Robert J. Pickett collection courtesy Kansas Aeronautical Historical Society*

Far right bottom: **The Henschel Hs 129B FE-4600 at Freeman Field in 1945.** *H. G. Martin photograph from Robert J. Pickett collection courtesy Kansas Aeronautical Historical Society.*

recorded at Wright Field on 25th September 1946 under overhaul for further flying but was 'salvaged' (scrapped) on 12th December 1946. When the aircraft was being dismantled an explosive charge was found in one wing; fortunately for 'Watson's Whizzers' *et al*, the detonator was defective and had failed to fire the charge!

FE-4010/T2-4010   Junkers Ju 388L-1   W Nr 560049
This aircraft was surrendered to US Forces at the Allgemeine Transport Gesellschaft factory at Merseburg in May 1945. It was flown from Merseburg to Kassel/Waldau (Y-96) for servicing by the 10th Air Depot Group on 20th May 1945. It was later, on 17th June, flown to Cherbourg/Querqueville and taken to the USA aboard HMS *Reaper*. The Ju 388 was taken to Freeman Field and, after reconditioning, made demonstration flights to the press there in September 1945. It was flown to Wright Field on 30th September 1945. By June 1946 it had returned to Freeman Field and was held in flyable condition. Technical Report F-TR-1138-ND was written on this aircraft and issued in October 1946.

Although initially assigned for transfer to storage at Davis-Monthan AFB, it was put into storage at No. 803 Special Depot, Park Ridge, Illinois, on 26th September 1946. It is at present in storage with the Silver Hill facility of the National Air and Space Museum.

FE-4011
Not traced, but probably Messerschmitt Me 262A-1a/U3, W Nr 500098, Watsons Whizzers No. 666 which crashed at Pittsburgh on 19th August 1945. '666' was a photo-reconnaissance aircraft, as were T2-4010 and T2-4012.

FE-4012/T2-4012   Messerschmitt Me 262A-1a/U3   W Nr *unknown*
This aircraft was surrendered to US Forces at Lechfeld and was named *Connie the Sharp Article*, with the number '444'. It was later re-named *Pick II* by Watson's Whizzers. It came to the USA aboard HMS *Reaper* and was flown from Newark to Freeman Field by Col Watson on 19th August 1945. While at Freeman Field it was reconditioned and given an overall smooth finish for performance comparison with the Lockheed P-80. This process almost certainly involved the removal of its photo-reconnaissance-type nose and its replacement by a fighter-type nose without camera bulges. On about 17th May 1946 Col Watson flew the aircraft to Patterson

Field for the start of this series of trials. It was flown at Patterson and Wright Fields on test work for 4 hours and 40 minutes (8 flights), being flyable at Wright Field in August 1946. Flight trials were discontinued after four engine changes were required during the course of the tests, culminating in two single-engined landings.

It was later handed over to the Hughes Aircraft Company. Howard Hughes proposed to enter the aircraft in air races in competition with USAF P-80s but this was officially frowned upon and the proposal was cancelled. The '262 had, in the meantime, been shipped to Hughes at Culver City, Ca, and was assembled and the engines run, but it was not flown by the Hughes company.

The '262 was disposed of to the Glendale Aeronautical School for use as an instructional airframe, until, after some years it was acquired by Edward T. Maloney for his Air Museum at Ontario, California. FE-4012 is currently with the Museum at Chino Airfield, California, marked as W Nr 111617, which is incorrect, the colour scheme being copied from the original 111617, which was scrapped on a dump near Munich at the end of the war.

FE-4600/T2-4600   Henschel Hs 129B-1/R2   W Nr *unknown*
This Hs 129 is the aircraft earlier identified as EB-105 (see Chapter Thirteen). It was at Freeman Field at the end of September 1945 when ex-Luftwaffe aircraft were on public display. It was still at Freeman Field on 17th May 1946. It was allotted for storage at Davis-Monthan AFB in Arizona but crashed at Gallatin, Tennessee, on 24th July 1946 while being ferried to Davis-Monthan by Lt Kenneth P. Almond. The aircraft ran out of fuel due to suspected tank leakage and was slightly damaged during the subsequent forced landing. It was taken to No. 803 Special Depot on 5th August 1946. When the Orchard Place storage depot was required for other purposes during the Korean War, FE-4600 was put up for disposal as scrap. The nose section was bought from the scrapyard by Earl Reinert in June 1951 and it remained in storage at his home until 1966. It then went on display at the Victory Air Museum, Mundelein, Illinois, which was formed by Earl Reinert and Paul Polidori. It remained on display until the Museum was dispersed following the death of Paul Polidori in a flying accident in 1985. In May 1986 the cockpit was purchased by Martin J. Mednis of Sydney, and taken to Australia. It is now being restored for display in his 'Der Adler Luftwaffe Museum'.

FE-4610/T2-4610   Messerschmitt Bf 108B-1   W Nr 8378

This aircraft was in the hands of Air Technical Intelligence at Villacoublay early in 1945, identified as 'GA-2'. It was used as a communications aircraft by the Air Technical Intelligence teams. It was transferred to the USA aboard HMS *Reaper*, with the intention that it should continue to be used for this duty in the USA, with an eye to its possible civilian certification in the US and use as a flying trophy by members of the team.

It is believed that the '108 was ferried from Newark to Freeman Field on 23rd August 1945 by Lt Robert Anspach. It was at Freeman Field on 17th May 1946 and was still there, in storage, on 1st August. This is the aircraft currently owned by the Planes of Fame Museum at Chino, California.

FE-4611/T2-4611   Bücker Bü 181 Bestmann   W Nr *unknown*

The two Bü 181s which later became -4611 and -4612 were captured at Merseburg or Halle shortly before the end of the war and were taken to the USA aboard HMS *Reaper* after serving as communications aircraft with Watson's ATI team, based at A-46 Toussus-le-Noble, which was the centre for collecting air freight for delivery to Wright Field. As this operation was closed down, the Bückers were flown to Villacoublay and then Cherbourg for shipment on board the *Reaper*. One of these two was test flown at Newark AAF on 20th September 1945 by Lt Bob Anspach and was ferried to Freeman Field by him on 4th October 1945.

This Bestmann was at Freeman Field in storage in May 1946; by August it was 'awaiting disposition'. Its W Nr is shown as 'K-2227' but this appears to be incorrect. It is now with the National Air and Space Museum on display at Silver Hill.

FE-4612/T2-4612   Bücker Bü 181 Bestmann   W Nr *unknown*

The origin of this aircraft was similar to that of FE-4611. This '181 was in store at Freeman Field on 16th May 1946 and by 15th August 1946 it was still there, 'recommended for salvage'.

FE-4613/T2-4613   Flettner Fl 282V-23   W Nr 280023

Code 'CI+TW'. One of the two Fl 282 was from Transport Staffel 40, surrendered at Ainring, the second was surrendered by Anton Flettner at Bad Tolz. Both this aircraft and FE-4614 were transported to the USA aboard HMS *Reaper*. This example was a two-seat version of the Fl 282 (FE-4614 was a single-seater variant). This

helicopter was flown by Prewitt Aircraft at Benedict Airport, Booth Corners, under the contract referred to under FE-4614; 4613 was flown for 95 hours – work done under contract Nos W33-038-ac15858 and -ac15926. Flight tests were conducted at Benedict Airport, Booth Corners, Pennsylvania, with the helicopter tethered and in free flight. The objectives of the tests were to determine power requirements, control response, stability measurements and a comparison between a straight and a 'butterfly' stabilizer. The test flights totalled approximately 20 flying hours. The flights were made by Prewitt Aircraft pilot, Dave Driskill, who had previously worked with Richard H. Prewitt when the latter had been Chief Engineer of the Kellett Autogiro Company. Reports of the test findings were published in November 1947.

FE-4614/T2-4614   Flettner Fl 282V-12   W Nr 280008

Code 'CJ+SF'. See FE-4613. After assembly and repair at Freeman Field, the helicopter was passed to the Prewitt Aircraft Co of Wallingford, Pennsylvania, under a contract (AAF W33-038-ac15926) to evaluate the stability and performance characteristics of the type.

FE-4614 was probably not flown by Prewitt, since -4613 was considered to be in better condition and it is believed that -4614 had been slightly damaged in an accident while at Freeman Field. Comparative tests were flown on -4613 using the different designs of tailplanes from the two aircraft. FE-4614 was handed over to Prewitt on 19th November 1946. This aircraft is also recorded as being tested by Grand Central Aircraft Inc in 1947, but this company has not been traced. Recorded as 'sold' in 1955.

Top left: **Bf 108 FE-4610 at Freeman Field in 1945.** *NASM*

Centre left: **Another, later photograph of the same Bf 108, but painted as T2-4610.** *Ashley Annis collection*

Bottom left: **Bücker Bü 181 Bestmann T2-4611 at Freeman Field in May 1946.** *Pete Bulban collection*

Top right: **The Flettner Fl 282 T2-4613 in flight at Benedict Airport, Booth Corners, Pa, in 1947, during trials by Prewitt Aircraft.** *USAF Museum*

Right: **The Fl 282 T2-4614 on arrival at Prewitt Aircraft, where it was cannibalised to make T2-4613 airworthy.** *USAF Museum*

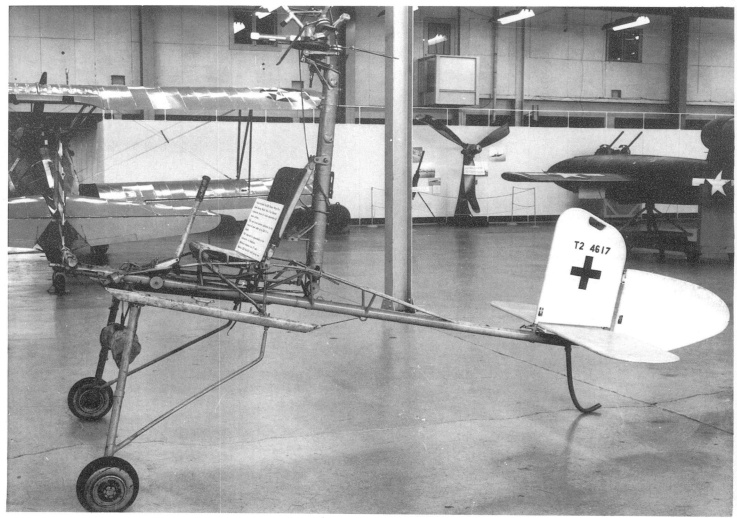

FE-4615/T2-4615   Doblhoff WNF 342V4   WNr *unknown*

This prototype helicopter was surrendered by its designer at Zell-am-See. It was shipped to Freeman Field but, after being held there for a time, it was transferred to Wright Field before May 1946. Some tethered flights were made at Wright Field under the supervision of Dr Doblhoff, prior to August 1946. Further flight trials were considered, but these would have required engineering development to have been carried out on the helicopter.

Because developments akin to the Doblhoff design were already under consideration by the Kellett Aircraft Corporation for its XR-17 helicopter, the WNF342 was sent to the General Electric Co at Schnectady, NY, for tests of its propulsion system in connection with the XR-17 project. In the meantime, Dr Doblhoff had visited General Electric and given it the benefit of his experience with the design concepts.

The XR-17 helicopter (later redesignated XH-17) used similar rotor-tip propulsion principles to the Doblhoff design. The XH-17 was later taken over by the Hughes Aircraft Company of Culver City, California. The WNF342 was used as a test-rig for component development to aid the XH-17 development programme. The work by General Electric was conducted under contract No. W33-038-ac10367, and was mainly concerned with studies of the propulsion control system. Work was completed in 1949 and reported in General Electric Co Report No. 87563. The final fate of the helicopter is unknown.

FE-4616/T2-4616   Focke-Achgelis Fa 330A   WNr *unknown*

This rotor-kite was at Freeman Field by 19th June 1946, assigned to the Display Branch. It was later 'bailed' (loaned) to Eastern Rotor Craft Inc of Pennsylvania, in 1947, for flight trials.

This example was one of two flown by Eastern Rotor Craft, which was contracted to carry out a full performance evaluation of the Fa 330 on behalf of Wright Field.

FE-4617/T2-4617   Focke Achgelis Fa 330A   WNr *unknown*

This Fa 330 was in storage at Freeman Field by 19th June 1946, being transferred to Wright Field during July 1946. This aircraft is now on display at the USAF Museum at Wright-Patterson AFB, Fairborn, Ohio.

FE-4618/T2-4618   Focke-Achgelis Fa 330A   WNr *unknown*

This Fa 330 was in store at Freeman Field by 19th June 1946. It was transferred to Wright Field during July. FE-4618 was test-flown at Wright Field, towed behind a truck. Four successful flights were made, followed by two in which the kite overturned on landing and was damaged. The damage was blamed on the tall wheeled undercarriage which had been fitted. This resulted in a high centre of gravity, which made the kite unstable on the ground and during the take-off phase. Previously, one of the Fa 330s had been rigidly mounted on a tiltable platform on a truck, which had been driven along a runway at speeds up to 35 knots to determine the adequacy of the rotor hub and blade strength.

Later, during 1948, it was test flown from a USAF patrol boat in Tampa Bay, adjacent to MacDill AFB, Tampa, Florida. The trials were initiated as a means of carrying out extended flights of the Fa 330, which were not possible under tow behind a truck confined to the length of the Wright Field runway. Another factor was consideration of a serious application – the possible use of the kite by the USAF as a means of extending the visual search range of small Rescue Boats.

The trials commenced in August 1948 and involved the construction of a platform on the aft deck of an 85-foot rescue boat. The kite was to be towed by a cable attached to a Navy Mark VII hydraulic winch installed on the boat. Several trials were conducted with the rotor kite tied down to the platform, before an attempt was made to carry out towed flight tests. The pilot was Capt Raymond A. Popson from the Flight Test Division at Wright Field. He was later killed in October 1953 in the crash of the second prototype Bell X-5 variable-sweep test aircraft.

Unfortunately, the kite broke away as it was launched, due to a mechanical failure of the cable connection. After the pilot was rescued from the sea, the site of the crash was marked with a buoy, but this was stolen, or washed away in a hurricane, before the kite could be recovered. The trials were therefore terminated. Although the pilot reported favourably on the trials, they were not continued. At the time the project ended, two further Fa 330s were available to conduct further flights. The test results were reported in Memorandum Report No. MCREXE-670-8-A of 31st December 1948, published by the Equipment Laboratory at Wright-Patterson AFB.

Note: Photographs show that T2-4618 was the kite involved in the MacDill AFB trials. The kite involved in the Tampa Bay trials was lost during these experiments. A correspondent recalls seeing such a kite in a war-surplus store in Tampa in 1969, which may have been the same kite after recovery. This may be the aircraft at Silver Hill or a quite different one which has since been painted as T2-4618.

Top left: **The fourth prototype Doblhoff WNF342 FE4615 making a tethered flight at Wright Field in 1946.** *USAF Museum*

Left: **The Focke Achgelis Fa 330A T2-4617 on display at Wright Field; the undercarriage was added by the USAAF to facilitate towed flight trials along the runways at Wright Field.** *USAF Museum*

Right: **The Fa 330 T2-4618 on board a USAF rescue boat adjacent to MacDill AFB, Florida, in 1948.** *USAF Museum*

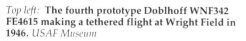

FE-5004/T2-5004   DFS 108-14 Schulgleiter (SG) 38
This primary glider was held at Freeman Field by 16th May 1946, assigned for display purposes. It was 'awaiting disposition' there by 15th August 1946.

FE-5005/T2-5005   'Primary Glider'   W Nr *unknown*
This glider (which was also probably an SG 38) was in store at Freeman Field by 16th May 1946. By 1st August 1946 it was assigned for transfer to Wright Field, but it is not known whether it, in fact, went there.
Note: It is probable that FE-5004 and '5005 are the two DFS SG 38s currently held in store with the NASM at Silver Hill.

FE-5038/T2-5038   Focke-Achgelis Fa 330A   W Nr *unknown*
In common with all the other Fa 330s taken to the USA, this example is believed to have been captured by the RAF at Kiel. This kite was 'bailed' (loaned) to California Aero Inc of Glendale, Ca, under bailment contract No. W33-038-ac18679 of 15th October 1947. It was also proposed to deliver Fa 330 T2-4616 as a source of spares for T2-5038, but the second example was deleted from the contract before delivery. T2-5038 was delivered to the Cal-Aero Technical Institute at Grand Central Airport, Glendale, on 2nd January 1948.

Cal-Aero proposed to carry out flight trials, but it seems that most of its effort was directed at providing a design exercise for its aeronautical engineering students. Cal-Aero proposed a powered development of the Fa 330 with a McCulloch 40-hp engine and modified fuselage structure, to be known as the XBK-1 Kite. So far as is known, no flight trials actually took place and the proposed XBK-1 was not constructed.

FE-5039/T2-5039   Horten Ho IIIf   W Nr 32
Captured at Rottweil am Neckar. This identity, and the number FE-5041, were allocated to two Horten Ho III flying-wing sailplanes brought to the USA from Germany. Both arrived in a damaged and incomplete condition. They were therefore not flown in the USA. Both of the Ho IIIs were shipped to Northrop for study at the same time as the Ho VI described next. This sailplane is in store at Silver Hill and is a prone-piloted single-seat version.

FE-5040/T2-5040   Horten Ho VI-V2   W Nr 34
The second incomplete prototype of the Ho VI flying-wing sailplane was surrendered at Bad Hersfeld and later shipped to Freeman Field. In 1947 it was 'bailed' to Northrop for study by pupils at Northrop Aeronautical Institute Inc. The petition for the loan of the aircraft was made jointly by Northrop and the Southern California Soaring Association. All three Horten sailplanes arrived at Northrop's Hawthorne facility on 22nd October 1947.

The Northrop concern had pioneered flying-wing design in the USA and the Horten sailplanes were therefore of particular interest to the company. A report on the Ho VI design was prepared by Stanley A. Hall, an employee of Northrop who was himself later to become prominent as a sailplane designer in the USA. Although it had been hoped to make flight tests with the Horten designs, they were judged to be in too bad a state of repair to be made airworthy.

The Ho VI was later transferred to the Smithsonian Institution and is currently in store with the NASM facility at Silver Hill, Maryland. This prototype of the Horten Ho VI has never flown, although the earlier Ho VI-V1 flew in 1944.

Junkers Ju 188   **W Nr 0590**

This Ju 188, coded 'F8+CM' of KG 40, was reported by the US Air Intelligence Organisation in Europe in May 1945, after examination in Austria or Northern Italy. It was recorded as 'to be flown to Florence for despatch to Wright Field'. It is probable that its shipment to the USA was cancelled, but this cannot be confirmed.

Messerschmitt Bf 108B-1   **W Nr 2246**

This Taifun, coded 'NF+MP', was captured by US forces in Tunisia in May 1943 and was taken over by the US Navy as a communications aircraft, based at El Aouina and later in Sicily, being on the strength of Cruiser Scouting Squadron (VCS-) 8, of the USS *Savannah*. In May 1944 it was handed over to Lt Leo D. Patterson (a pilot of the Squadron who had been instrumental in making the aircraft airworthy) and was shipped to the USA on board an aircraft carrier. Patterson registered the '108 as NX54208 after the war ended. In may 1946 he sold the aircraft to David S. Baker, only to repurchase the Messerschmitt in August 1955. In June 1956 the '108 was resold to William F. Waller, who like the previous owners lived in Burlington, West Virginia. In October 1958 the '108, by now registered as N54208, was sold again to Curt Heidenreich of Washington, DC. In May 1968 the Messerschmitt came into the ownership of Curtis Q. McWilliams, Raymond Hoffman and Glen L. Parks of Shamokin, Pa. Following McWilliams' death, Hoffman and Parks became the co-owners, in September 1985 re-registering the aircraft as N108HP. In 1990 it was sold to Lufthansa and taken to Frankfurt for rebuild. The rebuild was completed in May 1993 following which the Taifun was registered as D-EBEI and joined Lufthansa's Junkers Ju 52/3m D-AQUI as an historic aircraft flown for publicity purposes.

Left: **The Messerschmitt P 1101 prototype in Bell Aircraft hands after being damaged during ground handling (note the wrinkled fuselage structure).** *Jay Miller courtesy MCP*

Below: **The surviving Bell X-5 prototype 01838 on display at Wright Patterson AFB in 1974; compare with the P 1101.** *P. H. Butler*

Messerschmitt P 1101 V1   **W Nr** *unknown*

This was the prototype of an advanced jet fighter with a single jet engine and variable-sweep wings. The Bell X-5 was closely based on the P 1101 and the P 1101 was held by the Bell Aircraft Corporation of Buffalo, NY, for study during the development of the X-5. The P 1101 was damaged during ground handling in the USA and because of this no attempt was made to fly this aircraft. The P 1101 was surrendered at the Messerschmitt test facility at Oberammergau in southern Bavaria. It was taken to Wright Field for examination and was later, in August 1948, handed over to the Bell Aircraft Corporation for further study. An initial proposal made by Bell was to replace the Heinkel-Hirth He S-011 jet engine with an Allison J-35, to form the basis of a new interceptor design. The studies also included a proposal to replace the wing centre-section of the P 1101 with a new one which would permit in-flight changes of the sweep angle. The P 1101 had a wing which could be changed from 35 to 45 degrees on the ground, with three fixed positions. Bell also noted that the simple layout of the P 1101 permitted changes of engine installation with the minimum of effect on the fuselage structure. Bell proposals suggested the use of the P 1101 as an engine test-bed. Outline proposals were made for the installation of J34, J35, J46 and J47 turbo-jets, a ramjet, and a liquid fuelled rocket engine, as alternatives. Further studies, allied to the damage which the P 1101 had received during ground handling, led to the abandonment of these proposals. The proposal to fly the P 1101 was abandoned and the aircraft is believed to have been scrapped, because it was more expedient to build a new aircraft embodying the P 1101 design principles. The Bell X-5 was an enlarged development of the original concept, with provision to vary the wing sweep in the air – in the P 1101, the wing sweep could only be adjusted on the ground. The company formally proposed the construction of a variable-sweep research aircraft on 1st February 1949 and on 26th July 1949 a contract (W33-038-ac3298) was placed for the supply of two Bell X-5 aircraft. These had the Air Force serial numbers 50-1838 and 50-1839. The first X-5 made its first test flight from Muroc on 20th June 1951, with the second flying on 10th December 1951. The surviving aircraft, 50-1838, is with the Air Force Museum at Wright-Patterson AFB.

— **Nagler-Rolz NR 54V2**

This prototype helicopter, which was surrendered by its designer at Zell-am-See, was taken to the USA and was eventually taken into the NASM collection at Silver Hill, Maryland. Prior to this it was briefly on display at Wright-Patterson AFB in the early nineteen fifties. This aircraft was returned by 1975 to West Germany where it is on display at the Hubschrauber-Museum (Helicopter Museum) at Bückeburg.

— **Savoia Marchetti SM 82**

An example of the SM 82 Canguro (Kangaroo) three-engined bomber/transport was taken to the USA. The example concerned (Italian AF serial number MM 60317) was recorded at Patterson Field in non-flyable condition. It was sold for scrap to the Reconstruction Finance Corporation (the US government agency responsible for disposing of war-surplus material).

— **Focke Wulf Ta 154A**

An example of this twin-engined wooden night fighter was received in the USA, the type being listed among the exhibits to be shown to the Institute of Aviation Sciences during the Exhibition held at Freeman Field during September 1945. This aircraft was captured by the 54th Air Disarmament Squadron, at Lage in slightly damaged condition. It was shipped from Cherbourg to the USA on board the SS *Richard Gatling* in July 1945.

— **Focke-Achgelis Fa 223E**   **W Nr 0051**

After being grounded near Heilbronn on 25th May 1945 (see Chapter Sixteen) the Fa 223E was shipped to Wright Field. Components were sent to Prewitt Aircraft in 1947, for evaluation.

Details of the Japanese aircraft follow in Chapter Eighteen. Details of USN use of German aircraft appear in Chapter Sixteen (16.4).

The prototype Nagler-Rolz NR54V-2 photographed in the Helicopter Museum at Buckenburg in Germany. *Bob Ogden collection*

17.3   SUMMARY

To summarise the post-war trials of German aircraft in the USA, most of these were directed at the performance evaluation of jet and rotary-winged aircraft and novel planforms. The most significant of the trials are summarised in the individual histories of the following aircraft:

Flettner Fl 282 helicopter
Trials by the Prewitt Aircraft Co. (see FE-4613, -4614)

Doblhoff WNF342
Trials by the General Electric Co. (see FE-4615)

Focke-Achgelis Fa 330A
Trials by the USAF at MacDill AFB, and other tests of the type by Eastern Rotor Craft Inc (see T2-4616) and by California Aero Inc. (See individual history of T2-5038).

Horten sailplanes
Investigations of the Horten Ho III and Ho VI by Northrop (T2-5039, -5040, -5041). Later flight trials of the Ho IV at the Mississippi State University had a profound effect on sailplane designs on an international scale.

Darmstadt-München (Lippisch) DM-1
Wind-tunnel tests at the Langley Memorial Aeronautical Laboratories, to provide basic information for future delta-winged aircraft designs.

Messerschmitt P 1101
Investigations and subsequent design development by the Bell Aircraft Corporation, leading to the production of the Bell X-5 variable-sweep research aircraft.

Chapter Eighteen

Japanese Aircraft in the USA Post-war

The main batches of Japanese aircraft selected for evaluation in the USA after the surrender were concentrated at Yokosuka Naval Base, near Yokohama. Where it was possible to do so, the aircraft were made serviceable by Japanese personnel, before being ferried by Japanese pilots to Oppama airfield at Yokosuka. The ferry flights were made under escort by US military aircraft. In a few cases (e.g. the 'Rita') incomplete aircraft were finished under US supervision before flying to Oppama. Some aircraft, such as the suicide types, were crated where they were found and shipped as cargo in the hangars of aircraft-carriers. Most aircraft made the journey on aircraft-carrier decks, since they were too large to be taken below deck on the small lifts of the vessels concerned.

The shipments to the US were on board the Escort Carriers USS *Core* (CVE-13) and USS *Barnes* (CVE-20) during November, and the USS *Bogue* (CVE-9) during December, 1945. The basis for selection was to obtain four examples of each available type which had not previously been evaluated during the war. One example was to be for the USAAF, one for the USN, one for the RAF and one for later allocation or for use as a source of spares. It is not clear what happened to the aircraft allocated to the RAF; many of these in fact arrived in the USA but it may be that some were transferred to British control in Japan and possibly taken to the ATAIU-SEA at Tebrau in Malaya. Definite evidence of such an event has still to be found.

The three escort carriers carried between thirty-five and forty-five aircraft each. In addition the large H8K Emily flying-boat was transferred, on board the seaplane carrier USS *Cumberland Sound* (AV-17), also sailing from Yokosuka. The *Barnes* arrived at Norfolk, Virginia, on 7th December 1945 and commenced unloading forty-five Japanese aircraft on 10th December, for transfer to the Naval Air Station. The *Core* left Yokosuka on 16th November 1945 and docked at Alameda before returning to the Pacific.

It was at first intended that the USAAF aircraft would be delivered to Langley Field, Virginia, to be made airworthy for transfer

to Freeman Field. Personnel from Freeman Field had already arrived at Langley Field to work on the first batch of aircraft when their orders were rescinded. Due to a change of policy, it was directed, by Air Materiel Command order TSMCO2A-2-109 of 13th February 1946, that the Middletown Air Materiel Area (MAMA), Olmsted Field, Middletown, Pa, would become the sole Air Materiel Command repair agency for Foreign Equipment, including items designated as 'Class 32' for museum use.

The first such Japanese aircraft was, in fact, received at Middletown from Langley Field on 19th January 1946, and, by 30th June, fifty complete aircraft, and parts of nine others, had been received there from Langley Field and Newark. In addition, three aircraft had been flown out from MAMA to Wright or Freeman Fields and two others had been flown out of Newark after overhaul by MAMA personnel sent there on temporary duty (one of these aircraft being the 'Rita' T2-2210, which see, hereunder).

18.1   **UNITED STATES ARMY AIR FORCE AIRCRAFT ALLOCATED FE-/T2- NUMBERS**

FE-N50/   Kugisho MXY7 'Baka'
T2-N50   Navy Special Attacker Ohka
This was a purpose-built suicide attack aircraft. The 'N' in the FE-identity may indicate that its evaluation in the USA was in the hands of the US Navy. Certainly the USN had at least one example at NAS Norfolk in May 1947. Several examples of the type survive in museums in the USA, as listed at the end of this section. This example was in storage at the Middletown Air Depot, Pa, on 1st August 1946. On 18th September 1946 it was allotted for transfer to the Air Museum store at Park Ridge. It had previously been noted in the list of aircraft available for release to the aircraft industry on 10th March 1946.

Right: **The Mitsubishi Ki-83 in US markings, one of four prototypes completed before the Japanese surrender in 1945. This photograph is believed to have been taken at Matsumoto in Japan, before the aircraft was allotted the number FE-151.**
MAP/Real Photographs

FE-130/   Mitsubishi A6M5 'Zeke'
T2-130   Navy Type 0 Carrier Fighter Model 52
(See TAIC 7 in Chapter Fourteen)

FE-150/   Tachikawa Ki 94-II
T2-150   Army Experimental High-Altitude Fighter
This was the first prototype of a single-engined high-altitude
fighter which was only completed in August 1945. It had not made
its first flight at the time of the Japanese surrender on 21st August
and was surrendered at the manufacturer's works at Tachikawa,
close to Tokyo. It was shipped to the USA, being initially taken to
the Middletown Air Depot, Pa, for storage and servicing. It was
noted in the 10th March 1946 list of aircraft available for aircraft
industry evaluation. At 1st August 1946 this aircraft was at
Middletown – work to make it airworthy had been stopped but it
was allotted to the proposed Museum. In September 1946 it was
reported as under restoration for the Museum and was listed for
transfer to the Museum on 18th September. At Park Ridge in 1949.
There is no record of the aircraft after this date.

FE-151/   Mitsubishi Ki 83
T2-151   Army Experimental Long-Range Fighter
This was a twin-engined long-range fighter of which four pro-
totypes had been built before the end of the war. This example was
surrendered at Matsumotu. It was taken to the Middletown Air
Depot in February 1946 and was noted in the 10th March 1946 list
of aircraft available to the aircraft industry. At the end of Sep-
tember 1946 the Ki 83 was under restoration for the proposed Air
Museum, having been allotted to the Museum on 18th September.
At Park Ridge in 1949. There is no later record of the aircraft.

FE-152/   Rikugun Ki 93
T2-152   Army Experimental Heavy Fighter and Assault Plane
This was a twin-engined heavy fighter/ground-attack aircraft.
Only one prototype had flown before the Japanese surrender
although a second aircraft had been completed. It was this second
aircraft, captured at Takahagi, which was crated for shipment to
the USA. It was taken to the Middletown Air Depot. It was noted
in the 10th March 1946 list. The Ki 93 was under restoration for the
Museum in September 1946, having been assigned for transfer to
Park Ridge on 18th September, but there is no record of the aircraft
after 1949.

FE-153/   Nakajima Ki 87
T2-153   Army Experimental High-Altitude Fighter
This was a single-engined high-altitude fighter prototype of which
only one example (C/no 8701) had been completed at the end of the
war (see also FE-157 later). One incomplete example was crated at
Nakajima's Chofu factory for shipment to the USA. Both examples
were quoted in the 10th March 1946 list. At the time, FE-153 was at
the Middletown Air Depot, Pennsylvania. In September 1946 it
was 'under restoration' at Middletown for the proposed Air
Museum and was at Park Ridge in 1949. No further record.

FE-154/   Tachikawa Ki 77
T2-154   Army Experimental Long-Range Research Plane
This was a twin-engined long-range experimental aircraft, originally built (under the sponsorship of the *Asahi Shimbun* newspaper) as the Tachikawa A-26 with the intention of making record-
breaking flights. During the war the project was revived with the
intention of the aircraft being used for flights between Japan and
Germany, the second prototype being lost on the first such flight.
The first prototype was surrendered at Tachikawa's Kofu works at
the end of the war and was flown to Yokosuka in US markings. It
was shipped to the USA (probably on board the USS *Bogue*) and
was taken to the Middletown Air Depot. It was noted in the 10th
March 1946 list, and was last recorded there in September under
restoration, after allocation to the Museum on 18th September
1946. At Park Ridge in 1949. No further record.

The sole remaining Mitsubishi J8M1 Shusui FE-300 in the Air Museum at
Chino. *MCP*

FE-155/ Nakajima Ki 87
T2-155 Army Experimental High-Altitude Fighter
(See details under FE-153). On 1st August 1946, FE-155 was in storage at the Atlantic Overseas Air Materiel Center (AOAMC), Newark. It is presumed to have been scrapped there later in 1946. This example may have been an incomplete aircraft which had not flown.

FE-156/ Nakajima Ki 115a
T2-156 Army Special Attacker Tsurugi
This was a Japanese Army suicide attack aircraft of which 105 had been built during 1945. It was a single-seat aircraft with one radial piston engine. It was one of four captured at Nakajima's No. 1 Plant, Ota, Gumma Prefecture. Included in the 10th March 1946 list, although wrongly quoted in the list of 'Tony 1s' (Ki 61). FE-156 was still in store at Middletown on 1st August 1946, allotted for transfer to Park Ridge. This aircraft, C/n 1002, is still in store with the National Air and Space Museum facility at Silver Hill, Maryland.

FE-157 Nakajima Ki 87
Army Experimental High-Altitude Fighter
See FE-153 above. It is probable that this number is an erroneous report of FE-155.

Nakajima Ki-84 'Frank' FE-301 on static display in the USA after the war, possibly at Wright Field. Note that the 'FE-' or 'T2-' prefix was frequently not applied to the identity numbers of Japanese aircraft. MAP

FE-300/ Mitsubishi J8M1
T2-300 Navy Experimental 19-Shi Rocket-Powered Interceptor Fighter Shusui
(Note duplication with Italian allocation). This was a rocket-powered fighter based on the Messerschmitt Me 163B concept, but independently designed because one of the submarines carrying Me 163B data from Germany was sunk *en route*. Seven J8M1 had been built before the end of the war. This example, aircraft No. 403, is believed to have been captured at Mitsubishi's No. 1 Plant at Nagoya. The identity FE-300 is believed to be correct for this aircraft although two further Shusui were shipped to the USA, all three aircraft leaving Yokosuka on board the USS *Barnes* on 3rd November 1945.

It was included in the 10th March 1946 list, and by 1st August 1946, FE-300 was on display in Hollywood, Ca. This example is currently with the Planes of Fame Museum at Chino airfield, California. (See section 18.2 for further J8M1 examples).

FE-301/ Nakajima Ki 84 'Frank'
T2-301 Army Type 4 Fighter Hayate
The Ki 84 was one of the best Japanese fighter designs of the war, over 3,400 being built between 1943 and 1945. (See also FE-302 next). These two aircraft were captured at Utsunomiya South military airfield. Almost certainly they were those with the serial numbers 2366 and 3060 shipped on board USS *Barnes* from Yokosuka to the USA on 3rd November 1945. FE-301 was included in the 10th March 1946 list, was held at the Middletown Air Depot in May 1946 and by 1st August 1946 was in flyable condition at Wright Field, with the Public Relations Officer. This allocation implies that it was available to be flown to Air Shows and other events across the USA.

FE-302/   Nakajima Ki 84 'Frank'
T2-302   Army Type 4 Fighter Hayate

(See FE-301). This 'Frank' was shipped to the USA aboard the USS *Barnes* and was handed over to the USAAF on 7th December 1945. This example was also included in the 10th March 1946 list. After restoration work at Middletown, FE-302 was test flown on 16th May 1946. On 20th May it was delivered to Patterson Field, flying onwards to Wright Field on 27th May. After a further 8 hours of flight tests at Wright Field, it was flown to Park Ridge on 3rd July 1946 for the proposed Air Museum. The Flight Test report concluded that the type compared favourably with the NA P-51H and Republic P-47N. The type was criticised for its short range and lack of armour. It was also noted that the flight test programme had been hampered by frequent failures of the engine exhaust stacks due to the use of poor material, poor welding techniques and bad detailed design of the method of suspension. The series of Flight Test Reports was issued under Project No. NAD-25, with references in the series F-1M-1119-ND. There is no record of this aircraft after its arrival at Park Ridge and it was probably scrapped when the depot was reactivated during the Korean war.

FE-303/   Nakajima Ki 44 'Tojo'
T2-303   Army Type 2 Single-seat Fighter Shoki

The Ki 44 was a single-seat single-engined fighter of which 1,225 were built between 1940 and 1944. (See also FE-307). These two aircraft were captured at Kashiwa (Tachikawa military airfield). They were almost certainly serial numbers 1677 and 1841 which left Yokosuka for the USA on board USS *Barnes* on 3rd November 1945. Both examples were included in the 10th March 1946 list. FE-303 was at the Middletown Air Depot and arrived at Park Ridge on 4th October 1946, possibly after a brief period at Wright Field. At Park Ridge in 1949. No further record.

FE-304/   Kawasaki Ki 102b 'Randy'
T2-304   Army Type 4 Assault Plane

This was a twin-engined high-altitude fighter of which 238 were built in 1944 and 1945. (See also FE-308 to -310 inclusive). One of these was serial No. 1116, shipped on board the USS *Barnes*. Of these four aircraft, one was from the Kawasaki Akashi factory, near Kobe, while the other three were captured at Taisho (Osaka East military airfield). All four examples were included in the 10th March 1946 list. FE-304 was at the Middletown Air Depot in May 1946 and was under restoration there for the Air Museum in September 1946. At Park Ridge in 1949. No further record.

FE-305/   Kawanishi N1K2-J 'George'
T2-305   Navy Interceptor Fighter Shiden Kai Model 21

This was a single-seat single-engined fighter, developed from the N1K1 Kyofu floatplane fighter. 402 of this variant were built between 1943 and 1945. (See also FE-306). Both examples were included in the 10th March 1946 list as FE-N305, -N306 respectively. N305 was at Middletown and was ordered to be shipped to Park Ridge in September 1946. It is believed to have been surrendered at Omura. Two examples, c/nos 71 and 533, were at Yokosuka in October 1945, while two others were at Omura, awaiting ferrying to Yokosuka, pending shipment to the USA.

FE-306/   Kawanishi N1K2-J 'George'
T2-306   Navy Interceptor Fighter Shiden Kai Model 21

(See FE-305). FE-306 was in store at the Middletown Air Depot on 1st August 1946. It is owned by the US Department of the Navy; after storage for many years at NAS Norfolk, it has been on loan since about 1975 to what is now the New England Air Museum at Bradley International Airport, Windsor Locks, Connecticut, (Hartford/Springfield Airport), where it is on display.

FE-307/   Nakajima Ki 44 'Tojo'
T2-307   Army Type 2 Single-seat Fighter Shoki
(See FE-303). FE-307 was at New York in May 1946. On 1st August 1946 it was in temporary storage at Middletown, assigned for transfer to Park Ridge for the Museum. It has also been reported as being allotted to the USAF recruiting organisation for display purposes. No further record.

FE-308/   Kawasaki Ki 102b 'Randy'
T2-308   Army Type 4 Assault Plane
(See FE-304). This aircraft was at Middletown in May 1946 and was allotted to the USAF recruiting organisation in July 1946. On 18th September it was further allotted for transfer to the Air Museum. At Park Ridge in 1949. No further record.

FE-309/   Kawasaki Ki 102b 'Randy'
T2-309   Army Type 4 Assault Plane
(See FE-304). On 1st August 1946 this aircraft was in storage at the Atlantic Overseas Air Materiel Center (AOAMC), Newark, awaiting disposal.

FE-310/   Kawasaki Ki 102b 'Randy'
T2-310   Army Type 4 Assault Plane
(See FE-304). This aircraft was also awaiting disposal at AOAMC Newark on 1st August 1946.

FE-311/   Mitsubishi A6M8 'Zeke'
T2-311   Navy Type 0 Carrier Fighter Model 64
This was an improved version of the 'Zeke' with a Mitsubishi MK8P Kinsei 62 engine in place of the Sakae engine of the earlier variants. Only two prototypes of this version were completed in 1945. This example was surrendered at Misawa. By 1st August 1946 this aircraft was in store at Middletown Air Depot and on 18th September it was allotted to the Air Museum. No further record.

FE-312/   Kawasaki Ki 100
T2-312   Army Type 5 Fighter
This example was one of a number captured at Komaki. This Ki 100 was recorded on 1st August 1946 at Freeman Field as 'being crated for Museum'. No further record.

FE-313/   Kawasaki Ki 61 'Tony'
T2-313   Army Type 3 Fighter Hien
Single-engined single-seat fighter. Over 3,000 of the type were built between 1941 and 1945. This aircraft was captured at Itami (Osaka military airfield). It was included in the 10th March 1946 list

as 'FE-N313' and by 1st August 1946 this example was in storage at Middletown Air Depot. On 18th September it was allotted for transfer to the Air Museum. No further record.

FE-314/   Kawasaki Ki 100-I
T2-314   Army Type 5 Fighter
The Ki 100 was an adaptation of the earlier Ki 61 Hien with a radial rather than in-line engine. It did not have an Allied code name since the type was unknown to the Allies until the end of the war, although it has sometimes been referred to as the 'Tony 2'.

The examples shipped to the USA were captured at Komaki. FE-314 was included in the 10th March 1946 list as 'FE-N314'. By 1st August 1946 this example was on display at the University of Illinois, Champaign, Ill. where it remained until at least 1955.

FE-315/   Kawasaki Ki 100
T2-315   Army Type 5 Fighter
(See FE-314). Captured at Komaki. 'FE-N315' in 10th March 1946 list. On 1st August 1946 this aircraft was at Wright Field, in use for mobile display purposes. No further record.

FE-316/   Kawasaki Ki 61 'Tony'
T2-316   Army Type 3 Fighter Hien
(See FE-313). Captured at Itami (Osaka military airfield). 'FE-N316' in the 10th March 1946 list. On 1st August 1946 FE-316 was in store at the Middletown Air Depot; on 18th September it was listed for transfer to the Air Museum store at Park Ridge. No further record.

FE-317/   Kawasaki Ki 100
T2-317   Army Type 5 Fighter
(See FE-314). Captured at Komaki. Included in the 10th March 1946 list. On 1st August 1946 this Ki 100 was in store at the Middletown Air Depot. At this point it was assigned to the University of Illinois for display purposes. It is not clear whether this assignment was put into effect (see FE-314) since FE-317 was allotted for transfer to Park Ridge for the Air Museum on 18th September 1946. No further record.

FE-318/   Mitsubishi J2M5 'Jack'
T2-318   Navy Interceptor Fighter Raiden Model 33
Single-seat single-engined fighter. Thirty-four of this high-altitude version were made by Mitsubishi during 1944/5, while others were built by the Koza Naval Air Arsenal. Believed to have been captured at Atsugi naval airfield. FE-N318 to -N321 inclusive were included in the 10th March 1946 list. On 1st August 1946 FE-N318 was in storage at Middletown. No further record.

Far left: **Kawasaki Ki-102b 'Randy' '87' at Wright Field. This aircraft was probably FE-308. The number number '87' may be in the series of 'tail numbers' recorded against US Navy aircraft, which probably relate to the loading plans of the aircraft carriers which brought these aircraft to the USA.**
Howard Levy collection

Left: **Mitsubishi J2M 'Jack' in the USA, possibly at Middletown Air Depot.**
Edgar Deigan courtesy N. Malayney collection

FE-319/   Mitsubishi J2M5 'Jack'
T2-319   Navy Interceptor Fighter Raiden Model 33
(See FE-318). On 1st August 1946 FE-319 was in storage at
Middletown. No further record.

FE-320/   Mitsubishi J2M3 'Jack'
T2-320   Navy Interceptor Fighter Raiden Model 21
(See FE-318). In May 1946 this example was at Middletown Air
Depot, allocated for mobile display purposes. On 1st August it
was under restoration at Middletown. In September 1946 it was
reallotted for inclusion in the Air Museum collection at Park Ridge,
and was there in 1949. No further record.

FE-321/   Mitsubishi J2M3 'Jack'
T2-321   Navy Interceptor Fighter Raiden Model 21
(See FE-318). On 1st August 1946 this example was in store at
Middletown. No further record.

FE-322/   Mitsubishi A6M7 'Zeke'
T2-322   Navy Type 0 Carrier Fighter Model 64
(See FE-311). This example was possibly captured at Yatabe. On
1st August 1946 it was in store at Middletown and was reassigned
for transfer to the Air Museum on 18th September 1946. At Park
Ridge in 1949. No further record.

FE-323/   Mitsubishi A6M5 'Zeke'
T2-323   Navy Type 0 Carrier Fighter Model 53
In May 1946 this aircraft was at Middletown and by 11th September 1946 it was recorded as being 'on bailment' to the University of Kansas. Its fate is unknown.

FE-324/   Kawanishi N1K1 'Rex'
T2-324   Navy Fighter Seaplane Kyofu Model 11
Single-seat single-engined floatplane fighter. This example was
captured at Sasebo. Shipped to the USA on board the USS *Core*
from Yokosuka on 14th November 1945. Included in the 10th
March 1946 list. In May 1946 FE-N324 was at Middletown; in Sep-
tember 1946 it was recorded as being under restoration for the
Museum and it was assigned for transfer to the Museum on 18th
September. At Park Ridge in 1949. No further record.

FE-325/   Kawasaki Ki 45 KAIc 'Nick'
T2-325   Army Type 2 Twin-engined Fighter Toryu
Twin-engined night-fighter of which 1,701 were built. This example was surrendered at Fujigaya. It was shipped from Yokosuka to
the USA on board the USS *Core* on 14th November 1945. Included
in the 10th March 1946 list. It was handed over to the Flight Test
Section at Middletown on 25th April 1946 and was delivered to
Freeman Field on 10th May 1946. It remained in flyable condition
there until August 1946. It was finally recorded on 15th August as
'awaiting disposition'. A limited series of flight tests was carried
out under Project No. NTE-23, resulting in the issue of Technical
Report No. F-TR-1143-ND. The Report concluded that 'Nick' was
highly manoeuvrable and had very good handling characteristics,
but was significantly slower than comparable American types,
and materials and workmanship were considered inferior. No
further record.

Kawasaki Ki-45 KAIc 'Nick' T2-325 at Freeman Field. *US National Archives*

FE-326/ Kyushu J7W1
T2-326 Navy Experimental 18-Shi Type Interceptor Fighter Shinden

Unconventional single-engined single-seat fighter of canard lay-out with a pusher engine. This aircraft was the second of two pro-totypes; it had not flown at the time of the Japanese surrender and was captured at the Kyushu factory. Included in the 10th March 1946 list. On 1st August 1946 the Shinden was under restoration at Middletown, assigned for transfer to the Museum. It was recorded in a list of Middletown aircraft assigned for transfer to Park Ridge on 18th September 1946, with various special instructions indicat-ing that it was to be available for withdrawal from storage and

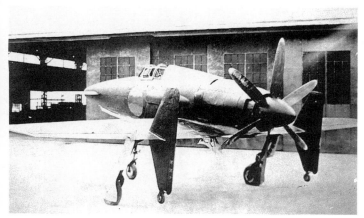

made airworthy in the event that an overhauled engine and other parts became available. It is now in storage with the Silver Hill facility of the National Air and Space Museum.

FE-700/ Nakajima J1N1-S 'Irving'
T2-700 Navy Type 2 Night Fighter Gekko Model 11

Twin-engined night-fighter. C/n 7334. This aircraft was probably surrendered at Atsugi. It was shipped from Yokosuka to the USA aboard the USS *Barnes* on 3rd November 1945. It was consigned to Langley Field, Virginia, and moved from Langley to the Middletown Air Depot at Olmsted Field, Middletown, Pennsyl-vania, on 23rd January 1946. The 'Irving' was included in the 10th March 1946 list of aircraft available to the aircraft industry, incor-rectly shown as 'FE-N1700', although it was still under overhaul at the time. It was test flown on 15th June 1946 and by 1st August was 'flyable' at Wright Field. By 4th October 1946 it was in storage at Park Ridge. It was later moved to the Smithsonian's Silver Hill facility and was eventually selected for refurbishing for display, a process which took from September 1979 to December 1983. It is now on display at Silver Hill.

Left: **Kyushu J7W1 Shinden canard fighter.** *NASM*

Below: **The Nakajima J1N1-S 'Irving' night fighter T2-700 on display at Silver Hill in 1988.** *Alan Curry collection*

FE-701/   Kawasaki Ki 45 KAI 'Nick'
T2-701   Army Type 2 Twin-engined Fighter Toryu
(See FE-325). C/n 4268. This example was surrendered at Fujigaya. Included in the 10th March 1946 list. It was at Middletown in May 1946. On 1st August 1946 it was recorded as 'flyable' at Park Ridge, although other sources show it arriving at Park Ridge for storage on 19th September 1946. It is now in storage with the Silver Hill facility of the National Air and Space Museum.

FE-1200/   Nakajima B6N2 'Jill'
T2-1200   Navy Carrier Attack Bomber Tenzan Model 12
Single-engined three-seat carrier-borne torpedo-bomber. Surrendered at Suzuka. Two 'Jill 12's, serial numbers 91112 and 91210, were on board USS *Barnes* when it left Yokosuka for the USA on 3rd November 1945. This aircraft is believed to be one of these two aircraft. Included in the 10th March 1946 list as 'FE-N1200'. It was at Middletown in May 1946 and in September was recorded as being under restoration for the Museum. It is believed to be the Tenzan which was at NAS Willow Grove for many years. This aircraft has recently been transferred to the NASM at Silver Hill. Its C/n is reported as 5350 and it may possibly be Navy 'tail number 12'.

FE-1201/   Kugisho D4Y4 'Judy'
T2-1201   Navy Special Attack Bomber Suisei Model 43
Suicide attack version of a carrier-based dive-bomber. (See also FE-1203 and the note at the end of this section). This example was surrendered at Nagoya. Included in the 10th March 1946 list as 'FE-N1201'. By 1st August 1946 this aircraft was under restoration at Middletown Air Depot. No further record.

FE-1202/   Kawasaki Ki 48 'Lily'
T2-1202   Army Type 99 Twin-engined Light Bomber Model 2
A standard light bomber of which almost 2,000 were built. (See also FE-1205 below). These examples were captured at Nasuno. Ki 48 serial number 1089, which was undoubtedly one of these two aircraft, was brought to the USA from Yokosuka on board USS *Barnes* in November 1945. Both FE-1202 and FE-1205 (which see) were included in the 10th March 1946 list. FE-1202 was at Middletown in May 1946 and in September 1946 was under restoration at Middletown for inclusion in the Museum. No further record.

FE-1203/   Kugisho D4Y4 'Judy'
T2-1203   Navy Special Attack Bomber Suisei Model 43
(See FE-1201 above and the note at the end of this section). Surrendered at Nagoya. Included in the 10th March 1946 list as 'FE-N1203'. On 1st August 1946 this 'Judy' was at Freeman Field 'loaned for display'; by 15th August the aircraft had been despatched to Park Ridge for Museum storage. No further record.

FE-1204/   Aichi B7A2 'Grace'
T2-1204   Navy Carrier Attack Bomber Ryusei Model 11
Single-engined carrier-based torpedo- and dive-bomber. (See also FE-1206 below). These aircraft were probably surrendered at Kisarazu. Both FE-1204 and -1206 were included in the 10th March 1946 list with 'N' prefices. FE-1204 was at Middletown in May 1946 but had arrived at Park Ridge by 25th September. FE-1204/ (T2-N1204) is in storage with the NASM at Silver Hill, Maryland; the C/n of this aircraft is 816.

FE-1205/   Kawasaki Ki 48 'Lily'
T2-1205   Army Type 99 Twin-engined Light Bomber Model 2
(See FE-1202). On 1st August 1946 this aircraft was in storage at AOAMC Newark, NJ. However, it appeared in a list dated 18th September 1946, of aircraft to be transferred from Middletown to the Air Museum. At Park Ridge in 1949. No further record.

FE-1206/   Aichi B7A2 'Grace'
T2-1206   Navy Carrier Attack Bomber Ryusei Model 11
(See also FE-1204 earlier). Captured at Kisarazu. FE-N1206 was held at Middletown in May 1946 but by July it had been allotted to the USAF recruiting organisation for display use. It was still in store at Middletown on 1st August. It appeared in the list of 18th September 1946 assigned for the Museum. No further record.

FE-1700/   Kugisho P1Y1 'Frances'
T2-1700   Navy Bomber Ginga Model 11
Twin-engined medium bomber. The three aircraft were probably captured at Matsushima. (See FE-1701 and -1702 later). One of these aircraft was serial number 4867 which was on board USS *Barnes* when it sailed from Yokosuka to the USA on 3rd November 1945. FE-1700 to -1702 are all included in the 10th March 1946 list with 'N' prefices to their identities. No record has been found of this aircraft being at either Freeman Field or Middletown.

Right: **The Kawasaki Ki-45-KAIc 'Nick' T2-701 at Olmsted Field (Middletown Air Depot) in 1946.**
US National Archives

Far right top: **The Nakajima B6N2 'Jill' T2-N1200 at Willow Grove on 12 September 1970. This aircraft has more recently been transferred to Silver Hill.**
Dick Phillips collection

Far right: **The Aichi B7A2 'Grace' FE-N1204 in store at Silver Hill in 1988.** *Alan Curry collection*

FE-1701/   Kugisho P1Y1 'Frances'
T2-1701   Navy Bomber Ginga Model 11
(See FE-1700 earlier). On 1st August 1946 this 'Frances' was awaiting disposal at the AOAMC, Newark, NJ.

FE-1702/   Kugisho P1Y1 'Frances'
T2-1702   Navy Bomber Ginga Model 11
(See FE-1700 earlier). In May 1946 this aircraft was at Newark and it arrived at Park Ridge for Museum storage on 22nd July 1946. Since it was recorded as 'flyable' at Park Ridge on 1st August 1946, it was probably flown there from Middletown. This example, c/n 8923, is in storage at Silver Hill.
Note: Kugisho is the correct acronym for the Naval Air Arsenal at Yokosuka.

FE-1703/   Nakajima Ki 49 'Helen'
T2-1703   Army Type 100 Heavy Bomber Donryu Model 2
Twin-engined heavy bomber. (See FE-1704 and -1705 later). All three aircraft were captured at the Training Air Division, Toyama. They were included in the 10th March 1946 list. FE-1703 was at Middletown in May 1946 and in September 1946 was allotted for inclusion in the Museum collection. No further record.

FE-1704/   Nakajima Ki 49 'Helen'
T2-1704   Army Type 100 Heavy Bomber Donryu Model 2
(See FE-1703 earlier). This aircraft was at Middletown in May 1946 and was recommended for 'salvage' in September 1946.

FE-1705/   Nakajima Ki 49 'Helen'
T2-1705   Army Type 100 Heavy Bomber Donryu Model 2
(See FE-1703 earlier). This 'Helen' was in storage at the AOAMC, Newark, NJ, on 1st August 1946, but assigned as scrap.

FE-2200/   Mitsubishi Ki 67 'Peggy'
T2-2200   Army Type 4 Heavy Bomber Hiryu Model 1
Twin-engined heavy bomber. (See FE-2201 to -2204 later). At least three of these aircraft were on board USS *Core* when it sailed from Yokosuka to the USA on 14th November 1945. These aircraft were surrendered at Kameyama (Kagamihara military airfield). All five aircraft are shown in the 10th March 1946 list. FE-2200 was at Middletown in May 1946 and was recommended for salvage (scrapping) in September 1946.

FE-2201/   Mitsubishi Ki 67 'Peggy'
T2-2201   Army Type 4 Heavy Bomber Hiryu Model 1
(See FE-2200 earlier). This 'Peggy' was in store at AOAMC, Newark, NJ, on 1st August 1946. It had been assigned for disposal as scrap.

FE-2202/   Mitsubishi Ki 67 'Peggy'
T2-2202   Army Type 4 Heavy Bomber Hiryu Model 1
(See FE-2200 earlier). This aircraft was at Middletown in May 1946 and was under restoration for the Museum in September 1946. It was assigned for transfer to the Museum in a list dated 18th September 1946. No further record.

FE-2203/   Mitsubishi Ki 67 'Peggy'
T2-2203   Army Type 4 Heavy Bomber Hiryu Model 1
(See FE-2200 earlier). On 1st August 1946 this aircraft was in storage at AOAMC, Newark, NJ, but had been assigned for disposal.

FE-2204/   Mitsubishi Ki 67 'Peggy'
T2-2204   Army Type 4 Heavy Bomber Hiryu Model 1
(See FE-2200 earlier). On 1st August 1946 this aircraft was in storage at AOAMC, Newark, NJ, but had been assigned for disposal.

FE-2205/ Mitsubishi G4M3 'Betty'
T2-2205 Navy Type 1 Attack Bomber Model 22
Twin-engined bomber. This aircraft was possibly from Clark Field rather than Japan, but equally may have been an example captured at Matsushima. A 'Betty' was certainly shipped to the USA from Yokosuka aboard the USS *Core* while there are reports that the 'Betty' flown at Clark Field came to the US (see Chapter Fourteen, section 14.4). FE-2205 was at Middletown in May 1946 and was allotted to the Museum store at Park Ridge in September 1946. Parts of this aircraft survive at the NASM Silver Hill facility.

FE-2206/ Tachikawa Ki 74 'Patsy'
T2-2206 Army Experimental High-Altitude Long-Range Bomber
Twin-engined high-altitude long-range reconnaissance bomber. Only 16 of the type were made. (See also FE-2207 to -2209 inclusive later). Two of these aircraft were surrendered at the Tachikawa factory and two at the IJAAF Test Bureau at Fussa (Yokota). All four aircraft were included in the 10th March 1946 list. FE-2206 was in storage at AOAMC Newark on 1st August 1946, but had been assigned for disposal.

FE-2207/ Tachikawa Ki 74 'Patsy'
T2-2207 Army Experimental High-Altitude Long-Range Bomber
(See FE-2206 earlier). FE-2207 was in storage at Middletown on 1st August 1946. It was listed for transfer to the Air Museum on 18th September 1946. No further record.

FE-2208/ Tachikawa Ki 74 'Patsy'
T2-2208 Army Experimental High-Altitude Long-Range Bomber
(See FE-2206 earlier). FE-2208 was in storage at AOAMC, Newark, on 1st August 1946, but was assigned for disposal.

FE-2209/ Tachikawa Ki 74 'Patsy'
T2-2209 Army Experimental High-Altitude Long-Range Bomber
(See FE-2206 earlier). FE-2209 was in storage at AOAMC, Newark, on 1st August 1946, but was assigned for disposal.

Far left: **A Kugisho P1Y 'Frances' at Newark in 1946, possibly FE-1701.** *Howard Levy collection*

Left: **A Mitsubishi Ki-67 'Peggy' at Newark.** *USAFM*

Below: **A Tachikawa Ki-74 'Patsy' in Japan.** *USAF Museum/Brundage collection*

E-2210/   Nakajima G8N1 'Rita'
2-2210   Navy Experimental 18-Shi Attack Bomber Renzan
This was the fourth of four prototypes of a four-engined heavy bomber, the first of which flew in October 1944. This example was incomplete at the end of the war at the Nakajima factory at Koizumi, north-west of Tokyo. The aircraft was completed on US instructions and flown to Yokosuka on 7th December 1945. It was then shipped to the USA aboard the escort carrier USS *Bogue* (CVE-) which left Yokosuka on 16th December 1945. The 'Rita' was off-loaded at New York during January 1946 and taken by barge to the AOAMC at Newark AAF.

eft: **The Nakajima G8N1 'Rita' T2-2210 being loaded on to a barge at Yokosuka.** *USAF Museum/Brundage collection*

ottom left: **The 'Rita' at AOAMC Newark in 1946.** *Dick Phillips collection*

elow: **One of the Kyushu Q1W 'Lorna' maritime patrol aircraft in US markings while en route to Yokosuka for shipment to the USA in 1945.** *hn Underwood collection*

The aircraft was flown from Newark to Patterson Field by Col Watson and Maj William Webb on 23rd June 1946. One later test flight was made by Col Al Boyd. As at 1st August 1946 it was recorded as 'flyable' at Patterson Field, with a note that it was being painted. It was included in the 10th March 1946 list of aircraft available to the aircraft industry and was then reserved for the proposed Air Force Museum, but was eventually scrapped.

FE-2650/
T2-2650
                    (Unidentified Gliders)
FE-2651/
T2-2651
These were probably troop-carrying gliders but have not yet been positively identified. By 1st August 1946 both were in storage at the Middletown Air Depot, after transfer from AOAMC, Newark. No further record.

FE-4800/   Kyushu Q1W1 'Lorna'
T2-4800   Navy Patrol Plane Tokai Model 11
Twin-engined anti-submarine patrol aircraft. (See also FE-4805, -4810 and -4811). These aircraft were probably surrendered at Hakata. They included serial numbers 37 and 170 which were on board USS *Barnes* when it sailed from Yokosuka to the USA on 3rd November 1945. This example was included in the 10th March 1946 list and on 1st August 1946 it was at Middletown. It was assigned for transfer to the Museum store at Park Ridge in the list issued on 18th September. No further record.

FE-4801/ Mitsubishi Ki 46-III 'Dinah'
T2-4801   Army Type 100 Command Reconnaissance Plane
Twin-engined reconnaissance aircraft. (See also FE-4802, -4806, -4807 and -4812 later). These aircraft included serial numbers 5444, 5453, 8053 and 8058 which were on board USS *Barnes* when it sailed from Yokosuka to the USA on 3rd November 1945. They had been surrendered at Kodama. This example was included in the 10th March 1946 list. At Middletown in May 1946. Allotted for Museum storage at Park Ridge in September 1946. At Park Ridge in 1949. No further record.

FE-4802/ Mitsubishi Ki 46-III 'Dinah'
T2-4802   Army Type 100 Command Reconnaissance Plane
(See FE-4801 earlier). This example was included in the 10th March 1946 list. It was under restoration at Middletown on 1st August 1946 and was assigned for Museum storage on 18th September. At Park Ridge in 1949. No further record.

FE-4803/ Nakajima C6N1 'Myrt'
T2-4803   Navy Carrier Reconnaissance Plane Saiun Model 11
Single-engined three-seat carrier-borne reconnaissance aircraft. (See also FE-4804, -4808 and -4809 later). These aircraft were surrendered at Kisarazu and were almost certainly serial numbers 735, 1308, 3379 and 4161 which were on board USS *Barnes* when it sailed from Yokosuka to the USA on 3rd November 1945. FE-4803, -4804 and -4809 were included in the 10th March 1946 list with 'N' prefices to their identities. FE-N4803 was at Middletown in May 1946 and was flown from there to Park Ridge on 22nd August 1946 for Museum storage with No. 803 Special Depot. This aircraft, C/no 4161, is in storage with the NASM at Silver Hill.

FE-4804/ Nakajima C6N1 'Myrt'
T2-4801   Navy Carrier Reconnaissance Plane Saiun Model 11
(See FE-4803 earlier). On 1st August 1946 FE-N4804 was at Wright Field 'for analysis'; it had presumably flown there from Middletown. No further record.

FE-4805/ Kyushu Q1W1 'Lorna'
T2-4805   Navy Patrol Plane Tokai Model 11
(See FE-4800 earlier). This example was included in the 10th March 1946 list. It was at Middletown on 1st August 1946, assigned to be salvaged, after parts from it had been used to service FE-4800.

FE-4806/ Mitsubishi Ki 46-III 'Dinah'
T2-4806   Army Type 100 Command Reconnaissance Plane
(See FE-4801 earlier). FE-4806 was at AOAMC, Newark, on 1 August 1946, awaiting disposal.

FE-4807/ Mitsubishi Ki 46 'Dinah'
T2-4807   Army Type 100 Command Reconnaissance Plane
(See FE-4801 earlier). This example was included in the 10th March 1946 list. It was in storage at Middletown by 1st August 1946. N further record.

FE-4808/ Nakajima C6N1 'Myrt'
T2-4808   Navy Carrier Reconnaissance Plane Saiun Model 11
(See FE-4803 earlier). On 1st August 1946 this aircraft was AOAMC, Newark, awaiting disposal.

FE-4809/ Nakajima C6N1 'Myrt'
T2-4809   Navy Carrier Reconnaissance Plane Saiun Model 11
(See FE-4803 earlier). FE-N4809 was at Middletown in May 19 and was allotted for display use by the USAF recruiting organis tion in July of the same year, although it was still in store Middletown on 1st August 1946 and was then assigned for A Museum storage on 18th September. No further record.

FE-4810/ Kyushu Q1W1 'Lorna'
T2-4810   Navy Patrol Plane Tokai Model 11
(See FE-4800 earlier). On 1st August 1946 this aircraft was in sto at AOAMC, Newark, awaiting disposal.

FE-4811/ Kyushu Q1W1 'Lorna'
T2-4811   Navy Patrol Plane Tokai Model 11
(See FE-4800 earlier). On 1st August 1946 this aircraft was in sto at AOAMC, Newark, awaiting disposal.

FE-4812/ Mitsubishi Ki 46-IV 'Dinah'
T2-4812   Army Type 100 Command Reconnaissance Plane
(See FE-4801 earlier). On 1st August 1946 FE-4812 was in storage Middletown Air Depot. No further record.

FE-6430/ Nakajima Ki 43 'Oscar'
T2-6430   Army Type 1 Fighter Hayabusa
Single-seat fighter. This may have been the 'Oscar' which arrive

Left: **The Nakajima C6N1 'Myrt' T2-4804 at Middletown Air Depot in 1946.**
US National Archives

at Wright Field on 21st July 1943. It was listed in the March 1946 list of aircraft available to the aircraft industry. This aircraft is also recorded as serial number C430. In May 1946 it was at NAS Anacostia; it was received at No. 803 Special Depot, Park Ridge, for Museum storage on 22nd July 1946, in company with an unidentified 'Zeke 52' and 'Frank' serial number 1446. While at Park Ridge, it wore the number '10' on its fin. It is probable that the FE- number of this aircraft is an erroneous report.

This example was later in Arizona during the 1950s. It was more recently on display with the Experimental Aircraft Association Museum, on loan from the NASM. The EAA Museum was originally at Hales Corners, Milwaukee, Wisconsin, but later moved to Wittman Field, Oshkosh, Wisconsin.

18.2 AIRCRAFT ALLOCATED TAIL NUMBERS BY UNITED STATES NAVY

In addition to the USAAF aircraft recorded in the previous section, many Japanese aircraft shipped to the USA were evaluated by the US Navy at the end of the war. Unlike the ex-Luftwaffe aircraft, the Japanese types did not receive standard USN Bureau of Aeronautics serial numbers but 'tail numbers' were applied. Although no complete record has been traced, examples of the numbers are indicated in this section. It is possible that the numbers related to the shipping allocations or loading arrangments at Yokosuka, in the same way as the ex-Luftwaffe aircraft shipped from Europe were allotted identity numbers at the port of embarkation.

2   Nakajima B6N2 'Jill'
Navy Carrier Attack Bomber Tenzan Model 12
Captured at Suzuka. At NAS Patuxent River in Maryland. Transferred from there to NASD Philadelphia, Pennsylvania, on 7th October 1947. Possibly the aircraft for many years on display at NAS Willow Grove. (See FE-1200 earlier).

14   Mitsubishi A6M5 'Zeke'
Navy Type 0 Carrier Fighter Model 52 (quoted as 62)
(Possibly a Model 62 'Zeke', captured at Yatabe). At NAS Patuxent River. Transferred to NAS Willow Grove on 4th December 1946. No further record.

19   Kawanishi N1K2-J 'George'
Navy Interceptor Fighter Shiden-Kai Model 21
At NAS Patuxent River. Transferred to the Naval Proving Ground (NPG) Dahlgren Junction on 11th October 1946, probably for use as a ground target.

20   Kawanishi N1K2-J 'George'
Navy Interceptor Fighter Shiden-Kai Model 21
At NAS Patuxent River. Transferred to NPG Dahlgren Junction on 11th October 1946, probably for use as a target.

21   Mitsubishi A6M5 'Zeke'
Navy Type 0 Carrier Fighter (Model ?)
At NAS Patuxent River. Transferred to NAS New Orleans on 23rd October 1946, for static display purposes. No further record.

22   Yokosuka D4Y3 'Judy'
Navy Carrier Bomber Suisei Model 33
Probably captured at Nagoya, and possibly Constructor's number 1620 or 1959. At NAS Patuxent River. Transferred from there to NPG Dahlgren Junction on 31st October 1946, probably for use as a target.

The Nakajima Ki-43 'Oscar' in the EAA Museum at Hales Corners, Wisconsin, in July 1974. *P. H. Butler collection*

Left: **Mitsubishi J8M1 Shiden 'Tail number A25'.**
US National Archives

Below: **The derelict Mitsubishi J8M1 Shiden 'Tail number 24' at NAS Glenview.** *E. Deigan courtesy N. Malayney collection*

Right: **Kawanishi N1K1-J 'George', photographed at its point of capture, Omura in Japan.** *USAFM*

Bottom right: **Kawanishi N1K1-J 'George' in store at Silver Hill in 1988.** *Alan Curry collection*

24   Mitsubishi J8M1
Navy Experimental 19-Shi Rocket-Powered Interceptor Fighter Shusui
At NAS Patuxent River. Transferred from there to NAS Glenview, north of Chicago, Illinois, on 3rd October 1946 for display purposes. Scrapped.

26   Yokosuka D4Y4 'Judy'
Navy Carrier Bomber Suisei Model 43
Captured at Nagoya. At NAS Patuxent River. Transferred from there to NPG Dahlgren Junction, Virginia, on 11th October 1946 for use as a target.

32   Kawanishi N1K2-J 'George'
Navy Interceptor Fighter Shiden Kai Model 21
Probably captured at Omura. At NAS Patuxent River. Transferred from there to NAS Willow Grove on 4th December 1946. This may well be the 'George' which was on static display at NAS Willow

Grove, which has since been transferred to the NASM at Silver Hill, Md.

34   Kawanishi N1K2-J 'George'
Navy Interceptor Fighter Shiden Kai Model 21
Details unconfirmed. Probably captured at Omura.

40   Kawanishi N1K1 'Rex'
Navy Fighter Seaplane Kyofu Model 11
At NAS Patuxent River. Transferred from there to NASD Philadelphia on 7th October 1946 for display purposes. Possibly the aircraft now at NAS Willow Grove.

41   Kawanishi N1K2-J 'George'
Navy Interceptor Fighter Shiden Kai Model 11
Captured at Himeji. At NAS Patuxent River. Transferred from there to NPG Dahlgren Junction on 11th October 1946 for use as a target.

42   Yokosuka D4Y4 'Judy'
Navy Carrier Bomber Suisei Model 43

Captured at Nagoya. At NAS Patuxent River. Transferred from
there to NAS Norfolk for onward shipment to the Naval Base,
Charleston, South Carolina, on 23rd October 1946, for display purposes. No further record.

45   Kawanishi N1K1 'Rex'
Navy Fighter Seaplane Kyofu Model 11

Captured at Sasebo. At NAS Patuxent River. Transferred from
there to the Naval Shipyard at Boston on 23rd October 1946 for display purposes. No further record.

47   Aichi M6A1
Navy Special Attack Bomber Seiran

C/no 1600228. At NAS Patuxent River. Transferred from there t
NAS Alameda, California, on 31st October 1946, for display pur
poses. This aircraft was a single-engined two-seater seaplan
intended for offensive operations against the USA and elsewher
To this end, it was designed to be launched from the large I-40
class submarines of the Imperial Japanese Navy. These wer
4,500-ton vessels capable of carrying three Seiran seaplanes in
watertight hangar. The submarines were equipped with catapul
for launching the aircraft. The seaplane entered service in 1944 an
the first attack on a US Navy base in the Pacific was about to b

Far right: **The Aichi E16A2 'Paul' 'Tail number 70'
at Floyd Bennett Field, New York.** *MAP*

Right: **The Yokosuka D4Y4 'Judy' 'Tail number 42'
in the USA.** *NASM*

Below: **The Aichi M6A1 Seiran submarine-
launched floatplane in storage at Silver Hill in July
1972.** *P. H. Butler collection*

launched on the day of the Japanese surrender. It is believed that this aircraft was one of two Seirans shipped to the USA from Yokosuka aboard the USS *Core* in November 1945. After display and storage at NAS Alameda for many years, this Seiran was transferred to the NASM facility at Silver Hill, Maryland, in 1962 and remains there in storage at the time of writing. In 1993, this Seiran was transferred to the restoration building at Silver Hill for refurbishing prior to display.

52   Aichi B7A2 'Grace'
Navy Carrier Attack Bomber Ryusei Model 12
Captured at Kisarazu. At NAS Patuxent River. Transferred from there to NAAS Mustin Field, Pennsylvania, for display purposes on 8th January 1947. No further record.

70   Aichi E16A2 'Paul'
Navy Reconnaissance Seaplane Zuiun
This single-engined two-seat twin-float seaplane, aircraft '16' of the 634th Kokutai (i.e. coded '634-16'), was brought to the USA on board the USS *Core* in November 1945. The Zuiun was taken to NAS Patuxent River and transferred from there to NAS Norfolk on 8th January 1947 for onward shipment to Floyd Bennett Field, New York, for use as a static exhibit. No further record.

A-3   Aichi M6A1-K
Navy Special Attack Training Bomber Nanzan
The Nanzan was a land-based trainer version of the Seiran described under '47' earlier. One example, with the serial number quoted as 46/91, was transported from Yokosuka to the USA aboard the USS *Barnes*. After delivery to NAS Patuxent River this aircraft was put into storage at NAS Seattle in October 1946 and was scrapped there soon afterwards. See photograph on Page 311.

A-25   Mitsubishi J8M1
Navy Experimental Interceptor Fighter Shusui
No details known. (See photo on page 252)

A-103   Nakajima Navy Special Attacker Kikka
This design was the first Japanese jet aircraft to fly and was of similar layout to the Messerschmitt Me 262. The examples taken to the USA were later prototypes which were incomplete at the time of the surrender. This example was at NAS Patuxent River and was then transferred to San Diego, California, on 18th October 1946. This may be the second incomplete Kikka held in store at Silver Hill.

A-104   Nakajima Navy Special Attacker Kikka
This example (as with A-103 earlier) was at NAS Patuxent River and was transferred from there to NAS Willow Grove on 23rd October 1946. No further record.

108   Nakajima Ki 84 'Frank'
Army Type 4 Fighter Hayate
Captured at Utsunomiya South military airfield. At NAS Patuxent River. Transferred from there to NAS Norfolk on 23rd October 1946 for onward shipment to NAS Jacksonville, Florida, for display purposes. No further record.

119   Nakajima Ki 84 'Frank'
Army Type 4 Fighter Hayate
Captured at Utsunomiya South military airfield. At NAS Patuxent River. Transferred from there to NAS Glenview, Illinois, on 3rd October 1946 for display purposes.
    By November 1947 the aircraft was in poor condition and was 'available for disposition'. See photograph on Page 310.

The following aircraft were also in the hands of the US Navy but no 'tail numbers' are known for them:

Kawanishi H8K2 Model 12 'Emily'
Navy Type 2 Flying-Boat

This aircraft, Constructor's number 426, belonged to the 801st Naval Air Corps (IJN) based at Takuma on the Japanese home island of Shikoku. It was flown from Takuma to Yokosuka on 13th November 1945 and was then shipped to the USA on board the seaplane tender USS *Cumberland Sound* (AV-17) during November 1945, being off-loaded at NAS Whidbey Island, Washington. This aircraft was tested by the US Navy at NAS Norfolk and NAS Patuxent River. It made only one recorded flight from NAS Norfolk to NATC Patuxent River on 23rd May 1946, afterwards being relegated to taxiing trials because of engine problems. The taxiing trials, under Project No. PTR 1411, were aimed at studying the type's hydrodynamic stability and characteristics of the spray generated during take-off. The tests took place between 22nd August 1946 and 30th January 1947, eventually being terminated by failure of an engine which could not be replaced. It was later put into storage at NAS Norfolk on behalf of the Smithsonian Institution and was seen there by the writer in 1972. It was returned to Japan in July 1979 and is now on display in the Museum of Maritime Science at Tokyo.

Mitsubishi A6M7 'Zeke'
Navy Type 0 Carrier Fighter Model 63

C/n 23186. Captured at Yokosuka, was shipped to the USA aboard the USS *Barnes* in November 1945. This was in the markings of the Yokosuka Kokutai. It was eventually turned over to the NASM. This aircraft may be FE-322 (see page 242).

It was loaned to the Bradley Air Museum at Hartford, Connecticut, but was damaged in a tornado on 3rd October 1979 which destroyed several museum exhibits and damaged many others. In March 1981 the 'Zeke' was transferred to the San Diego Aerospace Museum, where it has been on display since April 1984, after repair and restoration.

Nakajima J5N1 Navy Experimental 18-Shi
Interceptor Fighter Tenrai

This was a single-seat twin-engined fighter. Six prototypes were built, of which two (c/ns 11 and 16) were shipped to the USA aboard the USS *Barnes* in November 1945. Parts of one of these aircraft survive in store with the NASM at Silver Hill.

Nakajima Navy Special Attacker Kikka

In addition to the examples with 'tail numbers' A-103 and A-104 earlier, a third Kikka was received in the USA and came to be stored at NAS Norfolk by 1950. In 1960 this example was shipped to the NASM storage facility at Silver Hill, Maryland. It has been on display at Silver Hill since about 1972. The NASM also has parts of a second Kikka, which was also received from NAS Norfolk.

The Nakajima Kikka attack aircraft at Silver Hill in 1988. The aircraft is incomplete and the underwing 'engine' is a mock-up.
Alan Curry collection

Right: **The 'Emily' at NAS Norfolk in July 1972. In 1979 the flying-boat was returned to Japan, where it is now on display in the Museum of Maritime Science in Tokyo.** *P. H. Butler collection*

Centre right: **This ageing photograph of the 'Emily' at NAS Norfolk early in 1946 shows some details, including the Japanese fuselage insignia, not evident on the taxiing view, below.** *Pete Bulban collection*

Below: **The Kawanishi H8K2 'Emily' taxiing at Patuxent River in 1946.** *US National Archives 80G-265577*

— **Kugisho MXY7 'Baka'**
Navy Special Attacker Ohka
Several examples of the type were brought to the USA. Several of these were originally captured at Kadena Air Base on the island of Okinawa in 1945. One of the surviving examples is c/n 1049, marked as '1-18', which is currently in the Air Museum at Chino Airfield, California.

18.3   **AIRCRAFT OF UNKNOWN ORIGIN**

A number of Japanese Naval aircraft survive in museums and elsewhere in the USA for which the origins are unknown, but it is almost certain that they must relate to aircraft brought to the USA aboard the carriers *Bogue*, *Core* and *Barnes*. They include:

— **Kawanishi N1K1 'Rex' Navy Fighter Seaplane Kyofu**
C/n 514. At NASM, Silver Hill, previously stored at NAS Norfolk.

— **Kawanishi N1K1 'Rex' Navy Fighter Seaplane Kyofu**
C/n 562. Owned by the Department of the Navy. On display at the Admiral Nimitz Center, Fredericksburg, Texas since 1977. Previously stored at NAS Norfolk.

— **Kawanishi N1K1 'Rex' Navy Fighter Seaplane Kyofu**
Reported as C/n 565. At NAS Willow Grove, Pennsylvania.

— **Kawanishi N1K2-J 'George' Navy Interceptor Fighter**
Shinden Kai
C/n 62387. On display at the USAF Museum, Wright-Patterson AFB, Fairborn, Ohio. This 'George' was received at W-P AFB from the City of San Diego on 27th September 1959. (Note – the quoted C/n of this aircraft differs from any 'George' known to have been shipped to the USA).

— **Mitsubishi A6M2 'Zeke' Navy Type 0 Carrier Fighter**
C/n 11593. Owned by the USAF Museum, Wright-Patterson AFB, Fairborn, Ohio.

One of several Kugisho Ohkas in the USA is this example in the Air Museum at Chino, California. MCP

— **Mitsubishi J2M3 'Jack' Navy Interceptor Fighter Raiden**
C/n 3014. Owned by the Air Museum (Planes of Fame), Chino, California.

— **Kugisho MXY7 'Baka'**
Navy Special Attacker Ohka Model 11
C/n 1018 on display at the Marine Corps Museum, MCAS Quantico, Virginia.

— **Kugisho MXY7 'Baka'**
Navy Special Attacker Ohka Model 11
Example formerly at the now closed Victory Air Museum, Mundelein, Illinois. Now at the Yankee Air Museum, Chino, Ca.

— **Kugisho MXY7 'Baka'**
Navy Special Attacker Ohka Model 11
C/n 1049. At the Air Museum, Chino.

— **Kugisho MXY7 'Baka'**
Navy Special Attacker Ohka Model 11
Example with the NASM, Silver Hill.

— **Kugisho MXY7-K1 'Baka'**
Navy Special Attacker Ohka Model 11
Example on display at the USAF Museum, Wright-Patterson AFB, Fairborn, Ohio.

— **Kugisho MXY7-K1 'Baka'**
Navy Special Attacker Ohka
C/n 5100 on display at the Washington Navy Yard (Naval Historical Center).

— **Kugisho MXY7-K2 'Baka'**
Navy Special Attacker Ohka
C/n 61. With the NASM, Silver Hill.

— **Tachikawa Ki 106 Army Experimental Fighter**
The Ki 106 was an all-wood version of the Nakajima Ki 84 Hayate 'Frank'. Three prototypes were constructed in 1945, one of which was shipped to the USA and held at NAS Norfolk. The fate of this aircraft is unknown.

Chapter Nineteen

Museum Aircraft
in the USA

Towards the end of the Second World War, General H. H. 'Hap' Arnold, who was then the Commanding General of the United States Army Air Forces, based in Washington, DC, issued instructions to 'preserve in the United States all important items of enemy aeronautical equipment'. This task was delegated to the USAAF Air Technical Service Command (ATSC), which was made 'responsible for the procurement, reconditioning and preservation of enemy aeronautical equipment and the placing of such equipment in storage for post-war historical and scientific purposes, at least one each of every type of item used by the Enemy Air Forces'.

This intent resulted in the systematic collection of such equipment. Although in later years different priorities and perceptions led to the destruction of much of what had been collected, it was this single instruction from the Commanding General which ensured the survival of many items now on display at the NASM in Washington, DC, the Air Force Museum at Dayton, and in various privately-owned museums such as the Champlin Fighter Museum at Mesa, Ed Maloney's Air Museum at Chino and elsewhere.

As a result of Arnold's original order, many of the flyable aircraft collected at Wright Field, Freeman Field and other centres were sent to the ATSC's No. 803 Special Depot at Park Ridge, Illinois (located at what is now Chicago's O'Hare airport). The activities of the Depot were supervised by a Museum Section under the Office of Intelligence (T2) of Air Technical Service Command. The facility used the buildings erected to house the production lines of a Douglas Aircraft plant which had built six hundred and fifty-five C-54 Skymaster transports for the USAAF between September 1943 and October 1945. The collection housed at Park Ridge included many rare and famous American designs besides the German and Japanese equipment and the whole collection was stored pending the organisation of a major 'Air Museum' which took many years to come to fruition. With the outbreak of the Korean War in 1950, the plant became urgently required for the assembly and storage of military equipment and the historic aircraft were displaced onto outdoor hard standings, subject to the ravages of weather.

In August 1946 the US Congress had established Public Law 722, sponsored by Representative Jennings Randolph under the advice of General Arnold, which set up the National Air Museum. This was to become a separate bureau of the Smithsonian Institution. A leading member of the National Air Museum from its inception, and its Head Curator from 1952, was Paul E. Garber. In the trauma of 1950, when the aircraft were evicted from the Park Ridge facility, it was he who located an area of land near Washington owned by the US Federal Government – the location for the current storage and restoration facility of the National Air and Space Museum, now honoured with the name 'Paul E. Garber Facility'. It is also known as Silver Hill, its geographic name, and is at Suitland, Maryland, a mere seven miles from the Smithsonian Institution and the more recent National Air and Space Museum in downtown Washington. When taken over by the Smithsonian,

Silver Hill was a piece of derelict overgrown scrub land, but it was eventually turned into an adequate storage facility by the gradual addition of roads, 'temporary' buildings and other resources. Over the three to four years after 'eviction' from Park Ridge, the priceless Air Museum collection was gradually transferred to Silver Hill. Many more years were to pass before the National Air and Space Museum building on, the Mall, downtown, was authorised and built – it did not open until 1st July, 1976.

The other main beneficiary of the Arnold instruction of April 1945 is the Air Force Museum, located at the former Wright Field, now part of Wright-Patterson Air Force Base, Fairborn, near Dayton, Ohio. This grew from a museum which opened in 1923 at the original McCook Field at Dayton. This had transferred to Wright Field in 1927 but closed in 1940 during build-up of the Air Forces prior to the United States' entry to the Second World War.

In 1948 an Air Force Technical Museum opened at Wright Field and in 1954 it was permitted to acquire and display full-size aircraft. In 1956 the AFT Museum officially became the Air Force Museum.

A new purpose-built Museum display building was later constructed by the Air Force Museum Foundation. This building was donated to the USAF in August 1971 and dedicated in the following month in the presence of President Richard Nixon. The Museum building is a large structure, being built to house – amongst many other exhibits – a complete Convair B-36J ten-engined bomber of 1950 vintage, the largest land-based aircraft of its day.

In recent years, the activities of the USAFM have been expanded to include the 'Museum Program', which includes the support of museums located at other Air Force bases and civilian museums. Such support includes the loan of exhibits owned by the Air Force Museum.

The exhibits of these and other North American aviation museums are summarised in the lists below:

The Admiral Nimitz State Historical Park
This museum is dedicated to Admiral Chester Nimitz, Commander of the US Pacific Fleet for much of the Second World War. It is located at his home town, Fredericksburg, Texas.

Aichi D3A1 'Val'	C/n 3105, a derelict recovered from New Britain.
Kawanishi N1K1 Kyofu 'Rex'	C/n 562, precise origin unknown.

The Confederate Air Force
A Museum, previously based at Harlingen in Texas, dedicated to maintain Second World War aircraft in flying condition. The Museum, founded in 1957, is famous for its annual Air Show. The Museum has since moved to Midland, Texas.

Focke Wulf Fw 44 Steiglitz	N2497 (ex-OH-SZD & SZ-33 of Finnish AF)
Heinkel He 111H	(CASA built) N72615 (ex-T8B-124 of the Spanish AF)

Junkers Ju 52	(CASA built) N352JU (ex-T2B-176 of the Spanish AF)
Messerschmitt Bf 109	N109ME (Hispano built)
Messerschmitt Bf 109	N9938 (Hispano built)
Messerschmitt Bf 109	N9939 (Hispano built)
Mitsubishi A6M5 'Zeke'	N58245 - rebuild of Pacific island relic.

The aircraft below is held by the New Mexico Wing of the Confederate Air Force.

| Messerschmitt Bf 108D | N2231 (ex-G-AKZY, AM87, Luftwaffe). Under rebuild |

Experimental Aircraft Association (EAA) Museum

The EAA was formed in 1953, initially to promote the construction of home-built aircraft. It has since expanded to have divisions covering antique, classic, warbird and aerobatic aircraft.

The EAA Museum was set up in 1964 at Hales Corners, Milwaukee, Wi. A new museum building was completed at Wittman Field, Oshkosh, Wi, in 1983. Most of the exhibits are home-built aircraft, but others include:

Bücker Bü 133C Jungmeister	N515 (ex-HB-MKE and U-84 of the Swiss Air Force)
Messerschmitt Bf 109	N190BF (ex-N90601, G-AWHO, C4K-127) Hispano built
Nakajima Ki 43-2 Hayabusa 'Oscar'	C/n 6430 (On loan from NASM)
Nord 1002 (Bf 108)	N525R (ex-French Air Force No. 192)

The Fighter Museum

This museum, otherwise the Champlin Fighter Museum, is located at Falcon Field, Mesa, Arizona. It was founded by Doug Champlin in Oklahoma in 1969 and moved to Mesa in 1981.

| Focke Wulf Fw 190D-13 | NX190D (Ex FE-118) |
| Messerschmitt Bf 109 | NX109J (Hispano built) |

The National Air and Space Museum

The origins of the NASM are described in the introduction to this Chapter. The main Museum is on the Mall, in downtown Washington, DC. The Museum's Restoration Center, which also houses a subsidiary collection of exhibits on limited public display, is at Silver Hill in nearby Maryland. Some further items are held in storage at Washington's Dulles Airport for eventual display in a new museum to be built at the Airport.

Aichi B7A1 Ryusei 'Grace'	T2-1204, c/n 816	Silver Hill
Aichi M6A1 Seiran	C/n 1600228 (tail no. 47)	Silver Hill
Arado Ar 196A	W Nr 623183	Silver Hill
Arado Ar 234B-2	T2-1010, W Nr 140312	Silver Hill
Bachem Ba 349B-1 Natter	T2-1	Silver Hill
Blöhm u Voss Bv 155B-V2	T2-505	Silver Hill
Bücker Bü 181B Bestmann	T2-4611	Silver Hill
Darmstadt-München DM-1	? - (Lippisch DM-1)	Silver Hill
DFS 108-14 Schulgleiter 38	? - (possibly T2-5004)	Silver Hill
DFS 108-14 Schulgleiter 38	? - (possibly T2-5005)	Silver Hill
DFS 108-49 Grunau Baby	T2-2600	Silver Hill
Dornier Do 335A	W Nr 240102	Silver Hill
Fieseler Fi 156 (Morane MS 500)	C/n 85	Silver Hill
Focke-Achgelis Fa 330A	T2-4618	NASM
Focke Wulf Fw 190D-9	T2-120	(On loan to the USAF Museum)
Focke Wulf Fw 190F-8	T2-117	Silver Hill
Focke Wulf Ta 152H	T2-112	Silver Hill
Gotha Go 229 (Horten Ho IX)	T2-490	Silver Hill
Heinkel He 162A	T2-504	Silver Hill

Heinkel He 219A	T2-614	Silver Hill
Horten Ho II	C/n 6 ?	Silver Hill
Horten Ho IIIf	T2-5039	Silver Hill
Horten Ho IIIh	T2-5041	Silver Hill
Horten Ho VI	T2-5040	Silver Hill
Junkers Ju 52/3m (CASA-built)	ex-G-BFHD, T2B-255	Dulles Airport
Junkers Ju 388L-1	T2-4010	Silver Hill
Kawanishi N1K1 Kyofu 'Rex'	C/n 514	Silver Hill
Kawanishi N1K2-J Shiden Kai 'George'	C/n 5341	Silver Hill
Kawasaki Ki 45 KAI Toryu 'Nick'	T2-701	Silver Hill
Kugisho MXY7 Ohka 11 'Baka'	?	Silver Hill
Kugisho MXY7-K2 Ohka 'Baka'	C/n 61	Silver Hill
Kugisho P1Y1 Ginga 'Frances'	T2-1702	Silver Hill
Kyushu J7W1 Shinden	T2-326	Silver Hill
Macchi MC 202 Folgore	T2-498	NASM
Messerschmitt Bf 109G-6	T2-496	NASM
Messerschmitt Me 163B Komet	T2-500	Silver Hill
Messerschmitt Me 262A	T2-111	NASM
Messerschmitt Me 410A-2/U1	T2-499	Silver Hill
Mitsubishi A6M5 'Zeke'	T2-130	NASM
Mitsubishi A6M7 'Zeke'	C/n 23186	(loan to San Diego Aerospace Museum)
Mitsubishi G4M3 'Betty'	T2-2205 (incomplete)	Silver Hill
Nagler Rolz NR 54V-2		(loan to Hubschrauber Museum, Bückeburg, Germany)
Nakajima B6N2 Tenzan 'Jill'	C/n 5350	Silver Hill
Nakajima C6N1 Saiun 'Myrt'	T2-4803	Silver Hill
Nakajima Kikka	?	Silver Hill
Nakajima J1N1-S Gekko 'Irving'	T2-700	Silver Hill
Nakajima Ki-43 Hayabusa 'Oscar'	C/n 6430	(loaned to the EAA Museum)
Nakajima Ki-115a Tsurugi	T2-156	Silver Hill

Top right: **The Messerschmitt Bf 108D NX2231 Taifun of the Confederate Air Force at Harlingen, the one-time 'Air Min 87'.** *MAP*

Right: **The Mitsubishi A6M5 'Zeke' T2-130, on display in the NASM in downtown Washington.** *Alan Curry collection*

Below: **The rare two-seat trainer version of the MXY7-K2 Ohka stored at Silver Hill.** *Alan Curry collection*

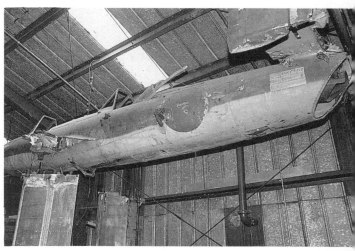

Arado Ar 396

One of the three Arado Ar 396 prototypes, which had been built by SIPA at Suresnes, was surrendered to the RAF at Leck and later handed over to the French authorities. The type entered production for the French military after the war as the SIPA S 10.

Blöhm und Voss Bv 144

The Bv 144 was a twin-engined high-wing transport designed for use by DLH (Deutsche Luft Hansa). Two prototypes were ordered but their construction was sub-contracted to the Breguet factory at Bayonne. The first prototype was flown in August 1944 but was taken over by the French before it could be flown away by the retreating German forces. This prototype was later flown in French markings, but its final fate is unknown.

Bücker Bü 181 Bestmann

Although large numbers of this type were transferred to France from British stocks, the aircraft was not in, and did not enter, production in France. Many of the examples initially used by the French Armée de l'Air were later civilianised. Details of known transfers from RAF stocks are given below:
VM143, 174, 181, 188, 199, 206, 215, 227, 231, 238, 243, 252, 259, 269, VM274, 278, 768, 770, 772 to 780 incl, 782 to 793 incl, 795, 796, 879, VN169 to 173 incl, VN782 to 787 incl. Also W Nr 099, 126, 374, 656, 877, 905, 995, 5937, 6031, 16108, 110094, 110104, 110294, 110408, 110411, 110736, 110799, 110854, 110855, 110948, 111180, 111194, 120043, 120047, 120058, 120066, 120226, 120243, 120247, 120515, 120547, 120744, 120905, 330126, 330244, 330282, 330321, 330354, 330703, 330715, 330716, 330721, 330727, 330790, 330791, 330796, 330802, 330803, 330817, 330823, 330843, 330875, 330893, 330897, 330913, 330918, 331155, 331359, 331360, 331369, 331446, 331447, 331452, 331534, 335987, 501323, 501604, 501694, 501998, 502001, 502037, 502051, 502054, 502111, 502161, 502180, 502203, 021/0131, 021/0144, 021/0209, 021/0257, 021/0390.
(Total: 135 aircraft)

The French military service of these aircraft was brief. The majority of the Bestmanns were handed over to the 'Service de l'Aviation Legere et Sportive' and civilianised. Details are given later in this Chapter.

Top: **This Ar 79B was probably the aircraft flown by the French military at Strasbourg-Entzheim during 1946. The markings of the short-lived Saarland (SL-) appear in this photograph, taken before the Saar voted to join the Federal German Republic in the nineteen-fifties. Photo, taken at Saarbrucken.** *MAP*

Above: **A Bücker Bü 181 Bestmann in French military markings.** *Thomas E. Willis collection*

Bottom: **The prototype Blöhm-und-Voss Bv 144 in French markings after capture at Bayonne.** *ECPA AIR G 9535*

Far right: **An example of the Focke Achgelis Fa 330A held by the French Musée de l'Air, photographed at Chalais Meudon in June 1963.**
P. H. Butler collection

Right: **A Focke Achgelis Fa 330A in French markings. Photograph possibly at Cuers-Pierrefeu.**
MA19275 Musée de l'Air courtesy Steve Coates collection

Left: **The Dornier Do 335V-14 (French 'No.1') at Lyon, still wearing its German code 'RP+UQ'.**
Serge Blandin collection

Right: **The ex-RAF Fieseler Fi 156C VM296 'WJC'.**
Jacques Mutin collection

In addition to the aircraft listed in the BAFO document quoted above, the French received at least two Do 335s which were among those surrendered to French forces at Mengen. The tests of the Do 335 were partly aimed at providing comparative data to the Arsenal company which then had its Arsenal VB10 under development. The VB10 also had two engines, although they drove co-axial tractor propellers. These aircraft were:

No. 1   Do 335V-14   W Nr 230014
Coded 'RP+UQ'. This was tested at the Centre d' Essais en Vol (CEV) at Bretigny. This aircraft was repaired at Mengen under French supervision and was ferried to Bretigny several months before the second aircraft.

It was reconditioned by SNCASO and then delivered to the CEV on 3rd June 1946. After taxiing trials on 24th February 1947, the Dornier made its first test flight at Bretigny on 13th March 1947. Further flights were made in May after which it was grounded until November for the repair of an item of ancillary equipment. The next flight was made on 21st November and further flights took place in December 1947 and January 1948. Further minor repairs took place, after which a final flight was made on 4th March 1948. On the following day, the test programme was cancelled. At this point the aircraft had flown for 9 hours 30 minutes and had made 10 landings.

No. 2   Do 335V-17   W Nr 230017

This single-seat aircraft was flown at the Centre d'Essais en Vol at Bretigny by Capitaine Roger Receveau. After being completed under French supervision in the Dornier facility at Mengen, and being test flown there on 2nd April 1947, the '335 was delivered to the CEV at Bretigny on 29th May 1947. This '335 was destroyed in a forced landing at Lyon-Bron following an engine failure on an unknown date.

Fieseler Fi 156

Production of the Fieseler Storch was undertaken from 1942 by Morane Saulnier at Puteaux and continued after the liberation as the MS 500 and (with different engines post-war) as the MS 501/502. Details of the Fi 156s transferred to France from RAF stocks were:

RAF serial numbers VH751, VM291 to 296 inclusive, VM472, VM824 to 829 incl, VM831 to 833 incl, VM835 to 839 incl, VM842, VM873, VM897, VN267.
Other aircraft, W Nr 1015, 1213, 4307, 4410, 4487, 5443, 5445, 5570, 5727, 5759, 5763, 5988, 018501/1, 110184, 110402, 110418 and 110419. Also MS 500 No. 136.

It is believed that ex-Luftwaffe examples were allocated French constructor's numbers in the sequence from 2001 after overhaul for use by the Armée de l'Air. A total of 65 ex-Luftwaffe Fi 156s is stated to have been taken over by the French government.

Examples of the Fi 156 captured in France, together with new aircraft from the Morane Saulnier factory, were flown by GR III/33 'Perigord'.

Focke-Achgelis Fa 330A Bachstelze

The Fa 330 rotor-kite was employed on German U-boats, mainly operating from French ports. Training of Kriegsmarine seamen as pilots on the type was carried out by the Germans using the large-scale wind tunnels at Chalais Meudon near Paris. After the liberation at least one Fa 330 was found here and was flown again in the wind tunnels by German pilots under Allied supervision. In 1946 further trials were made in which an Fa 330 was flown from the French submarine *Casabianca*.

The trials in the Chalais Meudon wind tunnel were carried out in late July 1945. Among the German pilots who took part was Hans Gerstenhauer, who was at the time held near Paris, supervising maintenance on the Fa 223 which was later to be flown to England. In early 1946, flights were made from the submarine *Casabianca* by Lt de Vaisseau (LV) Chatel, who was formerly an autogiro pilot with the French Navy. These trials were complete by March 1946.

There were two possible sources for the Fa 330s flown in France after the war, namely the batch of twenty-nine examples found by the RAF at Kiel, or examples abandoned by the Germans at Chalais Meudon. French documents make mention of the following W Nr for examples examined in France post-war:
100115, 100145, 100149, 100150.

The Fa 330s in the collection of the Musée de l'Air very probably came from Chalais Meudon. For many years after the war one example was on display in the former home of the Musée de l'Air at Chalais Meudon, only a few metres from the wind tunnels in which pilot training had been conducted during the war. One Fa 330 is on display in the Musée at Le Bourget; a second, less complete, example is in storage.

Gotha Go 150

One example was flown in French military markings during 1945/6 by Groupe Arnoult, based at Strasbourg-Entzheim. The Go 150 was a light twin-engined two-seat aircraft powered by Zundapp engines of 50-hp each. It was probably the same Go 150, W Nr 1159 of 33eme Escadre, which suffered an accident at Fribourg on 18th February 1946.

Heinkel He 46D

One example of the Heinkel He 46D army co-operation aircraft was abandoned by the Luftwaffe at Chateauroux in August 1944 and repaired by SNCASO. No details are known of its French service, although it was for many years in the Musée des Trois Guerres, Chateau de Diors, Indre, painted in French military markings. In 1981 the aircraft (W Nr 846) was transferred to the Musée de l'Air and is in storage at Villacoublay.

Heinkel He 111

In addition to the aircraft listed as supplied from British sources, one Heinkel He 111 was used by the French Armée de l'Air in the 1944/5 period. It is presumed to have been captured in France. The '111 was flown by GB I/31 'Aunis' alongside its Ju 88s, after being overhauled by SNCASE.

Heinkel He 162A

The seven examples listed as transferred to France from British sources were from the JG 1 aircraft captured at Leck. They were transported by rail to the Armée de l'Air depot at Nanterre near Paris and some were made airworthy for test at Melun or Mont-de-Marsan. The example flown as 'No. 3' by the French Armée de l'Air is now in the Musée de l'Air at Le Bourget; this is W Nr 120223. The W Nr and codes of the remaining six '162s have not yet been traced.

Left: **The sole French Armée de l'Air Heinkel He 111H, photographed at Toulouse in September 1945.** *Jacques Mutin collection*

Below: **A Heinkel He 162A coded '5' of JG 1, on a railway truck *en route* from Leck to France.** *S. Kahlert collection*

Junkers Ju 52

The thirty-six aircraft recorded as transferred to France from areas under British control equates fairly well with the total of 38 reconditioned aircraft given French identities '1001' to '1038' inclusive and there is a close connection between these two groups of aircraft. The thirty-six ex-British aircraft include twelve from the VM and VN batches of RAF serials listed in Chapter Eight, and nine seaplanes. The seaplanes came from I/TG 1, based at Sylt/Westerland and the nearby seaplane base at List. (See VM918, VM919, VM920, VM925, VM928, VM932, VM972, VM973, VM978, VM983, VN710, VN717).

The Ju 52/3m had been put into production in the former Amiot factory at Colombes during 1942 and it remained in production as the AAC 1 in the post-war period. AAC was also responsible for the reconditioning of the 38 aircraft mentioned in the previous paragraph.

Junkers Ju 88

The three aircraft listed earlier may have been types transferred for the evaluation of technical equipment. No details are known, but it is possible that the aircraft were the three Ju 88G-6 night fighter versions used by the French aircraft and guided-missile company Arsenal de l'Aeronautique at Villacoublay.

Prior to the end of the war, Ju 88As captured in France had been pressed into service with French Armée de l'Air units formed in the South of the country from personnel of the French Resistance and other organisations. The main unit was GB I/31 'Aunis', formed in 1944. This unit remained in being with the Ju 88 for some months after the war. The Ju 88s initially flown by this unit comprised sixteen aircraft found at Toulouse and overhauled there by SNCASO. Later, further Ju 88s captured at a Junkers overhaul facility at Villacoublay were refurbished at 'Ateliers Aeronautiques de Boulogne' (AAB). Seventy Ju 88s were repaired or rebuilt at AAB, most of them being Ju 88A-4s, but including examples of the A-6/U, G-6, R-2 and S-3 variants and the Ju 88A-4LT version. The A-4LT was a torpedo-bomber variant of the A-4 (LT – 'lance-torpilleur') modified for use by the Aeronavale, of which AAB converted four or five examples. In addition to GB I/31 'Aunis', the Ju 88 served with GB I/81 in Tunisia, the training unit at Cazaux, and the Centre d'Essais en Vol at Bretigny. The type also served with units 3S, 4S and 10S of the Aeronavale.

An evocative shot of a Ju 88A in French Armée de l'Air markings, taxiing past a line up of similar aircraft. *ECPA AIR 4555 ter*

— Messerschmitt Bf 108

Details of known transfers from RAF stocks are:
VH762, VM502, VM851 to 859 inclusive; also W Nr 1904, 3056, 5014, 5034 and 5043 for which no RAF serial numbers are recorded.

In addition to the above W Nr 1561 was registered as F-BBRH on 5th October 1948. In September 1953 this aircraft was sold in Denmark as OY-AIH where it is still currently registered. The origin of this aircraft is unknown but it cannot be entirely ruled out that it could be VH762 or VM858 for which no W Nr are known.

— Messerschmitt Bf 110

One example of the Bf 110, a day fighter variant, was used by the French Armée de l'Air in 1944/5. It is presumed to have been captured in France. It formed part of the equipment of GB I/34 'Bearn', a unit mainly equipped with Douglas Bostons and Martin Marylands. It is also reported to have been flown by GR III/33 'Perigord'.

— Messerschmitt Me 163B

It is believed that two of the four aircraft came from JG 400 at Husum and two from the Luftpark 4/XI store at Kiel/Holtenau airfield. It is not known whether the example identified as 'Air Min 203' (W Nr 310061), transferred from British stocks in the UK, is included in the total of four given in the statistics.

Three Me 262As were flown in France. 'No. 2' was flown by 'Watson's Whizzers' with the identity '3332' before being handed over to France by Watson. Two others came from British sources, one of these being a damaged aircraft found at Lübeck. Details are:

No. 1   Messerschmitt Me 262A

No. 1 brought to France by rail, arriving at the depôt at Nanterre. After rebuild at Chatillon, it was taken to Bretigny for final reassembly in February 1946. Its first flight was made by the SNCASO test pilot Daniel Rastel on 15 September 1946. No. 1 remained in the hands of SNCASO until handed over to the CEV, with which it made its first flight on 30th May 1947. It remained in service until 1948, making its last flight on 7th October.

No. 2   Messerschmitt Me 262A-1   W Nr 113332

Believed surrendered to Col Watson at Lechfeld. Flown from Lechfeld to Melun via St Dizier on 4th June 1945 and handed over to Col Badre of l'Armée de l'Air. It made its first flight in French hands on 16th June and on 22nd June was flown to Orange-Caritat by Capitaine Brihaye for further trials. On 6th September 1945, while it was being ferried from Orange to Bretigny by General

Housset, one engine failed and the aircraft force landed in a field at Tousson, near Nevers. The aircraft was subsequently repaired and made further test flights, its next being at Bretigny on 21st November. Remained in flying condition until October 1948. Test Pilots who flew the aircraft included Cpt Roger Receveau and Commandant Cabaret.

No. 3   Messerschmitt Me 262A

This aircraft was transferred to France by rail arriving at Nanterre. Rebuilt by SNCASO, making its first flight on 25th March 1947. After a number of flights by Daniel Rastel, it was handed over to the CEV and made its first flight with this unit on 18th August. After only a few flights, No. 3 was damaged beyond repair in a forced landing caused by engine failure.

A fourth aircraft, No. 4, was rebuilt by SNCASO but work on it was abandoned before any flights were made. A 'No. 5' is recorded as being reduced to spares, and Nos 6 and 7 were other Me 262s which were never made airworthy. No. 7 was a two-seat Me 262B which was reconditioned to take part in the development programme for the Leduc 010 ram-jet aircraft, but it seems it was never flown, because of a shortage of Jumo jet engines.

Siebel Si 204D

Twenty reconditioned aircraft, no doubt cannibalised from the thirty-nine aircraft transferred in Germany, entered service with the identities 1001 to 1020 inclusive. Details of known transfers from RAF stocks are given below:
VN101, 102, 104 to 107 incl, 109, 111, 113 to 129 incl, 131 to 135 incl, 137 to 140 incl, VP320.

The French forces in Indo-China after the Japanese surrender in 1945 utilised a number of Japanese aircraft. Details of these are incomplete but known information is as follows:

Aichi E13A1 'Jake'	six in use by Escadrille 8S of the Aeronavale
Mitsubishi Ki 21-I 'Sally'	two used by GT I/34
Ki 46-II 'Dinah'	one used by GT I/34 and crashed
Ki 51 'Sonia'	
Nakajima or Showa L2D2 'Tabby'	(licence-built Douglas DC-3) seven used by GT I/34
Nakajima Ki 43 'Oscar'	of which 12 at least were in use, 1945/6, by GC I/7 and GC II/7
Nakajima A6M2-N 'Rufe'	one in use in 1946, by Escadrille 8S of the Aeronavale
Tachikawa Ki 54 'Hickory'	four in use, 1946-1948, by SLAc 99

Right: **A Siebel Si 204D at Leck in French markings.** *S. Kahlert collection*

Top right: **Messerschmitt Me 262A 'No.2' of the Armée de l'Air, after its belly landing at Tousson on 6th September 1945.** *ECPA AIR 7110*

Far right: **An Aichi E13A 'Jake' in French Red Cross markings in Indo-China.** *ECPA Marine 12401*

Some of the above had also been used by the RAF unit at Saigon (Tan Son Nhut), known as 'The Gremlin Task Force'. This latter unit had carried out reconnaissance, leaflet dropping and transport flights in Indo-China prior to the arrival of French forces. The Ki 54s used by the French were probably all from the 'Gremlin Task Force'; they were coded with the numbers '8' to '11' inclusive. Of the 'Hickorys', two suffered recorded accidents:

'No. 2' - crashed 30 miles NW of Saigon after engine failure on 23rd April 1946. 'No. 4' - crashed into trees on take-off at Tha Ngon on 5th April 1946.

One of the Ki 21-I 'Sally' aircraft flown by GT I/34, identified as 'No. 6083', crashed and caught fire close to Tan Son Nhut on 20th April 1946.

One of the L2D aircraft flown by the same unit crashed on 30th July 1946 after both engines failed, probably due to running out of fuel, while it was preparing to land at Bien Hoa. The L2D was identified as 'No. 4265' and had completed 31 h 20 m flight time with GT I/34 at the time of the accident. The aircraft was scrapped after this incident.

Right: **A Tachikawa Ki-54 'Hickory' coded '11' in French Armée de l'Air markings in Indo-China.** *J. Mutin collection*

20.2   CIVILIAN AIRCRAFT

The following section lists, in alphabetical order of type, ex-German aircraft flown in French civilian markings in the post-war period.

Bücker Bü 131 Jungmann

Two Bücker Jungmanns were put into service in France after 1945. These were identified as F-BCSY 'FR-1' and F-BBXK 'FR-2'. F-BCSY was rebuilt with a Lycoming IO-360 engine and a cockpit canopy in 1969/70 becoming the 'CANU 01' with the registration F-PCSY; it is still in service. F-BBXK suffered an accident on 20th May 1953 and was scrapped in September 1955. FR-1 and FR-2 were probably captured by the RAF in Denmark and taken from there to Leck in December 1945. Three Bü 131s were found in Denmark, one at Vaerløse, and two at Aalborg East. The two aircraft were probably overhauled by Avions Maurice Brochet after delivery to France.

Left: **A poor but rare shot of a Nakajima Ki-43 'Oscar' in French markings in Indo-China.** *J. Mutin collection*

Right: **Bücker Bü 131 F-BCSY.** *MAP courtesy Eric Taylor collection*

Bücker Bü 133 Jungmeister

Two Bücker Jungmeisters were flown in France after 1945. One was W Nr 1131 which was flown to France by a American who had acquired it in Germany and who left it behind after his return to the USA. It was registered as F-BEDJ but had only a short life as such, being destroyed in an accident at Toussus-le-Noble on 5th June 1948. The second Bü 133 was identified initially as 'No 1'; it had served with the Armée de l'Air and was sold as scrap in 1948. It was rebuilt by Avions Maurice Brochet and registered as F-BBRI. In 1962 this Bü 133 was sold in the USA as N211U. The origin of the latter Jungmeister is not confirmed but it is possibly an example surrendered to British forces at Aalborg East in Denmark and later taken to Leck, where it is presumed to have been handed over to the French government. N211U was still currently registered in 1992.

Bücker Bü 181 Bestmann

Many of the Armée de l'Air Bestmanns were handed over to the 'Service de l'Aviation Légère et Sportive', a French government agency concerned with the development of private flying in France. These aircraft were overhauled, given new 'constructor's numbers' (FR-) and civilianised for use by French aero clubs and national pilot training centres. French identities FR-1 to FR91 inclusive are believed to have been rebuilt by Avions Maurice Brochet, at Neauphlé-le-Chateau. The remainder were possibly overhauled by another contractor. Some details are given below:

FR-1   W Nr   ?   ,   VM220, F-BBLP
FR-2   W Nr 330282,   F-BBLZ
FR-3   W Nr 110294,   F-BBMA
FR-4   W Nr 210340,   F-BBME
FR-5   W Nr 331547,   F-BBMN

FR-6   W Nr 330731,   F-BBMR
FR-7   W Nr   ?   ,   F-BBXD
FR-8   W Nr 330873,   F-BBNC
FR-9   W Nr 210178,   VM776, F-BBLN
FR-10   W Nr 210358,   F-BBMG
FR-11   W Nr 331396,   VN174, F-BBMI, N9269Z
FR-12   W Nr 110855,   F-BBNB
FR-13   W Nr   112,   F-BBLG
FR-14   W Nr 216168,   F-BBLJ
FR-15   W Nr 330844,   ex 'SV+NJ', F-BBNA
FR-16   not traced
FR-17   W Nr   228,   F-BBLR
FR-18   not traced
FR-19   W Nr 111192,   VM792, F-BBLO
FR-20   W Nr   ?   ,   F-BBLX, SL-ABI, D-EHIZ
FR-21   W Nr   ?   ,   F-BBLT
FR-22   W Nr 110401,   VN175, F-BBLL
FR-23   W Nr 331303,   VN782, F-BBMB
FR-24   W Nr 110402,   VM796, F-BBMJ
FR-25   W Nr 120502,   VM227, F-BBLQ
FR-26   not traced
FR-27   W Nr 110408,   F-BBMK
FR-28   W Nr   6348,   VN784, F-BBMF
FR-29   W Nr   ?   ,   F-BBLU
FR-30   W Nr   ?   ,   F-BBMP
FR-31   W Nr 110764,   'SK+EO', VM278, F-BBLY
FR-32   W Nr 330360,   F-BBMH
FR-33   W Nr 120518,   VM772, F-BBLA
FR-34   W Nr 120519,   VN785, F-BBMX
FR-35   W Nr 120547,   F-BBXF
FR-36   W Nr 331340,   F-BBHU

Above: **Bücker Bü 181 Bestmann F-BBMB with tricolour on fin.** *MAP*

Right: **The rare Focke Wulf-built Cierva C 30A 'F-BDAA' at St Cyr on 16th June 1963. This was in reality F-WDAA.** *P. H. Butler collection*

FR-37	W Nr 120046,	VM775,	F-BBMT
FR-38	W Nr 501659,	VN787,	F-BBMY
FR-39	W Nr ? ,	VM784,	F-BBMV
FR-40	not traced		
FR-41	W Nr 502161,		F-BBLI
FR-42	W Nr 120071,	VM790,	F-BBPX
FR-43	W Nr 656,		F-BBMO
FR-44	W Nr ? ,		F-BBML
FR-45	not traced		
FR-46	W Nr 258,	VN786,	F-BBXB
FR-47	not traced		
FR-48	W Nr 331351,	VN173,	F-BBLK
FR-49	W Nr 330750,	VM768,	F-BBMS
FR-50	W Nr 331331,	VM238,	F-BBLS
FR-51	W Nr 502061,	VM786,	F-BBLF
FR-52	W Nr ? ,		F-BBXA
FR-53	W Nr 021/0144,		F-BBLH
FR-54	W Nr 330799,		F-BBMZ
FR-55	W Nr ? ,		F-BBLM
FR-56	W Nr 330207,	VM782,	F-BBSA
FR-57	W Nr 110222,	VM777,	F-BBMU
FR-58	W Nr 110520,	VM788,	F-BBMM
FR-59	W Nr ? ,		F-BCSO
FR-60	W Nr ? ,		F-BBSC
FR-61	not traced		
FR-62	W Nr 501990,	VM206,	F-BBSI
FR-63	W Nr 502083,	VM199,	F-BBSE
FR-64	W Nr ? ,	ex-VM162(?),	F-BBXE
FR-65	W Nr 4022,	VM215,	F-BBXO
FR-66	W Nr 186,		F-BBSD
FR-67	W Nr. 757,		F-BBSJ
FR-68	W Nr 120066,		F-BBSG
FR-69	W Nr 501335,	VM783,	F-BBSB

FR-70	W Nr 120226,		F-BBXC
FR-71	W Nr 030,		F-BBSF
FR-72	no details		
FR-73	French military aircraft delivered to Indo-China. Damaged in accident at Bien Hoa, 5th August 1947		
FR-74	not traced		
FR-75	W Nr ? ,		F-BAYS
FR-76	not traced		
FR-77	not traced		
FR-78	W Nr 213,		F-BBXP
FR-79	W Nr ? ,		F-BBXQ
FR-80	W Nr 230,		F-BBXJ
FR-81	W Nr 392,		F-BBXI
FR-82	W Nr 120905,		F-BBXH
FR-83	W Nr 331563,	VM789,	F-BBXG
FR-84	W Nr ? ,		F-BBSH
FR-85	W Nr 331319,	VM791,	F-BBMC
FR-86	W Nr 120727,		F-BBMQ
FR-87	W Nr 110248,	VM259,	F-BBLV
FR-88	French military aircraft flown at Mainz-Finthen until at least December 1950. Later destroyed on 24th May 1951 in an accident at Mayence while being flown by Commandant Deroche, of Escadrille CPDA, Mayence		
FR-89	not traced		
FR-90	ex FR-33, F-BBSX, SL-AAL, D-EMAS		
FR-91	W Nr ? ,		F-BFAD
FR-92 to FR-100	not traced		
FR-101 to FR-133	W Nr & RAF serial numbers not traced. Registered F-BCRA to F-BCRV, F-BCRX to F-BCSG, and F-BCSP, respectively.		

It will be noted that not all the origins of the 'FR-' aircraft have been traced and also that some of the W Nr quoted for these aircraft do not appear in the earlier lists of W Nr above.

Of the above aircraft, at least the following still exist:

FR-11 (W Nr 331396): in 1975 this was registered in the USA as N9269Z; it was still current in 1983. It was on display at the Fritz Ulmer Collection at Göppingen, Germany, in 1985

FR-14/F-BBLJ, became OO-RVA and OO-BLJ; in store with the Musée Royal de l'Armée, Brussels.

FR-15 (W Nr 330844): this aircraft has been restored to display condition and by 1986 was with the Musée de l'Air at Le Bourget. Still present in 1989.

FR-20 current as D-EHIZ

FR-33/FR-90: current as D-EMAS

FR-38 currently held in West Berlin by the Museum fur Verkehr und Technik, marked as 'D-ESEL'.

FR-112 F-PCRL (ex F-BCRL) is on display at the Musée de l'Aéronautique de Nancy.

Focke Wulf Fw 44J Stieglitz

Two examples were flown in France post-war, F-BCNR (W Nr 251) and F-BCNE (W Nr 458). By 1952 both had been cancelled from the French civil register. Both aircraft were purchased by a new owner and together with the remains of a third aircraft (W Nr 593) were used to construct a 'new' aircraft which was registered as F-BFKK. This aircraft was largely built from F-BCNE. F-BFKK was cancelled from the register in 1962 but is currently being slowly rebuilt to fly once again. F-BCNE and F-BCNR may have been examples captured in the British Zone of Occupation. Two Fw 44s were flown to the collection centre at Leck, one from Travemünde on 8th January 1946, and another from an unknown place on 18th January.

Focke Wulf-Cierva C 30

One example of the Focke Wulf-built Cierva C 30A existed in France post-war. This was W Nr 1791 F-WDAA. Its origins are unknown. It was for some years at St Cyr l'Ecole and is believed to have been scrapped there in about 1963. Latterly it wore the false marks 'F-BDAA' which rightly belonged to a de Havilland Tiger Moth.

Heinkel He 72 Kadett

One He 72 was flown in France post-war – W Nr 486. It had been acquired in Austria in 1945 by a Capitaine Deroche, being captured at Nofels, near Feldkirch in western Austria and flown in French military colour with the code letter 'Z'. After the French military unit which Deroche commanded moved to France in September 1945, the Heinkel was delivered to Nevers on 22nd September and to Bourget du Lac on 1st November 1945. On 21st February 1946 it was flown to Baden-Oos where it remained with the based Section de Liaison after Deroche's unit, an Escadrille d'Aviation d'Artillerie with Piper L-4H Cubs was posted to Morocco in June 1946. It was civilianised in 1948 as F-BBHJ, being scrapped in 1961.

Klemm L 25

Four Klemm L 25 light aircraft were flown in France post-war. These were as follows:

F-PAAE W Nr 154 Origin unknown. Flown by the Aero Club de Constantine in Algeria prior to 1951.

F-PCDA W Nr 138 Origin unknown, although it had flown pre-war in Germany as D-1611 and then in the Saarland as TS-AAB and then EZ-AAB. It became F-PCDA on 25th June 1953 and then passed to the Transport & Technical Museum in West Berlin after its last Certificate of Airworthiness expired in 1963.

The DFS/14 SG 38 F-CAIC at Vannes-Meucon on 27th July 1964.
P. H. Butler collection

F-PDPT W Nr 581   Origin unknown. This aircraft was rebuilt in France in the latter part of 1947 and was registered on 12th February 1948. It had been registered in Germany pre-war as D-2931 but it is not known how it came to arrive in France. It was cancelled from the French register in 1952.

F-PAAZ W Nr 1038   This aircraft was found near Friedrichshafen in an area under French occupation post-war. It was restored to flying condition by French military personnel at the Centre de Kretz in 1948 and was flown intensively. Later it was at Salon de Provence and was sold there to a private owner with whom it was registered as F-PAAZ in December 1954. It had only a short life before being destroyed in an accident.

Klemm Kl 32
One Kl 32 was flown in France post-war. This is believed to have been brought to France by a US Army officer who had acquired the aircraft in Germany.

F-BCKX W Nr 1116   Registered in France on 22nd February 1947. Cancelled in September 1958 after it had been grounded for some years because of a lack of spares.

Klemm Kl 35B
Three examples were flown by the French after the war, as detailed below:

F-BBVZ W Nr 20814/24 and 'No. 1'. Registered in France on 15th October 1948, after sale by the French Air Force. Cancelled in February 1952.

F-BAIK 'No. 2' (W Nr not known). Registered on 21st June 1948. Believed to have been scrapped at St Cyr l'Ecole in about 1950.

F-OALS W Nr 20815/6. This aircraft was found by French occupation forces in Austria in 1945 and restored to flying condition. Sold for civilian use and registered as F-OALS on 28th May 1952. C of A suspended on 8th May 1953. This aircraft was flown by the French military at Treves in September 1945. No. 1 and No. 2 were almost certainly the examples captured by the RAF in Denmark and taken to Leck in December 1945 for transfer to France. One was captured at Haderslev and the other at Vandel.

20.3   SAILPLANES

A total of 378 gliders and sailplanes was also acquired from German sources. These aircraft included 175 DFS 108-14 SG 38, 40 DFS 108-30 Kranich II, 118 DFS 108-49 Grunau Baby, 20 München Mü 13 and twenty-five other assorted high-performance types.

A number of the German gliders and sailplanes still exist in France; details are:

DFS 108-14 SG 38	W Nr 124, F-CBHK With 'Les Aeroplanes', Montaigu, SE of Nantes
DFS 108-49 Grunau Baby	W Nr 14, F-CRDT With Escadrille Pegase, La Mole - St Tropez
DFS 108-14 SG 38	W Nr quoted as '157' With the Groupement pour la Preservation du Patrimoine Aeronautique, Angers. True W Nr 1493, built by J. Rathsens
DFS 108-14 SG 38	W Nr? At the Musée Aeronautique de Champagne, Brienne-le-Chateau

The Musée de l'Air holds several such sailplanes, as follows:

DFS 108-14 SG 38s	W Nr 31 and 173
DFS 108-30 Kranich II	W Nr 1399
DFS 108-53 Habicht	F-CCAG C/n '2' (but marked as F-CAEX C/n '1'
DFS 108-70 Meise	F-CRBT C/n 12/259
DFS 108-49 Grunau Baby	

Not all the 378 gliders and sailplanes brought to France received civilian registrations, since such registrations, in the series F-C..., did not begin to be allotted until 1952. Known allocations and their construction numbers given to gliders which survived after 1952 are as follows:

DFS 108-14 Schulgleiter (SG) 38

F-CACL No. 156	F-CACM No. 2	F-CAIC No. 125	F-CAJA No. 17
F-CAJB No. 35	F-CAJC No. 115	F-CASD No. 52 or 87	F-CASE No. 163
F-CAYV No. 11	F-CAYX No. 146	F-CBHK No. 124	F-CBHL No. 119
F-CBHM No. 187			
F-CRRK No. 19 (previously F-WRRK, later F-AZBJ)			

DFS 108-30 Kranich II

F-CACC No. 6	F-CACD No. 25	F-CACG No. 9	F-CACH No. 35
F-CADN No. 11	F-CANF No. 27	F-CAUD No. 10 or 16	F-CBBA No. 20
F-CBBB No. 5	F-CBBD No. 30	F-CRMY No. 1428	

Note: F-CANF later became F-CRJT. F-CATZ No 75 was a post-war Kranich III built by Focke Wulf.

DFS 108-49 Grunau Baby

F-CADD W Nr 004376	F-CAFI No. 52	F-CAFJ No. 56	F-CAFK No. 55
F-CAFL No. 57	F-CASF No. 11	F-CASG No. 103	F-CATB No. 5
F-CATC No. 58	F-CAVQ No. 135	F-CAXA No ?	F-CAXB No. 14
F-CBCD No. 15	F-CBCE No. 16 or 53	F-CBCF No. 105	F-CBCG No. 18
F-CBCI No. 50 or 184	F-CBCJ No. 13	F-CBCK No. 19	F-CBCL No. 21
F-CBCM No. 53	F-CBUU No. 45	F-CBUV No. 49	F-CBZH No. 12
F-CCBC No. 186	F-CCBE No ?		

Note: F-CAFL is reported variously as No. 57, 69 or 97; F-CBCF is reported as both No. 105 and No. 154; F-CBCL is reported as both No. 21 and No. 24; F-CAFI later become F-CRJB; F-CAXB later became F-CRDT.

DFS 108-53 Habicht

F-CAEX No. 1
F-CCAG No. 2 (is in the Musée de l'Air, painted as 'F-CAEX No. 1')

DFS 108-68 Weihe

F-CABU No. 9	F-CBGT No. 3 (later became F-CRMD and then F-CRMX)
F-CADE No. 4 or 20 (later became F-CRJC)	F-CBXX no. 55
F-CAER No. 39	

Note: F-CAEI No. 1 was a post-war built Focke Wulf Weihe 50.

DFS 108-70 Meise

F-CABH No. 1	F-CAGJ No. 9 (later became F-CRLY)
F-CABI No. 2 or 3	F-CACZ No. 6
F-CACI No. 7	F-CRBT No. 12
F-CACZ No. 10 (later became F-CRPJ)	

Note: F-CACI has also been recorded as F-CAGI - possibly both registrations were used; this aircraft later became F-CREA.

Göppingen (Hirth) Gö III Minimoa

F-CABL No. 1/206 (later to F-CRPY)	F-CAES No. 163
F-CADA No. 2 (ex D-14-280 later F-CROU)	F-CAGM No. 4 (later to D-1163)

Göppingen (Hirth) Gö IV Goevier

F-CARE No. 1/547 (later became F-CRPR)	F-CREY No. 2
F-CCBF No. 8	

München Mü 13 and Mü 13D

F-CABM (Mü 13D) No. 1 (later became F-CRKK)
F-CAEQ (Mü 13) No. 3 (later became F-CRRA)
F-CCBT (Mü 13) No. 2

Schweyer Rhonsperber

F-CABK No ?

Schleicher Rhonbussard

F-CAGU No. 789/5 (later became F-CRQI)	F-CAGV No. 6

A DFS/30 Kranich II in French hands in 1945. *ECPA AIR 6582*

In a few cases the gliders recorded above may in fact have been French-built versions of the same type - i.e., the Grunau Babies may be Nord 1300's and so on – due to incorrect entries in the official records. The F-CR.. registration series was issued for aircraft with Restricted Certificates of Airworthiness; many wartime-built sailplanes were transferred to this Category in later years because of concerns about the failure of Kaurite-type glue used for glider construction during the war period.

Top: **The DFS/53 Habicht currently in the Musée de l'Air collection, photographed at Chalais Meudon in July 1965. The registration is false, the true identity being F-CCAG.** *P. H. Butler collection*

Above: **An ex-German Grunau Baby, still in camouflage, in French hands in the immediate post-war period.** *ECPA AIR 6455*

20.4 FRENCH PRODUCTION OF GERMAN DESIGNS, POST-1944

Several types of German-designed aircraft were placed in production in French factories during the German occupation. In all cases production continued against new orders placed by the French government following the liberation. In addition, several sailplane designs of German origin were placed in production in France after 1945.

Below: **A Sipa S 10, the first French-manufactured Arado Ar 396 version to enter Armee de l'Air service.** *MAP*

Bottom: **One of the Dornier Do 24T flying-boats to be produced for the Aeronavale by SNCAN in the former CAMS factory at Sartrouville after the war. This photo taken at the factory.** *ECPA AIR 9196*

Arado Ar 396 (SIPA S 10 and developments)
The Ar 396 was under development (from the Ar 96B) by SIPA at Suresnes near Paris in 1944. Three prototypes had flown while SIPA was still under German control, one of which was surrendered at Leck and handed over to the French. The Ar 396 continued in production for the French military as the SIPA S 10 (of which 30 were built). 104 Sipa S 11/S 111 and 100 Sipa S 12/S 121 developments of the design were also delivered to the French Armée de l'Air.

Dornier Do 24T
The Do 24T three-engined flying-boat was in production by CAMS at Sartrouville from 1942 and following the liberation a further 22 examples of the type were completed for delivery to the Aeronavale. The type entered service with Flotille 9F in 1945 and the type remained in service until 1953. It is possible that a few surrendered Luftwaffe Do 24Ts also entered service.

Fieseler Fi 156C Storch (Morane-Saulnier MS 500/501/502 Criquet)
Several hundred MS 500/501/502 were built by Morane-Saulnier at
Puteaux with constructor's numbers from No. 1 onwards. These
mainly entered French military service, although in later years
many were civilianised for such duties as glider-towing. The
MS 500 was virtually identical to the Fi 156C-7 which was in production by Morane-Saulnier under German control. The MS 501
and 502 differed primarily in being re-engined with French-
designed power plants. The main production version, the MS 502,
had the Salmson 9Q radial engine. Later versions, such as the
MS 505, were examples re-engined after new production had
ceased.

Focke-Achgelis Fa 223 (SNCASE SE 3000)
The Fa 223 twin-rotor helicopter was chosen for post-war development and production by the French and was adopted by SNCASE
as the type SE 3000. At one point thirty examples were on order for
the French military (six for the Aeronavale, the remainder for the
Armée de l'Air), but this order was reduced to eight and then cancelled entirely. In the meantime two SE 3000 prototypes had been
flown, the first of these on 23rd October 1948 (F-WFDR). The second machine, F-WFRS, was flown in November 1950, by which
time the programme had all but been abandoned. The SE 3000 was
virtually identical to the Fa 223E apart from a slightly lengthened
nose and revised cockpit glazing.

Focke Wulf Fw 190A (Aerocentre NC 900)
The Fw 190 was in production in France under the German occupation. Production continued after the liberation of France, a total
of 64 Fw 190A-5 and 190A-8 being produced, initially by Ateliers
Aeronautiques de Cravant (AACr), at Cravant near Auxerre,
under the designation AACr 6. The first flight of an AACr 6 was
made on 16th March 1945. AACr was later absorbed by SNCAC
after which point the AACr 6 was redesignated as the NC 900. The
individual variants became the NC 900-A5 and 900-A8. One of
these aircraft was used by the Aeronavale, the remainder by the
Armée de l'Air. Units using the NC 900 included GC 3/5 'Norman-
die-Niemen', the CIC's (fighter training centres) at Tours and
Cazaux and the communications unit GAEL 87 at Paris/Le
Bourget. The Fw 190 on display at the Musée de l'Air at Le Bourget
is in fact NC 900 No. 62 from the French production line at Cravant. Production of the Fw 190 was also proposed by Ateliers
Aeronautiques de Colombes, under the designation AAC 5, but
the order for sixty aircraft was cancelled before any aircraft could
be completed.

Right: **The French-built Focke Wulf Fw 190A NC 900 currently displayed at
Le Bourget in the Musée de l'Air.** *Alan Curry collection*

Below: **A French built MS 500 Criquet still wearing invasion stripes and a
Cross of Lorraine, photographed (probably at Issy-les-Moulineaux) soon
after the liberation.** *ECPA AIR G 4749*

Bottom right: **The Heinkel He 274V-1 AAS 01 shortly before its first flight as
the Ateliers Aeronautiques de Suresnes AAS 01A in December 1945. Photo
taken at Orleans-Bricy.** *SHAA B87 2064*

Heinkel He 274 V-1, V-2 (AAS 01A and 01B)

The Heinkel He 274 was a development of the Heinkel He 177 bomber. Because of a lack of design capacity within the Heinkel organisation, the development of this aircraft had been sub-contracted to Société Anonyme des Usines Farman (SAUF) at Suresnes near Paris. The He 274 began life as a high-altitude version of the He 177 but, as development continued, its design diverged from its progenitor. It emerged as a four-engined aircraft with twin fins and a pressurised cabin for its crew. Its fuselage, originally identical to the He 177 apart from the pressure cabin, was considerably lengthened, its undercarriage arrangement was changed, and the wing was an entirely new design to achieve the high-altitude performance required of it. The He 274 V-1 was almost ready for its first flight when the advance of Allied forces in France forced the withdrawal of German personnel from the Suresnes factory. The prototype was completed under French control and made its first flight at Orleans/Bricy on 30th December 1945. In the meantime the SAUF organisation had been nationalised and became the Ateliers Aéronautiques de Suresnes and the prototype was thus redesignated the AAS 01A. The second He 274 prototype, the He 274 V-2, was later completed as the AAS 01B and made its first flight on 22nd December 1947, although in the meantime AAS had been absorbed into the SNCASO organisation. The aircraft were tested at the Centre d'Essais en Vol at Bretigny and were later used to carry and air-launch flying scale-models of the French SO4000 and NC 270 aircraft for test flights. Both aircraft were grounded towards the end of 1952 because of lack of spares; they were scrapped at Istres in 1953.

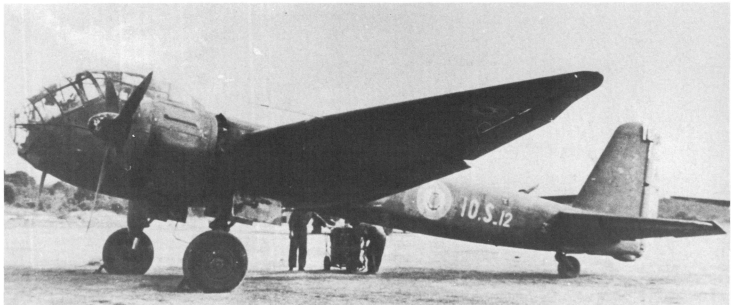

Junkers Ju 52/3m (AAC 1)

The Ju 52 was produced by the former Amiot works from 1942 and remained in production post-war as the AAC 1 'Toucan', Ateliers Aéronautiques de Colombes being the successor to the pre-war Amiot company. The post-war production total comprised 415 aircraft. AAC 1 aircraft served with the following Groupements de Transport of the French Armée de l'Air: GT 1/64 *Bearn*, 3/64 *Tonkin*, 1/63 *Bretagne*, 1/62 *Algerie*, 2/62 *France-Comte* and 2/61 *Maine*. AAC 1s also served with Escadrilles 4S, 5S, 22S and 56S of the Aeronavale.

Junkers Ju 188E

Four Junkers Ju 188 were reconditioned for the French Navy by Ateliers Aéronautiques de Boulogne. It is reported that a batch of ten Ju 188E aircraft was manufactured (or re-manufactured ?) post-war by SNCASO, also for the use of the Aeronavale. These served for a short period with Flotille 10S. Examples of the Ju 188 also served with the Armée de l'Air in the post-war period.

Top: **A typical AAC 1 'Toucan' of the Armée de l'Air, photographed several years after the war.** *MAP*

Above: **Junkers Ju 188 of the Aeronavale wearing its unit code '10.S.12' of Escadrille 10.** *J. Mutin collection*

Below: **Focke Wulf Fw 44 Steiglitz F-BFKK.** *MAP* (see page 275)

Top: **The Nord 1101 production version of the Messerschmitt Me 208 is exemplified by this Armée de l'Air aircraft No.182.** *MAP*

Above: **An early Nord 1000 'Pingouin' photographed at a French military airfield.** *NASM courtesy Norm Malayney collection*

Messerschmitt Bf 108/Me 208 (NORD 1000, 1100 series)
Production of the Bf 108 was transferred from Messerschmitt to SNCA du Nord at Les Mureaux in 1942 and the type remained in production post-war as the Nord 1000/1001/1002 'Pingouin' series, some 285 of the series being built after 1945. Prototypes of a tricycle undercarriage development, the Me 208, were built at Les Mureaux during the occupation and this version entered production as the Nord 1101 'Noralpha' post-war, some 200 being built.

This Aeronavale NC 702 'Martinet' coded '1.S.17' is typical of French Siebel Si 204D production. *MAP*

Siebel Si 204 (NORD NC 700 'Martinet' series)
From 1942 the Si 204 was in production by SNCA du Centre at Bourges. After the war it remained in production as the NC 700/701/702 series of which 350 were supplied to the French Armée de l'Air, French Navy and some civilian operators.

* * *

In addition to the powered aircraft, several types of German glider and sailplane were put into production in France, including the Grunau Baby (as the Nord 1300), Olympia-Meise (as the Nord 2000) and DFS Weihe (as the Victor Minie Aeronautique VMA 200). The VMA200s were assembled from 100 sets of parts found in the Kittleberger factory at Rheinau-Hoebert, near Bregenz. A version of the Hirth Goevier was also proposed as the Sud-Est PM 200 but only two were built. Production of the Nord 1300, Nord 2000 and VMA 200 was:

Nord 1300	Reported as 265 (but c/nos as high as 285 exist)
Nord 2000	105
VMA 200	32

Victor Minie Aviation was a private company based at St Cyr-l'Ecole. Société Nationale des Constructions Aéronautiques du Nord (SNCAN) was one of the regional companies of the post-war French nationalised aircraft industry.

20.5   **AIRCRAFT HELD BY MUSEUMS**

The main aerospace Museum in France is the 'Musée de l'Air et de l'Espace' at Paris-Le Bourget. This Museum originated as the Musée de l'Air at Chalais Meudon in 1921. A Museum building was opened in the centre of Paris in 1936, but it was damaged during the Second World War. The Museum reopened in 1950 at Chalais Meudon. With the planned opening of a new Paris airport at Roissy-en-France (now Paris-Charles de Gaulle), the opportunity arose to re-establish the Museum in the terminal building and hangars of the original airport at Le Bourget. The transfer of exhibits from Chalais Meudon took place from 1975, when the first stage of the Le Bourget exhibitions opened.

Aircraft held by the Museum which are relevant to this book include:

Bücker Bü 181 Bestmann	'SV+NJ' (C/n FR15, W Nr 330844)
DFS 108-14 Schulgleiter 38	No. 31 and No. 173
DFS 108-30 Kranich II	No. 1399
DFS 108-53 Habicht	F-CCAG no. 2 (marked as 'F-CAEX no. 1')
DFS 108-49 Grunau Baby	(in store)
DFS 108-68 Weihe	F-CBGR (French built VMA 200 Milan)
DFS 108-70 Meise	F-CRBT
Fieseler Fi 103	unmarked
Fieseler Fi 156C	No. 1034, marked as 'D-EMAW'
Focke-Achgelis Fa 330A	– (+ one stored)
Focke Wulf Fw 190A	No. 62 (French built NC 900)
Heinkel He 46D	No. 846 (in store)
Heinkel He 111	BR21-129 (Spanish built CASA 2.111E)
Heinkel He 162A	W Nr 120223 (French Air Force No. 3)
Junkers Ju 52/3m	No. 216 (French built AAC 1)
Messerschmitt Bf 109	C4K-156 (Spanish built Hispano HA 1112K)
Messerschmitt Me 208	(French built N 1101, Nos 133, 135, 177 – in store)
Siebel Si 204	(French built NC 702, Nos 282, 315, 317 – in store)

Chapter Twenty-One

Captured Aircraft
used in other Countries

This Chapter summarises aircraft used in countries other than the United Kingdom, the United States of America and France. It is presented in sections by alphabetical order.

21.1 AXIS AIRCRAFT IN AUSTRALIA

Two aircraft types of German origin were impressed into the Royal Australian Air Force during the Second World War. These were the Junkers G 31 and the Dornier Do 24K.

The twin-engined Ju G 31 transports had in pre-war days been used in New Guinea for transporting material from the coast to the Bulolo Goldfields. Two examples were impressed into the RAAF serialled A44-1 (W Nr 3010 ex VH-UOW) and A44-2.

The Dornier Do 24Ks were six survivors of the twenty-five Do 24 K-1 and K-2 variants delivered to the Netherlands East Indies Air Force prior to the German invasion of the Netherlands. The 25 aircraft had included examples supplied by Dornier and others built under licence by Aviolanda in the Netherlands. These aircraft received the RAAF designation A49, following their arrival in Australia from Java after the Japanese invasion of the Netherlands East Indies in March 1942.

German aircraft taken to Australia are listed elsewhere in this book. They include the Me 262A 'AM 81', Me 163B 'AM 222' (see Chapter Seven) and the Bf109G-14 W Nr 163824 (see under 'Museum Aircraft' in Chapter Twelve).

Japanese aircraft brought to Australia were at first under the aegis of the TAIC, a joint USAAF/USN/RAAF unit based at Eagle Farm, Brisbane. This unit recovered and rebuilt Japanese aircraft found in New Guinea and elsewhere which were test flown at Eagle Farm. These aircraft are detailed in Chapter Fourteen under the 'TAIU' entries; most of the aircraft were flown with numbers prefixed 'XJ' (for 'Experimental Japanese'). In 1944 the personnel of the Brisbane-based TAIU were transferred to Anacostia in the USA, together with some of the aircraft from Eagle Farm.

It is probable that RAAF units in the field did fly a number of Japanese aircraft. One known example is the Mitsubishi A6M5 'Zeke 52' handed over to No. 457 Squadron RAAF by the TAIU-SWPA at Clark Field, Manila, in the Philippines. So far as is known, this aircraft was not repatriated to Australia. Another example was the Mitsubishi Ki-51 Army Type 99 Assault Plane 'Sonia' flown by No. 4 Squadron RAAF at Keningan north-west Borneo, in November 1945. This wore the 'green cross' surrender markings and the code 'QE?' of No.4 Squadron. After hostilities ceased a number of Japanese aircraft were brought to Australia with the intention that they would be displayed by the Australian War Memorial in Canberra. These aircraft included:

The Me 262A Air Min 81 during the period it was displayed in Canberra by the Australian War Memorial. *AWM*

—   Mitsubishi A6M5 'Zeke' Navy Type 0 Fighter Model 52

This aircraft was 'BI-12' which had been flown by the ATAIU-SEA at Tebrau in Malaya. This aircraft is believed to have been scrapped.

—   Nakajima Ki-43-I 'Oscar' Army Type 1 Fighter Hayabusa

The origin of this aircraft, C/no 650, for many years in the Marshall Airways' Collection at Bankstown Airfield, Sydney, is unknown to the writer. Although originally intended for the War Memorial, this aircraft was bought by Sid Marshall when the Museum disposed of many of its assets in the 1950s, because of the lack of display and storage space. The Ki-43 was sold to J. Davidson and subsequently to Col Pay of Scone, New South Wales. The 'Oscar' is being restored to flying condition, as a long-term project, by Col Pay's aerial work company, Pay's Air Service.

Conceivably this aircraft could be one of those flown by the TAIU-SWPA at Eagle Farm, as described in Chapter Fourteen.

—   Mitsubishi Ki-21-IIa 'Sally' Army Type 97 Heavy Bomber Model 2A

This example was the aircraft which had carried part of the Japanese delegation from Borneo to Labuan Island for the surrender ceremony at the end of the war. The aircraft had belonged to the Headquarters Flight of the 3rd Kokugun (3rd Air Army). Between 10th and 15th February 1946 this was flown from Labuan via Darwin to Laverton, Victoria, by F/Lts Baker and Walters. This aircraft was later stored at RAAF Fairbairn, Canberra, for the Australian War Memorial, but was scrapped in about 1950 because of the lack of space and the deteriorating condition of the aircraft.

—   Mitsubishi G4M 'Betty' Navy Type 1 Attack Bomber

The origin of this aircraft is unknown. It was stored at RAAF Fairbairn with the 'Sally' and scrapped at about the same time.

—   Tachikawa Ki-54 'Hickory' Army Type 1 Transport

This example was also surrendered at Labuan after flying the Japanese General Baba from North Borneo to Labuan to sign the documents surrendering his forces. The aircraft was selected for transfer to Australia at the end of 1945 but by that time was no longer airworthy. It was therefore crated and sent to Australia by sea in April 1946. After arriving at No. 1 Aircraft Depot, Laverton, it was despatched to RAAF Base Fairbairn. It remained there for many years, latterly in a children's playground. In 1980, the fuselage of this aircraft was taken to the RAAF Museum at Point Cook, Victoria, where it remains at the time of writing.

21.2   AIRCRAFT SUPPLIED TO BELGIUM

The Belgian Government requested the supply of five Ju 52/3m aircraft from RAF stocks. After the unserviceable Ju 352A 'AM 110' located at Knokke airfield in Belgium had been offered and refused, four Ju 52s were delivered, as detailed in Chapter Eight. (See entries for VM930, VN747, VN750, VN751). It is believed that three of these were overhauled by Avions Fairey at Charleroi and then delivered to the Ministry of Communications as OO-SNA, OO-SNB and OO-SND. Details of these aircraft are as follows:

OO-SNA   Registered 18th April 1946.   Cancelled 17 April 1954.
OO-SNB   Registered 13 August 1946.   Cancelled 17 April 1954.
OO-SND   Registered 24 March 1949.   Cancelled 31 May 1951.

After cancellation these aircraft were handed over to the state disposal agency 'Domeinen' and are presumed to have been sold for

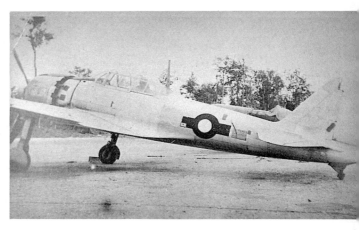

The Zeke 52 flown at Morotai by No.457 Squadron, RAAF after being overhauled by the TAIU-SWPA at Clark Field. *B. R. Robinson collection*

scrap. The four aircraft supplied by the RAF included one aircraft equipped for minesweeping which was to be used for spares – it is believed that this aircraft was VM930.

Other ex-Luftwaffe aircraft were flown in Belgium. These included the Bücker Bü 181 Bestmann OO-RVD WNr021969 'TP+CP', the precise origins of which are unknown. This aircraft is on display at the Musée Royal de l'Armée in Brussels. The Museum also holds Fieseler Fi 156C Storch WNr5503: this was interned in Sweden in April 1945 and later flew with the Flygvapnet as Fv 3822 (see under 'German Aircraft in Sweden', later).

The 'SABENA Old Timers' also holds two Junkers Ju 52/3ms, obtained from the Portuguese Air Force at Alverca. The identities of these aircraft are given later, under 'Norway'. One aircraft ex-FAP 6310, has been registered as OO-AGU (previously the registration of a SABENA Ju 52/3m) for demonstration flights.

21.3   AIRCRAFT SUPPLIED TO CANADA

Most of the Canadian involvement with captured aircraft was via the RAF. RCAF members of RAF units, and RCAF Squadrons under RAF control, flew many of these aircraft as related in earlier Chapters. After the war, several surrendered aircraft, including Heinkel He 162 and Messerschmitt Me 262 jets and Me 163B rocket powered fighters, were shipped to Canada. Examples of the jet types were used to examine jet engine operation in cold weather conditions; these tests were carried out at Winnipeg and involved ground running only. Examples of these He 162 and Me 163B aircraft survive today in the Canadian National Aviation Museum.

In addition to these aircraft, a number of gliders from German sources were taken to Canada after the war.

CF-ZPQ   München Mü 13d-3   W Nr 101

This aircraft was taken to Canada aboard a Royal Canadian Navy destroyer which sailed from Hamburg in 1945. It was built by Schwarzwald Flugzeugbau in 1944. After many years flying in Canada, initially with the McGill University Gliding Club, and latterly it would have been allocated the revised registration C FZPQ, this sailplane was sold to Robert E. Gaines of Marietta, Ga USA, in 1990 as N13MU.

CF-ZBH   Grunau Baby   WNr 1533

This Grunau was built by Edmund Schneider at Grunau and the WNr quoted is possibly that allotted by Schneider, although an RLM WNr(004496) has also been quoted for the aircraft. This glider was made airworthy by the Gatineau Gliding Club in 1947. It was still airworthy in 1985 with the Blue Thermal Association at Medicine Hat and in recent years it would have been allocated the revised national registration C-FZBH.

CF-ZBD   Grunau Baby   WNr *unknown*

This glider, for which the WNr is unknown, was previously 'LN+SR' of the Luftwaffe. (Note that the RAE received two more with consecutive codes, i.e. LN+SS, LN+ST). It was made airworthy by the Thunderbird Gliding and Soaring Club at the University of British Columbia, and first flew in Canada on 14th March 1948. The Grunau was grounded because of glue deterioration in its wings and the fuselage was sold to the Gatineau GC in May 1953. CF-ZBD was later flown with wings from another Grunau until it was destroyed early in 1965 when it was blown over in a severe storm while picketed out at the Quebec GC.

CF-ZAR   Grunau Baby   WNr 004497

This Baby was repaired by the Queens University GC at Kingston, Ontario. It was built by Edmund Schneider at Grunau with the WNr 1513, although the RLM WNr 004497 is also quoted. It made its first flight in Canada on 28 September 1947 and was flown by the QUGC until damaged in a landing accident on 18th July 1948. After lengthy rebuild, it reappeared in September 1956 as CF-ZCP. After flying with several more owners, CF-ZCP was donated to the Victoria Branch of the Canadian Museum of Flight and Transportation in 1982, for preservation.

CF-ZCB   Grunau Baby   WNr *unknown*

This aircraft was rebuilt by Rear Admiral H. G. DeWolf from two Grunau Babys retrieved from Germany. It was loaned to the Gatineau GC from 1951 after its rebuild was completed. Its registration was cancelled in May 1954.

21.4   AIRCRAFT USED IN CHINA

The war between Japan and China can be traced back to the 1931 invasion of Manchuria by Japan, albeit it that an attack on the heartland of China followed somewhat later. Formal Allied assistance to China awaited the Japanese attacks on Pearl Harbor and Malaya, although the American Volunteer Group (the 'Flying Tigers') was in place before these attacks. The AVG produced early reports on the legendary Mitsubishi Zero (Zeke), although it was not until 1942 that a 'Zeke' was rebuilt at Kunming and flown to Karachi in India for onward shipment to Wright Field, where it was flown as 'EB-2'.

With the defeat of Japan in 1945, large numbers of Japanese aircraft remained on Chinese territory. Even before the end of the war a civil war was in progress between the Nationalist government of Generalissimo Chiang Kai-Shek and Communist forces under Mao Tse-Tung. This war raged for several years with the Communist forces gradually advancing from the north of the country and overunning the Nationalist south. Ultimately the Chiang Kai-Shek regime withdrew to Formosa (Taiwan), where its successors still regard themselves today as the legitimate Republic of China.

Both sides in the Chinese Civil War used surrendered Japanese equipment.

The Tachikawa Ki-54 'Hickory' fuselage (far right) at the Beijing Aviation Museum in May 1993. *Leif Hellström collection*

The Nationalist Air Force used the following types:

Nakajima Ki-43 Army Type 1 Fighter 'Oscar' – flown by the 6th Fighter-Bomber Group in Shan-tong province from September 1945 to June 1946, when the unit was disbanded and the aircraft scrapped, primarily due to lack of spare parts.

Nakajima Ki-44 Army Type 2 Fighter 'Tojo' – a small number of this type was also flown by the 6th Fighter Bomber Group.

Kawasaki Ki-61 Army Type 3 Fighter 'Tony' – a small number of 'Tonys' was flown by the 18th Fighter Bomber Squadron, within the 6th Fighter Bomber Group.

Nakajima Ki-84 Army Type 4 Fighter Hayate 'Frank'– a number of 'Franks' were taken over by the Nationalist Air Force and served with the 18th and 19th Squadrons of the 6th Fighter Bomber Group until June 1946.

Kawasaki Ki-48 Army Type 99 Bomber 'Lily' – numbers of this twin-engined light bomber formed the equipment of the 5th Bomber Squadron within the 6th Fighter Bomber Group.

The Communist air force, the Peoples Liberation Army Air Force, initially operated in Manchuria and Japanese aircraft were used for pilot training. The types operated included:

Kokusai Ki-86 Army Type 4 Trainer 'Cypress' – more than ten, withdrawn by June 1946.

Tachikawa Ki-55 Type 99 Advanced Trainer 'Ida' – more than thirty, in service until 1953.

Mitsubishi Ki-30 Army Type 97 Light Bomber 'Ann' – three.

Mitsubishi Ki-46 III Army Type 100 Command Reconnaissance Plane 'Dinah' – two examples, one still in service with No.1 Squadron in 1949.

Tachikawa Ki-54 Army Type 1 Trainer 'Hickory' – a number of examples, flown by No.1 Squadron in 1949, and still in service as trainers until 1951.

Nakajima Ki-43-II Army Type 1 Fighter 'Oscar' – four examples

Kawasaki Ki-45-KAI Army Type 2 Fighter 'Nick' – three examples, flown by No.1 Squadron.

Nakajima Ki-44 Army Type 2 Fighter 'Tojo' – three examples, used for training in 1945.

Of the above, one Tachikawa Ki-55 exists in the Tang-shan Aviation Museum at Beijing, together with the fuselage of a Kawasaki Ki-48 'Lily'. The Beijing Aviation Museum holds the fuselage of Tachikawa Ki-54 'Hickory'.

Other types used included:

Kawasaki Ki-48 'Lily' light bomber

Nakajima Ki-34 'Thora' transport

Mitsubishi Ki-57 'Topsy' transport

Showa L2D3 'Tabby' transport

Nakajima Ki-61 'Tony' fighter

21.5   AIRCRAFT SUPPLIED TO CZECHOSLOVAKIA

The Czech government had requested the supply of a number of Ju 52/3m aircraft for the use of Bata Airlines. These aircraft were delivered but are believed to have been used by the government itself rather than Bata. (See entries in Chapter Eight for VM931, VN716, VN745). The State airline, CSA, used three Ju52/3m, OK-PDC, OK-TDI and OK-ZDO; it is not known whether these bore any relation to the ex-RAF aircraft.

In addition to aircraft supplied by the RAF, the Czech government had at its disposal many ex-Luftwaffe aircraft captured in its own territory as well as several aircraft production lines which had been established during the Nazi occupation. These included the following:

Arado Ar 96B
This aircraft was built by the Avia and Aero factories under the Czech AF designation C-2. 394 of the type were built between 1945 and 1949. Parts of one Ar 96B survive with the Vojenske Museum at Prague-Kbely.

Bücker Bü 131 Jungmann
This type was built post-war by Zlin under the Cz A F designations C-4 and C-104, 260 being built. The C-4 included twelve captured German-built examples. The C-104 (later redesignated C-4A) had the Czech-designed Walter Minor 4-III engine. The Bu 131 was not produced in Czechoslovakia under German control, but the drawings were available from a pre-war licence arrangement. Three examples survive with the Vojenske Museum, and one with the Narodni Technicke Museum in Prague.

Below: **OK-TDI, one of the Junkers Ju 52/3m flown post-war by the Czechoslovak government airline, CSA, pictured at Prague-Ruzyne shortly after the Second World War.** *Karel Hellebrand collection*

Bottom: **OK-RXE, a Czech-built Zlin C-104 version of the Bücker Bü 131 Jungmann, photographed at Prague-Kbely on 15th September 1990.** *Karel Hellebrand collection*

Bücker Bü 181 Bestmann
This type was already in production by Zlin and continued to be made for Czech Air Force service as the C-6, C-106 and C-206. Seventy-two Zlin 181 (C-6) were built in 1945/6, followed by 79 Zlin 281 (or C-206) re-engined with the Toma 4 motor in 1947/8 and then 314 Zlin 381 (or C-106) with the Walter Minor 4-III engine. Of the 314 Zlin 381, 154 were exported to Yugoslavia, Rumania, Egypt and other countries. The Narodni Technicke Museum (NTM) and the Vojenske Museum hold one example each of this type.

Fieseler Fi 156 Storch
The Storch was in production by Mraz at Chocen; 138 were constructed post-war under the Cz A F designation K-65 (later C-5). The NTM and the Vojenske Museum each has an example.

Focke-Achgelis Fa 223
Two of these twin-rotor helicopters were built by Avia and were flown under the military designation VR-3. The first of these, VR3-1 made its first flight on 12th March 1948. It was later flown by the Czech Air Police as OK-BZX. It was destroyed in an accident at Tyn nad Vltavou, in 1949. The second aircraft, VR3-2, flew for the first time on 5th July 1948. It was evaluated by the Czech Air Force, marked as 'V-25'. This aircraft was also destroyed in an accident in 1949, crashing at Hradec Kravde. These Fa 223s were from among the three incomplete production aircraft (S52 to S54 inclusive) found by Soviet forces at Berlin-Templehof in May 1945 and later handed over to the Czech authorities.

Messerschmitt Bf 109
This type was not in production in Czechoslovakia but large numbers of the type were abandoned in the country. A development of the Bf 109G was therefore produced by the re-manufacture of existing Bf 109 airframes using stocks of captured Jumo 211F engines. These were constructed by Avia and Letov as the S-199 and two-seat trainer CS-199. Some captured Bf 109G and Bf 109K airframes entered service as S-99s. A total of 450 S-199 aircraft were built for the Czech AF between 1947 and 1951 and a further twenty-five were exported to the Israeli Air Force (IDFAF) in 1948. Eighty-two CS-199 were constructed by Avia. The Vojenske Museum holds one example each of the S-199 and CS-199. The Bf 109G and Avia S-199 were both called 'Mezek' (Mule), as a tribute to their flying characteristics.

Messerschmitt Me 262
Avia constructed seven Me 262A single-seat jet fighters and three Me 262B two-seat trainers as the S-92 and CS-92 respectively. These were made by cannibalising Me 262 airframes and parts found in Czechoslovakia. Prague-Ruzyne had been an operational Me 262 base until the last few days of the war. The first S-92 flew on 27th August 1946, piloted by the Avia Chief Test Pilot, Antonin Klaus. The Vojenske Museum at Kbely holds an S-92 marked 'V-34' (S-92 No. 4) and a CS-92 marked as 'V-31' (CS-92 No. 5).

Siebel Si 204D
The Si 204 was in production in the Aero factory and continued in production for the Czech Air Force and in small numbers for the Czech airline, CSA. The Cz AF used the designation D-44 for the Si 204 in a transport role and C-3 as a trainer (C-3A navigational trainer, C-3B bomber trainer). 179 Si 204s were built between 1945 and 1949. The Vojenske Museum holds parts of two C-3 versions.

In addition to the aircraft built in Czech factories, other ex-Luftwaffe aircraft were used by the post-war Czech Air Force.

Top: The Fieseler Fi 156C Storch SP-AGO, one of a small number of the type flown post-war in Poland. *Hans Heiri Stapfer collection*

Above: An impressed Bücker Bü 133 Jungmeister, No. 1504, at No. 2 SFTS, Zwartkop. *MAP*

ZS-ABU	F 13HE	W Nr 2055	SAAF serial number 258
ZS-ADR	F 13KU	W Nr 2075	SAAF serial no. 1429, crashed at Durban, 3rd October 1940
ZS-AEA	F 13FE	W Nr ?	SAAF serial no. 259, crashed in South West Africa, 30th August 1943

Junkers A 50DU Junior

This was a two-seat all-metal trainer aircraft. Three civilian examples were impressed in March 1940:

ZS-ACJ to SAAF No. 2034, to Instructional airframe, SoC 7.44
ZS-ACK to SAAF No. 1551, to IS 9, SoC 12.43
ZS-ACL to SAAF No. 2035, to Instructional airframe, SoC 7.44

Junkers Ju 52/3m

The Ju 52 was one of the mainstays of the SAA fleet on the outbreak of war. The Ju 52s were at first taken over for use by the 'Airways Wing' of the SAAF, based at Zwartkop. The Wing was initially divided into Nos 17, 18 and 19 Squadrons of the SAAF, employed on transport and coastal patrol duties. In December 1939, the three Squadrons were amalgamated into No. 50 Squadron. The Ju 52/3ms later served in the Western Desert campaign. Eleven Ju 52/3m were impressed and their histories are:

ZS-AFD	W Nr 4061	To 660	Destroyed on the ground by enemy aircraft at Jigjigga, 29th March 1941
ZS-AJF		To 661	Sold as scrap 15th October 1946
ZS-AJG		To 662	Struck off charge 24th January 1946
ZS-AJH		To 663	Believed struck off charge 2nd August 1944
ZS-AJI		To 664	Sold as scrap 26th October 1946
ZS-AJJ		To 665	as ZS-AJI
ZS-ALO		To 666	as ZS-AJF
ZS-ALP		To 667	as ZS-AJI
ZS-ALR		To 668	Crashed 8th January 1941, North East of Mbeya
ZS-ALS		To 669	as ZS-AJI
ZS-ALU		To 670	as ZS-AJH

Junkers Ju 86Z and Ju 86K

The Ju 86 was designed as a twin-engined transport with a bombing capability. Although it served Deutsche Luft Hansa, Swissair and South African Airways as an airliner, many more aircraft served in the Luftwaffe and other air forces as a bomber. SAA operated eighteen Ju 86s; seventeen of these were Ju 86Z-1 and Z-5 airliners and one was a Ju 86K-1 bomber which it is presumed had been bought to provide the SAAF with some operating experience with the type, since it had always been intended that the SAA fleet would be incorporated into the SAAF in time of war.

The Ju 86s were allotted the serial numbers 641 to 658 inclusive and were at first operated in civilian colours by the 'Airways Wing', three aircraft being detached to No. 16 Squadron at Walvis Bay in South-West Africa for anti-submarine patrols. In May 1940, ten Ju 86s were passed to No. 12 Squadron SAAF on its formation. This unit flew to Nairobi/Eastleigh on 22nd May 1940 and commenced operations against Italian forces in Abyssinia following the declaration of war by Mussolini on 11th June 1940. One Ju 86 was shot down during these operations on 3rd September. On 1st May 1941, the surviving Ju 86s were handed over to a re-formed No. 16 Squadron at Addis Ababa. The Squadron was disbanded in August 1941, some of its personnel and equipment passing to No. 35 Flight, SAAF. Finally, the remaining Ju 86s passed in July 1942 to the newly-formed No. 22 Torpedo-Bomber Squadron, SAAF, at Durban, where they were soon replaced by Lockheed Venturas. Following active service the Ju 86s served with No. 5

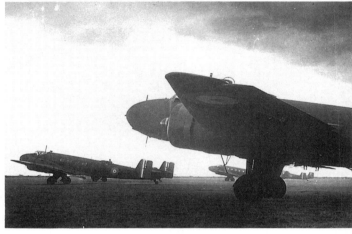

Top: **Junkers Ju 52/3m No. 661 of the SAAF.** *RAAF Museum P882*

Above: **A photograph showing Junkers Ju 86s of the SAAF in Kenya, the aircraft on the left being '647'.** *IWM SAF 149*

Wing, a conglomerate unit which carried out a variety of training and transport tasks. Finally, at the end of the type's career, the survivors went into service with No. 61 Squadron, SAAF, on communications duties.

ZS-AGE	Ju 86Z-1	ZS-AGF		ZS-AGG	
ZS-AGH		ZS-AGI		ZS-AGJ	
ZS-AJE		ZS-AJK		ZS-AJL	
ZS-ALN		ZS-ALV		ZS-ANA	Ju 86Z-5 W Nr 2017
ZS-ANB	W Nr 2018	ZS-ANC	W Nr 2019	ZS-AND	W Nr 2020
ZS-ANE	W Nr 2021	ZS-ANF	W Nr 2022	ZS-ANI	Ju 86K-1 W Nr 2041

The tie-ups between the civilian registrations and individual serial numbers in the block 641 to 658 are not known, but known fates are:

641   – written off at Derba Tabor on 23rd September 1941, with No. 35 Flight

21.16   GERMAN AIRCRAFT IN SPAIN

The Junkers Ju 290A-6 W Nr 110185 (originally coded 'KR+LP') of KG 200 was flown from Finsterwalde to Barcelona on 20th April 1945. Although other KG 200 aircraft are believed to have made later flights and to have returned to Germany, despite the imminent end of hostilities, this Ju 290 remained at Barcelona. In May 1950, after protracted negotiations, the aircraft was purchased by the Spanish government and taken into service with the Spanish Air Force. It served with the Escuela Superior de Vuelo at Salamanca/Matacan for a number of years until it was grounded by lack of spare parts. In Spanish Air Force service it was coded '74-23' ('74' being the code of the unit). It is believed that no Spanish Air Force type designation or serial number was allocated to the Ju 290 because of its unique nature.

It should be noted that the Franco government in Spain had close ties with the Axis following its backing of Franco during the Spanish Civil War. The Spanish Air Force retained many German and Italian aircraft supplied during the 1936-39 period. In addition, many types of German aircraft were produced under licence in Spain both during and after the Second World War. These included:

Bücker Bü 131, as the CASA 1.131 – 555 built, designation E 3.
Bücker Bü 133, as the CASA 1.133 – 50 built, designation E 1.
DFS 108-14 SG 38 primary glider, by AISA – 20 built.
DFS 108-30 Kranich sailplane, by AISA – 50 built.
DFS 108-49 Grunau Baby sailplane, by the Ejercito del Aire workshops, approximately 40 built.
DFS 108-68 Weihe sailplane, by AISA – 8 built.
Gotha Go 145, as the CASA 1.145 – 25 built, designation ES 2.
Heinkel He 111, as the CASA 2.111 – 236 built, designation B 7 (later B 2) and T 8 (transport conversions).
Junkers Ju 52/3m, as the CASA 352 – 100 built, designation T 2.
Messerschmitt Bf 109, as the Hispano HA 1109 (over 200 built), HA 1110 and HA 1112 (143 built).
Fiat CR 32 biplane fighter, by Hispano as the HA 132L (100 built).

Left: **C4K-156, the Spanish-built, Rolls-Royce Merlin-powered Messerschmitt Bf 109 (HA1112) in the Musée de l'Air at Le Bourget.** *MAP*

Below: **CASA 352, the Spanish-built Junkers Ju 52/3m T2B-272 at Cosford; this aircraft has since been painted to represent a pre-war aircraft of British Airways.** *Alan Curry collection*

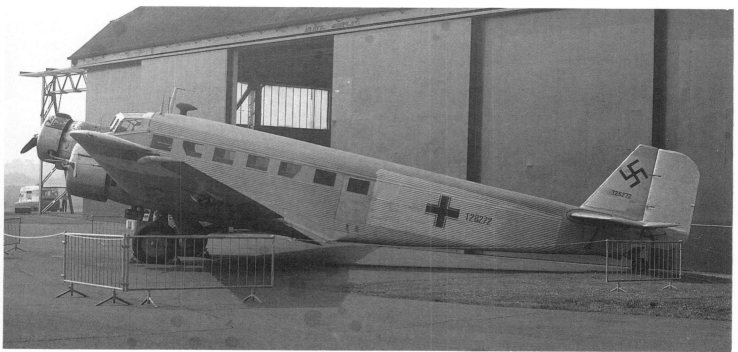

During the Second World War various German aircraft were supplied to the Spanish Air Force from German sources, including Dornier Do 24T-3 Air-Sea Rescue flying-boats, Fieseler Fi 156 Storch, Heinkel He 114 seaplanes, Junkers Ju 88A-4 bombers and Messerschmitt Bf 109F fighters.

The Museo del Aire at Cuatro Vientos, south-west of Madrid, has examples of the following types:

E1-14	Bücker Bü 133C
T2B-211	CASA 352 (Junkers Ju 52/3m)
T2B-254	CASA 352 (Junkers Ju 52/3m)
E3-8	CASA 1.131E (Bücker Bü 131)
T8B-97	CASA 2.111B (Heinkel He 111)
–	DFS 108-14 SG 38
EC-RAB	DFS 108-68 Weihe
EC-RAJ	DFS 108-68 Weihe
EC-RAM	DFS 108-68 Weihe
EC-RAQ	DFS 108-68 Weihe
HD5-2	Dornier Do 24T-3
–	Hispano HA 132L (Fiat CR 32)
L16-23	Fieseler Fi 156 Storch
B2-82	Heinkel He 111E - supplied by Germany during the Civil War
C4J-10	Hispano HA-1112K
C4K-158	Hispano HA-1112M
EC-MFG	Schneider Grunau Baby

21.17   GERMAN AIRCRAFT IN SWEDEN

Impressed Aircraft
Various civilian aircraft were impressed for service with the Flygvapnet (Royal Swedish Air Force). These included several of German manufacture, details of which follow:

Junkers Ju 52/3m
This type of aircraft was in service with AB Aerotransport, the Swedish national airline. Examples were impressed into the Flygvapnet from 1940 to 1944 as the 'Tp 5'.

SE-ADR	W Nr 4017 –	impressed as Tp 5 (no untraced). To SE-ADR in 1944.
SE-AFA	W Nr 5614 –	impressed as Tp 5 no. 907. Restored as SE-AFA in 1944.
SE-AFB	W Nr 5620 –	impressed as Tp 5 no. 909. Restored as SE-AFB in 1943.
SE-AFC	W Nr 5633 –	impressed as Tp 5 no. 908. Restored as SE-AFC in 1944.
SE-AFD	W Nr 5646 –	impressed as Tp 5 (no. untraced). To SE-AFD in 1944.

Klemm Kl 35
This type was used in Sweden as a trainer for the Flygvapnet as the Sk 15. The following additional civilian-registered examples were impressed:

Klemm Kl 35B

SE-AIF	W Nr 1595 –	impressed July 1940 as No. 5085. Restored to SE-AIF 19th December 1940.
SE-AIG	W Nr 1596 –	impressed July 1940 as No. 5075. Restored to SE-AIG 19th December 1940.
SE-AIH	W Nr 1587 –	impressed July 1940 as No. 5076. Restored to SE-AIH 19th December 1940.
SE-AIM	W Nr 1597 –	impressed July 1940 as No. 5077. Restored to SE-AIM 25th November 1940.

SE-AIN	W Nr 1630 –	impressed May 1942 as No. 5085*. Restored to SE-AIN 23rd September 1944.
SE-AIP	W Nr 1642 –	impressed July 1940 as No. 5086. To SE-AIP 26th October 1940. Impressed again 27th April 1942 as No. 5081*. To SE-AIP 23rd August 1944.
SE-AIW	W Nr 1731 –	impressed July 1940 as No. 5078. To SE-AIW 19th October 1940. Impressed again 18th May 1942 as No. 5082*. To SE-AIW 6th October 1944.
SE-AIX	W Nr 1725 –	impressed July 1940 as No. 5088. To SE-AIX 14th December 1940. Impressed again May 1942 as No. 5086*. To SE-AIX 15th September 1944.
SE-AIY	W Nr 1732 –	impressed July 1940 as No. 5087. Restored to SE-AIY 16th November 1940.
SE-AKB	W Nr 1664 –	impressed July 1940 as No. 5079. To SE-AKB 19th October 1940. Impressed again 18th May 1942 as No. 5075*. Not restored to civilian use.
SE-AKC	W Nr 1566 –	impressed July 1940 as No. 5080. To SE-AKC 19th October 1940. Impressed again 27th April 1942 as No. 5076*. Impressment ceased 6th October 1944 but this aircraft was not returned to civilian use.
SE-AKD	W Nr 1692 –	impressed July 1940 as No. 5081. To SE-AKD 19th October 1940. Impressed again 27th April 1942 as No. 5077*. To SE-AKD 6th October 1944.
SE-AKF	W Nr 1712 –	impressed July 1940 as No. 5082. To SE-AKF 19th October 1940. Impressed again 28th April 1942 as No. 5078*. To SE-AKF 23rd August 1944.
SE-AKG	W Nr 1713 –	impressed July 1940 as No. 5083. To SE-AKG 19th October 1940. Impressed again 2nd May 1942 as No. 5079*. To SE-AKG 2nd October 1944.
SE-AKH	W Nr 1711 –	impressed July 1940 as No. 5084. To SE-AKH 19th October 1940. Impressed again 2nd May 1942 as No. 5080*. To SE-AKH 15th September 1944.

Klemm Kl 35D

SE-AKK	W Nr 1767 –	impressed 26th May 1942 as No. 5083*. To SE-AKK 15th September 1944.
SE-AKL	W Nr 1768 –	impressed 26th May 1942 as No 5084*. To SE-AKL 15th September 1944.
SE-AKN	W Nr 1783 –	impressed 5th May 1942 as No. 5087*. To SE-AKN 20th September 1944.

Note: * means second use of this number.

German Aircraft supplied during the Second World War
Although Nazi Germany was very reluctant to supply war materiel to Sweden during the hostilities, twelve Fieseler Fi 156C-3 Storch were supplied during 1943 to supplement eight aircraft supplied or ordered before the war. The 1943 aircraft received the serial numbers 3809 to 3820 inclusive. Several of these aircraft were later sold to Austria and West Germany when they became surplus to Flygvapnet requirements. Details are:

Fv 3809	W Nr 110061	To D-EKLU - with the Museum Fridericianum, Kassel
Fv 3810	W Nr 110062	To OE-ADX, later D-ENTE

Fv3811 WNr110063 –
Fv3812 WNr110064 To OE-ADR, later D-EKMU
Fv3813 WNr110201 –
Fv3814 WNr110202 To OE-AKA
Fv3815 WNr110203 To Flygvapenmuseum Malmen, Linkoping
Fv3816 –
Fv3817 WNr110252 –
Fv3818 WNr110253 To OE-ADO, later D-ENPE, Technisches Museum, Vienna
Fv3819 WNr110254 To OE-ADS
Fv3820 WNr110255 –

Interned Aircraft
Arado Ar 95A-5
Three of these aircraft were interned in Sweden. WNr2346 and 2350 arrived on 21st September 1944 and WNr2351 on the following day. These were all seaplanes of 3/A Gr (See) 127, details being given below:

WNr2346 Originally 'DK+WH', and finally '6R+LL' of 3/A Gr 127
WNr2350 Originally 'DK+UL', and finally '6R+BL' of 3/A Gr 127
WNr2351 Originally 'DK+UM', and finally '6R+UL' of 3/A Gr 127

These aircraft were placed on the Swedish Civil Register as SE-ANT, SE-AOD and SE-AOE respectively. SE-ANT remained in service until cancelled on 1st October 1951; the other two aircraft were cancelled in 1947. SE-ANT was flown by Svensk Flygtjanst AB for most of its service in Sweden (this company was a contractor carrying out services for the Royal Swedish Air Force, such as target-towing etc, using military-type aircraft.) The other two aircraft were operated by AB Nordisk Aerojanst.

— Arado Ar 96B-1 WNr425262 & 4081
Coded '.U+9B' and 'CD+DH' arrived in Sweden on 30th August and 1st September 1944 respectively. They became SE-AOA and SE-AOB, and remained in service until cancellation from the register on 7th December 1954 and 31st January 1955, respectively. These aircraft were both built by the Avia works in Czechoslovakia. Their Swedish operator was AB Norrlandsflyg.

— Arado Ar 196A-3 WNr1006
Coded 'DH+ZF', an aircraft built by the French SNCASO works at St Nazaire, arrived at Sund in Sweden on 11th February 1943. It was placed on the Swedish Civil Register as SE-AOU but this registration was only briefly used. It is said that the aircraft's owner was a company set up by British intelligence. The Ar 196 was flown to Norway and handed over to the RAF at Fornebu on 26th May 1945. It was used by No. 333 Squadron of the RNoAF for a period, wearing British national markings, being flown both at Fornebu and Stavanger/Sola.

Later the aircraft returned to Sweden in 1946 and was re-registered as SE-AWY. It remained in service with AB Ahrensbergsflyg until cancellation from the Swedish civil register on 10th September 1947.

Bücker Bü 181
Several examples of the type (which was also licence-built in Sweden for service with the Flygvapnet/Royal Swedish Air Force as the Sk 25, 125 being made by A.B. Hagglund & Soner) force-landed in Sweden on various dates.
28 April 1944 – WNr330745 'PL+BN'. To SE-BFG.
24 March 1945 – WNr502174 'VN+NP'. To SE-BPY. later HB-UTA, D-EDOF.
25 May 1945 – WNr 108 'CR+YU'. To SE-BNK.

— Dornier Do 24T-1 WNr3343
Coded 'CM+RY' of Seenot Gr 81, force-landed at Hällevik in Sweden on 31st October 1944. It was taken over for service with the Flygvapnet/Royal Swedish Air Force under the designation 'Tp 24' and remained in service until 1952, with serial number '3343'.

Fieseler Fi 156C Storch
Six examples landed in Sweden, two on 4th April 1945, the remainder on 8th April. Their details are as given below; note that 'S 14B' is the Flygvapnet type designation for the Fieseler Storch.

— Fieseler Fi 156C Storch WNr110232
Coded 'BM+PL' (4th April). To S 14B with serial Fv 3826

Royal Swedish Air Force (Flygvapnet) Fieseler S14B No. 3826 at Nyköping on 13th February 1954 after being hit by an S31 (Spitfire 19). The Storch was repaired and returned to service; it had previously been a Luftwaffe aircraft 'BM+PL', until flown to Katusa, Ystad, on 4th April 1945.
Flygvapnet courtesy Peter Liander/Leif Hellstrom collection.

—   **Fieseler Fi 156C Storch**   W Nr 5503
Coded 'KR+QX' (4th April). To S 14B with serial Fv 3822. Subsequently to Austria as OE-ADT. Currently with the Musée Royal de l'Armée, Brussels, marked as 'KR+QX'.

—   **Fieseler Fi 156C Storch**   W Nr 5837
Coded 'DJ+PC' (8th April). To S 14B with serial Fv 3824. Subsequently to West Germany as D-EKLA.

—   **Fieseler Fi 156C Storch**   W Nr 1143
Coded 'NL+UU' (8th April). To S 14B with serial Fv 3821. Subsequently to Austria as OE-ADZ and then West Germany as D-EADZ.

—   **Fieseler Fi 156C Storch**   W Nr 5440
Coded 'PP+QA' (8th April). To S 14B with serial Fv 3825. Subsequently to West Germany as D-EBGY.

—   **Fieseler Fi 156C Storch**   W Nr 5806
Coded 'BD+VF' (8th April). To S 14B with serial Fv 3823. Subsequently to Austria as OE-ADU.

—   **Henschel Hs 126B-1**   W Nr 13156
Coded '6A+NL' of I/NSGr 12. Force-landed at Herrvik in Sweden on 28th October 1944. To SE-AOG and briefly operated during 1945 by Nordisk Aerojanst AB.

—   **Junkers W 34hi**   W Nr 317
Coded 'TF+NA'. Force-landed at Vombsjön in Sweden on 30th October 1944. To SE-AOC and briefly operated in these marks by AB Norrlandsflyg in 1945.

—   **Messerschmitt Bf 108B-1**   W Nr 2158
Coded 'L1+CF' of Stab V/LG 1. Force-landed at Limhamn in Sweden on 29th March 1945. To SE-BPZ, later PH-NFB, D-EFUM.

—   **Messerschmitt Bf 109E**   W Nr 0820
Coded '3' of II/JG 77. Damaged in force-landing on 24th October 1940. Not repaired, but was subject to detailed examination by SAAB.

—   **Messerschmitt Bf 109F-2**   W Nr 6741
Coded 'DJ+JW'. Force-landed in Sweden on 9th October 1943. Evaluated by SAAB.

—   **Messerschmitt Bf 109G-10/R2**   W Nr 770261 & 770293
Force-landed on 12th April 1945 at Rinkaby. These two aircraft were evaluated by the SFA/T.

—   **Messerschmitt Bf 109G-10**   W Nr 490137
Force-landed on 24th April 1945. Evaluated by the F/C.

—   **Siebel Si 204D-1**   W Nr 321583
Coded 'DI+QK' of L D Kdo 65. Force-landed at Bredåkra in Sweden on 19th April 1945. To SE-BPW. Subsequently sold to Denmark as OY-ADA and then to West Germany as D-IBAB.

Note: Various other aircraft landed in Sweden; these were either returned to Germany or, although stored for some time after the end of the war, were scrapped without further use being made.

Note: Also that a number of types of German aircraft were built under licence in Sweden, including the Bücker Bü 181 (125 built by A B Hagglund & Soner as the Sk 25), and Junkers Ju 86 (16 by SAAB as the B3). Large numbers of German sailplanes were also licence-built in Sweden:

DFS 108-49 Grunau Baby IIB-2
94 built by AB Flygplan at Malmo between 1942 and 1946, including 30 for the Flygvapnet with serials from 8101.

DFS 108-30 Kranich II
33 built by AB Flygplan in 1943/44, including 30 for the Flygvapnet with serials from 8201.

DFS 108-68 Weihe
25 built by AB Flygindustri, Malmo, including 18 for the Flygvapnet with serials from 8301.

DFS 108-70 Olympia-Meise
13 built post-war by AB Kockums Flygindustri of Halmstad. This company also built one Weihe and one Kranich post-war.

Examples of some of the aircraft mentioned survive in Swedish museums, as below:

Flygvapenmuseum Malmen, (Linkoping)
  Bücker Bü 181B (Sk 25) – Fv 25000 (Bücker built, ex-D-EXWB)
  Bücker Bü 181B (Sk 25) – D-EBIH ex-Fv 25114

D-EKLA, an ex Swedish Flygvapnet Fieseler Fi 156C (S14 No.3824 in Swedish service). Photographed at Munich-Oberwiesenfeld, 30th June 1962. *P. H. Butler collection*

Appendix A

Luftwaffe Unit Organisation and Codes

The Luftwaffe organisational structure was not directly comparable with that of the Royal Air Force or USAAF. The major flying unit was the 'Geschwader', very roughly equivalent to an RAF Group or USAAF Wing. Each Geschwader would have three to five 'Gruppen', roughly the equivalent of an RAF Wing or USAAF Group, which would be further divided into 'Staffeln' or Squadrons. Certain types of units, notably those concerned with reconnaissance, usually existed at 'Gruppe' level only instead of being organised into Geschwader. Geschwader normally had one specific duty – e.g. Fighter, Night Fighter, Transport, Bomber etc. Each Gruppe within a Geschwader was identified by a Roman numeral, while each Staffel was identified by an Arabic numeral. Thus III/TG 4 would be the third Gruppe of Transport Geschwader 4, while 3/TG 4 would be the third Staffel of the Geschwader. In most cases each Gruppe would have three Staffeln, and the structure would be adhered to rigidly so that, for example, if a Geschwader had a Staffel 15, this would always be the third Staffel of Gruppe V. Apart from its complement of Staffeln, each Gruppe and each Geschwader would have a 'Stabsschwarm' (Staff Flight) of aircraft flown by Gruppe or Geschwader senior officers. Such aircraft were of the same operational type as the constituent Staffeln although the Stabsschwarm would also fly any communications aircraft attached to the unit.

Aircraft of first-line fighter units were generally identified by an individual code number painted in a colour which identified the Staffel to which the aircraft belonged. Thus code references in the book indicate 'Red 8', 'Black 7', etc.

Aircraft of other front-line units were identified by a four-symbol code. The first two symbols, one of which would be a letter, the other a numeral, would indicate the main unit (Geschwader or Gruppe) while the fourth symbol would be a letter indicating the Staffel within the main unit. The third symbol would be an individual letter for the particular aircraft which would be painted in a colour also indicating the Staffel.

The 'fourth letter' codes indicating sub-units were as follows:

A – Geschwader Stabsschwarm (Gesch Stab), blue individual code letters

B, C, D, E, F – Gruppe Stabsschwarm for I, II, III, IV, V Gruppe, respectively, green individual code letters

H	K	L	M	N	P	R	S	T	U	V	W	X	Y	Z
1	2	3	4	5	6	7	8	9	10	11	12	13	14	15	Staffel, respectively with

1, 4, 7, 10, 13 Staffel – white codes
2, 5, 8, 11, 14 Staffel – red codes
3, 6, 9, 12, 15 Staffel – yellow codes

Thus 'G6 + RX' was aircraft 'R' of 13 Staffel within Geschwader or Gruppe 'G6' (G6 was the code for Transportgeschwader 4).

Aircraft on test at manufacturers' works were allocated in sequence identities/call-signs of four letters such that one aircraft might be 'KT + VJ' and the next 'KT + VK' and so on. These identities were frequently retained in service if the aircraft was used by a test establishment or a second-line unit such as a flying school. In other cases 'Versuchs' numbers, sequential code numbers, or, occasionally, the last three figures of the Werk Nummer, were used as alternative identities.

Unit abbreviations used in the text are as follows:

AufklGr	– Aufklärungsgruppe (Recon Wing)		SAGr	– Seeaufklärungsgruppe (Maritime Recon Wing)
FAGr	– Fernaufklärungsgruppe (Long Range Recon Wing)		SNG	– Seenotgruppe (Air Sea Rescue Wing)
FFS	– Fliegerführerschule (Pilot Training School)		SG	– Schlachtgeschwader (Ground Attack Group)
JG	– Jagdgeschwader (Fighter Group)		SKG	– Schnellkampfgeschwader (Fast Bomber Group)
KG	– Kampfgeschwader (Bomber Group)		StG	– Stukageschwader (Dive Bomber Group)
KüFlGr	– Küstenfliegergruppe (Coastal Patrol Wing)		TG	– Transportgeschwader (Transport Group)
LG	– Lehrgeschwader (Operational Trng Group)		TGr	– Transportgruppe (Transport Wing)
MSGr	– Minensuchsgruppe (Mine-sweeping Wing)		–	– Teilkommando (Detached Unit or Flight)
NJG	– Nachtjagdgeschwader (Night Fighter Group)		–	– Luftpark (Acft Storage Unit/MU)
NSGr	– Nachtschlachtgruppe (Night Grd Attack Wing)			

It should be noted that there were also various categories of special units:

– Independent Staffel reporting directly to a major Headquarters, such as Staffel 3/Versuchsverband der O K L. In this case the Staffel was attached to the test organisation of the Luftwaffe High Command (Oberkommando der Luftwaffe).

– Dedicated service trials units for new types of aircraft or equipment, which were generally entitled 'Kommando' or 'Einsatzkommando', suffixed by either the surname of the commanding officer or the name of the equipment/aircraft.

– 'Erprobungstellen' (or E-Stellen) – permanent trials units akin to the United Kingdom's Royal Aircraft Establishment at Farnborough or the Aeroplane and Armament Experimental Establishment at Boscombe Down, or the USAAF test center at Wright Field. Rechlin was perhaps the best known of these RLM units, but there were several others, including those at Travemunde for marine aircraft and Tarnewitz for aircraft armament.

Appendix B

IJAAF and IJN Unit Organisation

Imperial Japanese Army Air Force
The basic unit was the Sentai (Group) which consisted of three Chutais (Squadrons) and a Sentai Hombu (Headquarters Section). The Sentai might operate independently or be grouped into Hikodans (Wings). A Hikodan would have a Shireibu Hikodan (Command Section), a reconnaissance unit possibly up to Sentai strength and normally three Sentais of fighters or bombers. Two or three Hikodans constituted a Hikoshidan (Air Division) and two or more Hikoshidans comprised a Kokugun (Air Army).

Imperial Japanese Navy
The basic air unit was the Kokutai (Naval Air Corps). A Kokutai might operate independently or be grouped with others to form a Koku Sentai (Air Flotilla). Koku Sentais in turn might be organised into a Koku Kantai (Air Fleet) or Homen Kantai (Area Fleet).

Koku Sentais were also utilised as Carrier Divisions, such that a single Koku Sentai would provide the aircraft for a pair of aircraft carriers. This gave rise to the codings sometimes worn by Japanese naval aircraft such as 'BI-05', 'B2-20' etc. In these cases 'B' shows the aircraft to belong to the Second Koku Sentai. 'I' shows an aircraft of the first aircraft carrier in the Division, '2' an aircraft of the second carrier. The number to the right of the hyphen ('05', '20', etc.) was an individual code for the aircraft.

Land-based naval aircraft commonly wore a code comprising their Kokutai designation followed by an individual aircraft code – e.g. '634-16' was aircraft '16' of the 634th Kokutai. However, for security reasons, the Kokutai code might literally be a 'code' number which differed from the real Kokutai designation. Some Kokutai were identified by their base name rather than a number; in these cases the code to the left of the hyphen could be either a Kana (i.e. Japanese) character derived from the initial letter of the base name, or a Roman letter, or numerical call-sign.

Appendix C

German Aircraft Designations

German aircraft designations were allocated by the R L M (German Air Ministry) and formed part of the total engineering nomenclature of the Luftwaffe. Type numbers were normally allotted in chronological sequence, i.e. type 110 would be followed by type 111 (etc.) as the development of each new design was funded. It was not usual to allocate blocks of numbers to individual manufacturers, so the numbers were allotted on a fairly random basis to the different aircraft makers. However, if a new type were intended to replace an existing type from the same manufacturer, in some cases the number of the original design was incremented by 100 (or multiples of 100). Thus the Ju 88 led to the Ju 188, 288, 388 etc.

Strictly speaking, all aircraft type numbers were prefixed by the number '8'. Thus a Messerschmitt Bf 109 was an '8-109' and a Fieseler Fi 156 was an '8-156'. Drawings of aircraft parts, and makers' data plates, frequently show the '8'. The prefix derived from the Luftwaffe technical inventory system in which '8' indicated 'aircraft'. In the same system '9' indicated 'aero engine', '108' indicated 'sailplane' and '109' indicated 'jet engine'.

Starting with a basic type, such as a Focke Wulf Fw 190, the initial version would normally be the Fw 190A, with any new variant involving a major change of structure, engine, equipment or role resulting in a new series as the Fw 190B, followed by '190C, '190D, etc. Less important changes to the original Fw 190A would be shown by sub-series numbers – the first batch manufactured being Fw 190A-0 aircraft, the next modification standard being the Fw 190A-1, and then '190A-2, '190A-3, etc. In service modifications (or interchangeable equipment packs) were shown by a designation suffix, such as Fw 190A-6/R6 or Me 410A-1/U2. The letter 'R' indicated 'Rustatz' (Field Modification Kit), while 'U' indicated 'Umrust-Bausatz' (Factory Modification Kit).

Nakajima Ki-84 'Frank' FE-302 at Freeman Field in 1946 (see page 240). *Ashley Annis collection*

Nakajima Ki-84 'Frank' tail number 119, derelict at NAS Glenview near Chicago, probably in 1947 (see page 255). *Ashley Annis collection*

Appendix D

Japanese Aircraft Designations

The Imperial Japanese Army Air Force (IJAAF) and Imperial Japanese Navy (IJN) used different designation systems.

IJAAF

A type number was allotted to each IJAAF aircraft project, known as the Kitai (Ki) number. The Kitai numbers were allocated in chronological sequence. The first production version of the aircraft would have the suffix 'I' to its Kitai number, with subsequent versions being indicated by 'II', 'III', etc. The first production series of the first version would be the 'Ia', with minor variations introduced during production shown as later suffix letters ('-Ib', '-Ic' etc).

Each type would also have a designation related to its design duty, such as 'Army Type 2 Fighter'. The '2' in this designation derived from the last digit(s) of the year in the Japanese calendar during which the aircraft was accepted for service. The individual version would be given a Model Number, which was consistent with the Kitai designation. Thus a Ki-43-IIa would be an Army Type 1 Fighter Model 2A.

Most types also had an official popular name (e.g. the Ki-43 was the 'Hayabusa'). The main purpose of the name was for use in publicity or official war communiques, where use of the other types of designation might reveal information of use to Allied intelligence.

IJN

The IJN used a 'short designation' system, very similar to that used by the US Navy prior to 1962. Thus aircraft were identified by a letter-number-letter-number group which indicated the design duty of the aircraft, a sequence number showing how many designs had been accepted for that particular duty, a letter indicating which manufacturer had designed the aircraft, and a Model number. Minor modifications might be shown by a suffix

letter to the Model number. Thus A6M5 was the 5th Model of the 6th Carrier Fighter type, and was designed by manufacturer 'M' (Mitsubishi).

1st letter		*2nd letter*	
A	– Carrier Fighter	A	– Aichi
B	– Carrier Attack Bomber	D	– Douglas
C	– Reconnaissance Aircraft	K	– Kawanishi
D	– Carrier Bomber	M	– Mitsubishi
E	– Reconnaissance Seaplane	N	– Nakajima
G	– Attack Bomber	W	– Kyushu
H	– Flying Boat	Y	– Kugisho
J	– Land-based Fighter		
K	– Trainer		
L	– Transport		
M	– Special Floatplane		
MX	– Special Purpose		
N	– Fighter Seaplane		
P	– Bomber		
Q	– Patrol Plane		

Each type would also have a duty-related designation related to its year of acceptance, very similar to that used by the Army. Thus an A6M5 was also the Navy Type 0 Carrier Fighter Model 52.

Finally, popular names were used in the same manner as utilised by the IJAAF, except that the name indicated the duty for which the aircraft was designed (the IJAAF chose popular names at random).

General

Aircraft of both the IJAAF and IJN are often best remembered by their name under the Allied 'Pacific Code Name System', whose origins are given in Chapter Fourteen.

The Aichi M6A1-K Nanzan 'A3' photographed after capture by US forces. The Nanzan was a landplane trainer version of the M6A1 Seiran submarine-launched floatplane (see page 255).
Ashley Annis collection

Appendix E

Select Research Sources

Major sources for this book have been the UK Public Record Office files relating to the selection of aircraft for evaluation, the RAE Flight Logs for the relevant period, the Operational Record Books for the RAF Air Disarmament Wings, RSUs, DSRUs, MUs, and experimental units, Maintenance Command statistical returns for aircraft in storage, and Flight Test reports. Other records have included Aircraft Accident Reports provided by the Accident Investigation Branch, Aircraft Movement Cards and Aircraft Accident Cards made available for research at Ministry of Defence (AHB 2), and a copy of the British Air Forces of Occupation report on the 'Dissolution of the Luftwaffe' published in 1947. Specific PRO file references are listed below.

AVIA 1/13	RAE Flight Log, 19 June 1939 to 28 February 1941
AVIA 1/14	RAE Flight Log, 1 March 1941 to 3 June 1942
AVIA 1/15	RAE Flight Log, 4 June 1942 to 30 September 1943
AVIA 1/16	RAE Flight Log, 1 October 1943 to 13 February 1945
AVIA 1/17	RAE Flight Log, 14 February 1945 to 30 November 1945
AVIA 1/18	RAE Flight Log, 1 December 1945 to 20 October 1946
AVIA 1/19	RAE Flight Log, 21 October 1946 to 18 September 1947
AIR 27/2127	No. 616 Squadron
AIR 29/931	Nos 434, 435 and 436 DSRUs
AIR 29/932	Enemy Aircraft Storage & Servicing Unit
AIR 29/963	No. 6 MU
AIR 29/1454	No. 6 MU
AIR 29/1455	No. 6 MU
AIR 29/1505	No. 47 MU
AIR 29/1563	No. 390 MU
AIR 29/1568	MAEE
AIR 37/1442	The History of Disarmament in the No. 8302 Disarmament Wing Area
AIR 40 series of AI2(g) aircraft type files	
AIR 40/2022	Visits to Germany to collect German aircraft

The above references are representative rather than exhaustive. They give no clues to the many unproductive files which were also checked!

The following Accident Investigation Branch reports:

W 2303	Focke Wulf 190 trainer Air Ministry No. 37
W 2291	Heinkel He 162 AM 61
W 2273	Focke-Achgelis Fa 223E
W 2313	Fieseler Fi 156 Storch (unidentified)
W 2371	Dornier Do 335 AM 223

The following representative RAE 'Enemy Aircraft' Reports:

EA 14/20	Junkers Ju 88A-5 V4+GS dive-bomber, Electrical installation
EA 14/26	Junkers Ju 88A-1 M2+MK, Site examination
EA 26/2	Junkers Ju 87B-2 S2-LM, Examination at site
EA 234/1	Caproni-Campini, Structural features
EA 235/6	Messerschmitt Me 262, Experimental Interceptor I
EA 273/1	Fiat G 55, Site Examination

Appendix F

Select Bibliography

An Account of the Part Played by the Royal Air Force in Dissolving the Luftwaffe (volumes 1 and 2): Wigglesworth; AHQ BAFO, 1947.
The Captive Luftwaffe: West; Putnam & Company, London, 1978.
Catalogue of Enemy Aircraft Reports: Raitt; Royal Aircraft Establishment, Farnborough, 1969.
Combat Aircraft of World War Two: Weal, Weal and Barker; Arms & Armour Press, London, 1977.
Ceskoslovenska Letadla (II) 1945-1984: Nemecek; Nase vojsko, Prague, 1984.
Deutsche Luftwaffe uber der Schweiz 1939-1945: Ries; Verlag Dieter Hofmann, Mainz, 1978.
German Aircraft of the Second World War: Smith & Kay, Putnam & Company, London 1978.
A Historical Summary of the Royal Aircraft Establishment 1918-1948: Caunter; RAE Report AERO 2150A, 1949.
Impressments Log Vol IV: Moss; Air-Britain, London, 1966.
Japanese Aircraft of the Pacific War: Francillon, Putnam & Company, London, 1979.
Messerschmitt Me 262 – Arrow to the Future: Boyne; Jane's, London, 1981.
Monogram Close-Up series (Nos 3, 5, 6, 7, 8, 9, 10, 11, 12, 13, 17, 18 19, 20, 21, 22, 23, 24): Monogram; Boylston, Mass, USA.
Nurflugel – Die Geschichte der Horten-Flugzeuge 1933-1960: Horten & Selinger; H. Weishaupt Verlag, Graz, 1983.
Profile series (Nos 3, 15, 23, 29, 40, 46, 69, 70, 76, 82, 94, 99, 105, 113, 118, 129, 130, 141, 148, 160, 161, 164, 177, 184, 190, 203, 211, 213, 222, 228, 233, 234, 255, 261): Profile Publications.
Rotating Wing Activities in Germany during the period 1939-1945: Liptrot, HMSO, London, 1948.
Samoloty w muzeach polskich: Krzyzan; Biblioteczka Skrzydlatej Polski, Warsaw, 1983.
Warplanes of the Third Reich: William Green; Macdonald and Jane's 1979.

Periodicals
Aerofan (Associazione Italiana per las Storia dell'Aviazione).
Flyghistorisk Revy (Swedish Aviation Historical Society).
Journal of the American Aviation Historical Society.
Le Trait D'Union (Journal de la Branche Francaise d'Air Britain).
VGC Newsletter (Journal of the Vintage Glider Club of Great Britain).

A great many sources emanating from the United States were also used during the research, and were drawn from files at the National Air and Space Museum and the US National Archives in Washington D.C., the United States Air Force Museum at Dayton Ohio, the USAF Historical Research Center at Maxwell Air Force Base, Montgomery, Alabama, and numerous personal record collections held by persons concerned in the activities described.

Appendix G

Standard Abbreviations

AAC — Ateliers Aeronautique de Colombes (a post-war French aircraft company).

AAF — (US) Army Air Field or Army Air Force, depending on context.

AAEE — Aeroplane and Armament Experimental Establishment, Boscombe Down.

AHB — Air Historical Branch of the Air Ministry.

AOAMC — Atlantic Overseas Air Materiel Center (USAAF Depot located at Newark AAF, concerned with aircraft in transit to or from Europe).

ASR — Air-Sea Rescue.

A I 2 (g) — Air Intelligence section 2 (g) – the British Air Ministry department which was responsible for collating information on German aircraft and equipment.

BAFO — British Air Forces of Occupation, which later reverted to their wartime title of '2nd Tactical Air Force'. More recently, 'Royal Air Force Germany'.

CFE — RAF Central Fighter Establishment, based at Tangmere and Ford, until September 1945 when it moved to West Raynham.

CNAC — Canadian National Aeronautical Collection, at Rockcliffe near Ottawa.

C/n — Constructor's number.

CS(A) — Controller of Supplies (Air) – the authority which nominally 'owned' aircraft under test by the Ministry of Supply or successor procurement organisations.

CWE — Chemical Warfare Establishment, Porton Down.

DDL — Det Danske Luftfahrtselskab (Danish Airlines), now part of the Scandinavian Airlines System, SAS.

DLH — Deutsche Luft Hansa, the pre-1945 German national airline.

DNL — Det Norske Luftfahrtselskab (Norwegian Airlines), now part of the Scandinavian Airlines System, SAS.

DSRU — Disarmament Servicing and Recovery Unit. (RAF Engineering Support Unit to the Air Disarmament organisation).

EAF — Enemy Aircraft Flight of the CFE.

GAFEC — German Air Force Equipment Centre, RAF Stanmore Park. (Post-war RAF repository for ex-Luftwaffe equipment, part of No. 3 Maintenance Unit, Milton).

MAEE — Marine Aircraft Experimental Establishment. (RAF trials unit for marine aircraft and equipment, located at Helensburgh, Scotland, until it returned in August 1945 to its pre-war base at Felixstowe).

MAMA/ MAMC — Middletown Air Materiel Area/MAM Center (USAAF Depot located at Olmsted Field, Middletown, Pa).

MM — Matricola Militare – (Italian Air Force aircraft serial number).

MU — Maintenance Unit. (RAF storage/servicing unit).

RAE — Royal Aircraft Establishment, Farnborough.

RSU — (RAF) Repair & Salvage Unit.

SoC — Struck off Charge – RAF status assigned to aircraft no longer included in unit strength inventories (equivalent to US Navy status 'Stricken').

TVA — Luftwaffe Torpedowaffen Versuchsanstalt, Travemünde.

W Nr — Werk Nummern. (Constructor's serial numbers).

W&EF — Wireless and Electrical Flight (of the RAE).

RAF Damage Categories ('Category E' etc.)
Accidents to RAF aircraft were reported by letter or number categories which indicated the degree of damage. The system during the Second World War used letters, with an equivalent number system being introduced later. The Categories were:

Pre-1941	1941-1952	Post-1952	
U	U	1	Undamaged
M(u)	A	2	Repairable on site by unit
M	Ac	3	Repair beyond unit capacity
R(b)	B	4	Beyond repair on site
–	C	5(gi)	To ground instructional use
W	E	5	Write-off
–	E1	5(c)	To components
–	E2	5(s)	To scrap
–	Em	5(m)	Missing

Heinkel He 115 photographed at MAEE Helensburgh in July 1940, before the aircraft was repainted in RAF markings (see Page 36). *Norman Belcher collection*

Index

Fieseler Fi 156 Storch 'DAB' at No.151 RU Wevelgem in 1945. No identity is known other than the 'owner's' personal code letters (see Chapter Ten). *Jim Pickering collection*

This Fieseler Storch, VM874, served with 84 Group Communications Squadron and is believed to have been photographed at the unit's base at Celle. *Graham Skillen collection*